The Economic Transformation of China

The Economic Transformation of China

Dwight H Perkins
Harvard University, USA

World Scientific

NEW JERSEY • LONDON • SINGAPORE • BEIJING • SHANGHAI • HONG KONG • TAIPEI • CHENNAI

Published by

World Scientific Publishing Co. Pte. Ltd.
5 Toh Tuck Link, Singapore 596224
USA office: 27 Warren Street, Suite 401-402, Hackensack, NJ 07601
UK office: 57 Shelton Street, Covent Garden, London WC2H 9HE

Library of Congress Cataloging-in-Publication Data
Perkins, Dwight H. (Dwight Heald), 1934–
The economic transformation of China / by Dwight H. Perkins (Harvard University, USA).
pages cm
Includes bibliographical references and index.
ISBN 978-9814612371 (hardcover) -- ISBN 9814612375 (hardcover)
1. China--Economic policy--1949– 2. China--Economic conditions--1949– 3. Economic development--China. I. Title.
HC427.9.P468 2015
330.951--dc23

2014033036

British Library Cataloguing-in-Publication Data
A catalogue record for this book is available from the British Library.

In-house Editor: Alisha Nguyen

Typeset by Stallion Press
Email: enquiries@stallionpress.com

ABOUT THE AUTHOR

Dwight H. Perkins is the Harold Hitchings Burbank Professor of Political Economy, Emeritus, of Harvard University. Previous positions at Harvard include Associate Director of the East Asian Research Center (now Fairbank Center for Chinese Studies), Chairman of the Department of Economics, Director of the Harvard Institute for International Development, and Director of the Harvard Asia Center. Dwight Perkins has authored, coauthored or edited 21 books and over 100 articles on economic history and economic development of China and of other Asian and developing economies. His research and published writing about China began in the early 1960s and continues today. He has served as an advisor or consultant on economic policy and reform to the governments and other institutions in China, Korea, Malaysia, Vietnam and Indonesia and also to the Ford Foundation, the World Bank, and various parts of the US government and private corporations.

ACKNOWLEDGMENTS

Dwight H. Perkins gratefully acknowledges the publishers of the following essays for their permissions to republish the essays in this volume.

"History, Politics and 30 Years of Development and Reform," In Ho-Mou Wu and Yang Yao, editors, *Reform and Development in China: What Can China Offer the Developing World?* (London: Routledge, 2011), pp. 45–70.

"Government as an Obstacle to Industrialization: The Case of Nineteenth Century China," *Journal of Economic History*, Vol. XXVII, December 1967, Number 4, pp. 478–492.

"Centralization and Decentralization in Mainland China's Agriculture, 1949–1962," *Quarterly Journal of Economics,* Vol. LXXVIII, May 1964, pp. 208–237.

"Industrial Planning and Management," In Alexander Eckstein, Walter Galenson, and Ta-chung Liu, *Economic Trends in Communist China* (Chicago: Aldine, 1968), pp. 597–635.

"China's Economic Policy and Performance," In Roderick MacFarquhar and John K. Fairbank, editors, *The Cambridge History of China Volume 15 The People's Republic Part 2: Revolution within the Chinese Revolution 1966–1982* (Cambridge: Cambridge University Press, 1991), pp. 475–539.

"Reforming China's Economic System," *Journal of Economic Literature,* Vol. XXVI, June 1988, pp. 601–645.

"China's 'Gradual' Approach to Market Reforms," In Andres Solimano, Osvaldo Sunke, and Mario Blejer, editors, *Rebuilding Capitalism: Alternative Roads after Socialism and Dirigisme* (Ann Arbor: University of Michigan Press, 1994), pp. 177–206.

"The Challenges of China's Growth," Washington, The AEI Press, 2007, 53 pages.

"Forecasting China's Economic Growth to 2025," (with Thomas Rawski) In Loren Brandt and Thomas G. Rawski, editors, *China's Great Economic Transformation* (Cambridge: Cambridge University Press, 2008), pp. 829–886.

"China's Investment and GDP Growth Boom: When and How will it End?" In Masahiko Aoki and Jinglian Wu, editors, *The Chinese Economy: A New Transition* (New York: Palgrave MacMillan, 2012), pp. 35–59.

*I would like to express my thanks to Alisha Nguyen for her work overseeing the production of this book.

CONTENTS

INTRODUCTION

I. The Historical Foundation

China began efforts to modernize its economy in the late 19th century. Many of the building blocks needed for the construction of a modern economy were in place but progress toward sustained modern economic growth was slow and frequently interrupted. The building blocks that were in place included a population where a significant number of individuals were educated, some to a very high level at least in traditional terms, a commercial system that was sophisticated enough to keep almost all domestic commerce in local as contrasted to foreign hands, and a government that ruled over a country that had been unified for much of the past six centuries. The Qing and Republican governments, however, were under great pressure first from European imperial powers and then from Japan. China lost two wars to the European imperial powers, then to the Japanese, then again during the Boxer Rebellion to the combined Western and Japanese forces. The Taiping Rebellion was suppressed earlier but only after more than a decade of great destruction, and in the first half of the 20th century, the country was divided by local warlord control and by civil war between the Communists and Nationalists (Guomindang) plus an invasion by Japan that lasted for nearly eight years (14 years if one includes the separation of the Northeast from the rest of China by Japan in 1931).

Even when there were periods of peace and the Chinese government did not have to concentrate on warding off both foreign and domestic foes, the government made only feeble efforts to modernize its economy. The Confucian bureaucratic system combined with Chinese culture that had so effectively held China together over the centuries looked backward more than forward and proved to be very resistant to change. Even those in the government who wanted change had few resources at their command that could be used to invest in infrastructure or industry. The fall of the Qing Dynasty in 1911 did not change the situation dramatically. Governments that followed lacked the resources to make much of a difference in the economy although progress was achieved in limited areas with investments in modern industries in Shanghai and elsewhere and in railroads, but most of this progress relied on a few private entrepreneurs and even fewer foreign investors.

The end of the civil war that brought the Communist Party to power in 1949 was a major turning point in China's economic modernization. For the first time, China had a government that ruled unchallenged in the entire country (minus Taiwan, Hong Kong, and Macao) and had the resources to begin investing in modern economic growth on a large scale. However, the Cold War (and the hot war in Korea) isolated China from the high income market economies of the West and Japan and, together with Communist ideology, led China to choose a development strategy patterned on that of the Soviet Union. The Soviet command economy model was never a good fit with the Chinese economy and almost from the beginning China experimented with modifications to the rigidity of central planning and administrative control, as contrasted to market control, of most allocation decisions. It was not until 1978 that China began a process that was to lead to the complete rejection of the Soviet command model in favor of an economic system ruled primarily by market forces all be it still with a great deal of government intervention. The year 1978, therefore, was in many respects an even bigger turning point for the economy than the year 1949.

My personal involvement with China began in 1953 when I took a course on Chinese history taught by Professor Knight Biggerstaff at Cornell University. I began studying the Chinese language in 1954 and majored in what was then called "Far Eastern Studies". After two years in the US Navy, I went on to study economics at Harvard but my goal in studying economics was from the beginning the desire to use economic techniques to understand what was happening in China. My PhD dissertation dealt with the Chinese transition in the 1950s and early 1960s from a market economy to a centrally planned economy[1] and I published my first essay on China in 1963, more than 50 years ago as this is being written.

---

[1]This was published in 1966 as *Market Control and Planning in Communist China*, Cambridge: Harvard University Press.

The essays in this book cover to some degree the entire Chinese economic modernization experience from the 19th century to the 21st. The majority of essays were written after China began republishing economic data in 1979 after a two decade hiatus when the only data coming out of China had to be pieced together from statements by various Chinese leaders. Several of the essays, however, were published earlier based to a large degree either on pre-1949 historical materials or on the considerable amount of information that came out of China from journals and government publications during the 1950s. The 10 essays in this volume make no claim to being comprehensive although I have selected ones that cover broad topics. It would take several large volumes to be truly comprehensive dealing with such a large topic in such a large country and in fact much of what I have written about China has been in book form and thus is not included here.

The first essay chosen, "History, Politics and 30 Years of Development and Reform,"[2] gives a broad overview of the historical heritage that has had a direct influence on China's post 1978 development. It starts with the historical foundations that facilitated economic growth once there was a government willing and able to play its role in the process. It then moves on to a discussion of the efforts to build a modern economy with Soviet style central planning and to Mao Zedong's efforts to use his own political mobilization skills to first try to accelerate growth through the Great Leap Forward of 1958–1959. Then, with the failure of the Great Leap, Mao shifted his emphasis to trying to transform society through the Great Proletarian Cultural Revolution (1966–1976) that had some direct impact on the economy, but had its biggest impact on subsequent economic policy by discrediting Mao's approach to social change in the eyes of much of the Chinese population and of leading Communist Party cadres in particular.

Only one essay dealing with the 19th century is included in this collection, "Government as an Obstacle to Industrialization: The Case of 19th Century China."[3] This essay helped fill in a gap in our understanding of why the late Qing Dynasty government was unable even during periods

[2]In Ho-Mou Wu and Yang Yao, editors, *Reform and Development in China: What can China offer the developing world?* London: Routledge, 2011, pp. 45–70.

[3]*Journal of Economic History*, Volume XXVII, December 1967, No. 4, pp. 478–492.

of relative peace to do much to promote modern economic growth during the late 19th century. Based on Wang Yeh-chien's pioneering study of taxation under the Qing, I showed how the financial resources available to the Qing government were severely limited and barely enough to cover the expenses of the day to day running of the government and fighting off various domestic rebellions. There was relatively little money left over to build infrastructure or invest in industry even when government officials desired to do so. The contrast with early Meiji Japan in this regard was particularly pronounced. There was, of course, much more to the barriers to modern economic growth in the late 19th century than just the limited financial resources of the Qing Government. My own contributions to the analysis of this period, however, have mostly been in book form and thus could not be included here.[4]

II. Central Planning and Collective Agriculture 1955–1978

The next three essays deal with the pre-1978 economic developments of the People's Republic of China after 1949. The first of these, "Centralization and Decentralization in Mainland China's Agriculture, 1949–1962,"[5] deals with the agricultural sector where most Chinese lived and where success or failure in managing the sector had profound implications throughout the economy and society. The Chinese government during the early years after 1949 relied mainly on market mechanisms to give direction to production in this sector, but this changed with the decision to require all of the rural population to form agricultural producer cooperatives and then the even more radical People's Communes. While the motive for collectivizing agriculture was as much political control as it was economic, there were rational economic reasons for believing that collective agriculture could

---

[4]The books authored or edited by me that dealt with some of the broader historical development issues include, *Agricultural Development in China, 1368–1968* (Chicago: Aldine, 1969) (republished with a new introduction by Transactions Press in 2013); *East Asian Development: Foundations and Strategies* (Cambridge: Harvard University Press, 2013); (editor) *China's Modern Economy in Historical Perspective* (Stanford: Stanford University Press, 1975); *China: Asia's Next Economic Giant?* (Seattle: University of Washington Press, 1986).

[5]*Quarterly Journal of Economics*, Vol. LXXVIII, May 1964, pp. 208–237.

do more to promote production than individual household based agriculture. In theory, the collective form would make it easier to mobilize large amounts of "surplus" labor for rural infrastructure construction and rural cadres running the collectives would be more responsive to the adoption of improved technologies than conservative peasant households. In practice, particularly when these policies were integrated into a political campaign, the results did not come close to meeting the expectations of the Chinese leadership. Even during times when political pressures did not lead to irrational excesses, there was a constant struggle between the advantages for some efforts of central control and the disadvantages of that control for the growing of crops and raising animals. This study of agriculture was part of a broader study that looked at the transition of the Chinese economy to a centralized command system that formed part of my doctoral dissertation that was published subsequently as a book.[6]

The essay "Industrial Planning and Management,"[7] is a study of the challenges facing China in attempting to build a modern industrial sector using the mechanism of a Soviet style central plan. China's industrial structure involved everything from relatively modern large-scale plants to many smaller and more primitive enterprises even in the same industry. There were also major problems of getting reliable data on what was in fact going on within these enterprises. The central plans thus were at best crude guidelines for what enterprises should do. Crude guidelines, however, were the only coordination mechanism available given that market allocation of industrial inputs and most outputs had been eliminated. Inevitably, Chinese plant managers learned the methods practiced in the Soviet Union and Eastern Europe for following some plan targets rather than others and for getting critical inputs in sufficient quantity to meet their own production goals. The essay carries the story through the Great Leap Forward and into the early 1960s before the Cultural Revolution when China rebuilt its central planning and allocation system but did so mainly by first decentralizing the planning and control of most firms to provincial and lower level governments.

---

[6] See Footnote 1.

[7] In Alexander Eckstein, Walter Galenson, and Ta-chung Liu (1968). *Economic Trends in Communist China.* Chicago: Aldine, pp. 597–635.

The final essay dealing in part with the pre-1978 period is "China's Economic Policy and Performance" which appears in Volume 15 of the Cambridge History of China that covers the Cultural Revolution years (1966–1976) and then the first few years of the post-1978 reform period. While there was a blackout on the release of economic data during the Cultural Revolution, Chinese statistical authorities have done their best to reconstruct the economic indicators for the blackout period. These attempts with one exception are clearly superior to the earlier efforts by scholars outside of China including myself to construct economic data for the Cultural Revolution period from widely dispersed sources. One problem with the officially reconstructed data, however, is that 1950s prices are used to measure the growth rate of GDP. Because these prices were highly distorted in favor of industrial products, the contribution of industrial output to GDP is exaggerated. This flaw is easily fixed by recalculating GDP in year 2000 or later year prices. The revised figures make clear that there was growth during the Cultural Revolution period despite the years of disruption in the late 1960s, but the growth was slow and it is unlikely that the rural population experienced any improvement in their standard of living whatsoever. The urban population may have done a bit better because the tight restrictions on migration from the countryside had the effect of making it easier for urban women to find modern sector employment. Little or no urban housing was built during this period, however, so an urban family of three on average lived in an 18 m^2 apartment.

The institutions governing the economy during the Cultural Revolution did not change much and planning involved mostly doing a bit more each year of whatever an enterprise was doing the previous year. The leadership in the economic sphere was constrained by political pressures from the left and the fact that most of the economic leadership had been removed from office and sent to the countryside, May 7th Schools, or elsewhere. Communes existed and there were the beginnings of a rational rural small-scale industry program but the main unit managing agricultural was the 20 to 30 family production team, a sub-unit of the much larger Commune.

The years 1977–1978 following the arrest of the radical Shanghai group (the "gang of four") mainly involved the restoration of the central planning system in industry and a more rational approach to economic policy. The main economic efforts involved the continued emphasis on heavy industry, but at this time with firms encouraged to go abroad for imported machinery and other higher quality and higher technology inputs. The hoped for boom in offshore oil production, however, did not occur and the government soon learned that a greater reliance on imported inputs meant that the country had also to increase exports in order to pay for them. The major institutional and policy changes that stressed both exports and the beginning of what became the rapid dismantling of the rural Commune system, however, did not occur until the shift in power to Deng Xiaoping and his then close allies such as Chen Yun was fully established at the Third Plenum of the 11th Party Congress in December 1978.

III. China's Economic Reforms, 1978–2013

The Chinese leadership in 1978 had no clear picture of where they were attempting to go with respect to the economy over the next decade and beyond. Certainly, there was no decision at the Third Plenum to begin moving toward a market economy. Many and perhaps most of those who had played important economic roles in the past such as Chen Yun saw the main task as one of making the centrally planned command economy work the way it was supposed to. This involved rejecting the radical leftism of the Cultural Revolution with its anti-foreignism and anti-education platform, and it involved some use of market forces in areas where it was well established that the command system worked badly. But that view placed market forces in a clearly subordinate role to the centrally planned command part of the economy.

The first essays in this reform section of the book give an overview as I saw it at the time the essays were written. The first and second of these three essays were mainly written for professional economists interested in China's economic reforms that, at the time the essay was written, were far enough along (9 years and 14 years respectively) for a preliminary description and appraisal of the first stage of the reforms to be possible. The third was written mainly for an audience of Americans and others concerned with what policy toward China should be given the dramatic political and economic changes that had followed immediately on the death of Mao Zedong in 1976.

In March 1981, I presented a paper, "The International Consequences of China's Economic Development,"[8] at an American Assembly conference of policy-oriented China specialists that was published later that year. The prevalent view among most scholars and other policy analysts of China in the United States at that time, at least those that had a view, was that China's economy was likely to continue growing more or less at the pace of recent years and that any changes brought about by the reforms then known about outside of China, mainly the decision to look positively on international trade and imports of foreign products after years of trying to minimize the economy's dependence on foreign trade, would have a positive but modest effect on China's overall economic performance going forward. My own view was very different. The fact that China was turning outward and more generally following what appeared to be a more pragmatic set of economic policies meant that China's economy was likely to grow much faster than in the past. Simply by avoiding the enormous mistakes of the Great Leap Forward and the disruption of the Cultural Revolution, China's economy was likely to do much better than in the past. Thus, in this essay, I pursued the implications of a GDP growth rate that I suggested was likely to be between 6 and 8% per year. As it turned out, China grew over the next three decades at over 9% per year, faster than even I thought possible.

It is also very unlikely that the Chinese leadership itself in 1981 had much of an idea of the magnitude of the economic transformation that they had unleashed. Deng Xiaoping's background was in politics and military affairs not economics and the dominant economist on the standing committee of the Politburo, Chen Yun, was not for a rapid acceleration in the economic growth rate either in the early 1980s or earlier when the boom of the Great Leap Forward ended in disaster. It was also not apparent to the outside world, and was resisted by many cadres in China, that the rural reforms then underway would lead to the outright abandonment of the Commune system in favor of household farming. Deng himself at

[8]The essay appeared in Richard H. Solomon (ed.), (1981). *The China Factor: Sino-American Relations & the Global Scene.* Englewood, New Jersey: Prentice Hall, pp. 114–136. This essay is not included in the collection of this book because it was not possible to negotiate appropriate terms with the publisher.

key junctures supported the transformation that was occurring in rural China but he did so quietly in order not to generate overt opposition. Those rural reforms were to lead to an economic boom in the countryside, but more about that later.

It should also be noted that in 1981, the Cold War was still raging and US policy and China's policy in many spheres, notably toward the Soviet Union, were parallel to each other. China had only recently had military clashes with the Soviet Union on its borders. The issue facing the US at the time was whether US policy should change its approach to China given this situation. The essay also discusses the likely future of China's foreign trade and its likely influence on world trade. Here, the essay suggests that foreign trade would continue to grow fairly rapidly but not as rapidly as in fact what occurred. The essay suggests that foreign trade was likely to grow along with the economy as a whole or around 6 to 8% per year or a bit higher. In fact exports grew at 14% per year for the two decades of the 1980s and 1990s or roughly 10% per year after taking into account inflation. Still exports in 1999, at US$195 billion, were up from under US$10 billion in 1978 but still not the giant influence on world trade that China became in the next ten plus years when exports passed US$2,000 billion (in 2012).

By 1987, it was becoming increasingly apparent that the Chinese reforms were fundamentally transforming the nature and performance of China's economy even if it was still unclear just what the end point would be. The essay "Reforming China's Economic System,"[9] attempts a comprehensive overview of these reforms in agriculture, industry, foreign trade, and in macroeconomic policy and the distribution of income as of 1987. The core of the analysis of the reforms that increased the role of the market was to recognize that there were four elements that had to be in place if markets were to work well and raise productivity, five elements if one includes the fact that one must start with macroeconomic stability. The four elements were that (1) goods and services needed to be bought and sold on markets, not distributed by administrative means through government channels, (2) those buying and selling the goods and services needed to be motivated by the fundamental rule of effective

[9] *Journal of Economic Literature*, Vol. XXVI (June 1988), pp. 601–645.

markets — they had to be trying to a large degree to maximize profits, (3) prices had to reflect scarcities in the economy which meant they had to be set by supply and demand on markets, not by government fiat, and (4) the producing units in the economy had to be competitive.

The fact that China started market-oriented reforms in the agricultural sector made the transition to markets comparatively easy at least in technical economic terms. (1) Allowing increasing amounts of agricultural produce to be sold on the market meant mainly increasing the role of the small markets that already existed and gradually cutting back on state purchases. (2) Farm households unlike Commune cadres did not have to be taught to try to maximize profits or their net income, (3) prices on these rural markets readily reflected relative scarcities in the economy, and (4) farm households were too numerous and small to establish monopoly control over any part of the markets for their produce.

When China turned to attempting to introduce market forces into the industrial economy, however, the situation was quite different. Making industrial products available for purchase and sale on the market was straightforward. Prices on these markets quickly adjusted to reflect the relative scarcities of these products but a potential problem was created by allowing many industrial inputs for the powerful state-owned enterprises to continue to be distributed administratively at government set prices. This dual price system that resulted was to be one of several sources of rising corruption in the system and it did not disappear until much later in the 1990s. By the 1990s, producing enterprises had every incentive to try to move their products out of the administrative system onto the markets where prices and hence profits were much higher. Competition was also introduced in much of the system by allowing enterprises to sell anywhere in the country where before even county-level enterprises typically had a monopoly of their local county market.

The main problem was in changing the goals or objective functions of the management of the large state-owned enterprises. Managers continued to be motivated more by the desire to please their political superiors in the government and party and using their own political influence to get subsidies of various kinds rather than pursuing profits by expanding their markets or cutting costs. Later in Eastern Europe, efforts to solve this problem mainly involved the privatization of most state-owned enterprises, but that did not work all that well either and in any case China in the mid-1980s was not willing to even consider privatization. What made industrial development accelerate in China in the 1980s, therefore, was not the modest improvements in large state enterprise performance, but the surprising boom in township and village enterprises. These township and village enterprises were the main beneficiaries of the availability of key industrial inputs on the market as contrasted to the past when all inputs were controlled by the central planners.

Overall as the essay points out, the market-oriented reforms led to a large jump in total factor productivity in the economy as a whole. There was also the beginning of structural changes in the share of agriculture, industry, and foreign trade in GDP toward a more typical developing country pattern away from the very atypical pattern of the Soviet style economy of 1955–1978 with its emphasis on heavy industry, limited resources for agriculture, and a small share for foreign trade. More surprisingly, the 1980s also involved a significant improvement in the distribution of income of households due largely to the fact that it was in the rural areas, not the cities, where the most dramatic market-oriented reforms started.

Macroeconomic stability, however, was beginning to weaken as prices began to rise more rapidly, too rapidly for a Communist Party and population that had experienced the hyper inflation of the 1940s that had helped bring the Party to power. The rising inflation and increasing perceptions of corruption were to play an important role in the events that led to the tragedy of June 4, 1989. The financial system, mainly the large state-owned banks, also had been restructured to give the appearance of a modern financial system by separating the commercial banks from the central bank, but together with the state-owned industrial and commercial enterprises they continued to operate in many ways similar to how they had operated during the pre-reform era. This semi-reformed financial and state enterprise system was the main cause of accelerating inflation and that problem was not solved until after the turn to the 21st century.

The second essay in this reform section, "China's 'Gradual' Approach to Market Reforms", was presented at a conference at El Escorial, Spain in July 1992 that was devoted to reviewing and comparing the market oriented economic reforms recently underway in Eastern Europe after the dismantling of the Soviet Empire and in Latin America after the "Lost Decade" of the 1980s.[10] China's reforms by this time, in contrast, had been underway for nearly a decade and a half. The conservative reaction in China to the market reforms of the 1980s reinforced by the Tiananmen tragedy of June 4, 1989, had largely abated by 1992 and was strongly reinforced by Deng Xiaoping's now famous trip to southern China in January–February 1992 during which he decisively supported a renewed effort at market reforms.[11]

The El Escorial essay focused on the issue of what other countries undergoing market-oriented reforms might learn from China. The "big bang" or do everything at once approach being advocated for Eastern Europe and the states of the Soviet Union at that time was on the minds of many economists and this China essay, among other things, looks at whether the Chinese reforms were done "gradually" or "rapidly". As the essay points out, the return to household agriculture and the use of market forces to direct agricultural production was accomplished in the relatively short time span of five years, not as rapidly as some economists were advocating for Eastern European reforms, but rapid enough. Opening to foreign trade and rejection of attempts at autarchy were also accomplished rapidly. The boom in foreign direct investment, however, took much longer and did not really get underway in earnest until the 1990s. The agricultural reforms and trade opening were not only accomplished rapidly, but they also led immediately to large increases in both agricultural output and incomes and in exports of manufactures. That is they were an immediate economic success. In the trade sphere, the essay explores to

---

[10] "China's 'Gradual' Approach to Market Reforms," in Andres Solimano, Osvaldo Sunke, and Mario Blejer, (eds.), *Rebuilding Capitalism: Alternative Roads after Socialism and Dirigisme.* Ann Arbor: University of Michigan Press, 1994, pp. 177–206. The Spanish language version was translated and published a year earlier as *Las Reformas Economicas Contemporaneas: Experiencias Comparadas* in *Pensiamento Iberoamerican: Revista de Economia Politico.* Madrid: Instituto de Cooperacion Iberoamericana, July 1992–June 1993, Volume II, pp. 121–154.

[11] Deng's trip is not explicitly discussed in this essay. It was clear even at the time of the El Escorial conference that Deng had succeeded in reopening the debate over market reforms, but the full significance of his influence became more apparent over time, particularly to the world outside China, as major reforms were actually implemented.

what degree these successes were due to features unique to China, the presence of Hong Kong with its great knowledge of Western markets for example.

The major market reform issue that could not be solved so easily or quickly was the reform of large state enterprises. As the essay points out, the main challenge was to get enterprise managers to behave according to the key rule of behavior required by efficient markets, to attempt to maximize profits by their own efforts, by expanding sales or cutting costs, not by lobbying for government subsidies. The Eastern European economies and those of the former Soviet Union had attempted to accomplish this by privatization with mixed results, but China rejected outright privatization for most of the larger enterprises. The Chinese approach was to attempt to improve the performance of these enterprises by hardening their budget constraint and changing other manager incentives also with mixed success. China is still struggling with how to make state enterprises more efficient in 2014 as this introductory essay is being written. What sustained rapid industrial development in China in the 1980s into the 1990s was that smaller-scale enterprises under township and village governments after the beginning of urban reforms in 1984 were able to obtain the inputs they required on the market at market prices rather than having to negotiate for allocations through the central plan. These smaller local enterprises had to try to maximize profits because local governments could not afford to subsidize them.

This El Escorial essay also includes some observations about the similarity with the Chinese experience with the market reforms then just underway in Vietnam where I had begun working in 1989. The Vietnamese experience is particularly interesting in this comparative perspective because it had an economy more like that of China in many respects than was the case in Eastern Europe.

The American Enterprise Institute lecture and essay, "The Challenges of China's Growth,"[12] was given in May 2006 in Washington, DC and published in 2007 nearly 30 years after the beginning of the reform era in China. Part of this essay is devoted to describing the enormous changes that occurred in China over the previous three decades, but the focus of

---

[12]Washington, The AEI Press, 2007, 53 pages.

the essay is on the implications of this enormous growth for the future. There is a discussion of what future growth is likely to be which will be pursued further in the next two essays that are devoted mainly to that topic. But the essay also focuses on the problems that had arisen over time to a large degree because of the reforms. Many of these problems are sources of tensions in Chinese society in 2014 and are recognized as such by the Communist Party and Government leadership as evidenced by the list of reform areas outlined by the Third Plenum of the 18th Party Congress in November 2013.[13]

The issues discussed in this essay about what China needs to deal with going forward are all issues that the government knew it had to deal with and are included in the 60 points of reform outlined by the Third Plenum along with many others. In the AEI essay, they begin with the problems created by rapid urbanization of the population combined with retention of the household registration or *hukou* system that was originally used in the post-1949 period as a means to restrict rural to urban migration. That system no longer attempted to restrict migration, but it had created a two class system that makes it difficult to impossible for rural migrants to get access to many urban services and leads many of them to leave their children back in the village with their grandparents. Closely related to the migration issue is the fact that rural land, as contrasted to urban land, has never been regularly bought and sold on any market at market set prices. Instead it has often been confiscated by local cadres at below market prices and transferred to developers in exchange for payments to the local governments or to the local cadres themselves. But changing this system also involves solving the financial challenges facing local governments. In recent years, they have been asked by the central government to carry out and pay for various mandates, but to do so in situations where most local governments lacked the necessary revenue base.

A problem that first appeared in the 1990s is that to make state-owned enterprises more efficient, they had to let tens of millions of surplus

[13]"The Decision on Major Issues Concerning Comprehensively Deepening Reforms in Brief," *China Daily,* November 15, 2013. This decision is typically referred to as the 60 point of reform of the Third Plenum because it numbers the specific areas of reform in 60 points.

workers on their payrolls go, but a national welfare and pension system to support these workers as they transitioned either to new jobs or retirement was not yet fully in place. Further reform of the state enterprises remains a necessity if a reasonably high rate of growth is to be maintained, but how does one take care of the workers who were left behind by the rapid structural changes occurring? Other social issues that have come to the fore include the one child family policy that has led to a situation where the overall population is aging rapidly. It has also led to an unbalanced sex ratio. The Third Plenum called for small changes in the one child family policy but much more is likely to be required.

Environmental problems were serious in 2007 when the AEI essay was written, but they have become even more serious as time has passed. High rates of economic growth have overwhelmed the increasingly vigorous efforts of the government to gain control over air and water pollution. The problem is not unique to China — other countries at a comparable stage of development have had similar problems and managed to get them under control — but China is still struggling to find a solution. Given its heavy dependence on coal for energy, it is not clear whether it will be possible to have continued high economic growth and an improving environment.

The rise of China's economy has also had a substantial impact on the rest of the world. China's demand for energy and natural resources has impacted world prices in these commodities and China's rapid growth of exports to pay for the imports high growth requires has required adjustments in manufacturers and their employees throughout the world. China is now one of the two or three largest trading nations and what it does will have a major impact on how the international trading system operates, something that was not at all true even 15 years ago in the late 1990s. The rate of growth of Chinese exports has already slowed markedly from the extraordinary rates of 25% per year in 2000 through 2008 to a slower but still robust rate of 9.4% in 2009 through 2012 despite the slow GDP growth in many of China's export markets. These are nominal growth rates but even the slower rate, perhaps 8% in real terms, is likely to fall further in that even 8% implies that Chinese exports would reach four trillion dollars in 2022 (in 2012 US dollars) and eight trillion dollars by 2031.

Outside the economic sphere, China's growth of military expenditures at a rate comparable to or a bit faster than the GDP growth rate is shifting the balance of power in the Western Pacific and East Asia. More relevant to the kinds of issues in the essays in this volume is the fact that an educated middle class is rising rapidly in China. In 2004, a sample survey indicated that China's population that had a secondary school or tertiary school education had reached roughly 235 million people, a large number but still only 18% of the country's total population, but the number of people with this level of education has been rising rapidly as a very high percentage of those in school today go on to high school (*gaozhong*) and beyond. China will clearly have the numbers of educated that will be needed to staff a large and increasingly sophisticated economy, but will it make the political adjustments necessary to keep the more educated parts of the population reasonably content? This essay makes no attempt to answer that fundamental question.

IV. The Future

China's three plus decades of very high GDP growth fall into the category of catch up growth and once a country begins to catch up no country has been able to sustain anything like the kinds of growth rates achieved by the most successful East Asian economies during their first decades of sustained growth. The question for China is when will the inevitable slowdown occur? The final two essays in this collection attempt to give an answer to that question. The first of these essays, "Forecasting China's Economic Growth to 2025" (with Thomas Rawski),[14] attempts to answer this question looking mainly from the supply side. The core methodology used is the growth accounting framework pioneered by Robert Solow. The first task was to measure as precisely as possible the sources of growth in post-1949 China through 2005. It is possible to make rough calculations of the sources of growth that give a fairly reliable picture of the forces driving China's growth, but the economics profession tends not to take these calculations seriously unless one goes through the tedious

[14] In Loren Brandt and Thomas G. Rawski (2008). *China's Great Economic Transformation*. Cambridge: Cambridge University Press, pp. 829–886.

process of measuring everything as precisely as possible. This is particularly true for the measurement of the contribution of increases in education of the labor force even though the methodology, done carefully or using shorthand methods, understates the contribution of education in developing economies. In China's case, the most difficult issue until more recently was finding an appropriate price index for deflating the capital stock into constant prices. The work that was done by Rawski, myself, and a research assistant is as well as one could do with the Chinese data available in 2006.

The basic finding of the historical growth accounting analysis is that China enjoyed high total factor productivity growth beginning in 1952 and carrying through the first five-year plan period (1953–1957) although much of this productivity growth probably reflected continuing recovery from the ravages of the war with Japan. For the next 21 years (1958–1978), what little growth China achieved was made possible almost entirely by very high investment rates that steadily increased the size of the capital stock. Total factor productivity for the period as a whole was negative. After 1978, investment remained high (and as a percentage of GDP actually rose over time) but the major change that made possible the high growth rates was the large jump in total factor productivity. For the reform period as a whole (1979–2005), TFP accounted for 40% of total growth.

The main focus of the essay is to use this historical observation and the same methodology to explore what was likely to be possible going forward into the future. Because most of the work force that would exist through 2025 was already born, it was not a problem to come up with a reasonably reliable measure of the work force in future years all be it with certain assumptions about such things as death and retirement rates. Adding in the impact of education was also not that complicated because one could estimate the age profile of the population and schooling rates (that by 2005 were already a very high share of the age cohorts) going forward. For the capital stock, the issue was mainly one of experimenting with different rates of investment as a share of GDP but overall assuming that the investment would fall as the savings rate fell as the population aged. These data were then plugged into the growth accounting framework and the question asked was what level of total factor productivity growth would be needed to achieve either a 6% GDP growth rate or a 9% GDP growth rate. The results are in the essay but the general conclusion was that it would take total factor productivity growth rates comparable to or a bit higher than during the past 30 years to maintain 9% growth through the next decade and rates even higher than that in the second decade after 2005.

The challenge of keeping TFP growth rates at that high level for another one to two decades was thus a formidable one and it seemed more likely that the GDP growth rate would fall than stay at 9% with 6% being more realistic particularly in the second decade. As it has turned out so far (as of early 2014), China's GDP growth rate after 2005 grew for two years at an extraordinary 14% per year and then fell to an average of 9.5% for the next four years (2008–2011) but then fell further to 7.7% (2012–2013). The essay also points out that China's East Asian neighbor economies, notably Japan, South Korea, and Taiwan, all experienced a marked slowdown in GDP growth when their GDP reached US$13,000 per capita using the purchasing power parity definition of GDP per capita. Much of coastal China is already at that level or higher as of early 2014 and the national average GDP per capita is likely to reach that level within three or four years after 2013.

The remainder of the chapter then explores what China will have to do to maintain a high growth rate of GDP and TFP. The issues explored include the need to strengthen the legal system as it applies to economic disputes, further efforts to reform the state enterprises so that they would not continue to be a drag on overall growth, find the money to clean up pollution and take steps to further reform the financial system. These are all issues discussed in some of the earlier papers included in this volume and are on the list of 60 points of the Third Plenum of the 18th Party Congress.

The final paper, "China's Investment and GDP Growth Boom: When and How will it End?",[15] takes the discussion of the future prospects for China's economic growth a step further both by exploring what has happened in China since 2005 through 2010 (the paper was first presented to

---

[15]In Masahiko Aoki and Jinglian Wu (eds.), (2012). *The Chinese Economy: A New Transition.* New York: Palgrave MacMillan, pp. 35–59.

the International Economic Association meeting in Beijing in 2011) and by going in much greater depth into the demand side of the issue. China's high growth rate continued through 2010 but only by having the investment rate continue to rise to nearly 50% of GDP. The total rate of growth of total factor productivity fell as did the growth rate of the labor force. The other side of this very high investment rate was a very low and declining household consumption share of GDP. The official figure for household consumption as a share of GDP reached a low of 34.9% in both 2010 and 2011. Many analysts have presented evidence that this household consumption figure is biased downward by the way certain categories of expenditures are treated but even with adjustments to take this into account the Chinese figure has reached a level rarely if ever achieved elsewhere.

This demand-side problem was only secondarily due to a fairly high household savings rate. More important was corporate savings (and investment) that was unusually large and government savings (and investment). There was also a current account surplus although this peaked in 2007 at 8.8% of GDP and then fell to 2.6% in 2011. Low household consumption meant that a major source of growth in most countries, rising consumer spending leading to investment to provide the required consumer goods was lower than in other countries. The gap between the total demand needed to maintain full capacity production in the economy and the demand provided by consumption expenditures together with the investment expenditures needed to produce the goods for household and government consumption had to be filled with even more investment but investment in what?

China's answer to the question of additional investment in what was to pour enormous sums into investment in housing, transport infrastructure, and certain other kinds of government financed infrastructure. For a time, this added investment filled a real need. China's transport system during the period of Soviet-style economic planning had been badly neglected as was the case in the Soviet Union. Urban housing was also neglected to the point where at the beginning of the reform period housing for the average family of three was only 18 m^2. The investment boom of the first decade of the 21st century went a long way toward filling the demand gap. High-speed multi-lane highways that did not exist until 1988 rose to 74,000 km in 2010, new airports were built not only for the largest cities but also for all provincial capitals and many other cities, and a major start on a nationwide network of high speed trains was well underway. China also began to spend tens of billions (in US dollar terms) on moving large amounts of Yangtze River water to the parched north.

In the decade ending in 2000, private and government construction companies completed 11 billion m^2 of new housing and in the next decade this figure was raised to 14.5 billion m^2. The combined total of housing completed during these two decades was enough to house 880 million people with apartments of 90 m^2 for each family of three, a fairly luxurious amount of space in Chinese eyes. There was also, of course, much tearing down of old housing so this was not a net increase, but clearly the country was reaching a point where the need for further housing was reaching a saturation point. Private investors, with few alternative areas for investment, might keep on pumping money into real estate much of which would remain empty, and the government could finally begin to provide housing for those migrants who were registered as living in the countryside but were actually working in cities, but these housing investments would not sustain demand of the magnitude reached in 2001–2010. It is likely that further massive investment in transport infrastructure was also facing diminishing returns.

In effect, China's investment boom was propping up 9% growth but investment with a continued high rate of return of that magnitude was not sustainable. South Korean conglomerates in the 1990s similarly had sustained high growth in that country with an investment boom of this sort, but the investments were often poorly thought out and led to bankruptcies that contributed to Korea becoming engulfed in the 1997–1998 financial crisis. China was not heading for a financial crisis although many local governments that had helped finance the boom were in financial trouble. But one way or another high GDP growth was not likely to be sustainable through such measures. Either the investment rate would come down or the rate of return on that investment would fall.

THE HISTORICAL FOUNDATION

CHAPTER 1

HISTORY, POLITICS AND 30 YEARS OF DEVELOPMENT AND REFORM

To an outside observer unfamiliar with China's history since the country came in regular contact with the West or with its history since 1949, the accelerated growth and rapid structural transformation of the Chinese economy since 1978 came as a complete surprise and has widely been seen as a "miracle." A miracle implies that there is no real explanation for the acceleration in growth, the modernization of the economy and the urbanization of society. But China was not the first economy to enjoy such an abrupt change in economic performance. Growth in Japan, Republic of Korea, Taiwan Province, Hong Kong and Singapore all enjoyed two to three decades of near double digit growth that some considered a miracle but most analysts now describe as the product of various reforms in policy unleashing a pent up potential for growth. Because these economies were catching up with the high income countries of Europe and North America, their growth was particularly rapid until they began to catch up. What was different about China was that the number of people involved in this acceleration was far larger than anything that had occurred previously in history and, to date at least, accelerated growth appears to be going on longer than in the other economies that experienced accelerated growth and structural transformation.

For someone familiar with Chinese history over the past two centuries and particularly since 1949, the transformation of China since 1978 should have been less of a surprise, and, with the benefit of hindsight, can be readily explained. What is it about Chinese history that should have prepared us for this dramatic change in economic performance? And what role did politics and political leadership play in making the changes that unleashed China's pent up potential?

Our focus in the first part of this chapter will be on the conditions that existed in China prior to 1949 that help explain the present. The emphasis will be on the influences that created a unified Chinese state, the origins of the high value placed on education, China's pre-modern experience with long distance commerce, and the limited industrialization that occurred prior to 1949. We then will turn to economic developments in the years from 1949 to 1978 and how they influenced what happened after 1978. In the latter part of the chapter, we will begin with a brief discussion of the nature of Chinese politics in the nineteenth century and how political attitudes and beliefs in that period could still be found in the post-1949 era. The next part of the chapter will speculate about how political actions and movements in the first three decades of the People's Republic era shaped development in that period and had a major influence on developments after 1978. Up to this point, the chapter will have focused on what it is in China's history and politics that helps explain the country's economic performance during the 30 years of reform. In the final section, we will discuss what lessons other countries can draw from China's historical and political experience. Because only a small number of countries have experienced a history similar to that of China, there is much about the Chinese reform experience that cannot be easily adapted elsewhere. However, all developing countries can learn from comparing China's experience with their own, even if the lesson on occasion will be that they will have to do things differently.

I. The Historical Heritages of Unity and Education

China at the beginning of the 19th century was by far the largest country in the world in terms of population and it was also by far the largest in terms of gross domestic product (GDP). In 1820, all of Western Europe plus such countries as the United States and Canada had a total GDP of roughly $173 billion (in 1990 prices) while China had a GDP of $229 billion (Maddison, 2007, pp. 70, 105, 379). The GDP of the United States alone was only $12.5 billion. Of course China also had a larger population than the entire Western World and so per capita income in China in 1820 was roughly half that of Western Europe and the United States (Maddison, 2007, p. 382). England had begun to industrialize by 1820 but the other

Western countries were still primarily agricultural. In terms of agricultural and industrial technology, China was not far behind the West although the gap was beginning to widen and would become a chasm by the end of the 19th century. In everything from the growing of wheat to the manufacture of textiles and steel, China had introduced innovations centuries before they were in use in the West.[1]

China's economy was so large because China, unlike Europe and other parts of the globe, had developed a government system that was capable of maintaining unity across an unusually large geographic area and a population that by the early 19th century had reached 400 million. Among a certain generation of people in the West, the image of China comes from the warlord period of the 1920s when China's regions were ruled by different generals who periodically fought each other for control of one piece of territory or another, and from the 1930s and 1940s when China was divided between areas under Japanese occupation and areas controlled by the two sides in the civil war.

But the first half of the 20th century was the exception not the rule in Chinese history. From the founding of the Ming dynasty in 1368 to 1911, China was a unified country with only occasional outbreaks of the kinds of violence that split the country into more than one political unit (mainly the Manchu invasion and internal strife that brought about the end of the Ming dynasty in 1644, and the Taiping Rebellion that lasted from 1851 through 1864). There were also many centuries of unity prior to 1368 beginning with the original unification of China under the Qin Dynasty in 221 BC and continuing under the Han Dynasty for 400 years and another five centuries under the Tang and the Northern Song dynasties.

How was unity of unprecedented scope achieved and what relevance does it have to today? There were two key elements. One was that China developed a system of government that, on the one hand, was highly decentralized in the sense that local magistrates together with local elites

---

[1]There are many studies of individual technologies ranging from the development of steel technology in the Song Dynasty to the methods for growing wheat and other North China grain crops in the Tang Dynasty. The most comprehensive study of China's independent development of many aspects of science and technology is the well known multi-volume series led and co-authored by Joseph Needham (various years).

decided a wide range of local matters without first communicating with the capital, and yet, on the other hand, the capital had sufficient control over the localities to remove any magistrate who defied the wishes of the emperor's court. What made this possible was a shared set of values among the magistrates and elites obtained through long study of the Confucian classics and an examination system that ensured that only such people could hold government office. Military force, led by generals chosen by other means, was there to back up the emperor's wishes, but the government was dominated by civilian authority. China had solved the problem of unstable military alliances among feudal lords that dominated governance in medieval Europe.

The second key element in this unity was the fact that all Han Chinese shared a common rich culture and a common written language. Most Chinese going way back in history thus thought of themselves first as Chinese and only secondarily as people of Guangdong or Henan. Nor were there deep religious cleavages that might have provided a basis for breaking up China into hostile territories as in Europe. This same statement does not apply to the various tribes in China's western regions and north of the Great Wall, but within the territory where most Han Chinese resided there was no basis for regional loyalties that would enable a political-military leader to create a sustainable separate state in one region of the country or another. Put differently, one could create such a state but that state could not be sustained for long periods because the citizens of the new state would have no built-in natural loyalty to it. External forces could conquer the Han Chinese heartland and there could be civil wars within it, but ultimately only a government that ruled the whole territory was sustainable. The rise of modern ideas of nationalism in China after May 4, 1919, further strengthened this sense that all Chinese, at least all Han Chinese who today make up 91% of the total population, were part of one nation as well as one culture.

This sense of unity did not guarantee stability, as the first half of the 20th century demonstrated, but it provided a foundation on which stability could be built once one had a government capable of effective governance. China was not unique in this respect. Within East Asia, much the same can be said of Japan from the Tokugawa time on and Korea since it first achieved unity in the 7th century, but unity in these two countries involved populations similar in size to those found in major European nations. Where cleavages within a society along language, race and religious lines are deep, political stability is much more difficult to achieve, as various African countries in the 20th and 21st centuries have frequently demonstrated. Econometric tests reinforce the view that deep cleavages of this kind make stability more difficult, and in the absence of such stability and a stable environment for investment in particular, sustained economic growth is much more difficult if not impossible (see, for example, Alesina and La Ferrara, 2005).

Achieving stability by itself will not guarantee development, but it is a critical ingredient for development.

II. China's Commercial Heritage and Its Connection with Education

China's emphasis on the importance of education went beyond the role of education as the main vehicle for selecting government officials. Confucius, as is well known, put education and an educated man at the center of his value system and that value system has played a major role at all levels of Chinese society for more than 2,000 years. But there were other practical considerations as well why education and literacy became important to a much larger number of people than could possibly contemplate taking the three levels of examinations that could lead to a government appointment.

China was a commercial as well as an agricultural society and goods traveled over long distances. Cities were primarily the seats of the central and local governments with some notable exceptions, but the cities had to be supplied with products often from hundreds and even thousands of miles away.[2] China's capital city had a population of over one million people as early as the Song Dynasty if not before and supplying such a

[2]The trade in silk and tea is well known, but China during the Qing Dynasty and before had a large scale long distance trade in bulk products such as grain. Grain prices, as a result, tended to reflect supply and demand conditions over a wide area particularly along the Yangtze River from the surplus grain regions of Central China to the grain deficit region in Jiangnan. See the analysis in the collected works of Wang (2003), Volumes I, II and III.

city required tens of thousands of merchants, transport workers and the like. Commerce on this scale requires records and to use records an individual must be able to read at least numbers and some characters. We do not yet have a reliable estimate of the level of literacy in 19th century China but among males a basic level of literacy could have been as high as 30 to 45%.[3] Among the highest income 5 to 10% of the population, literacy must have been nearly universal and for many at this level literacy went way beyond basic.

A relatively high level of literacy by pre-modern standards did not lead to sustained economic growth prior to the 20th century, but it did lay the foundation for the creation of a modern high quality education system, at least when one compares the education system that existed in China in 1949 with what one found in much of the developing world on the eve of that world's attainment of independence from colonial domination. China's university system today compared with what currently exists in most low income countries is another way of making this same point. Sub-Saharan Africa would be at the low end of the education spectrum where at the time of independence in the 1960s, there were only a handful of universities in the entire continent and in many of the countries illiteracy was the norm.[4] Today in Africa, the level of education and literacy is much higher, but there is nothing comparable to China's university system either in terms of quantity and even more in terms of quality.

Education has expanded rapidly everywhere during the past half century including in Africa, but, while one can rapidly expand those who are literate, it is quite another matter to educate people to a level that can compete with the products of the universities of Europe and North America. A few individuals are bright enough and determined enough to come from an illiterate family and go initially to a poor rural school and rise up to become a PhD scientist, but such individuals are the rare exception in all societies. Most individuals who rise up the education

[3]Evelyn Rawski (1979, p. 23) suggests this figure. Her conclusion, however, is based on limited evidence and is not as yet widely accepted.

[4]Before 1939, there were only 10 real secondary schools in all of colonial Africa and as late as 1960 in Sub-Saharan Africa only 36% of the relevant age cohort were in primary school and a miniscule 3% were in secondary school (Perkins and Roemer, 1994, pp. 32–33).

ladder have educated parents and go to school with others much like themselves. It is no accident that Chinese (and Indian) students are a major component of the top science and engineering graduate programs in the United States. In part, this simply reflects the fact that these students are a tiny elite at the top of a very large pyramid given the size of China's (and India's) population, but that is not the whole story or probably even the most important part of the story. These scientific and engineering elites in China typically come from educated families and, once their talents are recognized, are put into schools where they are with other talented and highly motivated students like themselves and are taught by teachers who are fully qualified in scientific and mathematical subjects.

Nor is this rise in talent just a recent phenomenon. On the eve of the Communist Party's takeover of the Chinese government in 1949, China had more than 100,000 students enrolled in universities and nearly 50,000 of those were in science, engineering and medicine. The figures for the 1930s were smaller but even then there were 40,000 students enrolled in universities and nearly 15,000 of those were in science, engineering and medicine (Orleans, 1961, pp. 68–69). These figures are dwarfed by those of today with 18.85 million students enrolled in Chinese universities and with more than one million university level teachers. There are well over 200,000 post-graduate students enrolled in engineering, science and medicine and much larger numbers at the undergraduate level.[5] Numbers of this magnitude receiving a quality education today would not have been possible, however, if China had not started with a substantial number of university graduates in the 1950s and then expanded steadily on that base with the notable exception of the Cultural Revolution period (1966–1976).

As pointed out above, the Chinese story is not just a story of quantitative expansion. There has been a steady rise in quality, particularly since 1978, that has produced an educated elite that can compete with similar elites in high income countries. There is little doubt in this writer's mind, although no proof can or will be offered here, that an important part of the reason for the strength of Chinese students today has to do with these

[5]The overall enrollment data are for 2007 and the data on post-graduate enrollees are for 2006 (National Statistical Office, 2008, pp. 179–180; 2007, p. 791).

students' historical heritage. They grew up in families and a society that, for the most part, valued education highly. This high premium placed on education did not begin in 1978 or 1949 — it began more than two millennia ago. Circumstances such as war, poverty, and the Cultural Revolution have undermined educational opportunity, but the system bounces back in part because of underlying values that do not disappear even in the bleakest of times.

III. International Commerce and the Role of Overseas Chinese

Pre-modern commerce in China contributed more to the historical heritage than its contribution to the value of becoming educated. There is a large literature on the Western traders who came to China in the 19th century and helped expand China's exports in tea and silk and promoted Western imports of textiles, petroleum and much else including opium. Less well known is the fact that these Western traders played very little role in China's domestic commerce. Once imports were unloaded on the docks of Guangzhou or Shanghai, it was Chinese merchants who handled the transport and sale of these goods throughout China. Similarly, the export of tea and silk to Europe and North America was transported on foreign ships and handled from the Chinese port to the foreign port by Western firms, but these same firms played only a minor role in the original purchase of tea and silk from the Chinese producers and the transport of those products to the ports.

The supervisors of the people who played this role were called compradores and nationalist Chinese historians have been very critical of their collaboration with foreigners. It was these compradores and all of the other people involved in Chinese commerce, however, that ensured that domestic commerce and, over time, foreign commerce as well would largely be in Chinese hands. It was the fact that Chinese merchants learned how markets worked and acquired the skills needed to manage commercial transactions of all kinds. It was not that foreigners were unwilling to do these tasks. It was that foreigners could not compete with Chinese merchants in the domestic market and over time foreigners had increasing difficulty competing in China's export and import trade as well.

During the period when the Soviet style command economy dominated in China some of these commercial skills were lost but certainly not all of them. Farmers did not have to learn how to trade once the government allowed them to trade their produce freely. Nor did township and village enterprise managers need to be told how to use the market when after 1984 they were allowed to purchase their industrial inputs on such markets. Managing foreign trade, however, was another matter. Familiarity with foreign markets and foreign commercial practices did atrophy under the monopoly control of foreign trade by a handful of state trading companies. But China's historical heritage rescued China from the consequences of neglect in this area as well.

As is well known, tens of millions of Chinese emigrated to Southeast Asia and further abroad in the 19th and early 20th centuries, most of them as unskilled laborers. But these emigrants brought with them the basic skills needed to go into commerce once they had completed their labor obligations together with the knowledge of what commerce could offer in economic opportunity. Because there was little competition in commerce from the local population in these other Asian countries, and foreigners largely confined themselves to the high end of international commerce, overseas Chinese traders gradually moved up in scale and sophistication and came to dominate trade at all levels, particularly after independence was achieved by the various Southeast Asia nations. After 1978 they became increasingly involved in trade with China.

Of even greater importance, the traders in Hong Kong never had to close up shop in favor of state monopoly traders. The Western embargo on trade with China prohibited Hong Kong merchants from handling much China trade in the 1950s through the 1960s, but, when the embargo ended and even more when Chinese policy turned outward after 1976, Hong Kong traders were there to help move Chinese products into the quality and style conscious markets of North America and Europe. The share of Chinese exports handled through Hong Kong rose from 17% during the state monopoly trading period in 1975 to 40% by 1987 and the Hong Kong shares of Chinese textile fabric, machinery and clothing were 46, 87 and 62% respectively (Sung, 1991, pp. 105–107). The latter figures are far higher than what one would have expected if Chinese domestic ports had been in a position to compete on an equal basis with Hong Kong.

Hong Kong businesses were also the main source of foreign direct investment in the 1980s. By 2006, Hong Kong and Macao's share in total utilized foreign direct investment in China had fallen to 33%, still a high figure, but in 1988 the Hong Kong and Macao share was 66% of the total actually utilized foreign direct investment (National Statistical Office, 2007, p. 743; 1990, p. 655).

Could China have turned outward as dramatically as it in fact did after 1978 if support from Overseas and Hong Kong Chinese had been absent? Exporting petroleum and even many kinds of food products would not have been a problem. As a result of the break with the Soviet Union in 1960 and China's withdrawal from Comecon, the Soviet trading bloc, China had also acquired some knowledge in the export of textiles to Western and other quality and style conscious markets, but the numbers were very small. Almost certainly China's rate of export expansion would have been considerably slower in the 1980s and that would have meant tighter foreign exchange constraints and fewer imports. GDP growth as a result would almost certainly have been slower than the actual breakneck growth that actually occurred.

IV. Industrialization before 1949

The contribution of industrialization in China prior to 1949 is more difficult to assess. Certain Chinese industries such as the spinning and weaving of cotton and silk have hundreds or even thousands of years of history behind them.[6] But modern manufacturing did not really get started in China until the 1860s and 1870s when China built the Jiangnan Arsenal and the China Merchants' Steamship Navigation Company in Shanghai. Defeat by Japan in 1895 opened up China to foreign direct investment in manufacturing and the Japanese in particular took advantage of the opportunity and opened up a number of textile mills in Shanghai and elsewhere. But there were also a comparable number of Chinese owned textile mills and other industrial firms built during the first half of the 20th century. Overall, there was steady industrial growth in China from the 1890s

[6] See the extensive discussion of these and other industries in the Jiangnan area prior to 1850 in Li (2000).

through to 1937 when the Japanese invaded. If one includes Japanese sponsored industrial development in Japanese occupied Manchuria, industrial growth between 1912 and 1936 averaged 9.6% per year.[7] This growth in manufacturing was from a very small base at the beginning of the period, however, and as a share of GDP factory output in China was just over 2% (Rawski, 1989, p. 72).

There was more going on in the first part of the 20th century than industrial growth, however. There was the expansion of the railroad system, the construction of Shanghai as a modern commercial as well as manufacturing center, and the beginnings of a modern banking system among other developments. The best estimate of GDP growth that we have suggests that the GDP growth rate averaged between 1.3 and 2.5% per year between 1914/1918 and 1931/1936 which in per capita terms came to between 0.6 and 1.6% per year, not impressive in post-1978 terms but faster than many other parts of the globe at the time (Rawski, 1989, p. 330).

Much of the industry and infrastructure created during the period up through 1936 did not survive the war with Japan and the civil war. Much physical capital was destroyed during the war or moved inland ahead of the advancing Japanese forces. The equipment that survived the war was no doubt obsolete and not economical to transport back to the coast from where it had been transferred many years earlier. China was in economic chaos with hyperinflation in the late 1940s in any case and the civil war was raging so few were making long-term investments. In the Northeast, the Soviet army had most of the Japanese enterprises stripped and the equipment shipped back to the Soviet Union.

One thing that economists and others learned from the experience of World War II, however, is that physical infrastructure is less important than human infrastructure. Germany and Japan recovered quickly from greater physical devastation than what occurred in China because enough of the people who had run modern industry and the rest of the economic system had survived the war. These people knew what to do and how to do it. Presumably, something similar can be said about the managers and workers who ran the modern sector economic institutions in China. Those who

---

[7] Derived from Chang (1969, p. 131).

were Japanese, however, were repatriated to Japan and many who were Chinese left the mainland for Taiwan or Hong Kong or further afield. Still there would have been several million people who did not leave and were in a position to help China's modern economic sector recover and they did play an active role in the first years after 1949. Many of those with the highest modern sector skills in fields such as banking, however, were under a political cloud and were ultimately removed from positions where they could use their experience. In addition, the Chinese economic system by 1955 was well on its way to becoming a Soviet style centrally planned command economy and that kind of economy had little use for people who understood how a market economy operated. Factory workers and engineers could be used but not bankers and sales managers among others.

V. The Economic and Political Heritage from the Command Economy Era, 1949–1978

China's decision in the 1950s to adopt a Soviet style centrally planned command economy was an understandable choice given what was known at the time about economic development and the situation that China found itself in after the Communist Party took over the government. In the early 1950s, the Soviet Union was widely perceived to be an economic success story. By centralizing all economic controls under the state, the Soviet Union had managed to mobilize enormous resources from what was still a relatively poor economy although the cost in human lives and in the level of consumption of the population as a whole was large. Official measures of Soviet growth indicated that the increase in Soviet economic power was rapid and even Western revisions of those growth rates indicated that the growth rate was higher than in much of the rest of the world.[8]

Reinforcing China's leaning toward the Soviet model was the fact that the Western countries were in the first stages of the Cold War and were not likely to support a nation ruled by a Communist Party, particularly one that looked favorably on the Soviet Union and had fought a war with the United States in Korea. That war produced a total embargo on all trade between Western countries and China that lasted through the 1960s before

[8] See the estimates of Bergson (1961) and the brief discussion later in this essay.

being unilaterally abrogated by the United States and the other Western powers.

In many ways, it was remarkable that China could make the Soviet system work at all. That system required large numbers of people who could manage a very complex economic system. A plan had to be drawn up that provided information that became the basis for orders to individual enterprises as to what to produce and what inputs to use. The inputs were allocated directly to the enterprises through bureaucratic procedures based on the plan and the final product was allocated to end users also through administrative processes. Only consumers went to the market for their goods, and much of what they consumed was not really available through the market — one had to have ration coupons for most essentials.

China did rely heavily on Soviet advisors during the 1950s but advisors can help design a system, they cannot actually run it unless they are imported by the tens of thousands and that was not the case in China in the 1950s. Chinese had to draw up the plans and make them work for industrial sectors that ranged from users of decades old technology to producers using the latest Soviet techniques. Most developing countries with this level of government intervention would have descended into a long period of economic chaos and rising corruption as bureaucrats took advantage of their large discretionary powers to extract rents from factory managers and the general public, but this did not happen in China in the 1950s and 1960s. Through 1957, the system actually worked quite well although the centrally planned command system was not fully in place until 1956 or 1957.

One can only speculate as to what made the system work as well as it did. The morale and financial integrity of the government led by the Communist Party was at a high point after victory in the civil war. China's millennium of experience with running a large government bureaucracy probably also played a role. And there were enough well educated Chinese or educable Chinese so that the skills required could be developed to a functioning level in a relatively short time period.

The centrally planned system, however, did not function well for long. Chairman Mao Zedong was impatient with technology and bureaucratic procedures and attempted to use his political skills to achieve a "Great Leap Forward." The urban chaos that ensued led to a sharp drop in industrial output and the rural chaos of the first phase of the Peoples' Commune movement is widely seen as being the major contributor to a loss of possibly 30 million lives in the famine of 1959–1961. For a variety of reasons ranging from foreign policy and military base differences with China to a general abhorrence of Mao's approach to development, the Soviet Union withdrew all of its advisors in 1960 further exacerbating the situation, particularly in the industrial sector.

Recovery in the early 1960s was achieved by restoring the central planning command system in industry although modifying it to allow much of the planning to take place at the provincial level. In the rural areas, the basic accounting unit that determined the income of its members was transferred down from the Commune with 4,000 to 5,000 families to the Production Team with only 20 to 30 families, thereby resolving some of the most serious incentive problems for farmers. Economic recovery and renewed growth were achieved but were soon again brought to a halt by the "Cultural Revolution." We will not dwell on the specific goals of the Cultural Revolution because they had little to do with economic development. What matters most for our discussion is that the movement disrupted the economy for a number of years and promoted a general attack on educated people, anyone with foreign experience or contacts, and eventually almost everyone who held or had held a position of responsibility within the Communist Party and the government. The economic chaos was brought to an end by the intervention of the army but the political chaos continued right up until Mao's death in 1976 and the arrest of the group now known as the "gang of four."

Despite the impact of the Great Leap Forward and the Cultural Revolution, China did achieve some economic development after 1957 although not as much as the official GDP figures suggest. The official GDP figures indicate that the rate of growth was 5.3% per year between the end of 1957 and 1978 or 3.4% per capita, a quite respectable rate although not close to what was actually achieved after 1978.[9] This growth rate, however, by using the inflated industrial prices of the 1950s to weight

[9]National Statistical Office (1990, p. 35). The growth rates at the time were for Net Material Product (*Guomin shouru* in Chinese or national income). Net Material Product excludes most services but its growth rate in most cases in this period would be similar to that of GDP.

the contribution of industry to GDP, greatly exaggerated that contribution.[10] Using later year market determined prices lowers the GDP growth rate for this period to 3.9% (Perkins and Rawski, 2008, p. 839). While this lower rate still left room for a per capita rate of increase of 2.0%, consumers saw little of this increase. Officially "accumulation" increased from 24.9% of Net Material Product to 36.5% but the real increase was even larger because the prices used to calculate the accumulation rate in the 1950s overstated investment. The rate of investment in 1957 in 2000 prices was around 18%[11] making the rate of increase in consumption over the 1957–1978 period only 2.6% per year or 0.7% per capita and most of that increase probably went to the urban areas and to government consumption.[12] The rural areas with most of China's population experienced no increase in per capita consumption at all.

This stagnation in the standard of living of the Chinese population over a period of two decades despite a high rate of investment might not have seemed unusual if China had been located on some other continent, but China was located in East Asia where the neighboring societies most like China in other respects were growing during this period at 9% per year or 7% per capita. Most Chinese at the time were probably not aware of the rapid transformation that was happening nearby because major efforts were made to block such information from entering the country. But that embargo on information came to an abrupt end in 1979. Deng Xiaoping's trip to Japan in that year was covered on Chinese television and the pictures of Japan's modern industrial economy that came back were a shock.[13] Japan was much further ahead of China than it had been

---

[10]Industrial prices were inflated relative to agricultural and other raw material prices because the Chinese tax system, following that of the Soviet Union, used turnover and profits taxes on industrial products as the main source of government tax revenue.

[11]This figure was derived from the official accumulation and Net Material Product figures converted to year 2000 prices. The capital deflator was taken from Perkins and Rawski (2008, personal websites).

[12]These estimates were derived from the official net material product figures using the sources cited in the previous footnote.

[13]Deng Xiaoping also made a trip to the United States in 1979 that was carried on television in China, but most educated Chinese were well aware that the United States was much richer than China and had been so for a long time.

in the early 1950s. The flow of previously blocked information into China also made it clear that South Korea and Taiwan Province not to mention Hong Kong were experiencing a similar transformation. China was falling further and further behind. For a country whose leaders since the latter half of the 19th century had been concerned with making China wealthy and powerful, there was little doubt that China was doing something wrong and that change was required. In the late 1970s, however, there was no clear view as to what kind of change was required.

The 1960s and 1970s had created some economic wealth that could be used as a base for further growth. Much of this wealth, however, was in the form of heavy industries located in the Northeast or, after the Third Front effort of Chairman Mao, in mountainous regions in the interior of China. Those industries were a drag on Chinese economic performance throughout the 1980s and 1990s although they did create a substantial labor force that knew how to run technologically sophisticated factories. The labor force including the engineers and managers in the industries in cities such as Shanghai, however, played a more important role in the development after 1978. Despite being starved of funds from the central government in the 1960s and 1970s, Shanghai industry remained at the forefront of Chinese industry when it came to technological sophistication and it has retained that role to this day.

Also important during the early 1970s was the development of what was then called the "rural small-scale industry program." In many of the more advanced rural areas of China that program created a large cadre of workers and managers familiar with many aspects of a modern industrial enterprise.[14] When the government in 1984 freed up the availability of most industrial inputs for sale on the market at market prices, the people running these rural industries no longer had to beg the planners for what they needed to expand. The result was the boom in Township and Village Enterprises (TVEs) that was the most dynamic part of Chinese industrial development for the next decade.

Could a similar township and village enterprise boom have occurred in the absence of prior experience with rural industries under the rural

[14] See American Rural Small-Scale Industry Delegation (1977) for a snapshot of what these industries were like in 1975 prior to the beginning of the reform period.

communes? In the context of 1980s China, the probable answer is no. One reason for a negative answer is that the experience in the rural areas with organizing a factory, keeping its financial records, and managing its workforce would have been absent. But another reason is that China in the 1980s was not willing to support the rapid development of a fully private rural industry program largely because private enterprise in general was suspect and considered as a force that could undermine socialism. The TVEs, however, were collectively owned enterprises and as such were not a threat to the socialist system. Because the rural industries prior to the reform period started as collective enterprises imbedded in a system of collective agriculture, the collective TVEs were to a degree just a continuation of the way of organizing rural businesses that already existed. If the Communes had not existed, rural private entrepreneurs might have been able to take advantage of the 1984 reforms that freed up industrial inputs by forming small private firms, but it is unlikely that they would have or could have organized these enterprises along collective lines. Forming a collective while also starting a factory would have involved more innovation than could normally be expected.

One piece of support for the above argument is that Vietnam in its reform period would have very much liked to have experienced a boom in collective rural industries, but no such development occurred.[15] In Vietnam prior to their reform period (beginning in 1986 and 1989), rural collectives were devoted solely to agriculture. There was no experience with collective industry. Vietnam did not experience anything remotely comparable to China's rural industrial boom until it passed laws that explicitly recognized and gave legal support to outright private enterprises and that did not occur until the beginning of the 21st century. In the first decade of reform in both Vietnam and China, however, strong government support for private industrial efforts other than foreign direct investment was out of the question largely on political grounds.

[15]During the 1989–1999 decade, I gave dozens of lectures in Vietnam on the Chinese reform experience and other related issues and was regularly asked by members in the audience (mostly government officials) "how can we develop something similar to the Chinese township and village enterprises?" If there had been a good answer to that question, there is little doubt that the Vietnamese government would have provided support for such an effort.

The TVE boom in China in the late 1980s and early 1990s, however, involved more than the availability on the market of needed inputs and an ideological preference for the collective form over outright private ownership. Fiscal decentralization gave local governments a powerful incentive to promote these enterprises as a source of local revenue. When taxes on these enterprises were recentralized to the central government in the 1990s, however, local governments no longer had a fiscal incentive to promote these industries and most of them were rapidly privatized.[16]

VI. The Political Heritage

Up to this point, this chapter has focused mainly on China's economic and social historical heritage. Politics entered into this discussion mainly as part of the analysis of how China created a unified state over such a large territory. In this section, we will focus entirely on how domestic and international politics has shaped China's economic development.

Any discussion of Chinese politics is certain to be controversial, particularly when undertaken by an economist rather than a political scientist or a political historian. This statement is valid whether the discussion is about politics in the Qing Dynasty or politics after 1949. Our analysis, however, has a limited purpose. We are trying to understand how politics shaped major economic decisions and strategies made after 1949 and particularly after 1978. We are not trying to present a comprehensive view of the nature of Chinese politics nor are we trying to place China's political experience in a broad international context. Other countries can no doubt learn from China's political history, but our main task is simply to try to explain how politics in broad brush terms drove economic decisions in China. At the end of the essay, we will speculate briefly about the future, about what other developing countries and China itself going forward might learn from its own history and that of other countries that have gone through a period of sustained economic development.

---

[16]For a discussion of how fiscal incentives contributed to both the rise and fall of the TVEs, see Kung and Lin (2007). For further discussion of the reasons behind the rise of the TVEs, see also Jin and Qian (1998).

China's political history goes back for nearly three millennia to at least the time of Confucius. Our discussion, however, will begin with how the Chinese state responded to the impact of Western contact beginning with the Qianlong Emperor. A story often told is how the Qianlong Emperor in receiving the Macartney Embassy in 1793 declared that "our celestial empire possesses all things in prolific abundance" and turned down the mission's request for an expansion of trade beyond the port of "Canton" (Fairbank *et al.*, 1965, p. 77). In 1793, there was a considerable element of truth to the Emperor's statement. Industrial and agricultural technologies in Europe were not notably advanced over what existed in China at that time as pointed out above.[17] European importers of silk and tea from China, for the most part paid for their purchases in silver because there were not European goods of sufficient value to be worth taking on the several months long trip to China. The principal exception where European technology was superior was not in traded goods, but in military organization and tactics plus superior naval vessels and cannon, but that was not as apparent in 1793 as it was five decades later.

Defeat in two wars followed by treaties with the Western Powers in 1842 and 1858–1860 forcing open China's ports left little doubt about the military superiority of Western land as well as naval forces. What is relevant for this essay is the response of the Qing government to those defeats. There were modest efforts to improve China's military hardware (for example, the Jiangnan Arsenal in 1865 and the China Merchants Steam Navigation Company in 1872) and the beginnings of a few other Chinese owned industrial enterprises under the sponsorship of a few governor-generals in certain key provinces (notably, Li Hongzhang).

The dominant view of the imperial court in Beijing, however, was that China had little to learn from the West. Except for a few kinds of weapons and ships, China's way of doing things was superior. The problem was not how to fundamentally change the system in order to meet the external challenge. The goal of the Tongzhi Emperor's reign

---

[17]The definitive work on Chinese science and technology is the series led by Joseph Needham (various years), Pomeranz (2000) has looked explicitly at the comparison of the level of science and technology in China as compared to the west during the Qing dynasty among other periods.

was to restore the traditional system to its former integrity and glory. The biggest problem for the Qing government, after all, was not the small military battles with the West, but the massive Taiping rebellion within China that nearly overthrew the dynasty and killed millions of people in the process. During a period (1854–1894) when Japan was changing its economic and political system in fundamental ways, the dominant forces in Beijing were attempting to restore the old system as best they could.

Even defeat by Japan in 1895 with its military modernized along Western lines, the large indemnity of 200 million taels, and the loss of Taiwan to Japanese control did not fundamentally change the attitude of the imperial court except for a brief "100 days of reform in 1898" that was quickly overturned by the Empress Dowager and other court conservatives. Instead of reform, the court gave support to the Boxers *(yiho tuan)*, whose main unifying idea was opposition to foreigners and Chinese Christian converts, and who were easily defeated once the West had time to mobilize an international army made up of troops of all of the major imperialist powers.

The reason for reciting this well-known history is to make one point. Changing, the Chinese political system and the policies and institutions that were an integral part of that system was a very difficult task. The Chinese imperial system was not the product of a charismatic figure or two who served as emperors. It was a system built on a set of beliefs that were held by virtually all of those who attained a position as a government official and more broadly these beliefs were held by large parts of the population as well. With time and a different set of leaders at the court in Beijing, China might have been able to gradually adjust these beliefs to accommodate modern economic development, but it proved surprisingly easy for the court conservatives to defeat most of the modernizing reforms actually tried. From 1912 until 1949, on the other hand, the issue was not so much one of changing the Chinese system, but just who among an assortment of warlords and revolutionaries would rule China. Change and some modern economic growth did occur as pointed out above, but it occurred mostly on the periphery of Chinese society in or near the treaty ports or in the Japanese occupied northeast.

Even after 1949, it is not difficult to find some of the traditional attitudes of anti-foreignism and "China always knows best" present in some of the attitudes present and policies that were pursued. The most obvious cases occurred during the Cultural Revolution when it was frequently stated that one could rely on poorly educated farmers to develop the new agricultural technologies required or when anyone who suggested that importing advanced technology from the West was subject to severe criticism.[18] China's decisions particularly after 1960 to minimize dependence on foreign trade were due to much more than just anti-foreign or anti-imperialist attitudes, but the ease with which that approach to the international economy was accepted probably owes something to traditional beliefs about the outside world.[19]

VII. Politics and the Economic Choices in 1949–1978 and Beyond

When the Communist Party took over the Chinese government in 1949, the most immediate economic problem was the hyperinflation that had been raging for nearly a decade. Any government, whatever its politics, would have had to move to rein in inflation as soon as it was feasible to do so and the specific methods used were only indirectly influenced by politics. Basically, the growth in the money supply had to be brought down to a level that was consistent with the availability of goods on the market and that meant that the government, unlike its predecessor, could not finance its expenditures mainly by printing money.

The government after 1949 brought inflation to a halt quickly but the experience of the 1940s with prices rising by thousands of percent per month or even per week left a long-term political legacy. Future Chinese governments and the Chinese population more generally were very

---

[18]That did not prevent China from importing some key industrial products prior to 1976 such as large chemical fertilizer plants, but those wanting to go in this direction typically had a political fight on their hands with "left" critics and this criticism undoubtedly reduced such imports until after 1976.

[19]China in the 1950s and into the 1970s, of course, faced both credible dangers of a foreign invasion from either the West or the Soviet Union and it also was subject to the Western (and Japanese) trade embargo until 1968 although the embargo was lifted well before China turned outward with its economic policies.

sensitive to even modest levels of inflation, modest by developing country standards that is.[20] When inflation (the consumer price index) went above 10% per year in 1988 and again in 1993, the response of the government was rapid and vigorous even to the point of major personnel changes (bringing in Deputy Prime Minister Zhu Rongji as head of the People's Bank for example).[21] A vigorous effort to control inflation, of course, did not just serve political objectives. There is ample cross-country statistical analysis to show that low rates of inflation are also associated with higher GDP growth rates, but it is the relationship between price stability and political stability in China that undoubtedly played a larger role in the decisions to act quickly and decisively in bringing inflation below the double digit level (Fischer, 1991).

By 1955, China's leadership, as pointed out above, had made a firm decision to adopt a Soviet type development model and that decision also in part reflected political considerations although in a complex and indirect way. The Soviet model of economic development, with its emphasis on heavy industry and with its rejection of the use of market forces for everything but the distribution of some consumer goods and the purchase of subsidiary agricultural products, was seen in the 1950s as a model well suited to developing countries particularly large ones. The Soviet Union had achieved a high rate of investment and, in the 1950s and 1960s at least, a relatively high rate of growth in GDP.[22] The Soviet Union had also fought and won a major war against the nation that in 1939 and 1941 was the largest military power in the world, Nazi Germany.

---

[20]High income countries generally try to keep inflation around 2 to 3% per year and 10% or more is considered to be politically unacceptable and a threat to long term growth. Many developing countries, however, have continued to grow-rapidly despite inflation over 10% a year and it has not always been a major political problem unless it goes much higher (South Korea in the 1960s and 1970s for example, and many South American countries).

[21]Unlike in the United States and Western Europe, the head of the central bank in economies modeled on that of the Soviet Union was typically a weak position. The economy was run by the planning commission and bankers were there to support the planners in whatever the planners decided was desirable.

[22]The official national income growth rates for the Soviet Union were distorted in various ways but the most careful effort to reconstruct those figures eliminating these distortions still came up with a growth rate of 7.6% a year for the 1950–1955 period (Bergson, 1961).

China's decision to "lean to one side" politically (that is toward the Soviet Union) thus made the decision to also adopt the Soviet economic model a natural one. The fact that China fought a war in Korea with the United States beginning in 1950, faced a hostile Republic of China on Taiwan supported by the United States, and was subject to a complete embargo on trade with market economies, made it difficult if not impossible to adopt an alternative growth model similar to the one adopted in the 1960s by South Korea and Taiwan Province. In any case, in the 1950s, there were few in the development economics community that advocated a growth strategy based on export led manufacturing. The fact that the Soviet Union was willing to help China create a centrally planned command economy by supplying thousands of advisors made the decision that much easier.

The Soviet command economy model, in addition, had certain clear advantages for a government that was consolidating power over a nation that at the time had over 500 million people. Collectivizing agriculture, in particular, gave the state a high degree of control over the rural population as long as reliable political cadres could be put in charge of the collectives (agricultural producer cooperatives in 1955–1957 and rural people's communes from 1958 on). State ownership and control of industry had similar political advantages.

The centrally planned command economy model also allowed those in charge in Beijing to make major structural shifts in the economy in a relatively short time period. Initially, this meant the development from a very small beginning of a heavy industry sector focusing on machinery and steel. This emphasis could be justified in purely economic terms if one bought the Soviet closed economy model in which heavy industry was central to a high and rising rate of investment and a high and rising rate of investment also leads to a high rate of growth of national product. An emphasis on heavy industry makes much less sense if the economy is opened up and there is a large and rising level of foreign trade, but China could not have had a vigorous foreign trade regime because of the embargo. Even after China broke with the Soviet Union in 1960 (or vice versa), China was still subject to the embargo for another nine years.

In the late 1960s, as mentioned above, the command economy also made it possible for the government to move large parts of its by then expanded heavy industry sector into the interior of the country and into mountainous regions that, it was believed, would be relatively safe from military attack from either the Soviet Union or the United States. There was no conceivable purely economic justification for this move of "third front industries." It was a move dictated by the leadership's perception of the international political situation (Naughton, 1988).

The centrally planned command model, however, was much less suited to other aspects of Chairman Mao Zedong's approach to politics and political leadership in China. Chairman's Mao's greatest political strength was his ability to mobilize large numbers of people to carry out difficult goals. This talent had served the Communist Party well in the civil war but it did not fit well with a centrally planned command economy. That kind of economy requires a large bureaucracy that makes decisions on what to produce and where to use a product once produced and makes these decisions based largely on technical considerations. There is no room for politics or inspired leadership in setting the input and output goals of a centrally planned industrial enterprise. Many in the Chinese leadership as early as 1957 found this command system to be too rigid and were taking steps to loosen up that system by allowing in some market forces.

By 1958, however, Chairman Mao saw what he believed to be an opportunity to use his political mobilization skills to accelerate the development of China's economy and the "Great Leap Forward" described briefly above was the result. The method was to first remove from positions of influence everyone who was likely to be skeptical of such an effort and then to motivate the rest to go all out to achieve unprecedented results. The amount of energy released was enormous and unprecedented in world history. Hundreds of millions of farmers moved vast quantities of rock and dirt in what was hoped would provide rural China with a large increase in its physical capital mainly in the form of expanded irrigation and more efficient land use. In industry, factories were expanded and backyard iron and steel furnaces blossomed everywhere to melt up scrap iron and steel to make new crude farm implements and other tools. The problem was that there was no plan (or no market) coordinating this effort except on a political level and the result was a sharp drop in both agricultural and industrial output. The famine of 1959–1961, as pointed out above took millions of lives[23] and industrial output did not recover to the level of 1958 until 1964 (National Statistical Office, 1990, p. 414).

There were several political legacies of the "Great Leap Forward" that had a lasting influence. The first lesson for Chinese leaders, at least most of them, was that mass political mobilization was not a method for achieving desirable economic results. Even in agriculture where there was some basis in historical experience for using large amounts of rural labor to build irrigation systems, the lesson was that large Commune-sized agricultural production and accounting units might be good for mobilizing labor but they were a disaster when it came to managing crops. They also were not what were really needed to expand irrigation systems. Where labor mobilization could do the job, much of the work had been accomplished centuries earlier and these new efforts could improve the system only at the margin (Perkins, 1969, Chapter IV and Appendix H). In the other parts of China, with notable exceptions in some mountainous areas, labor mobilization was not what was required on places such as the North China Plain where water could only be reached by digging tube wells.

In industry, the backyard iron and steel furnaces were a failure largely because they were built through political mobilization without much consideration as to whether they would be useful in practice. By the early 1970s, the small scale rural industry described above was proving to make a real contribution to agriculture, but it was small scale industry based on careful calculations of local needs and done taking engineering requirements fully into account. In large-scale urban industry, central planning was re-established after 1961 although on a somewhat decentralized basis that made the province rather than Beijing the unit for coordinating inputs and outputs.

Even when it was functioning without political interference, however, the overall impact of the changes made in 1961–1962 led to recovery but only a modest rate of growth in GDP, as pointed out in the previous section. From a political perspective, the near stagnation in per capita income, particularly in the rural areas, did nothing to build support for the government or its policies, although the tight control of information from outside

[23]For analysis of the political content in the causes of this famine, see Kung and Lin (2003).

the country probably meant that slow growth was itself not that much of a political problem, especially given all of the other activities going on during the Cultural Revolution. As mentioned above, the potential political problems came when large numbers of people became aware of the economic performance of China's neighbors, but by then China was in the first stages of creating a boom of its own.

The biggest political legacy of the 1960s and early 1970s from the point of view of the economy, however, was derived directly from the politics of that period. The Great Proletarian Cultural Revolution was so extreme along so many dimensions that it led to a reaction that was equally strong. The Great Leap Forward did more direct damage to the economy, but it was the Cultural Revolution that fundamentally undermined political support for the kinds of Utopian social change goals and political mobilization policies pursued during the last half of the 1960s and into the early 1970s. Almost everyone with any foreign connection was subject to humiliating treatment that often led to suicide. Probably more importantly from the point of view of domestic politics, most of the senior members of the Communist Party and high officials in the government were stripped of their authority and sent to do menial jobs often under harsh conditions. Educated youth were also sent to the countryside typically under harsh conditions. It can plausibly be argued that many of the "sent down" youth gained a more profound understanding of the true nature and extreme poverty of the Chinese countryside. That was a positive outcome for the long-term future of China, but in the short term it did nothing to encourage support from these youth for the goals of the Cultural Revolution even though many of these same youth, somewhat blindly to be sure, had supported those goals in its initial phase. Today, many of these former sent down youth constitute a large part of the leadership of the Chinese government and the Communist Party although most of the most senior officials are from an earlier generation.[24] By the time the Cultural Revolution finally came to an end, support for the policies and political methods of that period was confined to a narrow group of

[24]This group is sometimes labeled the "fifth generation" of leadership or "generation of the Republic" (basically high officials who were born from 1950 through the early 1960s). For a brief discussion of the experience of this generation as sent down youth, see Li (2008).

"extreme leftist" politicians led by what is now called the "gang of four," and the "gang of four" was in jail.

There are other examples in other countries of years or decades of trauma that have led to a fundamental rejection of the policies of that period. The economically and socially disastrous policies of President Sukarno in Indonesia, for example, paved the way for the radically different although equally authoritarian policies of President Suharto. Eastern Europe's experience with an economic and political system dictated by the Soviet Union led to a complete rejection of that system once the Soviet forces that kept it in place were removed. It remains to be seen whether the disastrous policies of the Mugabe government in Zimbabwe will be followed by fundamental changes in policy under a new regime sometime in the future. Not all of the changes brought about by trauma are positive. The reaction against the short lived attempt by the Allende government in Chile with only minority support to fundamentally change society in a socialist direction was followed by the repression of the Pinochet years that for a time destroyed one of the most vibrant democracies in South America. A bit further back in history, the hyperinflation and heavy indemnity burden that led to the collapse of the Weimar government in Germany produced the Nazi regime of Adolph Hitler.

The related question for this chapter is whether the reforms of the post-1978 period in China were an inevitable result of the Cultural Revolution trauma that preceded it, or whether the changes could have gone in a very different direction? Put differently, how much of what happened after 1978 can be attributed to individual personalities starting with Deng Xiaoping and including many of the other leaders who led the reform effort? Counterfactual questions of this sort are not popular among historians, but they are worth asking in this context even if no definitive answer to such questions is possible.

As a matter of recorded history, there is no question that Deng Xiaoping led the reform effort and his basic approach of "seeking truth from facts" was central to how the reform effort evolved step by step based on accumulating experience. There was no plan designed by others that could be pulled off the shelf and implemented. It is also not seriously disputed that Deng Xiaoping had a level of political support that others in the leadership after 1977 could not have matched. This support came in part from his long years of playing a central role in the revolution that brought the Communist Party to power, but others still alive in the late 1970s had played important roles in the revolution. Probably more important was that many in leadership positions saw Deng as the ablest individual in the leadership, a person capable of getting things done and bringing order out of chaos. It is why Zhou Enlai advocated restoring him to a top position during the last years of the Cultural Revolution even though he was anathema to the "extreme leftists" then still powerful.

The other major political figure who could have taken over the leadership of economic reform and did in fact play an important role was Chen Yun. But, while Chen Yun was an important moderating force on economic policies in the 1950s and the early 1960s and was willing to experiment with some uses for market forces, he was fundamentally a believer in central planning and the command economy.[25] All of the evidence available to those of us not on the inside of Chinese decision making is that Chen Yun would have supported a restoration of a strong command economy modified to allow market forces in areas such as subsidiary agricultural output where central planning was ineffective. An argument he could have made is that central planning and the command economy were never given a fair trial, an argument that would have been hard to refute given that the command system, once in place, was only able to operate without political interference for two years in 1956–1957 and perhaps another three years in 1962–1964.[26]

Thus, in rejecting the economic radicalism of the 1958–1976 eras, it was not automatic that China would have moved to an open market economy as in fact occurred. There was a clear alternative that could have been tried and which would have been more consistent with typical approaches of most Communist Parties in power. Central planning, the command economy, and only limited opening of the economy were still

[25]Chen Yun, as is well known, used the metaphor of a bird in a cage to describe the nature of the desired economic system. The bird (economic decision makers) was allowed to fly but only within the confines of a cage (the central plan). For some of Chen's earlier views, see Lardy (1983).

[26]This author is unaware whether Chen Yun did in fact make such an argument, but such an argument would have been consistent with his view that central planning should take the lead economic role.

seen by a wide spectrum of people in the 1980s as the correct way for socialist economies to be managed. Furthermore, there was an individual with the knowledge and the respect of most of those in power after 1978 who could have led this revitalization of a centrally planned command economy.

The return to central planning did not occur because Deng Xiaoping in part had no preconceived view as to what kind of economy would be best for China. His concern was one not unlike the reformers of late nineteenth century China — he wanted to make China "wealthy and powerful" and was prepared to try anything that worked to achieve that goal. In the 1980s, he turned to certain key individuals who demonstrated that they could make changes that would lead to higher growth in production and income. Those individuals in turn listened to others who from the outset knew they had to open up the economy and do something about rural poverty, but who only step by step came to realize that they were moving toward a full market economy, although in the 1980s no-one in a leadership position was willing to say that was the goal. When problems with reform occurred in 1988–1989 (inflation and corruption among others) and political events brought to positions of power those opposed to many market oriented reforms, it was Deng Xiaoping who made his famous trip to the south in 1992 and by stating his approval of the more controversial reforms of the 1980s effectively put the engine of reform back on a track toward a full market system.

It is not possible, therefore, to separate the nature of China's economic reforms between 1978 and the early 1990s from the personality and political strength of an individual, Deng Xiaoping, even though he himself probably designed few of the specific policies pursued. He knew what he wanted as an end product and he had the vehicle, a restored Communist Party, to implement what he wanted. The actual designers of the specific policies were an eclectic group made up of politicians and their advisors who listened to all manner of others inside and outside of China and who also responded to "facts on the ground." In the latter category of facts on the ground was the rapid response of farmers to the opportunity, first applied in only a few poor provinces, to go back to household agriculture. Later in the decade it was the surprise blossoming of township and village enterprises when they were given ready access through the market to the inputs they needed to use their entrepreneurial skills. In the background was the ongoing economic boom in the four "Tiger economies" that increasingly influenced how those in China thought about what kind of reforms were likely to be most successful.

A comprehensive intellectual and political history of the first phase of the reform period between 1978 and 1997 has yet to be written and, given its complexity, it will be a difficult task. It has some features in common with vigorous economic reform efforts elsewhere in the world including in South Korea between 1961 and 1979, and in Indonesia in the 1970s and 1980s, among others. In each case, there was a strong leader supported by able subordinates who were more technocrats than politicians. They also had an organization capable of carrying out their wishes (the Communist Party and government bureaucracy in China, the military and the government bureaucracy in South Korea, and less effectively the military but with primary reliance on market forces in Indonesia). During the most successful reform periods in these three economies, the leaders supported reforms that would raise income and production regardless of their ideological content. This changed in Indonesia in the 1990s when President Suharto became heavily concerned with more personal goals, but in both China and South Korea the reforms outlasted their first leader despite the assassination of President Park and the problems initially connected with the succession to Deng Xiaoping.

VIII. The Lesson of China's Historical Experience for Others

This brief review of certain aspects of China's historical economic, social and political heritage raises the question of whether another developing country can learn from China's reform experience and adopt for its own ends some of what China accomplished during its 30 years of reform. Or is the path China took dependent on that country's unique historical background? Certainly political unity and stability across a large area is not easily achieved if it does not exist, as many of the nations that were formed by colonial borders drawn in ways unrelated to underlying economic and cultural divisions of the new nations have demonstrated. These nations, whether in West Africa or the Middle East, will have to find their own path to unity and stability. The political stability required for long-term investments in these countries will be impossible without a higher level of unity than now exists in many of these countries.

China's historical experience with education also cannot be copied but there is no need for other nations to try to do so. There are a variety of paths to universal literacy and high quality schools at the primary, secondary and tertiary levels. But a country that does not now have highly educated elite cannot simply create one within a few years by following a standard educational development strategy. It can take generations of education to produce tens or hundreds of thousands of scientists and engineers who can compete with the best in the world and can work on the frontiers of technological knowledge. A nation that began independence with high levels of illiteracy, with a few hundred or a few thousand university graduates, and with a weak and small secondary school system, should not think about becoming a manufacturer of commercial aircraft (as Indonesia tried and failed to do in the 1970s through the 1990s) or become a launcher of commercial satellites into space. There are a number of other developing countries that clearly do have an adequate base for such efforts, but there are many others that do not. For those that do not, the challenge is to build a first class education system step by step because sustained economic development to levels of income comparable to what is found in high income countries is impossible without it.

The richness of China's pre-modern commercial skills is something that other countries can more readily achieve if the right incentives for commercial development are in place. All countries have their own commercial traditions and many large commercial firms in China and among Chinese in Southeast Asia grew from tiny unimpressive beginnings into giant international enterprises. Chinese policies actually tried for 30 years (1949–1978) to suppress most of these talents, but ultimately failed to do so. Most countries that have tried to promote the development of indigenous commercial firms have succeeded in doing so. China began with an advantage in this sphere for historical reasons, but it did not give Chinese merchants a permanent advantage.

On the other hand, replicating China's support from the commercial talents of Hong Kong and the Overseas Chinese more generally is a kind of resource available to only a few countries. India, for example, could take more advantage of the overseas Indian Diaspora and in recent decades it began doing so. Lebanon would be another nation with a similar opportunity if it could establish stability at home, but there are not many others.

China's pre-modern industrial experience and its first 30 years of industrialization beginning in 1949 mainly gave the country a small cadre of people who could manage industrial enterprises, or at least the engineering aspects of such enterprises, and a larger number of workers with experience in industry. There is not a great deal that other countries can learn from this experience except for a few lessons of what not to do, mainly from the 1949–1978 period. Do not start by running such enterprises through a central plan and a command economy structure that rejects market forces, do not start with an emphasis on large-scale heavy industries. Even China's experience with rural industries is mostly relevant to the very special context in which this development occurred. No one is going to suggest that other developing countries should collectivize agriculture and the rural economy more generally in order to promote the Chinese style collective township and village enterprises. On the positive side, China does demonstrate that there are a wide variety of rural enterprises that can contribute in a major way to industrial development at a particular development stage, but, from an organizational point of view, it is much easier to create the incentives and infrastructure that will facilitate the growth of private rural industrial and commercial enterprises than it is to create collective enterprises.

What at the most general level can other countries learn from the politics of reform in China? Probably, the most basic lesson is that economic and political disaster can contain within it the seeds of fundamental change for the better. This idea is not new although most analysis focuses on more short-term crises of the kind that require a rescue by the IMF (see, for example, Grindle and Thomas, 1991). In China's case, the disaster lasted off and on for nearly 20 years. To take advantage of the disaster, however, one must be able to bring to the fore a leader who has a clear vision of the nature of the challenge and is supported by an organization capable of implementing that vision. How does one get such a leader and implementing organization? The organization has to be already in place because one cannot create an effective government bureaucracy or even a modern and disciplined military overnight.

The leaders discredited for causing the crisis are likely to be removed from office, but that then leaves the country with the challenge of finding a new leader or leaders of the right kind. It is not difficult to find someone who has the necessary power. The political process will frequently throw up a powerful figure capable of building a coalition of supporters. But finding someone with a vision, and not just any vision but the correct vision for the time, is much more of a challenge. Certainly, there is a strong element of luck involved in the rise of an individual like Deng Xiaoping in China as there probably was with any number of other great figures in history.

The historical experience of all countries is to some degree unique. One can learn from others about what worked in their particular context and why it worked, but then must think hard about what is realistic in one's own context. China had a functioning bureaucracy going back for centuries and many kinds of reform require a reasonably efficient government bureaucracy, but such institutions cannot be created in a decade or two. If one does not have such institutions one must rely on policies that can be implemented without much government help — generally this involves reliance on market forces to shape private business activity.

There are also many negative lessons that one can learn from the experience of others. China, because it had a functioning government bureaucracy and a reasonably well educated and easily trainable population, could make a centrally planned command economy work, but not very well. Most analysts would draw from this experience the negative lesson that it makes little sense for a developing country to adopt such an economic system however strong and competent its government bureaucracy and China's own experience would lend some support to this view on the pitfalls of central planning.

Are there any lessons for China itself from this brief review of its political history? Perhaps, the main lesson is that a political system that worked well in a particular context may not work well at all in a different context. The imperial bureaucracy and belief system of traditional China worked well for centuries but was unable to cope with the Western challenge. The mass mobilization and related political skills of Mao Zedong were well suited to making a revolution, but not to running an economy. Deng Xiaoping with his vision and leadership skills was the right person to lead the first phases of the reform effort, but it takes very special circumstances to produce such a leader and to give him the tools to make the fundamental changes required. Those circumstances are not likely to be repeated in China. Going forward another decade or two, China is likely to be well on its way to high income status and an urbanized and increasingly well educated society. Managing that kind of society is likely to require a very different kind of government from what exists in China today or at any time in the past.

References

Alesina A and E La Ferrara (2005). "Ethnic diversity and economic performance". *Journal of Economic Literature,* 43, pp. 762–800.

American Rural Small-Scale Industry Delegation (1977). *Rural Small-Scale Industry in the People's Republic of China.* Berkeley, CA: University of California Press.

Bergson, A (1961). *The Real National Income of Soviet Russia since 1928.* Boston, MA: Harvard University Press.

Chang, JK (1969). *Industrial Development in Pre-Communist China: A Quantitative Analysis.* Chicago, IL: Aldine Publishers.

Fairbank, JK, EO Reischauer and AM Craig (1965). *East Asia: The Great Transformation.* Boston, MA: Houghton Mifflin.

Fischer, S (1991). "Macroeconomics and development". *NBER Working Paper* No. W3702.

Grindle, MS and JW Thomas (1991). *Public Choices and Policy Changes: The Political Economy of Reform in Developing Countries.* Baltimore: Johns Hopkins University Press.

Jin, H and Y Qian (1998). "Public versus private ownership of firms: Evidence from rural China." *Quarterly Journal of Economics,* 113(3), pp. 773–808.

Kung, JK and Y Lin (2007). "The decline of township-and-village enterprises in China's economic transition." *World Development,* 35(4), pp. 569–584.

Kung, JK and JY Lin (2003). "The causes of China's great leap famine." *Economic Development and Cultural Change,* 52(1), pp. 51–73.

Lardy, N (1983). *Chen Yun's Strategy for China's Development: A Non-Maoist Alternative.* Armonk: M.E. Sharpe.

Li, B (2000). *Jiangnande Zaoqi Gongyehua.* Beijing: Shehui Kexue Wenxian Press.

Li, C (2008). "China's fifth generation: Is diversity a source of strength or weakness." *Asia Policy,* 6, pp. 53–93.

Maddison, A (2007). *Contours of the World Economy, 1–2030 AD.* Oxford: Oxford University Press.

National Statistical Office (1990). *Zhongguo Tongji Nianjian 1990.* Beijing: China Statistics Press.

National Statistical Office (2007). *China Statistical Yearbook 2007.* Beijing: China Statistics Press.

National Statistical Office (2008). *Zhongguo Tongji Zhaiyao 2008.* Beijing: China Statistics Press.

Naughton, B (1988). "The third front: Defense industrialization in China's interior." *The China Quarterly,* 115, pp. 351–386.

Needham, J (various years). *Science and Civilization in China* (multiple volumes). Cambridge: Cambridge University Press.

Orleans, L (1961). *Professional Manpower and Education in Communist China.* Washington: National Science Foundation.

Perkins, DH (1969). *Agricultural Development in China, 1368–1968.* Chicago, IL: Aldine.

Perkins, DH and TG Rawski (2008). Forecasting China's economic growth to 2025. In *China's Great Economic Transformation,* L Brandt and TG Rawski (eds.). Cambridge: Cambridge University Press.

Perkins, DH and M Roemer (1994). Differing endowments and historical legacies. In *Asia and Africa: Legacies and Opportunities in Development,* DL Lindauer and M Roemer (eds.), pp. 25–28. San Francisco: Institute for Contemporary Studies Press.

Pomeranz, K (2000). *The Great Divergence: China, Europe and the Making of the Modern World Economy,* Princeton, NJ: Princeton University Press.

Rawski, E (1979). *Education and Popular Literacy in Ch'ing China* (Michigan Studies on China), Ann Arbor: University of Michigan Press.

Rawski, T (1989). *Economic Growth in Prewar China*, Berkeley, CA: University of California Press.

Sung, Y (1991). *The China-Hong Kong Connection: The Key to China's Open Door Policy,* Cambridge: Cambridge University Press.

Wang, Y (2003). *Qingdai Jingjishi Lunwenji,* Banqiao City, 3 volumes, Taibei Xian: Daoxiang Press.

CHAPTER 2

GOVERNMENT AS AN OBSTACLE TO INDUSTRIALIZATION: THE CASE OF 19TH CENTURY CHINA

Few generalizations find wider acceptance among specialists on China than that which holds that the Chinese Imperial Government was hostile to commerce and industry and that this hostility was a major element in the country's failure to achieve modern economic growth. There is, of course, an important element of truth in this generalization, but analysis of the issues involved has generally suffered from a failure to make clear just what it was that the Chinese government in the 19th century should have done to promote development.

This chapter is made up of two parts. In the first, there is a brief summary of recent findings by a number of historians to the effect that the reputed official hostility to commerce has been greatly exaggerated. Many Ch'ing government officials not only understood commerce, but were deeply involved in it themselves. Included in this section is an argument, based on some recent research of my own, to the effect that the size and nature of China's commerce in the 19th century and before were limited by essentially economic conditions. Government hostility, where it existed, played only a marginal role.

The more significant question, however, is whether a reasonably sophisticated commercial system leads readily into industrialization. The answer, of course, is that it does not. A number of additional steps, particularly the introduction of a new technology and increased capital formation, are necessary. For the late-developing countries — that is, every nation except England — the government can play an important role in both areas. The failures of the Ch'ing government of 19th century China were in these areas. China's retarded industrialization was more a result of sins of omission than of commission.

I. Chinese Commerce: Attitudes versus Economics

The standard view of Chinese commerce used to be that it was a despised profession. Merchants were at the bottom of the social ladder, according to official doctrine, following after officials, peasants, and artisans. Commerce was a parasitic activity that could be milked at will, and if it was destroyed in the process, that was no cause for concern. Furthermore, merchants held themselves in low repute. Whenever possible, they bought or educated themselves into the official class. Operating under such conditions, Chinese commerce was never able to develop beyond a certain level.

Scholars familiar with other premodern societies will recognize this portrait. The low position of merchants in the formal social structure was common to Tokugawa Japan and Europe (in the Middle Ages and later), as well as to China. Japanese merchants also bought their way into the samurai class whenever possible. Nevertheless, these countries did somehow succeed in developing modern industry, and there is little reason to believe that the low repute in which men of commerce were held was a significant drag on the process.

In recent years, a number of scholarly efforts have gone a long way toward shattering the image of Chinese commerce portrayed by official Confucian ideology.[1] Although a statute of the year 1394 prohibited officials above a certain rank from participating in trade, even then many official families ignored the statute and engaged in a wide variety of commercial activities. By the 18th and early 19th centuries, Imperial Government policy had evolved to the point where merchants were commonly being rewarded with high ranks and titles. In the words of Ping-ti Ho, "it may be said that in Ch'ing times the social distinction between officials and rich merchants was more blurred than at any other time in Chinese history except for the Mongol Yuan period."[2] Another source estimates that 17% of all gentry income came from trade and financial

[1]This analysis of attitudes toward commerce has benefited from the reading of an unpublished paper by Thomas G. Rawski, The Role of the Chinese Merchant Community in Treaty Port Commerce, 1860–1875.

[2]Ho (1962), p. 82.

activities, almost as much as was obtained in government service.[3] In fact, a case can be made that it was difficult to carry on large-scale trade unless one was a member of the gentry or official class. Most such activities required constant contact with officials, contact that was not easy to sustain for individuals lacking the proper social background. The sale of titles and degrees, which was practiced on a large scale in 19th century China, increased the flexibility of the system by making it easier for merchants to attain gentry status. The practice did not, however, originate in the 19th century, and it only modified and did not basically change the merchant-gentry relationship.

Nor was government policy as vigorously anticommerce as has been supposed. Given the role of official families in trade, it would be surprising if government actions did really do much harm to commercial activities. In the words of Thomas Metzger, there was in contrast "constant official propaganda against greedy officials who regarded merchants as 'fish and meat.' Respect for private property or more especially bureaucratic dependence on well-to-do merchants for cooperation in implementing policies is a common theme in Ch'ing governmental documents."[4]

By contrast with British commercial policies of the 19th century, to be sure, Chinese imperial efforts do not appear particularly enlightened, but then British policies prior to the 19th century are not very impressive by that standard either. Like so much premodern trade, that in China was riddled by government and private or guild efforts to establish monopoly controls and profits. Sometimes these were successful; often they were not. If profits or taxes became too high, illegal alternatives quickly manifested themselves.

Perhaps, the most onerous of Ch'ing commercial policies was the *likin* tax or tax on internal trade. The formal rate of this tax ranged from 1% of the value of the good to as much as 10%.[5] Furthermore, the tax was frequently levied more than once on a single commodity. Thus, although the most common tax rate was 2% per tax station, the actual rate paid by journey's end was often higher. What made the tax so onerous in the 19th

---

[3] Chang (1962), p. 327.

[4] Metzger (1966).

[5] Lo (1936), p. 62.

century, however, was that foreign goods were not taxed and thus gained some advantage over domestic products. In addition, the arbitrary manner in which many tax stations were administered brought an element of uncertainty into internal trade.

But the tax was not excessive if one abstracts from foreign competition and arbitrary administration. Much of the burden of the tax could be readily passed on to the consumer.[6] Seldom was the tax administered so harshly that it destroyed commerce in an area altogether. Taxations did lead to internal smuggling, but most goods appear to have traveled through legal channels.[7] Generally, the transport costs entailed in avoiding a tax station were much higher than the tax. Even if international competition is taken into account, it is doubtful that the *likin* played more than a marginal role in giving foreign goods competitive advantage over those produced domestically.[8] Chinese sources are full of complaints to the effect that the *likin* gave foreigners unfair advantage and about the height of the *likin* tax in general, but then Chinese sources are full of criticisms of taxes of all kinds. Most of these taxes seem to an outside observer to be rather low, not high.[9]

[6]This statement assumes that the demand for commodities which paid taxes was price-inelastic. As most of these goods were basic necessities which were only a small percentage of the total consumer budget (e.g., salt and sugar) or luxuries which made up a larger but still small portion of a typical gentry budget (e.g., silk and tea), this assumption should not be very controversial.

[7]A good discussion of the various trade routes and the amount of legal and illegal trade in various areas can be found in Royal Asiatic Society, "Inland Communications in China," in *Chinese Economic and Social Life,* pp. 15, 18, 20–21, 27, 30, 56, 104, 118, and 157.

[8]Foreign goods, after all, did pay a 5% ad valorem import duty. In addition, many foreign goods did not have any domestic competition at all. Cotton textiles, the most important foreign import in the late 19th century, did have domestic competition. Much of this competition, however, was from producers who paid no *likin* tax in any case (because their commodities did not enter long-distance commerce). As for those producers of textiles who did pay the transit tax, their inability to compete over the long run resulted from the greater production efficiency of the modern plants (Chinese even more than foreign).

[9]For example, Chinese sources for the 19th century and earlier are full of complaints about the burden of the land tax. Yet this tax on the average was at most 3 or 4% of the value of farm output. For the way in which this percentage was arrived at, see my Six Centuries of Agricultural Development in China (1368–1967) (in process), Ch. vii. Many of the taxes complained about represented rates near to or even below the average.

A useful question to ask at this point is whether China's commerce in the 19th century was limited to any significant degree at all by the commercial policies of the Ch'ing government. No precise answer is possible, but there is reason to doubt that if the government had not taxed or otherwise interfered with trade there would have been any large expansion in that trade.[10]

First, one can eliminate from this discussion any analysis of the government's impact on commercial relations within a standard or intermediate market town area.[11] Government officials were not located in either of these two tiers of the marketing structure and it is difficult to see how their activities could much influence trade that did not leave the area. This rural commerce was carried on by petty traders or the farmers themselves and constituted perhaps three-quarters or more of all the trade in the Chinese empire in the 19th century.[12]

Analyses of the relationship between commercial development and industrialization, however, generally deal not with petty rural traders, but with large-scale commerce and wealthy merchants who handled trade between distant points. Only long-distance trade paid the *likin* tax. This trade was also the only kind worth interfering with from a financial point of view.

What we know about this long-distance commerce suggests that official interference and taxation was only one of several elements limiting the size of that trade, and probably not one of the more important ones. The key determinants of the scope and nature of long-distance commerce were transport costs, the existence of commodities that could be efficiently produced in only a few regions, and the size of the gentry class.

Because of high transport costs, low-price bulky goods were effectively eliminated from long-distance trade in many parts of the country. Grain, for example, when carried on the back of a pack animal, cost as

[10]This discussion of the determining factors in China's domestic trade is based on a much longer analysis in Ch. iv of my Six Centuries of Agricultural Development in China (1365–1967) (in process).

[11]For a fuller discussion of the market town structure, see Skinner (1964), pp. 3–43.

[12]The figure "three-quarters" is a low estimate based on data for the 20th century carried backward to the 19th century with the aid of a number of assumptions together with various estimates of long-distance trade in the 19th century.

much to transport 200 miles as it did to grow in the first place.[13] Transport on easily navigable waterways was, of course, less expensive. Yangtze river freight rates were one-third to one-fifth land rates in Hopei and Shansi Provinces. Still, to carry grain from a rice surplus area such as Hunan to the deficit regions of Kiangsu and Chekiang, a distance of 1,000 miles, cost as much as the original price of the grain. Thus, grain shipments on the Yangtze river and elsewhere seldom exceeded several hundred thousand tons a year if one excludes short hauls of less than 100 miles.[14] This amount represented only a small fraction of the total value of long-distance trade of 19th century China.

The commodities that did make up the greatest proportion of long-distance trade, in terms of both quantity and value, were such items as tea, silk, salt, sugar, cotton and cotton textiles, and a few valuable metals. Generally, the value of these commodities per ton was high. A ton of tea, for example, was four or five times as expensive as an equivalent weight in grain. Raw cotton was slightly more expensive than tea. A shipment of cotton from Hankow to Shanghai, therefore, would only raise its cost by 10 to 15%.

Even a markup of 10 or more percent, however, is worth paying only if there is no cheaper alternative. Thus, most of the goods in long-distance trade not only had a high value per ton, but were also commonly items that could be efficiently produced in only a few regions. Sugarcane was grown in Kwangtung, Fukien, and Shantung. Salt was extracted in Szechwan and parts of Kiangsu. Tea and silkworms had to be raised under special conditions. Mines near the surface in such provinces as Yunnan provided certain metals. The comparative advantage of a particular region, therefore, was largely determined by its natural resources (including weather).

A province with few navigable waterways and lacking unique and easily transportable natural resources simply did not contribute much to

---

[13]This statement is based on the assumption that the price of grain where it was produced was 1.5 to 2.0 taels per 100 catties. Transport costs over land in such provinces as Shansi, Hopei, and Shantung were between 0.25 to 0.3 tael for 100 catties per 100 li (one li = 0.36 mile) (Source: Royal Asiatic Society, "Inland Communications in China," *Chinese Economic and Social Life*, pp. 175–176).

[14]Grain shipment data for various centuries can be found in numerous local gazetteers and memorials to the throne. See my Six Centuries of Agricultural Development in China (1368–1967) (in process), Ch. v.

long-distance trade. Much of northern China, for example, an area containing over 30% of the population of the empire, accounted for only a little over 10% of all long-distance trade.[15] Officials in north China may have been more rapacious than those in the south, but this certainly was not the principal limitation on the size of trade.[16] In fact, it may be possible to make a case that northern officials interfered more (if they did) partly because there was less trade to milk and perhaps also because, with less trade, there was less opportunity to learn about the needs of commerce and the financial benefits that could be obtained from currying to those needs.

The third important element in shaping long-distance trade was the size and wealth of the gentry class. A high proportion of this trade, perhaps as much as a third, operated to provide the gentry class with various luxuries.[17] Silk was entirely a luxury good. Tea was consumed in large amounts by the wealthy. The poor more often than not substituted water. Kiangsi pottery, a luxury item, was shipped all over the empire. Pottery for peasant use could be more efficiently produced nearer home. These examples could be readily multiplied. It would indeed be surprising if the gentry official class vigorously pursued a policy whose principal effect was to raise their own cost of living.

---

[15]The trade percentage used here was derived from *likin* revenue and tax rate data in Lo Yu-tung. The provinces included are Shansi, Shensi, Honan, Shantung, and Hopei. The *likin* data are full of biases but they are adequate for the purpose to which they are put here.

[16]To establish really that northern officials were more rapacious than those in the south would require a great deal of research into relevant documents. For what it is worth, one fairly astute Western observer in the 1840s stated that Peking was a particularly unattractive place for trade because of much greater official interference there, but this situation may have been because of the great concentration of officials in the capital (Martin (1847), p. 107). There is also evidence that the route from Sian in Shensi Province was "dreadfully burdened with custom houses" (Royal Asiatic Society, "Inland Communications in China," p. 30).

[17]According to Chung-li Chang, p. 327, gentry income per year in the late 19th century was about 675 million taels. According to my own estimates, total long-distance trade (foreign and domestic) was valued at about 900 to 1,000 million taels (Ch. iv of Six Centuries). If a quarter of gentry income was spent on goods in long-distance trade, then gentry consumption together with the goods shipped out to pay for the gentry consumption goods would be valued at 350 million taels.

The key point of this discussion, however, is that it was transport costs and the location of natural resources that determined the size of China's interregional or long-distance trade. Most commodities that could be cheaply carried (in terms of transport cost expressed as a percentage of value) did enter long-distance commerce in large quantities. It is difficult to see, given China's preindustrial society, just what additional commodities could have been traded in substantial amounts. It was out of the question, for example, to ship much coal in 19th century China.

With the coming of modern industry and the railroad in the 20th century, trade grew rapidly. This growth coincided with the final disintegration of the old imperial system, but it is difficult to see how changing official attitudes toward commerce much affected that growth. In fact, the Communists today are in many respects less in sympathy with the needs of commerce than 19th century officials. In any case, many of the commodities that have gone to make up the rise in trade in the 20th century could not possibly have been efficiently shipped any distance in 19th century China, whatever the attitude of officials. In 1958, for example, coal represented 39.8% of the total tonnage carried on Chinese railroads; ores, iron, and steel represented another 10%.[18]

Thus, government policies must have played only a marginal role in China's interregional commerce. Particularly high taxes or arbitrary officials may have limited trade in a few areas, perhaps driving the trade to alternate routes and even killing it altogether. But such effects were exceptions, not the general rule.

II. Commerce and Industry

The discussion up to this point has, to a certain degree, been asking the wrong question. The fact that the Ch'ing government took reasonably good care of the needs of premodern commerce reveals little about whether that government created conditions under which modern industry could develop.

---

[18] The figures are from Hunter (1965), p. 81. The original source was A. L. Il'in and M. P. Voronichev, *Zheleznodo-rozhnyi transport Kitaiskoi nar. res.*

There is no natural or irresistible movement from commercial development to industrialization. The experience of China alone is testimony to this. Chinese commerce in the 11th century AD looked much as it did in the 19th.[19] Trade in the 19th century was larger, but primarily because population in the 19th century was also greater. The new entrepreneurs of Japan's modernization did not arise primarily from the Tokugawa merchant class.[20] Guilds, which controlled much of China's commerce and large-scale handicrafts, were not dynamic forces for change in Europe either.

Undoubtedly, the existence of a sophisticated commercial system created some of the conditions that made industrialization possible. The ability to run a fairly large organization for profit was no mean or irrelevant skill. The comparatively developed state of China's premodern commerce created important attitudes toward profit maximization and the role of the market in that profit in even the poorest of peasant farmers. These attitudes and skills must have played an important part in the economic success of so many overseas Chinese. Yet commercial sophistication was in itself not enough in China (or among the Chinese of Southeast Asia).

A short paper is not the place to attempt to outline all the conditions that had to be met in China before industrialization could proceed, even if I knew what they all were. There were, however, two basic areas in which the existing situation was clearly inadequate and in which the government could have done something — capital formation and technological change, the two key elements in modern economic development. There is also a third condition that must at least be mentioned — political stability. It is difficult for any country to achieve industrial development if artillery shells are constantly landing among the machinery and railroads are used primarily for moving troops.

I shall ignore one condition which is often assumed to be relevant to the question of the role of the government in the early stages of Chinese industrialization. Whatever the merits of centrally planned economies of the Soviet type in the 20th century, an economy owned and directed by the state in the 19th century would have been a complete anomaly. A government

[19]For a discussion of Chinese trade in the 11th century, see Balazs (1957), pp. 587–593.
[20]Hirschmeier (1964), pp. 248–249.

with the best of intentions toward industry could not have hoped to run such an economy efficiently. There was no pattern to follow, not even a theoretical model. By contrast, the Soviet Union in the 1930s had an already established industrial base.

Thus, the proper question is not whether the Chinese state was in a position to build an industrial economy by itself, but whether it could create the conditions that would make it possible for the private sector to carry out that development. When analyzing the role of the Ch'ing government in the 19th century the issue is whether that government contributed to capital formation and technological change in privately run industry.

III. Government Policy Toward Industrialization

On almost every count, the policies of the Chinese government in the 19th century were not so much wrong as inadequate. I shall turn first to the problem of capital formation and then to that of technological change.

One of the first steps of the Meiji government in Japan was to remove all land from ownership or control by the old feudal aristocracy. Feudal dues became central government taxes thereby basically solving that government's financial problems, at least for a time. In addition, the bonds placed in the hands of the old aristocracy provided them with the capital to start new enterprises.

No remotely comparable step was undertaken by the Ch'ing government. The principal major source of increased revenue for the Chinese government was that received from customs duties on international trade, a trade that had been imposed on the Ch'ing government by the force of Western arms. Even when customs duties are included, however, central government revenues at the end of the 19th century came to less than 100 million taels or between 1 and 2% of the country's gross national product,[21] an extraordinarily low figure.

[21] Gross domestic product in 1933 prices was 30 billion yuan (Liu and Yeh (1965), p. 66). Foreign trade price indexes, which generally moved with domestic prices, indicate that domestic prices in the 1890's were about 30 to 40% of prices in 1933. Gross domestic product thus becomes 9 to 12 billion taels. Even if real product in the 1890s were half the

Under the circumstances, the government could not begin to afford to spend much money on modernization of any kind.[22] Only feeble efforts, for example, could be instituted in the direction of building and equipping a modern army. Japan's military program, by way of contrast, played an important role in making the Japanese government aware of the need for a broad industrial base to support that program. The disparity between Chinese and Japanese effort in this sphere was demonstrated in Japan's overwhelming defeat of the Chinese armies in 1895. Nor could the government, if it had desired, have given much financial support to a modern education program or subsidies to new industries. Instead, the government was often a net financial drain on the few industrial firms that were set up.

One can only wonder what would have happened in China if central government revenues had been 5% of gross national product or even 10% (in 1957 under the Communists, the figure was 30%). After the failure of the *Tung Chih* Restoration (1862–1874), the government was in the hands of those with an active antipathy toward modernization,[23] but would they have been so rigid if government funds had exceeded administrative expenses? Or might the efforts of men such as Li Hung-chang have appeared more impressive and hence ultimately more worthy of support, particularly if they promised some real relief from foreign domination?

If the government could not contribute directly to industrialization or efforts in support of industrialization, it could still have promoted institutions that enhanced private capital formation, domestic or foreign. The problem in the late 19th century was not how to reduce peasant consumption so as to extract a larger surplus. The needs of modern industrial development at that time were modest. They could have been met, for a time at least, by a banking system capable of channeling existing savings into modern industrial investment.

---

level of 1933, which is unlikely, the figure would become 4.5 to 6 billion taels. For price data, I used the Nankai index numbers of foreign trade prices and J L Buck's data on prices paid and received by farmers (the latter only go back to 1906 for most regions).

[22] I first became aware of the significance of the disparity in government revenues between China and Japan in discussions with Professor Albert Craig.

[23] The standard work on the *Tung Chih* Restoration is that of Wright (1957).

Setting up a banking system capable of making long-term investments in industry is no simple matter. China's traditional banks, like those in many other countries, were designed to service the needs of internal commerce. Loans for commercial activities, however, are for short periods of time and can be secured against the commodities being traded. Industrial loans must be for a long period and cannot be so safely secured. While the Japanese government began experimenting with national banks for this purpose in the 1870s, the Chinese government did not begin to take steps toward a modern banking system until the late 1890s and the first decade of the 20th century.[24] Even then efforts in this direction were too limited to have much effect on industrial development.

The lack of modern industrial banks meant that industry had to obtain its capital directly from wealthy individuals. It is customary to argue that wealthy Chinese preferred to buy land or lend their money out to peasants at high interest rates because such practices were "traditional," prestigious, and safe. Perhaps so, but it would have taken an extraordinarily courageous individual with wealth, living say in the interior, to send money to individuals whom he did not know to invest in enterprises about which he knew little. On top of this, if those who received the funds absconded, there was little recourse. With a modern banking system, this individual could in effect hire experts to handle these matters for him, thus reducing the risk considerably.

As it was, industrial enterprises in the late 19th century had to rely for funds on the few wealthy individuals who were familiar with modern industry, principally the treaty port compradors. The funds of these compradors were limited and they had numerous alternative uses for them. In the late 19th century, as a result, Chinese industrial firms were constantly on the verge of collapse due to undercapitalization.[25]

The other major source of money for industrial enterprises came from abroad. In 1895, the Japanese followed up their military victory with, among other things, a demand that China allow direct foreign investment in industry. In the words of Chi-ming Hou, "foreign capital played a significant role in bringing about whatever economic modernization existed

[24] See Frank (1942).

[25] This discussion is based on the analysis of Feuerwerker (1958).

in China before 1937."[26] But Ch'ing government policy could take none of the credit.[27]

Government efforts to promote technological change in China did exist, but they too were feeble. By the late 19th century, of course, Chinese industrial technology was a long way behind that of the West. Generally, the farther behind a country gets in the development of technology the easier it becomes for the government to play an important role in bringing in the new techniques. Bureaucrats are notoriously poor innovators, but, if they have access to tax revenues, they can greatly reduce the risks and costs of innovation for the private sector in a late-developing country.

Ch'ing government policies in this area can be subsumed under two broad headings: the construction of pilot industrial plants and a general reform of the educational system.

Goverment-sponsored pilot industrial projects have seldom proved to be successful ventures from a financial point of view. This statement holds true in large measure for Japan and for such European nations as France, Prussia, and Austria, all of whom invested large sums in such projects.[28] It comes as no surprise therefore, to find that Chinese efforts in the late 19th century by themselves failed to lead a broadly based industrialization drive.

Still these firms in China, particularly the textile mills, did train workers and managers and familiarized Chinese investors with many of the problems of setting up modern industrial enterprises in China. How much credit the Ch'ing government deserves for these projects is a debatable point. They were carried out under the protection of a few comparatively enlightened viceroys, not under the protection or control of Peking. But then these viceroys were part of the government and were, like the rest, trained in the traditional manner. Perhaps more relevant is the fact that most of the management and capital for these firms came not from the government but from treaty port merchants.

It would be going too far to say that all the lessons learned from experiences with these semigovernmental enterprises were beneficial. The

[26] Hou (1965).

[27] Few Chinese, then or now, would want to take credit for allowing foreign investment in Chinese industry.

[28] See discussion of Landes (1965), pp. 100–106.

complete government take-over of a textile mill in Wuch'ang, for example, made it difficult for a time for others to obtain funds for additional mills.[29] Discouragement of this kind did not last long, however. Most of the pilot textile projects were begun in the early 1890s.[30] By the late 1890s, China's modern textile industry was well launched with over one million spindles in operation in 1899 and over 5 million by 1922.[31] Whether the semigovernmental efforts really played a major role in starting this development or whether it would have proceeded just as quickly without the encouragement of men such as Li Hung-chang, it is impossible to tell.

The other sphere in which governmental efforts contributed to technological progress was education. Chinese students were sent abroad as early as the 1870s. Modernizing education was a key plank in the reform program of such men as Chang Chih-tung and later K'ang Yu-wei and Liang Ch'i-ch'ao. Particularly after 1900, the Ch'ing government began to set up more modern schools. These schools may not always have been ideally designed from the point of view of economic development. But then even today no one really knows what constitutes an "ideal" expenditure on various educational resources. The key fact is that the Chinese government spent very little money on education, ideal or otherwise. Private contributions to missionary schools from Americans and Europeans had a much greater educational impact in this period.

IV. Conclusion

If the imperial government of China was an obstacle to industrialization, it was more because of what it did not do than because of harmful efforts which it did undertake. The image of a rapacious government attempting to crush commercial and industrial firms or to tax them to death through indifference is overdrawn. Occasionally such things happened, but more often, the government cooperated with commerce to the mutual benefit of officials and merchants. When similar methods were attempted in the sphere of modern industry, the results were not so successful, but such efforts were

29 Chu (1965), p. 26.

30 Feuerwerker, *China's Early Industrialization*, p. 222.

31 Fong (1934).

not financially profitable in many other countries either. They were, however, a first and probably necessary step for any bureaucratic state.

The real problem was that although the Ch'ing government (including the various progressive viceroys) did take a number of positive steps they were few and feeble. In a sense, China provides a test of the proposition that a government in a late-developing nation not only can, but must, take steps to aid economic growth if the country is to avoid a long slow process of institutional change prior to industrialization. Key areas where the government must take on major responsibilities are in the fields of education and banking reform.[32]

The obvious next question is, why were the efforts of the Ch'ing government so inadequate? The usual answers to this question stress the intellectual milieu of the Confucian tradition and contrast it with that of Japan, particularly as regards the two countries' differing attitudes toward change. The tenacity of the Confucian tradition in keeping closed to progress the minds of many or most Ch'ing officials was certainly an important factor in the resistance to modernization. But there were a number of very powerful officials who did see the need for change. One can easily criticize their perception of how change was to be brought about. Few nations, if any, however, have been blessed in the early stages of industrialization with leaders who saw clearly the path ahead, and that includes Meiji Japan.

A nation learns about industrialization, not by intellectualizing in study groups, but by building factories and then correcting for what goes wrong. One of the great failures of the Chinese government of the 19th century was that it never did enough toward industrialization for anyone to know whether it was moving in the right direction or not.

Confucian conservatism certainly accounted for some of this lack of movement. But the failure of the government resulted from more than the inadequacies of the Confucian tradition or dominance at the court by the most conservative elements. Even the most progressive could not really do

---

[32] There is an implicit assumption here that government failures — not the social structure, attitudes, or foreign interference — were the major drag on Chinese growth. I believe this to be the case, but this paper is too short to attempt to deal with the various explanations for Chinese failures that are based on the pernicious influence of the Chinese social structure or foreign interference.

anything, and what paralyzed them most of all was probably the lack of funds. Financially, the Chinese government was an almost unbelievably weak instrument for such a monumental task. The contrast with Japan is striking.

References

Balazs, E (1957). "Une Carte Des Centres Commerciaux de la Chine" [A map of Chinese commercial centers]. *Annales: Economies Sociétés Civilisations*, October–December, pp. 587–593.

Chang, C-L (1962). *The Income of the Chinese Gentry*. Seattle: University of Washington Press.

Chu, SC (1965). *Reformer in Modern China: Chang Chien*. New York: Columbia University Press.

Feuerwerker, A (1958). *Chinas Early Industrialization*. Boston, MA: Harvard University Press.

Fong, H-T (1934). *Chung-kuo chih mien fang-chih-yeh* [China's cotton textile industry]. Shanghai, p. 8.

Frank, M (1942). Tamagna. *Banking and Finance in China*. New York: Institute of Pacific Relation.

Hirschmeier, J (1964). *The Origins of Entrepreneurship in Meiji Japan*. Boston, MA: Harvard University Press.

Hou, C-M (1965). *Foreign Investment and Economic Development in China 1840–1937*. Boston, MA: Harvard University Press.

Hunter, H (1965). "Transport in Soviet and Chinese Development". *Economic Development and Cultural Change*, xiv(1), October.

Landes, DS (1965). Japan and Europe: Contrasts in Industrialization. *The State and Economic Enterprise in Japan*.

Liu, TC and KC Yeh (1965). *The Economy of the Chinese Mainland*. Princeton, NJ: Princeton University Press.

Lo, Y-T (1936). *Chung-kuo li-chin shih* [A history of the *likin* tax in China]. Shanghai: Commercial Press.

Martin, RM (1847). *China: Political, Commercial and Social*. London: John Madden.

Metzger, T (1966). "Ch'ing commercial policy". *Ch'ing-shih wen-t'i*, February, p. 4. (mimeograph).

Ping-ti Ho (1962). *The Ladder of Success in Imperial China*. New York: Columbia University Press, p. 82.

Skinner, GW (1964). "Marketing and social structure in rural China," Part I. *Journal of Asian Studies*, 24, pp. 3–43.

Wright, M (1957). *The Last Stand of Chinese Conservatism*. Stanford, CA: Stanford University Press.

CENTRAL PLANNING AND COLLECTIVE AGRICULTURE, 1955–1978

CHAPTER 3

CENTRALIZATION AND DECENTRALIZATION IN MAINLAND CHINA'S AGRICULTURE, 1949–1962*

From the beginning of Communist control over the Mainland of China, the major objectives of Chinese farm policy have been to raise agricultural output and the marketed portion of that output together with the maintenance of political security and control. The regime has attempted to accomplish these aims with minimal state investment in the rural sector. The importance of obtaining a substantial and increasing marketed surplus derived first of all from the fact that agricultural and processed agricultural products have made up approximately three-quarters of all Chinese exports. Second, although the rural–urban shift in population has been small in percentage terms, the absolute number of city dwellers increased between early 1950 and the end of 1956 by over 30 million people or 55%, all of whom had to be fed.[1]

Unlike the situation in the Soviet Union, however, a substantial and increasing marketed surplus could not be achieved independently of increases in farm production. Under Stalin collectivization and heavy industrialization could be pushed without fear that the Soviet population would starve for economic reasons either in the short or long run. In China, a prolonged agricultural crisis such as that which occurred in the Soviet Union, coupled with a 2% growth in population, would be economically and perhaps politically disastrous to the present regime.

*Acknowledgments are due to Professors Abram Bergson and Simon Kuznets for advice and assistance at all stages of the research and writing of this paper and to Professor Walter Falcon for his comments on the final drafts. The research was done at Harvard University and in Hong Kong under a fellowship from the Ford Foundation Foreign Area Training Program.

[1]Yin (1960).

Therefore, whereas the USSR could achieve most of its goals through the introduction of centrally determined compulsory delivery quotas, Communist China had to rely more heavily on control devices that had less detrimental effects on production.

This chapter is an attempt to show how, in light of these considerations, Communist China has dealt with the problem of controlling and directing the agricultural sector. The principal focus is on the choice between decentralized versus centralized controls, and between the market and various types of administrative directives. The market is, of course, a form of decentralized control, but a number of administrative measures undertaken by the Chinese, such as the rural communes, have also involved important elements of decentralization.[2]

The significance of Mainland China's experience in this field lies, first of all, in the fact that since 1949, the Communists have made vigorous efforts to achieve a breakthrough not only in industry but in agriculture as well. As a result, they have faced and attempted to deal with a number of important issues of interest to other underdeveloped countries with similar economies. Second, the fact that China is today a totalitarian state with a predilection toward and ability to enforce centralized controls makes it an interesting case study of the limitations of centralization under the most favorable political conditions and conversely of the advantages of various forms of decentralization in the agricultural sector of an underdeveloped economy.

The remainder of this essay deals with the nature of the controls selected by the regime and the reasons behind the various choices. The material is presented historically because the major points can best be brought out in this way without the reader becoming unnecessarily confused by the many shifts and turns in Chinese Communist agricultural policy.

I. Price Policy, 1950–1953

In 1950, as a result of nearly 13 years of war and civil war, agricultural production and the rural market situation were chaotic. Production was

---

[2]The term "decentralization," as used here, means simply the transfer of authority over a given activity from a smaller to a greater number of individuals or groups. The greater number also implies being closer to the actual scene of operations.

perhaps only two-thirds of the prewar level and the amount that was marketed had fallen to 21% of total output from a prewar level estimated in one source at as high as 53%.[3] The factors behind the general drop in output need no elaboration; the measures taken to restore it were primarily the maintenance of political stability, the repair of damaged irrigation systems, and other similar efforts. The fall in the marketed portion, however, was somewhat more complex. The depressed level of average per capita farm income accounted for part of the reduction. This was further aggravated by the land reform which had been completed in the main by the end of 1952. Available data unfortunately are not adequate for the task of estimating the effect on marketing of the elimination of the landlord class. Although rents were high, most landlords owned only a little more land than their nonlandlord neighbors. Nothing even remotely like the landed states of Czarist Russia existed in China. Nevertheless, the lopping off of the wealthiest class and the transfer of its land to the poorest group probably had a considerable effect on the market. This is supported by a 1955 survey which found that even rich peasants (a rung below landlords) marketed 43.1% of their grain as compared with 25.2% for middle peasants and 22.1% for poor peasants.[4] Although the redistribution of land undoubtedly had some positive economic benefits in the form of increased incentives toward land improvements, these may have been partially offset by the fact that landlords had formerly often rented to rich peasants who had more capital and better knowledge of advanced techniques of farming than poor peasants.[5] In any case, land reform was primarily motivated by the desire to destroy the class most inimical to the Communists and to solidify support from the poor and middle peasants. Any redistribution in favor of the wealthier peasants would have been unthinkable on political grounds, whatever its economic benefits.

There were two other causes of the decline in the marketed portion of farm produce which were not the result of political considerations and

[3]Buck (1930). Buck's figure is not fully comparable with the official Communist one.

[4]These figures were based on a survey of 13,245 households in eighteen provinces, reported in Tung (1959).

[5]Fei and Chang (1948). *Earthbound China*. Yang (1959).

hence were more amenable to economic policies undertaken by the Communists. They were first the relatively greater reduction in the production of industrial consumers' goods leading to a large shift in the relative prices of industrial and agricultural products against agriculture, and second, the greatly reduced market for certain specific types of products produced in the rural areas.

Although the shift in relative prices in favor of agriculture after 1950 was primarily a result of the rapid recovery of the production of industrial consumers' goods, the regime's policy-makers contributed to the shift by making it possible for the market forces of supply and demand to work freely. They did this by rapidly restoring normal channels of commerce and then not interfering with their functioning. The first step was to bring the hyperinflation under control so that the populace would have some confidence in the currency and end such practices as hoarding and barter trade.

This meant primarily bringing the budget rapidly into balance[6] and expanding the position of state trading companies in handling certain key commodities, particularly grain and cotton textiles. The latter measure was desirable in part because speculative movements in China at that time tended to be destabilizing. A spiral once started was difficult to stop, particularly after the regime had automatically geared urban wages to a cost of living index based on a few major consumers' goods. Once

Table 1. Index of relative prices of industrial to agricultural products (1930–1936 average = 100).

1950	1951	1952	1953	1954	1955	1956	1957 (estimate)
131.8	124.4	121.8	109.6	109.2	111.3	107.0	103.0

Sources: *T'ung-chi Kung-tso* data office. "Price Gaps between Industrial Products and Farm Products: Their Changes in Post Liberation Years." *T'ung-chi Kung-tso*, No. 17, September 14, 1957, in *Extracts from China Mainland Magazines*, 104, October, 22, 1957, p. 20.

[6]Official data published several years later indicate that the budget was balanced by 1951, but data published at the time can be reconstructed to show that balance was not achieved until 1952. If foreign credits and bond sales are excluded from revenue, there were also deficits from 1953 through 1956. Perkins (1963).

inflation had been brought under control, perhaps the most important of the regime's policies in this area was the negative one of refraining from using its market power over certain consumers' goods to obtain monopoly profits. This situation contrasts with that during the "scissors crisis" of 1922 and 1923 in the Soviet Union. There industrial firms held products off the market in order to keep prices high and hence also reduced the quantity of agricultural goods which the peasants were willing to market.

The role of state policy in promoting the development of certain products was a more active one. The goods hardest hit by the war were luxury products and products the bulk of which were exported or used as industrial raw materials. An example of an industrial raw material of this type would be cotton whose output in 1949 was 47% of the 1933 level, while that of a luxury product might be tea or tobacco whose 1949 outputs were 16 and 4% of their 1933 levels respectively.[7] Many other special goods and handicrafts disappeared from the market altogether.[8] Since the bulk of export earnings came from commodities of this type (foodgrains were only a relatively minor export item), any producers' goods industrialization program depended heavily on their recovery. The consumers' goods industrial sector was even more dependent on them since they were the source of the bulk of its raw materials.

The main devices used by the state in its attempt to restore production of these items to their prewar level were centrally determined purchase prices, backed up by various marketing arrangements that gave price adjustments greater impact. The long experience of the Chinese Communists in dealing with the rural scene apparently left them with little doubt that the Chinese peasant would respond to price incentives. The correctness of this judgment is backed up by a number of prewar

---

[7]The 1949 data are taken from State Statistical Bureau (1960). *Ten Great Years* (Peking: Foreign Languages Press), pp. 124–125, and the 1933 data are from T C Liu and K C Yeh (1963).

[8]The percentage of such unsaleable commodities in East China was 30–40% of the total output of local special products in the area. *Shanghai Chieh-fang Ch'ien-hou Wu-chia Tzu-liao Hui-pien.* Shanghai: People's Press, 1958, p. 385.

studies of Chinese agriculture. These demonstrate that the Chinese peasant was economically rational within the scope of his limited knowledge and his need to minimize the risk of starvation or other economic disaster.[9]

The regime made its most vigorous and effective use of price policy in its efforts to promote cotton, the most important of the industrial crops. As early as 1950, official minimum purchase prices for cotton were guaranteed to the farmer; the minimum was set at about the prewar level and then raised again in 1951. Also in 1951, the state introduced advance purchase contracts whereby the farmer was paid in part for his crop prior to sowing, in exchange for which he promised to plant a certain number of *mow* in cotton.[10] In effect, this was an interest free loan which, because rural interest rates were very high, raised the real value of the cotton crop to the farmer well above its value at the official price.[11] It was also further insurance against adverse price movements at the time of the harvest. The success of these measures is immediately apparent from the data in Table 2. By 1951, cotton production and the sown area were above the prewar levels and they climbed still higher in 1952, so high in fact that the regime felt that excessive attention to the cotton crop might interfere with the even more important goal of increasing grain output. As a result, advance purchases for cotton were abolished in 1953 and the purchase price was lowered relative to that of grain, although one compensatory move was made by changing the basis for computing the agricultural tax on cotton.[12] The effect was greater than anticipated, however; the state

[9]See discussion of the evidence presented in these studies in Perkins, *op.cit.*, pp. 40–50.

[10]Joint Cooperative Board (1951). "Temporary Methods of Handling 1951 Advance Cotton Purchase." *Hsin-hua Yueh-pao*, 18, April 25, p. 1338. A *mow* is a sixth of an acre.

[11]A more precise statement would be that interest rates would have been very high (they were several per cent per month and higher before 1949) if the Communists had allowed private moneylenders to operate freely.

[12]The tax on cotton was to be computed at the regular rate of 11% on the basis of what the land produced when sown to grain. Since the yield of cotton in value terms was considerably above that of grain, the result was a lowering of the agricultural tax on cotton land. Editorial, "Clearly Understand the New Cotton Grain Price Ratio in Order to Complete Agricultural Production Duties," *Ching-chi Chou-pao,* 14, 1953, pp. 2–3.

Table 2. Cotton prices, production and sown area.

	Official cotton–grain price ratio[a] Area's principle grain crop				
	Millet	Wheat	Rice	Production[b]	Sown Area[c]
1933	7.9	7.0		1,900	67.9
1946	5.5	5.0	5.5		
1950	8.0	7.0	6.5	1,385	56.8
1951	8.5	8.0	8.5	2,061	82.3
1952	8.0–9.0	7.5–8.5	8.0–9.0	2,607	83.6
1953	6.75–8.0	6.25–7.5	6.75–8.0	2,349	77.7
1954	7.5–8.25	6.75–8.0	7.25–8.25	2,130	81.9
1955	7.5–8.25	6.75–8.0	7.25–8.25	3,037	86.6
1956	7.5–8.25	6.75–8.0	7.25–8.25	2,890	93.8
1957	7.5–8.25	6.75–8.0	7.25–8.25	3,280	86.6
1958	7.5–8.25	6.75–8.0	7.25–8.25	4,200	85.8

Notes: [a]Unit: Catties of grain per catty of 7/8 inch middle grade cotton (2 catties = 1 kilogram).
[b]Unit: 1,000,000 catties.
[c]Unit: 1,000,000 *mow* (6 *mow* = 1 acre).
Source: See Perkins, *op. cit.*, pp. 63–65.

reinstituted advance cotton purchases in 1954 and raised the purchase price part way back to the 1952 level.

Centrally determined prices were also important in varying degrees to the production and marketing of peanuts and other sources of edible oils, tea leaves, certain fibers such as jute and green hemp, tobacco, silkworms, and wool. There is less evidence available regarding these commodities, however, than there was in the case of cotton. A minimum ratio between the price of fibers and grain similar to that for cotton, for example, was set in 1950 and 1951.[13] The price of tea, even though already greater in 1950 relative to the price of rice than the 1930–1936 average, was raised from 4.9 to 5.7 times the price of middle grade rice in 1951

[13] Financial and Economic Committee (1951). "Regulations Concerning the Relative Price of Fibers and Grain and the Settling of Purchase and Grain Fertilizer Supply Problems," March 17, *Hsin-hua Yueh-pao*, 18, April 25, p. 1341.

and to 7.86 times it in 1953.[14] Tea production recovered more slowly than either cotton or fibers; the reason was not a lack of response to price changes but the much longer time needed to rehabilitate tea production. Only in the case of oil-bearing crops, a major export as well as food item, did the regime refrain from raising purchase prices, apparently for fear of significantly impinging on grain acreage.[15] Rapeseed, the most neglected of all the oil-bearing crops, hardly recovered at all.[16] Advance purchases were also instituted in the case of all the above crops but not until after 1954; hence, they did not play the role in recovery that they did in the case of cotton.

Although many products had not recovered to their prewar levels by 1952, the Chinese Communists would seem to have had reason to be satisfied with the rapid rate with which rehabilitation of both output and marketing had been achieved. The marketed portion of farm production had risen from 17% of gross agricultural output in 1950 to 27% in 1952 and to 28% in 1953 (absolute increases of 62 and 92% respectively).[17] Nevertheless, by the end of 1953, it had become apparent that affairs in the agricultural sector were not proceeding so well as the regime required. The year 1953 marked the beginning of the first five-year plan. Investment had been raised 84% above the 1952 level, exports were 28% higher, and the urban population had increased by 6 million persons or 8.4% since the beginning of the year.[18] This rapid growth was sustained for a time by the good harvest of 1952, but in 1953 the weather which had been particularly good in 1952 reverted back to normal and the production of many crops fell while that of grain rose by only 1.6%.

---

[14]"Our country's Development of Tea Leaf Production, *"T'ung-chi Kung-tso,* 3, February 14, 1957, p. 33.

[15]"Directive on Increasing Production of Oil Materials Crops," (December 25, 1953), *Hsin-hua Yueh-pao,* 1, January 25, 1954, p. 157.

[16]Taso (1956).

[17]These figures are obtained by dividing gross agricultural output by total sales of agricultural and subsidiary products, adjusting the latter for purchase price changes. The raw data are from State Statistical Bureau, *Ten Great Years, op. cit.,* pp. 16, 168.

[18]H and Y C Y in, *op. cit.*, pp. 4, 63.

The most serious of the difficulties created by this situation occurred on the grain market where in 1953 the state's sales of grain were running several billion catties ahead of its purchases.[19] The problem of acquiring adequate amounts of marketed grain had existed from the beginning of the regime and was one of the major reasons why the agricultural tax was a tax in kind, 90% of which was paid in grain. The apparent decline in grain purchases over and above the tax between 1950 and 1952–1953, in spite of substantial increases in output, was probably the result of an increase in the rural demand caused by a rising farm population, the redistribution of income as a result of land reform, and the rising level of per capita peasant income.[20] Since the income elasticity of demand for grain at such low absolute levels of income is substantial, this was a source of significant additional demand.

As a result of this rapidly increasing demand for grain, the Chinese Communists were faced with a dilemma at the end of 1953. They could alleviate the pressure on the grain market by cutting back the investment program, but substantial cuts would have required indefinite acceptance of a slow rate of industrial growth. Alternatively, they could have obtained the necessary grain deliveries through the market by raising grain purchase prices. The price rise would have had to have been so great, however, that it would have forced the regime to transfer a large portion of its investment resources from the producers' goods sector to consumers' goods. Since these two possibilities were unacceptable, the remaining choices were either to abandon the market and obtain the necessary grain deliveries by means of compulsory quotas or to take even more radical centralization measures in an attempt to increase the rate of growth in agricultural output.

---

[19] Some idea of the state's deficit can be derived from the fact that state purchases in 1953–1954 were 80% above 1952–1953 whereas sales were only up 33%. Applying these percentages to the data in Table 3 would mean a deficit of 4 billion catties; and the deficit would be even larger if grain exports were taken into account. Yang (1957).

[20] Official Communist estimates of gross agricultural output show an increase of 30% between 1950 and 1953. Communist estimates of agricultural production and income for the 1950–1953 period cannot be considered reliable, but there is little reason to doubt that per capita farm incomes rose rapidly from their very low wartime levels, perhaps by as much as 20%.

II. Introduction of Compulsory Quotas, 1954–1955

In November 1953, the alternative decided upon was the introduction of compulsory grain delivery quotas. The authority to set the absolute level of these quotas rested with Peking, although various levels of local authority had some leeway for adjusting the proportion of the local quota that would fall on each individual member of the group. This move achieved the desired end as evidenced by the fact that grain deliveries during the 1953–1954 grain year were 39% above the previous grain year. Unlike the Soviet Union, the Chinese introduced compulsory quotas without an accompanying radical reorganization of agricultural institutions. Such action was feasible probably because the rural party apparatus, which was far more highly developed in China than in the Soviet Union, made any additional changes unnecessary. Even this relatively modest change in marketing technique, however, was not without cost. Compulsory quotas also had to be introduced for cotton and edible oil-producing materials and eventually for most of the major crops. Since the bulk of these crops was marketed in any case, presumably the main reason for making them subject to quotas was to prevent farmers from reducing resources expended on industrial crops in an attempt to restore their grain consumption. This widespread use of quotas not only reduced the potential effectiveness of purchase price adjustments, but undoubtedly harmed peasant incentives as well. Although the disincentive effect of the quotas was probably not solely to blame, the recovery of farm production, which had been so rapid between 1950 and 1952, slowed down in 1953 and 1954. In the case of soybeans, rapeseed, jute and hemp, and silkworms output actually declined. Furthermore, the sluggishness in most instances, excluding grain and cotton, came long before output of the various crops began to approach even prewar levels.

The impact of agriculture's poor performance began to be felt fairly quickly throughout the economy. The compulsory quotas kept the rate of increase in marketings from falling very far in 1954 (from 18 to 13%), but there was very little increase in 1955 (2.5%). Exports of farm and processed farm goods fell from 81.6 to 74.5% of total exports between 1953 and 1955 and their absolute amount increased by 28% as compared with

Table 3. Grain purchases (Including soybeans) (Unit: 1,000,000 catties of husked grain).[a]

1950	1952–1953	1953–1954	1954–1955	1955–1956	1956–1957	1957–1958	1958–1959
66,850	61,000	84,600	90,270	85,990	83,430	92,910	111,300

[a]2,000 catties = 1 metric ton.
Source: See Perkins, *op. cit.*, pp. 438–41.

37% over each of the previous two years. More significantly, the rate of increase in consumers' goods industrial production, the bulk of whose raw materials were supplied by agriculture, fell from 26.7 to 14.2% in 1954 and output actually declined slightly in 1955. In the producers' goods sector, the rate of increase, which was closely related to the level of imports, also dropped from 36.5 to 19.8 to 14.5% per year during this period. The lag in agriculture was by no means the sole cause of these declines. State investment in 1953 had been increased too rapidly to allow for its effective utilization and inflationary pressures had to be brought back under control in 1954. It is also probable that part of the industrial growth in 1953 resulted from some of the same elements of recovery from wartime destruction which made the 1950–1952 rates so high. Nevertheless, the main cause of the difficulties was agriculture and the Chinese Communist leadership was well aware of this fact.[21]

Once again, therefore, the regime was faced with an important set of choices. The situation as it stood was unsatisfactory and the potential for solving it by raising the compulsory delivery quotas had been exhausted. In 1955, the state discovered that it had actually purchased too much and had forced peasants to consume grain which would otherwise have been used for seed and fodder for their hogs. The 1956 quotas, therefore, had to be reduced, not increased. The alternatives of reducing the investment in industry or shifting to consumers' goods

[21]E.g., Mao Tse-tung (1955). *The Question of Agricultural Cooperation.* Peking: Foreign Languages Press, pp. 22–26. Mao talks of the connection between agriculture and industry only in general terms. Specific reference to the problems of 1953 through 1955 and their relation to the need for agricultural cooperativization can be found in Tung Ta-lin (1959). *Agricultural Cooperation in China.* Peking: Foreign Languages Press, pp. 21–22, and in Hsueh (1960).

production were no more acceptable than they had been in 1953. With regard to the first possibility, the state in fact was planning to increase industrial investment sharply in 1956. As for the second, it is doubtful that it would have had any effect on the marketed portion of agricultural output in any case since the quotas were taking about all the grain the peasants could spare.

The real problem was that agricultural production had to be increased, but without raising state investment in the farm sector since this would have jeopardized the priority given to industrial producers' goods. The task was made more difficult by the fact that most land which could be brought under cultivation easily and cheaply was already being farmed.[22] The choices open to the regime, therefore, were to get the peasants to invest more of their own funds, to mobilize rural labor to construct capital projects, or to introduce new technology. The first and the third objectives could have been accomplished in the context of a free peasant economy through the concentration of income and land in the hands of the rich peasant class, a solution that would have been an anathema to the Chinese Communists on both political and ideological grounds. Barring such a solution, there was no easy or quick way by which these aims could be accomplished through the existing market system. Unless the regime were willing to raise farm purchase prices and hence shift investment funds to the consumers' goods sector, peasant savings could be increased in only a small way. Equally important, the mobilization of even a single village appeared to the regime to face virtually insurmountable barriers of conflicting self-interest between those who did the work and those who benefited from it. This problem is evidenced by Chinese difficulties in this area prior to the Communist period[23] and the failures of the Indian community development program under not entirely dissimilar circumstances.[24] Finally, the regime

[22] The Chinese Communists were so convinced that increasing the area of cultivated land was less economic than the more intensified cultivation of the existing area that in 1958 they actually reduced the total cultivated area by over 10 million acres.

[23] An example of these difficulties is described in C K Yang, *op. cit.*, p. 24.

[24] One of the major problems in India was that the people who did the work did not receive the benefits of their work or at least not proportionate benefits.

believed that the encouragement of new technology would probably have been a slow process, at least until the peasants had acquired the habit of experimentation. No such transformation was likely to take place soon since the peasants were in the main uneducated and the consequences of a mistake could be disastrous. To the Chinese Communists, therefore, the only solution to the dilemma of how to increase agricultural output without abandoning more fundamental goals appeared to require the removal of the individual peasant's power over many key aspects of farm production and the centralization of that power in hands more responsive to the wishes of the state.

III. Centralization through Cooperatives, 1956–1957

Centralization was accomplished in the winter of 1955–1956 by the abolition of private farmland and the formation of cooperatives with party cadres at their head endowed with full authority.[25] It was believed that, because these cadres could control the use of the cooperatives' output, they could set aside a larger portion of output for investment purposes than had previously been the case. Most of the difficulties in the way of effective utilization of seasonally unemployed labor for road and irrigation works construction would also be eliminated since the benefits would accrue to the whole village and could, if necessary, be prorated to give the greatest benefit to those who had done the work. Finally, it was felt that the introduction of new technology would no longer pose much of a problem since the cadres could be ordered to use any technique which the party desired. In addition, cooperativization would of itself make possible more efficient use of the land through the elimination of excessive fragmentation of plots. Among other things, these small plots wasted land by increasing the need for boundaries. Also after the land was pooled, crops could be planted on the land best suited for them. In the past, each farmer had to plant enough grain on his own land whether or not it was suitable for grain — to ensure that his family would not starve if the market for

[25] Democratic features were written into the cooperative charters, but all evidence indicates that the cadres in charge of each cooperative were not subject to the collective will of the individual members in any major way.

his nonfood crops collapsed. The larger plots would also make possible the efficient use of various types of machinery, not so much tractors and other labor-saving devices which would have been pointless, but items such as better plows that would improve the way in which the land was cultivated.[26]

The one obvious drawback to the cooperatives, their effect on individual incentives, was apparently considered by the regime to be a problem of the period of transition to the new form rather than a long-run fundamental feature of the system itself. The Chinese were certainly not unaware of the experience of the Soviet Union and Eastern Europe where collectivization had proved to be a drag on all attempts by those countries to raise agricultural production. There were strong arguments, however, for assuming that Chinese agriculture was different and that, in any case, the Communist party in China had a far greater understanding of how to handle the peasants than its Russian or Eastern European counterparts. The very success of the Communist revolution in China after all had depended primarily on the party leadership's understanding and manipulation of the peasant situation. In addition, China could learn from and make a point of not repeating Stalin's mistakes. Finally, after reading through the vast amounts of Communist literature on the subject, one finds it hard to escape the belief that the Communists were convinced that socialism, if properly combined with individual self-interest, could provide a superior system of incentives to that of capitalism and the market.

None of the above is meant to imply that because the Communists believed there were solid economic reasons for cooperativizing Chinese agriculture, cooperativization was motivated solely by economic considerations. If these promising economic elements had not existed, however, the Communists could not have risked doing what they did on purely political grounds. The political advantages of the cooperative form were obvious. By eliminating individual land holdings and placing

[26] One of the best listings of the expected advantages to be attained from cooperativization can be found in the Chinese Communist Party Central Committee, "Decisions on the Development of Agricultural Producers' Cooperatives" (December 16, 1953), quoted in R Carin, "China's Land Problem Series," Vol. 2 (mimeo.), pp. 87–89.

control over the peasant's economic life in the hands of loyal party personnel the single remaining potential source of political opposition was eliminated. Furthermore, it was desirable to carry out this political coup at an early stage, since otherwise the highly organized party apparatus in the countryside built up during the civil war and land reform was in danger of atrophying for lack of use.[27] The regime had in fact been laying the groundwork for the cooperative movement ever since the completion of land reform. The exact timing of the movement could have been altered slightly, but it would have been difficult to put it off or conversely to push it up by more than a year.[28] Once it was underway, the speed with which it progressed probably depended primarily upon the amount of serious opposition it engendered, which by all appearances was very little.

The contrast between the motives behind the Chinese and the Russian decisions to collectivize is striking. Both were partially influenced by political motives, and both felt the need to achieve more direct influence over the economic aspects of agriculture, but there the similarity ends. The Russian decision was a conscious rejection of the market as a means of mobilizing an already existing potential agricultural surplus. The Chinese decision was not so much a conscious rejection of the market. Compulsory quotas in China do not appear to have been extended to any large degree. There was a brief attempt in 1956 at central planning of agricultural production and particularly of the acreage sown to various crops, but it was not successful and was quickly abandoned. The regime went back to attempting to manipulate the relative importance of the different crops by adjusting prices. The Chinese decision was thus an attempt, by means of a partial centralization of authority, to add certain functions such as the promotion of technological advance, functions which until then had not been performed at all or at least had not been controlled in any systematic

---

[27] There was criticism of some cadres during this period for thinking that their job was finished once land reform was completed and that they could allow future developments to follow their natural course.

[28] Land reform and the Korean War were not over until 1953 and some time was needed to get the country prepared for a new movement. Once decided upon, the changes had to wait until after the fall harvest so as to have a minimum impact on production.

way. A second reason behind Soviet collectivization was the need to free labor from the farm so as to provide an industrial work force. The mechanization of Russian agriculture which helped make this possible was brought about by the formation of Machine Tractor Stations.[29] These stations were used to increase centralized control of the production of the individual collectives, over and above that achieved by planning and compulsory quotas. Since the problem in China has been how to keep the population from leaving the rural areas, an institution comparable to the Machine Tractor Stations would have been irrational. The main thing which the Soviet experience did for China, outside of providing a case study in how not to go about collectivizing, was to recommend the use of the collective form of organization in agriculture as something that any good socialist country should accept rather than reject as a radical and bold innovation of unknown effect.

Although the Chinese leaders thought they were increasing centralized controls only in certain specific areas of agricultural production, it quickly became apparent that they had in fact accomplished a higher degree of centralization than they realized at first. The most conspicuous area was that of farm subsidiary products. There are literally thousands of such products usually made in the home or grown on small plots in the individual peasant's spare time. Together they make up nearly 30% of Chinese farm output.[30] It was the intent of the regime that the production of these items would continue to be carried out largely in the traditional manner. Cooperative regulations were written to ensure that each family would have a small private plot and sufficient time to work it. Success for the cadres, however, was judged only by the results of collective efforts. The cadres, as a result, were strongly motivated to cut down on both the size of the private plots and the amount of spare time allowed to the peasants.[31] Another feature of cooperativization was that the rural free market

[29] The mechanization of Russian agriculture was a necessity regardless of its aid in transferring labor from the farm because of the widespread slaughter of cattle during collectivization.

[30] Perkins, *op. cit.*, p. 127, fn. 32.

[31] One study based on 28 separate surveys showed that the actual size of retained plots averaged 3% of the per capita cultivated acreage instead of the allowed maximum of 5%. Sung (1957).

was closed and the purchasing of subsidiary items taken over by state and cooperative stores. These stores were geared to the handling of major items, had little if any knowledge of the supply and demand conditions of the myriad subsidiary products, and no ready way of acquiring such knowledge. Thus, they usually set purchase prices too low and seldom made adjustments, often refusing to handle the items altogether. With this combination of factors it is not surprising to find that subsidiary production fell off sharply in China in 1956.[32] The first step taken by the state to overcome these difficulties was to reopen the free market and to remove rigid price controls on minor commodities. This move appears to have had the desired effect, although it created some difficulties in the purchasing of major crops which were sold on the free market at high prices before the compulsory quotas had been met.[33] In 1957, the regime also increased the size of the private plots and attempted to reduce cadre interference with private activities. With respect to hogs there were additional efforts, such as a regulation requiring the cooperative to pay a fair price for manure used collectively. The solution by the Chinese Communists in 1956 and 1957 of the problems of subsidiary production, therefore, was to restore private initiative and decentralized control through the market.

A second area where the regime overcentralized without fully realizing what it had done was in its control over the relative weight given to major crops. As already mentioned, the central planning of these crops had faltered on the inability of the planners to gather sufficiently accurate data within a reasonable amount of time. Even the efficient setting of compulsory quotas for grain was not easy. The excessive raising of these quotas in 1955, for example, caused some hardship and a drop in hog production.[34] The solution at the time had been to lower the quotas and fix

[32]For evidence of this fall in output, see Perkins, *op. cit.*, pp. 127–128.

[33]The state apparently ended most of these difficulties with a directive by the State Council, "Regulations on the Restrictions on Certain Agricultural Products and Other Commodities Which Are Subject to Planned Purchase or Unified Purchase by the State" (August 9, 1957), translated in K C Chao (1959). *Economic Planning and Organization in Mainland China*, Vol. 2. Cambridge: Center for East Asian Studies, Harvard University, pp. 43–47.

[34]After reaching 101 million head in June, 1954, the number of hogs fell to 84 million by June, 1956. Chinese Communist Party Central Committee and State Council, "Decision on

them for a period of three years so as to maximize peasant incentives and minimize other harmful aspects of the quotas. In the latter part of 1956 and in 1957, the authorities had to revert back to controlling the relative levels of production of major crops through the purchase price mechanism. In particular, an attempt was made to raise the level of output of crops other than grain and cotton by sharp price increases. Rapeseed prices were raised from 50 to 70% in the key producing areas in September 1956, and the prices of oil producing materials in general were raised another 10 to 30% in the first quarter of 1957.[35] Tea prices in mid-1956 were already 7% above 1955 and were raised another 7% by the end of the year, and domestic cocoon prices which had fallen off in 1953 had again reached the prewar level by 1957.[36] Often in the past less dramatic shifts in the price of cotton and other crops had resulted in the desired recovery in output. But in 1957, the production of every crop whose price had been increased fell while that of both grain and cotton rose. It is always difficult to pinpoint cause and effect in something as complex as agricultural production, particularly when allowance must be made for the quality of the statistics. However, this 1957 phenomenon and to a large extent the poor performance of crops other than grain and cotton from 1956 on was probably mainly a result of the regime's preference for crash programs and concentration on key points, a philosophy of unbalanced growth with a vengeance. A second lesser factor may have been the moderate increase in the scope of rationing on the consumers' goods market, which would have made the effect of price changes less significant in terms of real purchasing power. As to the first factor, this writer has not seen one reference where the main goal of the cooperatives has been described as the maximization of income or profit.[37] The basic planning

---

the Development of Live Hog Production" (February 28, 1957), *Chung-hua Jen-min Kung-ho-kuo Fa-kuei Hui-pien*, 5, January–June 1957, p. 231.

[35] *T'ung-chi Kung-tso*, 11, June 14, 1957, pp. 26–27.

[36] Tientsin *Ta Kung Pao*, June 23, 1956, and "Our Country's Development of Tea Leaf Production," *T'ung-chi Kung-tso*, 3, February 14, 1957, p. 33.

[37] It is, of course, possible that such a reference exists, but this would not fundamentally alter the point made in the text. If a goal such as that is to be followed, it must be well publicized. The closest the regime came to setting such a goal was when it told cadres to make sure that 90% of their membership experienced a rise in income after cooperativization.

aim was usually stated in terms of coordinating cooperative plans with those of the state. This meant the concentration on key points, which in the case of agriculture meant a crash program to increase grain output and to a lesser extent that of cotton. There is some question whether the average cooperative cadre was sophisticated enough to maximize something as complex as an entire village's income or even to measure it accurately. In any case, the attempt was never made, with the result that crop acreage ceased responding to the market.

During 1957, the central authorities attempted to increase local initiative by reducing the size of some of the larger cooperatives and decentralizing some of the authority within the cooperatives to the production brigades.[38] In addition, existing duties were clearly defined so that they would not be intefered with or usurped by higher authorities and so that responsibilities and rewards of an individual would be more closely tied to his job performance. Since the performance for grain and cotton was not unsatisfactory, these measures were probably undertaken not only for their effect on incentives in general, but because they would correct some of the above described imbalances arising out of overcentralization of control.

Even for activities over which the regime had purposely centralized authority there were complications although none so serious as those cases already mentioned, where the centralization had been unintentional. Local construction projects were carried out on a much greater scale, but were still limited by conflicts of interest at the village level and above. It is also probable that the rates of savings and investment by the individual cooperatives were raised.[39] Control over the rate of savings was achieved by merely setting a maximum percentage of total income which could be saved, and then letting the pressure from the cooperative

---

[38]Chinese Communist Party Central Committee, "Directive on Doing Agricultural Producers' Cooperative Production Management Work Well" (September 14, 1957), *Hsinhua Pan-yueh-k'an*, 19, October 10, 1957, pp. 136–137.

[39]One relatively reliable survey of 228 cooperatives shows a significant increase in the cooperatives' capital in 1957 over 1956 which, if true, tends to confirm the belief that the rate of savings and investment was raised. (*T'ung-chi Yen-chiu* data office, "Research Materials on Income Distribution in 228 Agricultural Producers' Cooperatives in 1957," *T'ung-chi Yen-chiu*, 8, August 23, 1958, pp. 10–11).

cadres ensure that that maximum would be reached. There was also a limited amount of funds issued to the cooperatives by the central government in the form of loans, which influenced the coops' rate of investment. It is worth noting, however, that in 1956 and 1957 when the central government wished to increase its direct investment in the cooperatives,[40] it relied less on budget allocations or loans of funds and more on price reductions of agricultural producers' goods sold to the cooperatives. The state could have financed the large increase in producers' goods sold to agriculture from 1956 on through budget allocations and loans. The absence of a highly developed planning apparatus, however, would have meant that the goods would have gone to the cooperatives with the swiftest or most persuasive cadres and not to those who could afford them and use them effectively. As it was, the central authorities had no easy time getting these cadres to use their own investment funds efficiently. The temptation to build unproductive or inefficient showcase projects was great.

One of the best documented examples of the difficulties involved in getting cadres and the central government to make efficient use of the resources earmarked for agriculture is the case of the double-wheeled double-bladed plow. This case also has the advantage of pointing up the fact that the state's ability to carry out rapid technological change in agriculture was not an unmixed blessing. These plows had worked well in a number of areas in 1954 and 1955, and, with the upsurge of cooperativization, the authorities decided that every well-equipped cooperative needed a full quota of such tools. Production and sales plans were raised first from 400,000 to 5 million plows and then scaled down to around 2 million. The leadership cadres of the cooperatives were either forced to buy plows they did not want, or did so because they felt no cooperative was complete without several double-wheeled double-bladed plows. As things turned out, the plow was unsuited to large areas of the country so that by the middle of 1956, although 1.4 million plows had been produced (at considerable cost in terms of disruption of other industries), only 800,000 had been sold and of those 40 to 50% were not being used. The result was that

[40]Most state investment in agriculture went to such things as major water conservation projects which were not handled through the cooperative organization.

their production was stopped entirely and not renewed on any considerable scale until 1958.[41] This was an extreme case, but similar lesser occurrences must have happened frequently, particularly since so much emphasis was placed on a cadre's party loyalty and ideological purity, qualities perhaps only coincidentally possessed by the better farmers. The Communist leadership on occasion has recognized this difficulty by calling on the cadres to pay more attention to the views of the older and hence more experienced peasants.

The fruits of centralization in 1956 and 1957, therefore, were not very impressive. Overall agricultural production continued to creep upward, but only very slowly.[42] The problems which existed in 1955 had not been resolved. The 1956 attempt to raise significantly the rate of investment and industrial growth had to be abandoned. Industrial growth in 1957 was slower than in any year except 1955. The advantages of centralization had proved illusory for three basic reasons. First of all, it turned out to be impossible to centralize certain functions without interfering with the proper carrying out of others. Some of these problems were only the result of unforeseen difficulties which were bound to occur when any fundamental change in an organization takes place in so short a time. There was no need for the difficulties with subsidiary production to continue, for example. The excessive concentration on grain and cotton, however, was more fundamental. Second, it proved difficult to find an adequate substitute for the incentive provided by the knowledge that one's reward depends solely on one's own effort and skill. Finally, the advantages of centralization in raising the rate of investment and promoting technological change did not prove to be great. This was largely because the rural cadres were not sufficiently skilled to carry out these efforts efficiently.

At the beginning of 1958, therefore, the regime in a sense was in worse shape than in 1955. The same conflict between the basic goals of

---

[41]This account is based on "Why Is There a Stopping of Production and an Obstruction of Sales of Double-Wheeled Double-Bladed Plows," *Chi-hua Ching-chi*, 9, September 23, 1956, pp. 1–4.

[42]The official estimates show a rise of 4.8 and 3.5% respectively (State Statistical Bureau, *Ten Great Years*, *op. cit.*, p. 118.), while the Liu-Yeh estimates are 3 and 5% (T C Liu and K C Yeh, *op. cit.*, p. 560).

the regime and the inadequacy of agricultural production existed as before, but in addition, the regime had brought its major weapon (the cooperatives) to bear and found it wanting. Perhaps given time and a willingness to move further toward more genuine cooperation rather than "commandism," the Chinese Communists might have found a way out which would not have involved a substantial reduction in the emphasis on heavy industry. Instead in 1958, they attempted to solve the problem by an even bolder and more radical reorganization of agriculture, the communes.

IV. Communes and Anarchy, 1958–1959

The commune movement which got underway in the summer of 1958 was hailed as one of the most revolutionary developments in the history of mankind by both Communists and anti-Communists alike, although the adjectives used differed. The rural communes were in fact considerably less radical than their publicity, but they did make several profound changes. To understand fully why the communes were set up in the first place, one would have to go deeply into the inner dynamics of the Chinese Communist Party. The leadership's disillusionment with greater relaxation of control in general as a result of the abortive "hundred flowers" or free speech campaign, for example, made any further relaxation even if confined to the economic sphere out of the question. The answer to the problem of the sluggish development of agriculture, therefore, had to be found elsewhere. It could not be found, however, by centralizing economic decisions in Peking. Even the modest attempts in this direction with regard to planning had proved unworkable. The solution decided upon, which was applied to industry as well as agriculture, was to tighten the grip of party personnel at the local level and then to remove virtually all constraints except ideological ones emanating from the central government. Pressure was then put on these local party cadres to achieve spectacular economic results through the exercise of their own energy and ingenuity. A combination of decentralized decision-making together with a maintenance of ideological reliability on the part of those making the decisions had proved successful in guerilla warfare, and it was hoped it would do as much for the economy.

The stated reasons for expanding the basic unit in agriculture from an average size of under 200 families (the cooperative) to 4,000–5,000 families (the commune) were linked with the added functions which a larger unit could undertake.[43] (An unstated reason probably was that it was easier to ensure proper party control when only 26,000 units had to be staffed instead of the previous 700,000.) The most important economic function which a larger unit could undertake was the organization of much larger quantities of labor for work on water conservation projects and in local industries. The larger unit, it was felt, was also big enough to be able to exercise control over local commercial, credit, and industrial establishments which previously had had to be controlled on a nationwide or provincial basis. The cooperatives, as already mentioned, were limited in the size of the water conservation projects they could undertake by the need to reconcile the interests of each village involved. Second, no single cooperative could hope to find enough surplus labor or managerial skills in its own small group to staff anything but an extremely small industrial firm even on a seasonal basis.

This move to increase the size of the basic administrative unit in the rural areas was not so wholly in conflict with the attempts in 1956 and 1957 to reduce the size and authority of cooperatives over agricultural production as at first appears. At least in theory, it was not. According to the commune regulations control over agricultural production itself was to remain where it was. As in the case of the cooperatives, centralization was carried out with the idea of increasing the number of activities handled at the local level rather than centralizing control over already existing activities. Once again, however, theory and reality were far apart. The major problem was that, when control over a few activities was centralized, it was difficult to prevent a gravitation of all other decision-making powers to the center. This tendency of gravitation toward centralization occurred partly because of the difficulty of coordinating decisions at different levels within the commune and partly as a result of the atmosphere within which the communes' party leadership operated. There was no hard and fast rule that would have allowed commune heads to plan for use of labor on large

[43] E.g., see the brief discussion of what the communes were supposed to achieve in Chao (1960).

water conservation projects without in some way coming into conflict with demands on that same labor from production brigade heads (the heads of the old cooperatives) for use in farming. Since the commune leadership contained the more senior party personnel, they invariably won out — whatever the economic merits of their case.

This situation was made even worse by the extreme pressure on commune leaders to achieve spectacular results, together with the fact that all restraints on their exercise of initiative had been removed. The decentralization of almost all authority for organizing the communes down to the commune itself effectively removed all constraints on cadre interference in subsidiary production, in determining the rate of savings and consumption, and in the planting and harvesting of the major crops. Even where there were specific regulations against such interference as in the case of responsibility for planning the major crops, it was safer to deviate toward the left, i.e., toward greater centralization and reduction of individual control, than to follow the regulations literally.[44] Pressure from the top was by no means the only cause of the overzealousness of the lower level party cadres. Their own thorough indoctrination in Communism, together with their relative youth, undoubtedly gave them overconfidence in their own ability together with faith in the inherent superiority of more "Communist" forms of organization. All the propaganda put out by the central party organs on the general theme of the rapidly approaching "Communist" millennium certainly did nothing to discourage such views.[45]

Whatever the causes, the result of the commune movement was a vast increase in rural construction work combined with a severe accentuation of all the problems created by the cooperatives. Private plots were abolished altogether and along with them went the free market since it no longer served any function. The time which peasants had to devote to crops grown on these plots had been encroached upon under pressures from the "great

[44]Even on something as fundamental as the size of the communes the deviation was toward a size much bigger than what was recommended (4,600 families versus the recommended size of 2,000 families per commune).

[45]For a discussion of the spate of articles on the approach to communism, see "Transition to communism (I) and (II)," *China News Analysis*, 278–279 (May 29 and June 5, 1959).

leap forward" even prior to the introduction of the communes. After the communes were established, this encroachment was carried to such great lengths initially that the peasant's time for family subsidiary occupations was eliminated and even his time for sleeping was reduced.

Perhaps even more serious than the centralization of authority in the heads of the communes and the removal of limits on cadre encroachment on the private sector was the concurrent removal of all external means of guiding the commune leadership toward rational economic decisions. Even under the cooperatives, cadre success tended to be reckoned only on the basis of ability to increase grain and cotton output. In 1958 and 1959, the decentralization down to the commune organization itself of the State Statistical Bureau's power to collect agricultural production statistics and the resulting falsification of all farm data[46] made it impossible for higher level organs to know whether a particular measure was successful, even within the narrow scope of their emphasis on grain and cotton. Statistics could no longer be used to appraise performance. Rational planning in accordance with any criteria at all was made even more difficult for the commune leadership by the competition in target-raising carried on among individual communes, and the resulting need for constant plan revision. No sooner would a particular commune have raised its grain output target than one of its neighbors would set an even higher goal, and the whole process of planning in the first commune would have to be begun again. It is not surprising, therefore, that agricultural purchase price adjustments played an even smaller role than previously. Under the cooperatives the cadres commonly came from the village they were responsible for and were probably somewhat influenced by the membership's desire to maximize their income. Commune heads were too far removed from individual peasant reactions to have felt any such pressure directly, and the falsification of statistics made it difficult to obtain information indirectly even if they had so desired. What is surprising is that the central government and party organs reacted to the continuing poor performance of most of the industrial crops by raising their purchase prices even further, in the

[46] For a full discussion of the changes in the state statistical organization in 1958, see Li (1962).

belief that this would somehow raise their output.[47] Some indication of the results of these efforts can be gathered from the fact that in 1959 the regime ceased publication of all crop production figures, except for those of grain, cotton, and soybeans.

In addition, financial restraints operating through limits on the availability of funds were undermined by the huge influx of money into the rural areas in the form of large increases in agricultural credit and budget allocations directly to the communes.[48] In agriculture, as elsewhere, this easy money policy further accentuated the tendency to ignore income and profit goals and concentrate on a few key physical output targets. The cooperatives had to pay their own way and this limited how far the cadres could go in building nonproductive establishments or ones that would not become productive until some date far in the future. It also provided them with an incentive to respond to purchase price adjustments. Such financial restraints were not effective for the communes.

Finally, one cannot ignore the effect which the commune organization had on the incentive of the individual peasant to put forth his best effort. Some of the features relevant to the question of incentives, however, were not so significant as their publicity made them appear. The "part wage part free supply" distribution system, for example, was in reality not very different from the procedure existing under the cooperatives. There the peasant was paid both in money and in kind, with the latter being determined partly by work done and partly by need. The communes took this same food, plus that which had once been grown on private plots, served it in the messhalls, and called it free supply. The wage portion was somewhat of an innovation in that peasants were probably paid at more regular

[47]The purchase prices of soybeans, sugar cane, sugar beet, and peanuts were raised. State Council, "Directive on Adjusting Several Types of Commodity Prices" (October 16, 1959), *Jen-min Shou-ts'e*, 1960, p. 388.

[48]*China News Analysis*, No. 258 (January 2, 1959), p. 5, states (on the basis of the *Jen-min Jih-pao*, December 18, 1958) that agrarian loans made by the banks in 1958 wore equal to the total amount during the first five-year plan. Loans were also large in 1959 and in addition there was 1 billion *yuan* investment in the People's Commune, 1.24 billion *yuan* for various operating funds, and large funds from local authorities in addition to the regular state investments in agriculture.

intervals, rather than having to wait until the harvest was sold before their shares could be divided up.

In the area of individual incentives, the most significant change brought about by the communes was that the basis upon which wages were calculated was the income of the whole commune, rather than that of the cooperative or production brigade. In effect, this removed the reward given to the individual peasant one step further from direct connection with the amount of work he performed. Elaborate bonus systems for brigades, teams and individuals were set up just as they had been under the cooperatives, but these were far from adequate substitutes for the built-in bonus system which existed when the individual depended completely on his own performance for his reward. Of equal importance were the egalitarian tendencies of the rural cadres. Although the spate of articles and speeches on how China was on the verge of making the transition from socialism to communism were not meant to have immediate practical application, they could not help but influence the decisions of rural cadres. Their success depended not only on obedience to the party directives of the moment, but on anticipation of future directives as well. Even prior to 1958, the regime had had to make special efforts to get the cooperative cadres to make sufficient allowances for the disincentive effects of the leveling of incomes both within and among cooperatives. Part of the motive behind the reduction in size of the cooperatives had been to take better account automatically of incentive differentials in income. In 1958 the further separation of work from reward was at least partly responsible for the subsequent agricultural crisis.

The commune movement, therefore, proved first of all that more centralized control of labor allocation could not work effectively. There were economic advantages to increasing the number of hours worked, by making individuals work longer and during seasons when they would otherwise have been idle. These advantages, however, were more than offset by the decreased quality of labor resulting from the many disincentives attached to this form of organization and the inefficiency with which labor was used because of the inadequate managerial skills of rural cadres. Communist ideology and party pressures accentuated these disadvantages, but they probably would have existed to some degree in any case. The commune movement also proved that the authorities in Peking could not abandon all responsibility for setting basic guidelines within which lower level cadres could operate. Cadre self-interest in such areas as subsidiary production and objective reporting was bound to be in conflict with the best interests of the state.

The Chinese Communists paid a heavy price for this knowledge, but the price was obscured for a time by the good harvest of 1958. When the central authorities finally realized that the net effect of the communes on agricultural production had been deleterious, they were forced to face the fact that their ambitious industrialization program was, at least for the time, up against basic and unpostponable requirements of agriculture.

V. Revisions, 1960–1962

The time that it took the central authorities to realize the seriousness of the crisis they had helped create and to act on this knowledge was longer than on previous occasions. This was in part the result of the decentralization of most controls formerly exercised at the center down to the commune, although the deep ideological commitment to the commune movement was also an important factor. The most serious aspect of the loss of central control was the loss of the means of attaining accurate information as to what was really going on at the lower levels. Without the accurate reporting of the State Statistical Bureau, the top leaders were probably unaware that a crisis was brewing until it was well under way.[49] They were also unable to ascertain fully the crisis' true causes. To accomplish this latter objective would have required detailed seasonal and area breakdowns in data, so that the effects of poor organization could have been separated out from the effects of the bad weather which affected most of China between 1959 and 1961. The decentralization of authority also prolonged the time needed to deal with the difficulties in agriculture. The leaders not only had to decide what needed to be done, but they had either to convince the commune cadres to do it or else to reestablish central lines of authority so that they could be ordered to do it. The latter method was quicker but on the

[49] If they had been fully aware of the impending difficulties, they would presumably have taken measures to avoid or soften the negative propaganda effect by such measures as not giving so much publicity to grossly falsified production data.

whole inefficient. From the beginning of the Communist regime, the system of agricultural controls was based on the principle that any central directive must be applied with considerable flexibility and imagination at the operational level so as to take into account local conditions. It was generally assumed that to ensure that this would be the case, convincing the cooperative and commune cadres of the advisability of taking a particular action was superior to putting it in the form of a military order. Under the communes, the cadres had been given even greater leeway to take initiative, particularly in the direction of more radical moves. As a result, it was difficult to get them to move back in the opposite direction, especially when the central authorities themselves seemed reluctant to put their full weight behind reversing the trend.

The first move back was the gradual reintroduction of a semblance of a free market in the rural areas.[50] By early 1959, the regime was aware that subsidiary production had suffered heavily, at least partly because of overtight commercial controls. Initially, it attempted to cope with the problem by renewed emphasis on contracts and special meetings where such contracts were drawn up, but it met with considerable reluctance on the part of commune cadres who felt that such contracts would merely reduce their freedom of action. Consequently, the authorities began experimenting with reopening rural markets in particular areas — culminating in a directive on September 25, 1959, calling for nationwide adoption. Prices, however, were to be kept under much tighter control than under the previous free markets, and state commercial organizations were told to keep a sharp lookout for a resurgence of capitalism.

By the summer of 1960, the regime went a step further by encouraging the restoration of small private plots and of limits on the amount of labor time which the commune could require of its members.[51] That these measures did not meet with complete enthusiasm on the part of local cadres is evidenced by the fact that the authorities still found it necessary to explain why they were restored and answer criticism of

[50] For a fuller discussion of the various administrative changes involved in the reintroduction of rural trade fairs (free markets), see Donnithorne (1961).

[51] Greene (1961), states that, when he was in China, peasants were in fact being encouraged to develop small private plots.

them well into the middle of 1961. The state also continued to rely heavily on various collective expedients for raising pigs and vegetables until the beginning of 1962. During 1961, further steps were also taken to loosen price controls at the rural trade fairs and expand the amount of trade taking place there.[52]

Finally in 1961, the regime also began to take a number of measures aimed at correcting the general disincentive effects of communization, by passing control over production and incomes down to lower level units. In a sense, this emphasis on the role of lower level units began with the December 10, 1958, resolution which reaffirmed that it was the brigade which was to organize agricultural production and the team which was to arrange labor allocation. It was not until the beginning of 1961, however, that ownership and hence the calculation of profit and loss and wages was passed down to the production brigades.[53] In early 1962, a further step was taken in the transfer of the basic level of ownership down to the production team. Thus, after four years of experimenting with larger units, the regime was back to a unit which may have been even smaller than the one with which it started. These adjustments were brought about by changes in the level of ownership rather than by reducing the size of the communes and brigades, probably because the regime could accomplish the same ends either way, and unlike most farm related actions, the first could be carried out quickly and easily by an administrative order. It also had the added advantage that it allowed the regime to claim that the communes were still very much in existence.

Although generally successful, these moves managed only to restore the situation to conditions which had prevailed in 1957, if that. There was nothing about these policies that could have been expected to do more toward solving the fundamental dilemma facing the regime. Apparently the 1962 harvest was fairly good, but nowhere good enough to sustain a

[52]For further discussion of these measures see Perkins, *op. cit.*, pp. 167–170.

[53]E.g., *Jen-min Jih-pao* editorial, "The Three-Level Ownership System with the Production Brigade as the Basic Level is the Basic System for People's Communes at the Present State," *Jen-min Jih-pao*, December 21, 1960, translated in *Survey of the China Mainland Press*, No. 2408, January 3, 1961, p. 10.

substantial and lopsided investment in industrial producers' goods. As a result, the basic conflict between the needs of agriculture and those of rapid industrialization had to be resolved temporarily at least by shifting resources from the former to the latter.

VI. Centralization versus Decentralization

It should be clear from the above discussion that almost from the beginning, the Chinese Communists have faced a basic conflict between their desire to build a heavy industrial base as rapidly as possible and China's low level of per capita agricultural output. As early as 1953, the regime was forced to abandon the market in favor of centrally determined compulsory quotas for major crops. Where for Stalin a similar centralization of control over marketed agricultural output had provided a long-run solution of over twenty years duration, the relative poverty of China made these quotas only a temporary respite of little more than two years in length. In fact, by harming individual farmer incentives, they probably hastened the need for measures which would get at the real problem, that of agricultural output. From 1955 on, the key question was how to raise agricultural production without in any way reducing the state's investment in producers' goods industry. This was a goal that ultimately proved to be beyond China's capabilities, but between 1955 and 1959 both within China and without there was a belief that it could be achieved by partial centralization of authority over certain aspects of agricultural production. Guided by this belief, the Chinese Communists tried first the cooperatives and then the communes.

In a limited sense, both types of organization accomplished what they were set up for. Centralization made possible the utilization of rural underemployed labor in various construction projects. Furthermore, the greater the degree of centralization, the larger were the size and number of projects that could be undertaken. The communes were even large enough to build and staff various industrial and commercial establishments. In addition, the more decision-making was centralized, the easier it was to encourage the trial of new techniques and to raise the rate of rural savings. The accomplishments along these lines, however, were not very great. The cadres were too often insufficiently skilled or overly doctrinaire to use the added resources or new techniques efficiently.

Even these modest advantages of centralization, however, were bought at heavy cost. A serious but by no means the only cost was the decline in peasant incentives, which accompanied the removal of the direct connection between individual effort and the produce of the land. This decline was more serious, the larger the unit which controlled agricultural output and the larger the unit on the basis of whose income individual wages were determined. The efficient use of resources in controlling farm production was also more difficult, the more centralized decision-making became. The Chinese Communists recognized this latter danger, but failed to take account of how difficult if not impossible it was to centralize control over labor and financial allocation for one purpose (construction) and not for another (farm production). This problem was further complicated by the lack of any adequate criteria by which cadres could hope to plan successfully their unit's activities. This problem became more aggravated, too, as the unit became larger and the contact between villagers, who could be counted on to encourage maximization of income, and cadres became more remote. The tendency to concentrate on grain and cotton at the expense of other crops might have been somewhat reduced if it had been possible to centralize planning all the way up to Peking, but the lack of adequate and timely data made the one move in this direction a complete failure. The lack of response by cadres to price changes made it impossible for the central planners to achieve indirectly what they could not accomplish directly.

The one area where centralization proved to be unqualifiedly detrimental in its effects was in subsidiary production and marketing. The regime had to learn twice over that these commodities could only be handled efficiently by individual peasants working on their own under the stimulus of a free market. The problems with subsidiary output also illustrate one of the major dilemmas facing the authorities in Peking, whenever they attempted to reorganize agriculture. If a reorganization were to be effective, plenty of leeway had to be allowed for adjustment to local conditions by lower level cadres. Because these same cadres were also under extreme pressure to prove their enthusiasm and ideological purity, however, the adjustments made were often more closely related to the political atmosphere of the times than to local economic conditions. Moreover, even without these pressures, there were real conflicts of interest between cadres and the central government of which private plots and free time were the most conspicuous example. Therefore, although the central authorities could not become too involved in the details of the various reorganizations, they could not afford to decentralize all of their authority to lower level party cadres as they did in 1958.

By I960 and 1961, the Chinese Communists finally became aware of this conflict between the anticipated advantages of centralization and its costs. During the entire course of their experimentation in the rural areas, they had failed to discover any combination of centralized and decentralized control which on economic grounds was any better than the combination which had existed prior to the cooperatives. As a result, they were ultimately forced to make the decision that these reorganizations had been designed to avoid, namely, to cut back investment in producers' goods industry and shift it to agriculture.

The difficulties which the Chinese Communists have run into in their attempts to make either the cooperatives or the communes work effectively cast doubt on whether there are any realizable advantages from centralization in agriculture even in overpopulated and labor-intensive countries such as China. Political and ideological considerations aside, there appears to be little that centralization accomplishes which cannot be done better through extension services, taxes and market controls in the context of a free peasant economy. In Communist China, however, political and ideological considerations cannot be put aside. The political and ideological advantages to the regime of the collective form of organization in agriculture have been too great for this organization to be abandoned except under the most desperate circumstances. The real question for China, therefore, is not whether cooperatives or communes work better than a free peasant alternative, but whether they can be made to work at all. Can agricultural output and marketings under the cooperatives be increased with sufficient speed to support the industrialization program and perhaps modest increases in the standard of living as well?

On this point, the evidence against the cooperatives, at least, is not conclusive. Perhaps with time, the skills of the cadres will improve sufficiently to reduce many of the costs of centralization. It may also be that the political and ideological pressures on these cadres will be reduced and that a number of minor adjustments will result at the local level which will damp down disincentives. Always working in the opposite direction, however, will be the need of the totalitarian state to maintain tight political control. Even if a modified form of the cooperative does prove workable, there is no assurance that the Chinese Communists will abandon their attempts to find a more radical solution to their basic dilemma. The evidence available is insufficient to determine whether the present retreat from centralization is meant to be a long-run policy or only a temporary respite.

References

Buck, JL (1930). *China's Farm Economy*, Institute of Pacific Relations. Shanghai: Commercial Press, p. 196.

Chao, KC (1960). *Agrarian Policy of the Chinese Communist Party*. New Delhi: Asia Publishing House, pp. 163–164.

Donnithorne, A (1961). "The organization of rural trade in China since 1958." *The China Quarterly*, 8, October–December, pp. 77–91.

Fei, H-T and C-I Chang (1948). *Earthbound China*. London: Routledge and Kegan Hsiao, p. 77.

Greene, F (1961). *Awakened China*. New York: Doubleday.

Hsueh, M-C (1960). *The Socialist Transformation of the National Economy in China*. Peking: Foreign Languages Press, p. 90.

Li, CM (1962). *The Statistical System of Communist China*. Berkeley, CA: University of California Press.

Liu, TC and KC Yeh (1963). *The Economy of the Chinese Mainland: National Income and Economic Development, 1933–1959*, Vol. II. Santa Monica: Rand Research Memorandum 3519, p. 455.

Perkins, DH (1963). "Price Formation in Communist China," Unpublished PhD thesis, Harvard University, 1963, Appendix C.

Sung, H-W (1957). "A discussion of the problem of retained plots of land in agricultural producers' cooperatives". *Ching-chi Yen-chiu*, 4, August 17, p. 13.

Taso, J-H (1956). "Questions of Raising the Procurement Prices for Rapeseed." *Liang-shih Kung-tso*, October 14, translated in *Extracts from China Mainland Magazines*, 58, November 26, pp. 25–27.

Tung, T-L (1959). *Agricultural Cooperation in China*. Peking: Foreign Languages Press, p. 23.

Yang, CK (1959). *A Chinese Village in Early Communist Transition*. Cambridge: Technology Press, p. 46.

Yang, C-P (1957). *Chieh-fang I-lai Wo-kuo Kuo-min Ching-chi-chung Chi-chung Chu-yau Pi-li Kuan-hsi Pien-hua*. Shanghai: New Knowledge Press, p. 44.

Yin, H and YC Yin (1960). *Economic Statistics of Mainland China (1949–1957)*. Cambridge, MA: Center of East Asian Studies, Harvard University, p. 6.

CHAPTER 4

INDUSTRIAL PLANNING AND MANAGEMENT

THE CHINESE COMMUNISTS consistently stress the importance of planning to China's economic growth. In one sense or another, of course, nearly every nation plans its economy. But for China and other economies that to some degree follow the Soviet model, "planning," particularly in the industrial sphere, takes on the more specific meaning of control exercised through centrally determined output targets. This chapter will investigate exactly how Peking plans in the industrial sector, why changes in planning techniques have been made over time, and how suitable the alternative methods are for China.

Analytically, planning can be divided into three parts: (1) the determination of broad policy goals (e.g., producer goods versus consumer goods, autarky or reliance on foreign trade, etc.); (2) decisions on specific plan targets for output, costs, etc.; and (3) the implementation of those targets. In practice, the lines between these three parts are not sharply drawn. At times, broad policy goals are taken for granted or largely ignored, and planning starts at the specific target level. More important, decisions on what targets are to be and how they are to be implemented are intimately connected. For example, a target may be set higher or lower depending on which will elicit the most effort from the enterprise involved. Or planners may channel resources at their command into one sector or another simply because they are able to control what is going on in that sector, not because to do so is to make the most efficient use of their resources.

All these problems have arisen in China and will be discussed below. In spite of such difficulties, however, the discussion will be carried out in terms of the three suggested phases.

I. Economic Goals

The goal of rapid economic growth has been second only to the security of the Chinese Communist state itself. In fact, economic growth has been considered to be a fundamental guarantee of that security.

Increases in industrial and agricultural output serve national security in a number of ways. They may make possible a rising standard of living for the people as a whole or for major groups within the society, thus promoting domestic political tranquility. Heavy industrial development is the one key prerequisite to an armaments industry. Growth of certain heavy industries may also make possible reduced dependence on foreign trade, not only for the military but also for further economic development. It should be pointed out that "heavy industry," as the term is used by the Chinese Communists, is not synonymous with producer goods industry. While it includes defense industries, it excludes producer goods industries still operating with relatively primitive technology. Further, heavy industries tend to be large in scale, thus excluding many small-scale producer goods enterprises from the category.

During the first decade of Communist control of the Chinese mainland, it was the advantages of heavy industrialization that held the regime's attention. It was by means of heavy industry and eventually modern weapons that China would achieve great power status. Those same industries, particularly machine-building and steel, would also make possible economic autarky, which at that time, before the deterioration in Sino-Soviet relations, was desired more for its own sake than for its immediate military advantages. With increasing hostility between China and the Soviet Union, autarky has taken on even greater importance for reasons of both security and economic development. Although China has been able to import some needed industrial equipment from the West, the regime undoubtedly considers this a precarious source of assistance at best. In the words of Po I-po, "The socialist industrialization of our country entails building an independent comprehensive and modern industrial system..." (1963, p. 22).

Once a decision to promote autarky has been made, emphasis on producer goods industry becomes necessary in order to raise future living standards, whatever the military implications. A given investment in consumer goods industry may yield a higher return than an equivalent expenditure on producer goods,[1] but if one does not want to rely on exporting consumer goods in exchange for imports of producer goods, then economic growth comes to an end. Thus, although producer goods are not synonymous with heavy industry, the differences are not great. Even if investment is concentrated in agriculture, the major inputs other than labor are primarily the products of heavy industry (e.g., chemical fertilizer, power machinery, etc.).

Communist China's emphasis on heavy industry, however, has not resulted solely from rational calculations such as these. Heavy industry as the path to economic growth had become a part of the regime's ideology, in effect a goal in itself. Marx had tended to look on economic development and the growth of large-scale heavy industry as one and the same, and the example of the Soviet Five-Year Plans (FYPs) further solidified the place of this model of growth in the regime's ideology. Even if the ideological element had not been present, however, Peking's lack of experience and resulting need to rely on Soviet support would have made it difficult to follow a different path.

As Chinese economic experience grew, this unquestioning reliance on the Soviet model began to wane. Perhaps as early as 1955, the regime began to have doubts about the emphasis on machine-building and supporting industries. The main cause of these doubts was the poor performance of agriculture. As it became increasingly apparent that organizational reforms alone would not raise farm output, Peking was forced to transfer resources to sectors that would directly benefit agriculture.[2] The greatest shifts in resources apparently took place after 1961 or 1962, but there were lesser changes as early as 1956.[3]

This change, given Peking's desire for autarky, did not mean a reallocation of investment funds away from heavy industry so much as a change in direction from one set of heavy industrial products to another. However, this statement must be qualified to the degree that the need to

[1]There is, of course, no necessity for consumer goods to yield a higher rate of return than producer goods, particularly if prices reflect planners' rather than consumers' preferences.

[2]For a further discussion of these problems, see Perkins, 1966 (Chs. III–IV).

[3]In 1956, state investment in agriculture was raised from 6.7% to 8.0% of the total; it reached 8.6% in 1957, and 9.9% in 1958 (SSB, 1960, pp. 59–60).

maintain work incentives has caused the regime to lower the rate of investment and thus indirectly transfer resources to consumer goods. In addition, the increasing emphasis on agriculture did involve a transfer of funds from industries producing machines that would produce more machines to machines that would produce end products.

The continued substantial investment in heavy industry can be seen from the fragments of evidence available on industrial performance since 1962. Chemical fertilizer output in the first half of 1964 was 53% above the same period in 1963, and 1963 output was 40% above 1962 (Kao Kuang-chien, 1964, p. 25). Tractor production in the first half of 1963 was 30% above the comparable period in 1962 (Fang Chung, 1963, p. 40). Nor has the shift been toward agricultural supplies only. In weaponry and related fields, the Chinese not only exploded their first nuclear device on October 16, 1964, but are apparently able to produce (not just assemble) MIG-21's (*New York Times,* December 30, 1964). Furthermore, petroleum output in 1963 reached an estimated 6.5 million tons, four and one-half times the level of 1957.

Thus, although the economic content of Chinese Communist goals has changed somewhat over time, the emphasis on autarky and military-strength has insured that a large portion of state-controlled investment has gone to heavy industry. This fact, together with a more general understanding of China's economic goals, is fundamental to any appraisal of the effectiveness of Chinese Communist planning technique.

II. Drawing Up the Plan

Balance

There are two significantly different problems involved in drawing up an industrial plan. One is deciding how to allocate current production and stocks of goods among individual enterprises so as to maximize current output according to certain criteria, and given existing plant capacity. The other is determining the direction of investment; i.e., where plant capacity is to be expanded and by how much. This section deals with the first of these problems — that of coordinating or balancing inputs and outputs, given existing plant capacity.

At the heart of a typical annual plan, for China as for any Soviet-type economy, are a number of targets set for each industry and enterprise. In China, prior to November 1957, there were 12 different kinds of targets. After 1957, the number of such targets that were classified as compulsory was reduced to four, but the reasons for this concerned the problem of implementing the plan, not of drawing it up. The other eight targets continued to be computed, but were for advisory purposes only. About 5 of the original 12 could be classified as physical goals: (1) output of major products, (2) total number of employees, (3) trial manufacture of new varieties of products, (4) total number of employees at year's end, and (5) certain technical-economic norms. If these norms are broken down into their component parts — consumption of raw materials, level of mechanization, and rate of equipment utilization — the number of physical targets increases to seven.

The remaining seven targets involve prices or money: (6) gross value of output, (7) cost reduction rate and (8) cost reduction quota, (9) total wage bill and (10) the average wage, (11) labor productivity, and (12) profits. Except for input targets, targets were the minimum, and an enterprise was expected to exceed the designated figure. In the case of raw material and labor inputs, the targets were set at the maximum.

The major problem in setting the targets for output and material consumption is one of coordination or balance. Many of the outputs of one enterprise are the inputs of another. Any given product, in fact, may be crucial to the manufacture of hundreds of others. The process of achieving coordination in a centrally planned economy is commonly referred to as "material balances planning."

The difficulties involved in attaining balance, however, should not be exaggerated for a country such as China. Because China is underdeveloped, it produces a far fewer number of commodities than a developed economy. In 1957, Chinese central planners dealt with 729 individual items (Hsueh Mu-ch'iao, 1957, p. 24), but it is likely that the number for which coordination was seriously attempted was much fewer. The number of commodities actually distributed by the state in a rationed and "unified" (i.e., coordinated) manner was 28 in 1952; 96 in 1953, the first year in which annual planning was put into operation; and 235 in 1956 (*TCKT*,

1957, p. 26).[4] This compares with the more than 1,500 commodities that were centrally allocated in the Soviet Union in the 1950s.

The fact that China is underdeveloped makes the planners' coordinating task easier in another respect as well. There are fewer interdependencies between industries and sectors in an underdeveloped economy. For example, under the existing plan, textile and cigarette output in China depend almost exclusively on the cotton and tobacco crops of the previous year. The same can be said of most other products of light industry. In China, in particular, substantial unused plant capacity in most such industries makes it possible to expand output greatly before any consideration has to be given to investment in new plants and equipment (Chu Jung-chi, 1956, p. 22). In recent years, interdependence has been increased by the regime's policy of expanding those light industrial products that depend on industrial rather than agricultural raw materials. In Shanghai, for example, only 39.5% of total light industrial output in 1962 depended on agricultural raw materials as compared with 63.9% in 1957 (Shih, et al., 1963, p. 9). This change, however, is undoubtedly partly accounted for by a lack of agricultural raw materials due to preceding bad harvests. Most Chinese light industry is still heavily dependent on agriculture.

Unlike the case in heavy industry, most of the products of light industry go directly to the consumer. A reduction in output in this sector, therefore, does not cause a chain reaction through all other sectors. Consumers suffer a decline in consumption, but this is important to overall production only to the extent that it affects incentives. Even consumer tastes in an underdeveloped economy are comparatively easy to predict: they will take virtually any reasonably priced item placed on the market. As per capita incomes rise, questions of style and quality become paramount and make

---

[4] Whether or not formal material balance sheets were drawn up for this number of commodities is not clear. There are statements which indicate that such formal procedures were followed for only a much smaller number of commodities. Nevertheless, if 235 commodities were distributed in a coordinated manner, something approximating the materials balances procedures, by whatever name, must have been followed.

An additional problem in using these numbers arises from uncertainty surrounding the question of whether commodities are defined in the same way in both China and the Soviet Union, and even within China at different times. The differences are probably not great enough to negate the value of such comparisons, but one cannot be certain.

central planning difficult and often very inefficient,[5] but this is a problem not faced in China at present.

Even within heavy industry, the degree of interdependence can be overemphasized. Table 1, showing the Soviet Union's intersectoral balances in 1959, illustrates this point.

The balances for the Soviet Union were selected because its industrial development has followed a pattern that China until recently has attempted to emulate. In fact, as Chenery and Clark (1959) have shown, interindustry relations tend to be similar in all industrialized economies, so that almost any such country's input–output table would probably present essentially the same picture as that of the Soviet Union.[6]

First of all, it is apparent from the table that the heavy industrial sectors (columns [a] to [e]) are almost entirely independent of inputs from outside (except for trade and transport). Furthermore, the degree of interdependence within each sector is limited. Current output of power and fuels depends only on inputs of power and fuels in any quantity. Ferrous metals depend primarily on ferrous ores, nonferrous metals, and fuel and power. Only machinery and metalworking draw heavily from all other heavy industry sectors. This whole picture changes if new investment or expansion of plant capacity is considered, but we are only concerned for the present with the problem of coordinating current output, given existing plant and equipment.

Planning heavy industry, then, becomes increasingly complex as development proceeds not because of increasingly complex patterns of interdependence so much as because of the increasing number of commodities within each sector, which are following already established allocation patterns.[7] Broad sectors thus can be planned individually without regard to what is happening in more than one or two other sectors. Since in China the number of commodities involved in any given sector is

---

[5] An excellent discussion of this problem as it has arisen in Hungary can be found in J. Kornai (1959). The recent Soviet experimentation with greater emphasis on profits started with consumer goods industries partly for this reason.

[6] I am indebted to Herbert S. Levine for a number of observations relevant to the Soviet input–output table.

[7] This statement is obviously an oversimplification, but a more precise statement would add much to length and little to clarity.

Table 1. Soviet Union, intersectoral balances (1959) (gross output of each commodity = 100) consuming sectors.

Producing sectors	(a) Ferrous	(b) Non-ferrous	(c) Fuels	(d) Machinery	(e) Chemicals	(f) Construction	(g) Transport	(h) Trade	(i) Other	(j) Final demand	(k) Gross output
(a) Ferrous ores and metals (1, 2)[a]	16.4	—[b]	—	46.9	—	22.3	—	—	2.8	7.8	100.0
(b) Nonferrous ores and metals (3, 4)	11.9	29.0	—	27.9	3.1	—	—	—	—	23.8	100.0
(c) Fuel and power (5, 7–11)	8.0	2.7	18.3	5.0	2.7	7.0	10.2	—	21.6	23.7	100.0
(d) Machinery, metal-working, autos, etc. (6, 12–20)	—	—	—	14.7	—	9.1	—	—	12.7	58.5	100.0
(e) Chemicals, abrasives, etc. (21–23)	—	—	2.1	9.5	22.3	4.0	—	—	33.9	25.2	100.0
(f) Construction and construction materials (27–33)	—	—	—	—	—	18.4	—	—	—	80.9	100.0
(g) Transport (36)	4.2	—	25.0	8.0	4.9	15.6	—	—	38.8	—	100.0
(h) Trade (37)	2.1	—	7.5	8.8	—	3.9	—	—	81.3	—	100.0
(i) Other (24, 26, 28–32, 34, 35, 38)	—	—	—	—	—	2.8	—	—	37.1	56.2	100.0

Source: Joint Economic Committee, *Annual Economic Indicators for the USSR*, February, 1964, pp. 202–205.

Notes: [a] The data in the table in the source were aggregated and the percentages of gross output were computed by the author. The row numbers in the original source are included for each row in Table 1. [b] Where the amount was less than 2% of gross output — were entered in the table rather than the precise figure for purposes of clarity.

comparatively small, the intrasector coordination problem does not appear to be insurmountably difficult.

The underdeveloped nature of China's economy, however, is not an unmixed blessing to those charged with drawing up the material balances. The main problem arises from the fact that Chinese industrial output is produced by a large number of enterprises varying widely in scale, and using techniques that range from the very primitive to the most modern available. This difficulty was accentuated by the emphasis on small-scale industry in 1958 and 1959, though it did not originate then. Approximately, one-third of gross industrial output in China was produced in firms that used only the simplest kinds of hand-powered machinery (see Table 2). Altogether there was nearly 170,000 individual industrial firms, 140,000 of which employed fewer than 15 persons (fewer than 30 if no mechanical power was used).

Table 2. China's industrial firms.

	Gross value of industrial output in nonmodern enterprises			Number of enterprises	
	(In million yuan) (1)	As % of total industrial output (2)	Total (3)	Large- and medium-scale (4)	Small-scale (5)
1949[a]	6,100	43.6	126,035	—	—
1950	8,230	43.1	—	—	—
1951	10,440	39.6	—	—	—
1952	12,280	35.8	167,403	27,527	139, 876
1953	15,890	35.5	176,405	31,379	145,026
1954	17,990	34.6	167,626	31,187	136,439
1955	17,790	32.4	125,474	—	—
1956	20,020	28.4	—	—	—
1957[b]	22,760	29.1	—	—	—
1958	29,730	25.4	—	—	—

Source: See Perkins, 1966 (pp. 108–109). The data on gross value of output in non-modern enterprises are crude estimates at best, particularly for the years 1949–1951 and 1958.

Notes: [a]Data for 1949 through 1956 are in constant 1952 prices. [b]The 1957 and 1958 data are in constant 1957 prices.

With that many firms operating with such primitive technology, it was impossible to collect statistics of sufficient quality to allow central planners to truly coordinate all industrial inputs and outputs. Within a given industry, for example, consumption of raw materials and other inputs per ton of output was likely to differ considerably. The difference in average cost between a large- and small-scale copper ore-dressing plant was 32% (Secretariat of National Conference, 1959, p. 9). Cost disparities among different plants for 21-count yarn were 70%; wheat flour, 100%; grade "C" cigarettes, 50%; and matches, 150% (*KJJP,* 1956).

In China, the problem of achieving balance among so many disparate firms has been accomplished by a number of measures that have considerably reduced the scope of the central material balances. Although the number of commodities subject to centralized allocation has gradually been increased, a portion of each has regularly been set aside and sold on the market. In early years, this practice was necessitated by the inability of central authorities to attain the necessary control over allocation. In Shanghai, for example, the state initially controlled only 9.8% of the market supply of metals and machinery, and by the final quarter of 1952 still had only 56.2% (*Shanghai chieh-fang* ..., 1958, pp. 380–381, 395). Even in 1956, when the state could have had complete control, 8.6% of all cement, 2.8% of steel products, and 40.9% of coal output were sold in the market (*TCKT,* 1957, p. 26). Much of this (particularly coal) went to consumers and agriculture, but part was presumably bought by small-scale industrial enterprises. The existence of this marketed portion has been one element, although not the most important one, in the Chinese Communist decision not to follow the Soviet practice of setting heavy industrial product prices at 5% above average cost. Instead, partly in order to restrict demand, these prices were held at the high levels prevailing during the Korean War.

More important, Peking has made a number of attempts to remove a large portion of small-scale and consumer goods output entirely from the province of the centrally planned balances. Initially, in 1956, this took the form of allowing various small-scale handicraft-type firms to produce for the market and buy their raw materials from that market without having to deal through state wholesaling agencies or to compete ultimately with large-scale firms for planned allocations (Ch'en Yun, 1956).

In late 1957, the regime ordered a major decentralization of control over production and distribution, placing responsibility at provincial and lower levels (Chinese Communist Party, 1957, pp. 96–99; 100–101). Once the rural communes had been set up, management of many of the smaller firms devolved onto the commune leadership. Although these decentralization measures were shortly to be caught up in the extremes of the "Great Leap Forward," they were not conceived in that atmosphere.

Most of the firms transferred down were either small-scale, consumer-oriented, or both. Generally, their raw materials came from the province or region in which they were located, as did their buyers. Local authorities, it was thought, would know local conditions best and could thus achieve the most efficient coordination of activities. A certain amount of general guidance was still to come from the central plan, but basically the central authorities were excused from responsibility for coordinating a significant portion of industrial output and allocation. Unlike the system proposed by Ch'en Yun in 1956, the 1957–1958 decentralization did not involve a significant increase in the role of the market. It was more like an attempt to divide the problem of drawing up material balances into several independent parts.

The fact that the system worked badly from the start was not that it was wrong in principle, but that it was implemented in a way that made efficient coordination impossible. (This, however, is the subject of the last half of the chapter.) The basic validity and importance of the principle of decentralized control over these secondary industrial products is testified to by the regime's continuance of the system in one form or another ever since. By 1965, all industrial enterprises were entitled to produce what they liked after they had fulfilled the state plan targets, providing they did not use materials allocated to them under the plan (Ma Wen-kuei, 1964, p. 24). Presumably, this provision has had little significance for large-scale heavy industrial establishments, most or all of whose output is centrally planned. It is rather a way of perpetuating decentralization of responsibility away from the central planning authorities to, in this case, the enterprise itself.

Up to this point, the problem of attaining coordination or balance has been treated as a question involving only output targets (in physical or value terms) and input coefficients (items 1, 5, and 6 of the 12 targets listed in Section I). In practice, these targets, particularly that for gross value of output and later for output of major products, were the heart of the material balances. The other targets were of far less importance, although nominally it was as much a violation of law to slight them as to disregard output targets. Many of the reasons for these priorities concern problems of plan implementation and the kind of men charged with that implementation. In part, however, priority for output targets flows directly from the nature of the balancing problem.

If the profits target is not met in each firm, the national treasury will not be prevented from financing the government budget, for either a number of firms will overfulfill their targets, or taxes can be made to fill the deficit. Similarly, an excess hiring of labor or payment of wages is a problem only for those trying to prevent inflation on the consumer goods market (Perkins, 1966, Ch. VIII). Most unskilled and semiskilled labor is a comparatively homogeneous input and thus can be readily transferred from one occupation to another. With China's surplus of unskilled labor, there is not even any real need, from the point of view of production, to insure that demand for labor by industry as a whole is limited.

On the other hand, an excessive use of steel or petroleum by one firm means that all other firms must either find substitutes (no easy task in the short run) or curtail output. Similarly, if the aluminum industry fails to meet its output target, all aluminum users suffer, as do the consumers of their products in turn. Therefore, given the decision to achieve coordination of inputs and outputs through centralized allocation and material balances planning, the emphasis on output targets follows naturally.

The function of the other targets, of which the profits target is the most important, is in part simply to help enforce the production targets. More important, however, is their role in promoting quality, variety of output, and more efficient use of inputs. In principle, these functions could be carried out by setting production targets so that they could be completed only if inputs were used efficiently, and by establishing a proper pricing policy (so that gross value of output correctly reflected quality). In practice, though, the task of implementing any set of targets is formidable, requiring not only these other kinds of plan targets, but a variety of other measures as well (as will be discussed in later sections).

It has been suggested in some sources that in the early 1960s, the profits targets actually replaced the output target in the scale of priorities (Schurmann, 1964). In China, during 1961–1962, there was a certain amount of debate on this point in economic journals and elsewhere, not unlike the debate surrounding the Liberman proposals in the Soviet Union (and the much more extensive discussion in Eastern Europe). However, there has been no evidence to indicate that Peking has actually put these proposals into operation, as the Soviet Union did for a large number of consumer goods industries in 1964 and 1965. In fact, there is considerable evidence to the contrary.[8]

Such a change in priorities in favor of profits could have taken one of two somewhat different forms. Profits targets could have been set in such a way as to be the main means of enforcing what was still expressed (and drawn up) in the plan in physical output terms. Planners' preferences, expressed in the material balance tables, would still determine what was produced, but the enterprise's only immediate concern would be profits. A much more radical move would be to allow industrial firms to produce directly for the market (consumers' preferences) and judge their performance by the profits they made in that arena. This alternative was in 1965 being tried for certain consumer goods industries in the Soviet Union, and has often been an element in the method of operation of small-scale industrial enterprises in China. From all appearances, however, neither alternative has ever really been tried in China's major industrial enterprises. A more complete understanding of why this has been the case must await the analysis in subsequent sections of this chapter.

Investment in new capacity

Decisions on where and in what, products new investment will be made are quite different, in terms of the demands put on central planners, from

[8] The "Seventy Theses for Industry" promulgated in draft form in early 1962, for example, follow earlier directives in calling for obedience to all plan targets, with output targets listed ahead of profits. (These were reproduced in rough form from memory by a refugee for the Union Research Institute. I am indebted to Mr. Chao Yung-ching for making them available to me.) See also many articles such as Hsiao Liang, 1962. This article, along with a general discussion of the virtues of imaginatively obeying the state plan, includes the passage:

> It is necessary, on the basis of a comprehensive balancing to specify concretely what a particular enterprise should produce, how much of the product it should produce, when its product should leave, to which unit it should supply, from where its raw materials should come, and so forth.

drawing up the material balances. Investment plans and the material balances, of course, are not unrelated. Increased output due to increased plant capacity and related inputs must balance out with all other products, new and old, but comparatively large errors in estimating increases in output are reduced in significance when total production is taken into account. The degree to which this simplifies matters, however, should not be exaggerated. Prior to 1960, annual increases in output in sectors where the Chinese Communists concentrated their resources (heavy industry) often loomed large in proportion to total output. Between 1952 and 1959, the output of producer goods factories in China (value added) had increased sixfold (Liu and Yeh, 1965, p. 66).[9]

The more difficult problem for those planning new investment is to decide the direction economic development is to take; i.e., what new products are to be invested in and to what extent. This task, however, is simplified considerably by the nature of Communist China's overall economic goals, particularly the emphasis on autarky and military strength. The alternatives open to Peking were further reduced by the regime's desire to emulate the Soviet economic performance.

The key to both autarky and a modern armaments industry is a machine-tools industry. Machine tools in turn require steel and electric power, which in turn use coal and various ores and metals (see Table 1). Furthermore, these industries (particularly steel and machine tools) make maximum use of modern technology. Although the Chinese Communists had some choice of scale and technology, they had to import modern steel and machine tool plants *in toto* from the Soviet Union. Investment planning, therefore, primarily involved deciding how large total expenditure on new plant and equipment was to be, and then buying the relevant set of plants from the Soviet Union,[10] at the same time ensuring that supporting industries wholly domestic in origin were not neglected.

---

[9] Because of the dubious reliability of the 1958–1959 data, the Liu and Yeh estimates are intended to be conjectural.

[10] Approximately, one-third of all Soviet exports to China were for "complete plants," generally meaning the import component of the 156 (later 166) projects that the Soviet Union had agreed to help China build.

At least before 1960, deciding the overall rate of investment was a vitally important, but not very complex decision. It was vitally important not only because of its political impact, but also because the resulting level of consumption, and any changes in it, were a major determinant of individual work incentives and hence of productivity. The relative lack of complexity arose from the low level of output existing when the Communists took power and from the pace with which development proceeded through 1957. In effect, the regime could channel most of the increase in output in these early years into investment, while ensuring that enough was left over to make possible some increase in per capita consumption. As the rate of increase in production began to slow down in 1954 or 1955, particularly in consumer goods, it was no longer possible to push up savings so easily, but by that time China had nearly reached the rate of the Soviet Union in the 1930s and could afford to level off.[11] After output fell off (from 1960 on), investment was cut back sharply, but what principles were used in determining the extent of the reduction are not known.

Once the decision on how much to invest was reached, the questions of which products to invest in and what scale and technology to use remained. As already indicated, this was not as difficult a task as might be supposed, as long as investment was concentrated on an autarkic heavy industrial sector patterned on the Soviet model. The major difficulty, just as in the problem of achieving balance, was how to deal with small-scale traditional industries. Prior to 1958, however, this difficulty was minimized by making such enterprises largely responsible for whatever investment in themselves they were capable of making.

State investment in industry controlled through the central plan was concentrated on a number of key large-scale projects. There were 694 above-norm projects[12] in the First Five-Year Plan (FFYP), published in

---

[11] This at least appears to be the implication of Po I-po's remarks in his speech to the Eighth Party Congress (1956), although it is stated in somewhat vaguer terms. Comparison of Soviet and Chinese rates of accumulation is complicated somewhat by valuation problems. The Soviet 1937 rate at current ruble factor cost was 25.9% (Bergson, 1961, p. 237). The Chinese 1957 rate was 23% in 1957 prices, 26% in 1952 prices, and 15% in 1933 prices (Liu and Yeh, 1965, p. 80).

[12] "Above-norm" refers to projects in which total investment was above a certain figure, the norm. Above-norm projects were subject to much stricter controls than below-norm

mid-1955 but meant to cover the years 1953–1957. Of these 694 projects, 455 were to be completed during the FFYP, the remaining during the Second FYP. At the heart of the program, however, were the 156 projects for which the Soviet Union had agreed to provide assistance. More than 44% of all investment in industry was to go to these projects, and another 7% to 144 projects designed to directly support them [*FFYP,* 1956, p. 39]. By the time the plan was published in 1955, 29 of these Soviet aid projects were wholly or partially completed.

By 1957, the number of above-norm projects had been raised to 921, with 537 already in operation, including 68 of the Soviet aid projects (instead of the 45 in the plan) (Po I-po, 1958, p. 12). By 1958, the number completed had risen to 1,037 (*Ten Great Years,* p. 67) and another 671 were reportedly finished in 1959 (Li Fu-chun, 1960, p. 2), although data for 1958 and 1959 are of dubious quality.

In deciding which above-norm projects to initiate, the state had first to draw up annual (and five-year) output targets for key commodities. To translate these output targets into individual projects, a further decision on what scale and technology to use had to be made. Very little work has been done on how the Chinese made this latter decision.

The impression given by a superficial reading of materials readily available is that Peking never felt that the choices involved were particularly difficult to make. Probably, part of the explanation for this apparent lack of concern is that Chinese choices were severely limited by what the Soviet Union was willing and able to offer.

Even as the impact of the Korean War embargo declined and the range of alternatives increased, studies of other underdeveloped countries suggest that the Chinese would not go far wrong by simply selecting the most advanced technology available to them. The most modern steel processes, jet airplanes, and the like are not only labor-saving, a virtue of little benefit to China, but capital-saving as well. A similar line of reasoning is probably not valid for most light industries, but Chinese investment was primarily in heavy industry. It must be reiterated, however, that this issue has yet to be adequately dealt with for China (and for most other

---

projects. The norm for most industries varied between 10 and 30 million *yuan,* depending on what was produced.

underdeveloped countries), and a definitive conclusion must, therefore, await further analysis.

Once a project was approved, its actual rate of output of steel or machinery depended on when the project was allowed to start, how fast it was completed, and how fast the completed project reached capacity output. Given the uncertainties involved at each stage, the number of "tons" of output in any individual year could only be guessed at. Otherwise, it would be difficult to explain the widely different rates at which annual output targets were completed. The relevant data are presented in Table 3. Changes in output are used rather than total output, since new investment is related primarily only to changes. In light industry, success in meeting annual production goals was even more erratic than in heavy industry because of dependence on harvest fluctuations.

With this erratic relationship between planned and actual output, it would appear that annual output targets were intended only as a very rough first approximation used to decide the allocation of key materials. As the months passed and bottlenecks appeared, allocations must have been speeded up in certain cases and slowed down in others in order to overcome the most severe imbalances. It is likely that within a few months of their publication, the annual targets had only very limited operational significance.[13]

It was not so much that China was unable to plan well enough to use more sophisticated procedures. Of course, in early years, planning was at a very rudimentary level. In 1953, the first year for which annual plans in industry had much meaning, production targets were revised three times in the course of the year (Rostow, 1954, p. 274). But, with Soviet assistance, the more conspicuous difficulties were overcome. If a comparison of Soviet and Chinese FYP performance is any guide, Chinese planning by 1955 was no worse than that in the Soviet Union in the 1930s (see Table 4). The point is that, given Peking's goals and the underdeveloped state of the economy, more sophisticated planning techniques were, on the whole, not

[13] It is, of course, true that Soviet-type planning does not call for the exact completion of output plans, but instead for overcompletion. The evidence for "erraticness" in Table 3, however, is not simply that the index numbers are not always 100, but that their departure from 100 differs so much between commodities and between years for each commodity.

Table 3. Annual plan target completion record.

$$\frac{\text{Realized output}}{\text{Planned output}} = \text{Index}$$

	1953	1954	1955	1956	1957	1958	1959
Steel	143.2	164.9	—	96.9	169.5	295.1	164.6
Electricity	112.9	134.2	—	161.4	121.1	231.2	100.0
Cement	210.8	208.7	—	105.0	112.7	—	75.2
Coal	—[a]	197.8	—	108.1	284.2	671.6	70.7
Petroleum	103.9	163.7	—	83.8	87.5	—	—
Cotton yarn	148.1	193.5	—	113.3	97.6[b]	—	111.6
Paper	785.7[c]	185.7	—	135.3	—	—	—
Sugar	—	38.8	—	32.3	—	—	—
Cigarettes	—	30.1	—	36.2	—	—	—

Sources: All realized production data (except 1959) are form *Ten Great Years*, pp. 95–100 and Yin and Yin, *Economic Statistics of Mainland China*, pp. 50–51.

1953 plan data: See Wu Yuan-li, *An Economic Survey of Communist China*, pp. 257–258. The 1953 output data in *Ten Great Years* may not be the same as those used in constructing the plan indices, thus causing some error in the figures in the table.

1954 plan data: Derived from data in State Statistical Bureau, "Report on 1954 Development of the National Economy and the Effectiveness of the State Plan," September 21, 1955; *HHPYK*, October 28, 1955, No. 10, p. 166; and Teng Hsiao-p'ing, "Report on the 1954 Draft State Budget," June 18, 1954, in *I-chiu-wu-szu-nien Kuo-chia Yu-suan* (Peking: Financial and Economic Press, 1954), p. 16.

1956 plan data: *Jen-min Shou-ts'e*, 1957, p. 426.

1957 plan data: Po I-po, "Report on the Results of the 1956 National Economic Plan and the Draft 1957 National Economic Plan," *Fa-kuei hui-pien*, No. 6, pp. 155–157.

1958 plan data: Po-Ipo, "Report on Proposed 1958 National Plan," February 3, 1958, *HHPYK*, March 10, 1958, No. 5, p. 18.

1959 realized output and plan data: Many 1959 targets apparently were set by looking at the original targets for 1962 in the draft Second FYP, except for commodities such as coal, for which 1958 output had already surpassed the 1962 target. Realized output data, of course, have no relation to the true production situation. Li Fu-chun, "Report on the Draft 1958 National Economic Plan," April 21, 1959, *Fa-kuei hui-pien*, No. 9, pp. 45–46; and Li Fu-chun, "Report on the Draft 1960 National Economic Plan," March 30, 1960, *Second Session of the Second National People's Congress of the People's Republic of China*, p. 4.

Notes: [a]The plan called for little or no increase in coal output. Actual output rose by over 3 million tons. [b]The plan for cotton yarn called for a decrease in output in 1957. [c]The planned increase was very small.

Table 4. Plan completion record: China and the Soviet Union.

	Soviet Union						China		
	First Five-Year Plan (1927–28 to 1932–33)			Second Five-Year Plan (1933–1937)			First Five-Year Plan[a] (1953–1957)		
	Target[b]	Actual	%	Target	Actual	%	Target	Actual	%
Coal[c]	68	64.4	94.7	152.5	128.0	83.9	113	130	115.0
Oil[c]	19	21.4	112.6	44.3	28.5	64.3	2.01	1.46	73.1
Electric power[d]	17	13.5	79.4	38.0	36.2	95.3	15.9	19.3	121.4
Cement[c]	5.4	3.48	64.4	7.5	5.45	72.7	6.0	6.86	114.3
Steel[c]	8.3	5.93	71.4	17.0	17.73	104.3	4.12	5.35	129.9

Source: For Soviet data, sec A. Bergson, *The Economics of Soviet Planning*, 1964, Table 5.2, p. 84. Chinese data are in *First Five-Year Plan*, pp. 48–49; and State Statistical Bureau, "Communique on the Results of Implementing the First Five-Year Plan, 1953–1957," reprinted in *Contemporary China*, Vol. iii, p. 205.

Notes: [a] The Chinese FFYP was in reality a three-year plan since it was not promulgated until 1955.
[b] The target figures for the Soviet FYP were expressed in terms of "minimal" and "optimal variants."
[c] In million metric tons.
[d] In billions of kilowatt-hours.

very important. Complex calculations of rates of return and capital-output ratios were of limited use when trade embargos and technologically determined input–output coefficients severely limited the choices of what kind of factories to build. However, when the regime in 1958 turned away from concentration on large-scale heavy industrial plants and from following the Soviet pattern, deciding what plants to put up was no longer so simple a task. More elaborate investment criteria had to be used, particularly in deciding when a small-scale enterprise ought to be built.

As already pointed out, small-scale enterprises played a large role in Chinese industry long before 1958 (see Table 2), but it was not until that year that they achieved relatively high priority status. In the general cutback in investment in late 1956 and 1957, for example, materials and funds for below-norm projects bore the brunt of the reduction (Fang Fa, 1956, p. 41; *CHCC*, 1956, p. 40). Early in 1958, small- and medium-scale enterprises continued to be placed in a low priority position, with only 387 million *yuan* being allocated in the plan for such investment by local authorities (*CHCC,* 1958, p. 40). As the Great Leap Forward got underway, the whole picture changed, and by the end of the year 5,260 million *yuan* had been spent outside the plan, presumably mainly by local authorities on small- and medium-scale plants. In 1959, another 5 billion *yuan* was spent in this way (*Ten Great Years*; Li Fu-chun, 1960).

Although carefully calculated rates of return, or some comparable investment criteria, probably should have been used in deciding whether to build particular small-scale plants, in practice they were not. In fact, the only constraint on local authorities was apparently whether or not it was physically possible for them to build the plant with materials obtained locally. The extremes in 1958 and 1959, however, resulted more from the way in which plans were implemented under the Great Leap spirit than from the lack of adequate investment criteria used in drawing them up in the first place.

Even during periods when greater restraint was exercised, it is doubtful that the investment criteria used were adequate to the task of ensuring efficient use of local investment funds. The principal advantages the regime expected from small- and medium-scale enterprises were these (Kao Chen-teh, 1957; Sung Ping, 1957):

(1) A lower amount of investment was required per unit of output, and the time required to build a plant and put it into operation was less.
(2) Quality of output would be raised.
(3) Savings on transport cost could be achieved.
(4) Fewer building materials and machinery would be required.
(5) Employment, particularly employment outside urban areas could be raised more rapidly.

This list presumably also constituted the criteria by which small-scale projects were accepted or rejected. The first four items could be subsumed under a general concept of profitability or rate of return, if China's price structure were meaningful. The employment criterion, to the degree that it was more than a desire to maximize the rate of return by means of capital-saving devices, cannot be so subsumed.

Whether China's price structure was sufficiently meaningful to make possible the effective use of a single profitability measure is too complex a question to deal with in detail here. However, the main point, already mentioned previously, is that Peking has never followed the Soviet practice of pricing producer goods at average cost plus a 5% margin. Instead, these and most other industrial prices were frozen at levels prevailing during the Korean War, with only relatively minor adjustments afterwards. Most such adjustments have been made to overcome particularly irrational prices,[14] but in 1955–1956, there was a general lowering of industrial producer goods prices. At the time, it may have been intended to carry these reductions further, but, if so, the attempt was abandoned.[15] The principal reasons for maintaining prices at these levels involved problems of implementation and control, and will be discussed later. The point here is that China's price structure probably reflected, at least to a degree, the underlying Chinese supply and demand conditions. The further the regime moved from the conditions at the time when prices were frozen, the less this was true. On the other hand, Peking's ability to avoid serious inflation eliminated price distortions arising from this source.[16]

Whether or not the price structure was suitable, rate of return or profitability criteria seem to have played a rather limited role in Chinese investment allocation decisions. They played a part in the decision to emphasize small-scale enterprises in the first place, but evidently had little influence on which small-scale firms were set up. The much higher rate of return on investment in restoring old plants and on construction in well-established industrial centers was a major reason why such areas as Shanghai continued to a significant degree their pre-1949 industrial supremacy (Chu Jung-chi, 1956), but sophisticated criteria were hardly necessary to reach these rather obvious conclusions. The greater profitability of light industry was mentioned in the discussion surrounding the decision in 1956 and 1957 to increase the share of industrial investment funds going to that sector (Ho Cheng, 1956). On the other hand, several writers pointed out that

---

[14] For example, area differentials in petroleum prices had been set prior to completion of rail lines to the northwest oil fields, and had to be revised (Fan Jo-yi, 1957, p. 28).

[15] There was considerable debate in the economics literature as to whether China should or should not follow a price policy for producer goods similar to that of the Soviet Union (Fan Jo-yi, 1957; Nan Ping and So Chen, 1957).

[16] It will be argued later that plan implementation was partly effected by a policy of overfull utilization of resources (excess demand or inflationary pressure). This pressure made market allocation for many key industrial products impossible even if it had been desired. The degree of pressure did not tend to increase over time and thus did not necessitate raising prices.

higher returns in light industry were simply the result of the government's high price policy for these commodities, prices which in those authors' eyes did not reflect the commodities' true worth.[17] When, in addition, it became clear that output in this sector could be raised only if raw materials from agriculture were available, the state in 1958 sharply reduced the proportion of light industry investment and shifted it, in part at least, to agriculture (*CHCC*, 1958, pp. 37–41).

Thus, in deciding how to allocate investment in new plant and equipment, the Chinese Communists relied on crude and rather unsystematic criteria. Most decisions were predetermined by the regime's desire to build large-scale plants of Soviet design and to stress heavy industry and autarky. Given these aims, more sophisticated techniques of allocation were largely unnecessary. One can question whether it was proper to emphasize heavy industry, or whether military or other needs required so much investment in the interior, but these were problems related to fundamental aims of the regime. Right or wrong, they did not result primarily from the methods used in planning.

When it was decided to stress small-scale industries, the lack of adequate investment criteria did have a detrimental effect, but it should not be exaggerated. Most of the excesses in small industries during the Great Leap Forward were not caused by the inadequacy of the criteria available to local planners, but by the failure of these lower level cadres to apply any criteria at all. One can also ask whether these decisions might not have been better made if the regime had relied on the market rather than on centralized planning. Such questions, however, cannot be answered without a thorough investigation of the problems of plan implementation, to which we now turn.

III. Plan Implementation

Introduction

Most literature on planning in underdeveloped countries deals with problems of investment allocation, but the main barriers to successful growth

[17]What these authors meant by the "true worth" or value of a commodity is a subject in itself. See, for example, Wang Tieh-sheng, 1957.

have far more frequently been failures in implementation.[18] Setting up a system that makes possible effective plan implementation is no easy task. Not only must the regime see to it that enterprises comply with central plan directives, it must also ensure that those directives are carried out flexibly and imaginatively to achieve economic efficiency.

In attaining efficient compliance, a centralized socialist system of planning has both advantages and disadvantages compared with a market-controlled industrial sector under private ownership. On the one hand, the number and strength of control devices available to the centralized, non-market system are much greater than in the private market economy. On the other, there are many more activities that must be controlled. State regulations in a market economy are designed primarily to prevent selected forms of "antisocial" behavior or to encourage firms (by subsidies, etc.) to pursue certain particularly desirable activities that the system itself would not automatically promote. Within the broad ranges set down by these regulations, the enterprises may do as they like, coordination and efficiency being achieved by allowing the least successful to go out of business.

In an economy centrally planned and controlled by means of targets set for physical output and other factors, however, the state decides in some detail the directions that enterprise activities are expected to take, and so must establish means for checking each aspect. In a private market economy, for example, it does not matter to the state (except for tax purposes) whether the enterprise has an elaborate accounting system that allows it and the state to know exactly how well it performed in every respect. If such a system is necessary to the firm's efficient operation, it will adopt it or go bankrupt. By contrast, in a centrally controlled state

[18] In actual practice, it is not easy to distinguish between failures due to a plan itself and those due to the implementation of that plan. The problems discussed in this section generally would have arisen regardless of what particular numbers appeared in the output plan (unless perhaps there was a radical change in basic priorities); nor could these numbers have been designed so as to overcome implementation problems. It does not follow, however, that any sets of numbers would have done as well as those selected. In fact, if the distinction between planning and implementation is meaningful, and if the plan itself was drawn up properly as was generally argued above, then some arbitrarily chosen set of numbers would have increased the number of bottlenecks, etc.

economy, the lack of such an accounting system would make central direction of the enterprise virtually impossible.

In the discussion that follows, Chinese Communist efforts to implement the central plan for industry will be dealt with in two parts. The first presents the formal control structure and changes that have been made in it over time. The second analyzes how that formal structure has been undermined by a variety of elements, foremost among which is the need to choose the leaders of enterprises for their political as well as their technical qualifications.

The formal control structure

The key to control of industrial activities in Communist China (as in the Soviet Union) is the responsibility system in its broadest sense; i.e., the principle that each unit's activities should be clearly defined so that its performance can be properly judged and reward or punishments dealt out accordingly. A unit may be an individual, a workshop, an enterprise or a larger organization; but the key unit is the enterprise.

Each enterprise in China is an independent economic accounting unit responsible for only its own profits and losses.[19] State plans drawn up by the central authorities were broken down into specific targets for each enterprise, but it was the enterprise's own basic responsibility to translate these targets into orders and directives for its subordinate units. The central government judged each enterprise's success or failure in meeting these targets; and the enterprise in turn appraised the performance of its own divisions and individual personnel. When individual units below the central government level dealt with each other, it was usually on an enterprise-to-enterprise basis. Enterprises, for example, had the right to draw up purchase and sales contracts with each other.

Although the enterprise was an independent unit in the sense described above, its ability to take independent action was, according to the regulations at least, severely limited. Enterprise plan targets were set by the state, and purchase and sales contracts, as well as bank loans, had to be strictly in accordance with the plan. Individual firms could influence the

[19]This brief discussion is based largely on Schurmann, "Industrial Management in China."

central plan during the period when it was being drawn up. The process of drawing up the plan, in fact, was one of almost continuous negotiation between higher and lower levels. Ultimately, however, authority rested with and was exercised by Peking. Enterprise independence was independence of responsibility, not of authority.

This system, of course, was essentially the same as the Soviet *khozraschet* system and was consciously patterned after it. Other key elements of the structure were one-man management and the production territorial system. One-man management was a key part of what was intended to be a clear-cut vertical command structure. It not only made possible an unimpeded flow of command, but also enabled the regime to attach to individuals the responsibility for success or failure. The production territorial system ordered the chain of command between the enterprise and the central government. In essence, it subordinated all industrial units producing similar types of products and located in the same geographical region to a single superior unit, which in turn was responsible to the national ministry responsible for those particular products.

Even the formal aspects of this system began to undergo changes at least as early as 1956; but before looking at those changes, it will be useful to deal with other formal techniques used to back up the central plans. Several of these measures are either readily understood or have been dealt with earlier in the chapter in other contexts, needing only brief mention here.

Perhaps foremost in importance among these measures is the centralized allocation of key industrial raw materials, machinery and other inputs. Any enterprise that attempts to set out on its own, counter to directions set down in the plan, immediately runs into bottlenecks resulting from shortages of inputs. Furthermore, allocations called for by the plan are backed up in turn by formal contracts between enterprises involved in selling and purchasing these materials.[20] In addition, plan targets are supposed to be set so that unless a firm uses all materials allocated to it efficiently, it will be unable to surpass its targets. Finally, there is generally planning for overfull use of resources; i.e., more inputs are called for in

---

[20] Contracts have been used for a number of other purposes as well, including, for example, restricting the activities of private industrial enterprises prior to 1956. For a fuller discussion of industrial contracts, see Pfeffer, 1963.

the plan than will be actually allocated, giving, at least in theory, an added incentive to use materials efficiently.

Other key elements in the control process are the various methods set up by the state to ensure the accurate flow of information from the enterprise up to the central authorities. Under the State Statistical Bureau, the Chinese Communists have attempted to establish uniform statistical procedures throughout the industrial sector, beginning with a survey of all state and joint industrial and mining enterprises in 1950.[21] Although there was a major setback in statistical collection procedures in 1958 and 1959, industrial statistics in other years, particularly those for large-scale heavy industry, have generally been adequate to the demands put upon them. The major exceptions would appear to be the data for small-scale industry and for items difficult to measure properly (e.g., costs per unit of output: value of fixed capital, etc.)[22] There has also been a problem of getting data early enough to allow central planners to draw up a plan and make the necessary adjustments before the year for which the plan was designed was nearly past. This latter problem, however, was more one of plan formulation than of plan enforcement. Timeliness was somewhat less crucial to those whose job was to reward or punish enterprises for past behavior.

Finally, behind these various types of essentially physical and administrative measures, and the information channels connected with them, there was a complex system of financial controls. Considering both the importance and the complexity of these financial controls, it is desirable to analyze them in some detail.[23]

Financial targets (profits, cost reduction, the wage bill, etc.) appearing in the annual plans, for example, were conceived of partly as devices for backing up the physical output and input targets, and partly as substitutes

---

[21] The establishment of a state statistical system is discussed in detail in Li, 1962.

[22] The term "adequate" does not imply that there was no falsification or distortion of output and other "relatively good" data by industrial enterprises. To the contrary, *T'ung-chi kung-tso* (TCKT) and *T'ung-chi kung-tso t'ung-hsun* (TCKTTH) are full of examples, but not sufficiently serious examples to negate the statements made in the text. For a much more thorough discussion of these issues, see Yin, "The Reporting of Industrial Statistics in Communist China."

[23] The discussion of the role of financial controls in plan implementation is based on Perkins, 1966 (pp. 99–135).

for an excessive proliferation of physical targets. That is, it was simpler to put a limit on the total wage bill than to specify the number of workers in each salary grade.

The key element of financial control, however, was not financial targets, but controls over sources and uses of enterprise funds. The most important were sales ("industrial and commercial") and profits taxes. These taxes took away a large portion of the funds coming into an individual enterprise and turned them over to the state treasury, where central planners could reissue them or not as they saw fit.

In addition, there were elaborate rules governing how enterprises could obtain funds for their own use and how they could use them once obtained. Enterprise funds for use in meeting everyday expenses (working capital) had to be kept separate from investment funds. The latter were financed out of the budget, and actual payment was handled by a special bank, which closely supervised all expenditures to make sure that they complied with the central plan. Even new investment financed out of profits that an enterprise had been allowed to retain had to be used according to the central plan and under supervision of the construction bank (Ministry of Finance, 1956). Furthermore, only a small portion of retained profits could be used in this way, the remainder being divided among bonuses, welfare funds, and various working capital needs. In any case, total retained profits prior to 1958 were very small. If budget data are an adequate indicator of profit plan overfulfillment (on which calculation of retained profits was based), then enterprise income from this source would have been negligible in 1955 and 1956, less than 3% of total profits in 1957, and less than 9% in 1954.[24]

Sources of working capital were somewhat more complicated. Each enterprise had income from sales of its output, after deductions were made for profits and sales taxes. These deductions were taken out several times a month. Otherwise, the very high rates of profit on both consumer and producer goods would have provided firms with so much working capital that serious financial discipline would have been virtually impossible.

[24]These estimates are probably somewhat too low since they were obtained by taking 40% of total profits actually paid into the treasury in excess of the planned amount. In fact, many enterprises exceeded the target while others fell below it, but the latter did not have 40% of profits below plan taken away from them.

Since sales revenue was seldom synchronized with outlays, particularly in rapidly growing firms or ones with wide seasonal fluctuations in activity, funds were required over and above what could be obtained from sales. These needs were met out of a combination of allocations from the budget and loans from the People's Bank. The former were made without interest or need to repay; the latter had to be repaid and carried an interest charge.

Whatever the source of funds, individual firms never had much freedom in using them, at least according to the regulations. Not only was use of working capital for fixed capital investment purposes prohibited, but such funds could not be used to increase the wage bill beyond the target figure. More important, enterprises had to draw up detailed income and outlay plans for approval by higher level authorities. This plan then formed the basis upon which loans were given and budget allocations made. Even the enterprise's own deposits (it was only allowed enough cash for three days' operations) were, according to regulations, not to be used for other than approved purposes (Financial and Economic Committee, 1950).

Still, even in theory the enterprise did retain a limited capacity (and in practice this ability was far from limited) for easing its own financial situation, to the extent that it could readjust the inflow and outflow pattern of its funds. The major areas where this could be done, i.e., through such activities as delaying payment and purchasing on credit, however, were declared illegal from the beginning.

It is clear, then, that financial controls were not conceived of as substitutes for physical or administrative controls, but as backstops to those controls. With such a variety of financial restrictions augmenting equally numerous physical and administrative measures, it is a wonder that industrial enterprises had any room whatsoever for maneuvering. But in fact, they were occasionally able to act as if they were subject to no restrictions at all. Before turning to how the system worked in practice, however, it is desirable to look briefly at the formal measures taken to modify the system of control described above.

Formal decentralization measures

The same elements that made drawing up the material balances and investment plans difficult, in particular the existence of a large number of small-scale firms with widely varying techniques, also contributed to the problems of plan implementation. It is doubtful whether many of the firms ever entered into the planning process in a significant way.

Nevertheless, these enterprises had to have materials to work with and money to pay for them. As indicated in a previous section, the materials for such firms were generally obtained locally. The later decentralization (1958) that gave control over the output and inputs of these enterprises to provincial and lower level authorities was probably in part only formal recognition of a situation that had always existed to some degree.

Control over enterprise finances was also partially decentralized, but by price policy rather than by the actual transfer of administrative authority to lower levels. Relatively high prices (see Table 5) for all industrial products (in contrast to the Soviet policy of pricing producer goods at 3–5% above cost) made it unnecessary to provide higher cost (usually

Table 5. Profit rate on selected commodities (% of average cost, including taxes).

Commodity	Rate
All commodities (1957)	50
Consumer goods	
Cotton cloth (1957)	107
Cotton yarn	43
Cotton cloth	52
Cigarettes	160–335
Sugar	40
Grain	15–20
Average of light industry (including commerce) (1955)	47
Producer goods	
Electric power (1956)	101
State iron and steel enterprises	25
Average of heavy industry (1955)	43

Source: See Perkins, 1966 (Table 10). Where the year is not given, it is not known precisely, but is generally 1956 or 1957. These percentages were taken directly from Communist sources or were computed by the author from official price and cost data.

small-scale) firms with subsidies or with as large allocations of funds for working capital, tasks that would have created formidable administrative burdens. Local branches of the People's Bank and other local financial units still exercised supervision over an enterprise's use of its own funds, but there was less need to coordinate that control with higher level authorities in order to prevent excessive issuance of funds. Avoiding subsidies, with their attendant administrative burdens, was probably a more important reason for keeping a high price policy than the previously mentioned fact that such a policy also made possible a limited market distribution of certain producer goods.

Closely related to the regime's high price policy was its stress on profits taxes over sales taxes.[25] In the Soviet Union between 1928 and 1940, the sales (turnover) tax provided from three to more than 10 times as much revenue as the profits tax (Holzman, 1955, p. 217). This contrasts sharply with China, where profits tax revenue surpassed that received from sales taxes in 1954, and by 1959 was double the sales tax revenue. Both profits taxes and sales taxes served essentially the same function, that of removing most income over cost from enterprise control. If this had been accomplished by a higher uniform sales tax for each industry, however, firms producing at relatively high cost per unit would have had to receive subsidies or go out of business. The Chinese Communists did pay a certain price for this policy. High profits taxes and low sales tax rates lowered a firm's incentive to reduce costs, since there was little danger, whatever the cost, that it would have to ask the state for a subsidy.

These price and tax measures did not allow any great degree of decentralized operation of industry. Control of industry was effected primarily by physical means, which were still highly centralized. Beginning with the Eighth Party Congress in 1956, however, the regime began to take steps to reorganize industrial controls generally in the direction of decentralization, although of a very limited kind.

The removal of restrictions on enterprises' dealing directly with each other or with alternative sources of supply in the purchase and sale of

---

[25]The term generally used by the Chinese Communists is "industrial and commercial taxes." These taxes are expressed as a percentage of price and hence are similar in nature to sales taxes or what in the Soviet Union are called "turnover taxes."

non-key commodities has already been discussed. There was also an attempt to upgrade the importance of profits and the profits target. In 1955, the Ministry of Finance issued a directive stating that enterprises could retain 40% of profits made over and above the plan profit target in 1954, and that these funds could be used to meet shortages in circulating capital and for certain very limited basic construction purposes (Ministry of Finance, 1955). In 1956, this regulation was liberalized slightly, in that such funds could be carried over into the next year and bonuses were to be given specifically for exceeding planned profits (Ministry of Finance, 1956). In both directives, all enterprise bonus funds were to be taken out of profits in excess of plan before making the 40–60 split.

Major changes in formal financial controls and targets, however, were not made until late 1957 and 1958. The number of compulsory targets, for example, was reduced from 12 to 4 in 1957. Output targets continued to have priority, but the change was probably intended to enhance the importance of the other three targets, particularly profits. In May, 1958, the method of calculating profits retained by the enterprise was changed to a fixed percentage of total profits,[26] usually around 10%, or significantly higher than previously. This change was a further step in enhancing the importance of the profits target.

In addition, in 1957 and 1958, there was the already discussed decentralization of administration, giving authority over many industrial enterprises to provincial and lower level authorities. Along with the basic transfer measure went a number of other measures dealing with related financial and market aspects of this transfer (Sung Hsin-chung, 1961). Unlike the measures dealing with retained profits and the number of targets, however, these transfers of authority did not really enhance the role of the market in controlling industry. Instead, they were primarily designed to enable local authorities to implement plans that they drew up, which were still essentially physical in nature. Even the increased retention of profits itself may have at times only enhanced the independence of the enterprise without increasing its responsiveness to the market.

---

[26]The actual calculation for each firm was based on that firm's expenses in certain areas (on trial of new products, etc.) and so varied between firms (State Council, 1958).

Although the various measures described above involved decentralization through both the market and administrative measures, both methods were designed to deal with the same problem, that of effectively controlling many firms using diverse technology without stifling local initiative. In many areas, the formal changes made between 1956 and 1958 have remained intact ever since. Others have been modified by either retightening the reins or relaxing control further. Examples of the former would be the reduction in the size of the portion of profits that the enterprise could retain (Sung Hsin-Chung, 1961), and the apparent rehabilitation of various plan targets other than the four listed in 1957.[27] An example of relaxation would be the regulation allowing enterprises to exchange excess materials with other enterprises (only when it would increase output of producer, not consumer, goods) (Ma Wen-kuei, 1964).

In early 1962, there was also some debate in economic journals over whether decentralization and further use of market controls, especially profits, should be carried further.[28] Although this debate may have led to some enhancement of the role of the profits target, there is no evidence to suggest that it was carried very far, certainly not to the point where the profits target attained first priority and even less near the point where partial consumer sovereignty was restored — as it was for many industrial consumer goods in the Soviet Union in 1964–1965.

Formal regulations, however, tell only a very inadequate part of the story of plan implementation in Communist China. Often these regulations were ignored altogether or their original purpose distorted.

---

[27] See the "Seventy Theses" (1962) mentioned in footnote 8. The other eight targets were never abolished but only relegated to an advisory role. Regulations (such as No. 24 of the "Seventy Theses") calling firms to comply with several targets other than the basic four may not involve a major change of policy, but only a vaguer working of the directive, but this does not appear as likely as the interpretation in the text. A published source giving essentially the same information, but for a somewhat later date is K'uanglih-an *et al.* 1963 (p. 34).

[28] The debate, such as it was, began with an article in Ching-chi yen-chiu in March, 1962, and was ended by or at the 10th Plenum of the Eighth Party Congress. For a fuller discussion, see CIA, 1963.

Plan implementation in practice

The major source of difficulty arose out of the nature of the Communist Party control apparatus and the personnel who manned it. The essence of minority Communist control in China is that all key positions, military, political, or economic, be held by Party members of demonstrated loyalty. On occasion high formal titles are bestowed on non-Party personnel, but in all such cases, a subordinate Party member exercises real control. Party members of sufficient standing to be appointed factory managers, heads of factory Party committees, and higher positions, however, have usually built their reputations in guerrilla warfare against Japan and the Nationalists. Although thoroughly indoctrinated in Communist ideology, they generally have had little or no formal education.[29] This combination of Marxism and lack of sophistication has generated attitudes incompatible with the efficient use of such tools as financial targets and controls and, in fact, with the rational allocation of resources in general.[30] Reality and Russian experience and advice forced modifications in these attitudes, but did not submerge them completely.

Modification of these attitudes was further restricted after 1956 by the shift in the locus of power within factories from the factory manager (one-man management) to factory Party committees (Li Hsueh-feng, 1956). It is not really clear why this shift was made. Part of the explanation may be that the regime did not want to decentralize control even slightly without first guaranteeing the political loyalty of those receiving increased authority. It may also be that the Chinese Communists felt that Party committees, by being closer to the workers, could more effectively mobilize these workers even for purely economic purposes. As events turned out, this shift in power contributed in a major way to the excesses of the Great Leap Forward in 1958 and 1959. Recognizing this fact and its economic consequences, the regime in the early 1960s shifted back to placing primary control over enterprises in the hands of factory managers (Po I-po, 1963, p. 28). In 1964 and 1965, though, this reverse trend was in turn checked

---

[29]This discussion is based on refugee interviews and such sources as Hsia Yen, 1959; Ai Wu, 1961; Chandrasekhar, 1961; *TCKTTH*, 1957. For a fuller discussion see Perkins, 1966.
[30]Aside from its political implications resource allocation has little or no place in Marxist ideology (Wiles, 1962, pp. 50–56).

by a renewed intensification of ideological education and pressures within enterprises ("learn from the People's Liberation Army," etc.); it, however, was largely confined to attaining political rather than economic objectives.

The attitudes generated by these pressures, and by the backgrounds of the factory leadership personnel involved, manifested themselves first of all in a tendency on the part of factory managers and Party secretaries to ignore all plan targets other than that for the physical output of major products or (pre-1957) the gross value of output. (Such a situation was also in part a result of the nature of material balances planning, as pointed out earlier in Section II.) Nor were the factory managers (or Party secretaries) alone to blame. Similar attitudes were manifested by the central planners themselves (Ishikawa, 1960, pp. 92–93).

A similar emphasis on production targets existed in the Soviet Union, but there it was a result of bonuses being paid primarily on the basis of performance in meeting the production targets only; although the decision to use this basis may itself have been the result of factors similar to those for China. In China, bonuses appear to have been small; in any case they were not supposed to be paid to enterprise leadership cadres.[31]

Equally serious was the tendency on the part of plant managers to ignore, whenever possible, not just the financial plan targets, but most financial regulations. However, this lax attitude toward financial controls did not exist because the various financial authorities lacked sufficient legal power to carry out their duties. Final authority for determining whether an enterprise was to receive a particular loan or budget disbursement rested with the People's Bank or the Ministry of Finance and with central and local governments. Industrial firms were never free to demand funds for expenditures above their approved plan, and there was no automatic loophole in the regulations such as existed in the Soviet Union, where enterprises could obtain funds for up to a 10% overpayment of the wage fund in any month following one in which the enterprise had stayed within the authorized amount. Also unlike the Soviet situation, the

[31]This statement is based on refugee interviews, on the fact that bonus laws seem always to be worded so as not to apply to managers, and on criticisms of bonuses given to enterprise cadres. There is also some evidence to the contrary (*JMJP*, 1957).

interests of those with power to grant overpayments were not intertwined with the interests of the individual enterprise.[32]

In spite of the apparently strong position of the authorities, financial control was tight only sporadically. In many cases, enterprise cadres simply disobeyed the regulations. For example, the 1950 regulation setting up many important aspects of financial control specifically stated that state-owned enterprises were not to obtain credit from each other in any form, but could obtain such credit only from the People's Bank (Financial and Economic Committee, 1950). Yet in the second quarter of 1954, this type of credit made up 17.2% of the total working capital of enterprises under the five industrial ministries (People's Bank, 1955, p. 270). In numerous other instances, funds earmarked for one purpose were used for another, and various devices were utilized to inflate costs so that a larger portion of profits could be retained by the enterprise (Pilmin, 1955, p. 37).

More serious than the enterprises' disobedience was the lack of sympathy with tight financial control at even the highest levels within the Party. This attitude toward tight financial control also extended, in many respects, to careful planning in general. It arose out of the same elements that caused factory managers to disregard financial targets and controls, but its effects were more farreaching. How serious they were depended heavily on the prevailing political atmosphere. When Party discipline and Communist ideology were the paramount concerns, careful planning and tight financial control were eschewed. During periods when political controls were more relaxed, technical and economic-minded personnel (both in and out of the Party) were more apt to be listened to.

This can be seen more concretely by reviewing briefly the Chinese Communist experience with administrative and financial controls since 1949. From 1949 through 1955, there was slow but steady progress toward tighter administrative control over the availability of funds going to individual enterprises. Faster progress was impossible because of the

---

[32]For information on the Soviet case, see Holzman, 1955 (p. 37). The independence of the Chinese financial authorities can be seen from the eminence of the Ministers of Finance (Po I-po and Li Hsien-nien) who were among the top echelon in the Communist hierarchy, from the fact that the People's Bank had a position comparable to that of a ministry, and from criticisms of that independence (Chang Ch'uan-shu, 1958).

complexity of problems to be overcome and the limited experience that could be brought to bear. The state began working out basic plan targets in 1951 and 1952, for example, but as already pointed out, the actual introduction of annual plans did not begin until 1953, and the First FYP (1953–1957) did not come out until 1955. In 1956, following the collectivization of agriculture and the socialization of industry and commerce, an attempt was made to raise the industrial growth rate sharply by increasing investments in basic construction by 59% over the previous year (*Ten Great Years*, p. 55).

The resulting inflationary pressure and depletion of stocks, however, forced the regime to retrench in 1957 (investment declined by 7%). Disregarding the experience of the previous two years, the regime initiated in 1958 a Great Leap Forward in all sectors of the economy, raised investment by 93%, and issued loans to enterprises so freely that deposits in the People's Bank rose in 1958 by an amount equal to the total increase during the previous five years (Ch'en Hsi-ya, 1959, p. 29).

The events of 1958 are worth further analysis because they vividly illustrate forces that have existed during the entire period of Communist rule. Disappointment with economic performance in 1957, and, more important, the avalanche of criticism during the brief "hundred flowers" or free speech campaign, led in the latter half of 1957 to a strong counteractive attempt by the Party to restore Party discipline and the preeminence of Communist ideology. This attempt was so successful that it effectively cowed the voices of caution and restraint, particularly in the economic sphere. It explains, for example, the complete lack of financial discipline in 1958 and 1959. The financial authorities had been intimidated by criticisms that they were ignoring Communist principles and placing too little faith in the masses by maintaining tight financial discipline (Chang Ch'uan-shu, 1958; *JMJP*, 1958).

It was not only the financial authorities who were constrained. The basic idea of the Great Leap was that tremendous economic advances could be achieved if Party cadres in factories and communes were given free reign to exercise initiative. Any constraints on this initiative would simply hamper progress. In the light of this reasoning, even central planning was considered excessively restrictive. Plan targets, therefore, no longer had to balance each other, but merely be set high enough to give the cadres a really "Great Leap" to try for. The process lost all touch with reality when statistics were subjected to similar considerations. They were no longer objective criteria for appraising plan performance, but only an additional means of heaping praise on activities considered desirable by the cadres; i.e., they were grossly falsified to show that any procedure recommended by the cadres had, in fact, achieved the predicted results. The Great Leap, therefore, was not a decentralization through the market, as some of the formal regulations seem to indicate (see preceding section, "Formal Decentralization Measures"), but a decentralization of authority subject to no constraints other than those of Party discipline and ideology. As already indicated, the ideology of the Chinese Communists had little to say about problems of allocation, so that the not-surprising result of this decentralization was economic anarchy. The experience of 1958 and 1959 was, of course, extreme, but it reveals basic forces that have been present since the advent of Communist rule.

The economic costs of the Great Leap Forward were high. They became increasingly apparent through 1959 and into 1960, and were aggravated by the concurrent crisis in agriculture and by the Soviet withdrawal of all Russian technicians in 1960. Yet, it was not until the ninth plenary session of the Eighth Party Central Committee in January, 1961, that steps were taken to reinstitute plan discipline by reducing the scale of capital construction and reemphasizing various financial procedures. In fact, tight financial control was not fully achieved until after 1962, if then (*Ta-kung pao,* 1961; *Nan-fang jih-pao,* 1962). One of the key documents upon which reimposition of rigorous controls in industry was based, the "Seventy Theses," was not even promulgated until 1962, and then only in draft form as a basis for further discussion and revision.

Some idea of how heavy the costs of disruption resulting from the Great Leap really were can be seen from the fact that state factories, in the first half of 1961, completed only 15.9% of the planned target for the manufacture of military weapons, equipment, accessories, and parts, the highest priority sector in Chinese industry (*Kung-tso t'ung hsun,* 1961). This same sector was undoubtedly particularly hard hit by the Soviet removal of trade and technical support, but this was certainly not the only reason.

It is even more difficult to isolate the effects of lax administrative and financial discipline in periods when the situation was less extreme than after 1958. For example, one of the most serious problems plaguing the regime from the outset was maintaining quality. The authorities were continually launching drives to get firms to raise the quality of their output; and many changes in the administration of prices were undertaken so that firms would be concerned with quality, but there is no way of measuring the effects of these efforts precisely. The regime has stated, for example, that 99% of the pig iron smelted in early 1963 was up to standard, and 95% of forging and rolled stock were top grade (Ma Wen-Kuei, 1964), but what this means other than that quality undoubtedly improved from the low standards during the Great Leap is difficult to say. However, being unable to make very precise statements about the issue does not mean that it is unimportant. Failure to maintain quality was one of the main sources of disruption during the Great Leap, and has been a major source of inefficiency during all periods of lax control.

Lax administrative and financial control also had a significant effect on costs of production, particularly consumption of raw materials. For example, in 1956 when discipline was weak, coal mine costs (per metric ton) in Liaoning province rose 16% above 1955; costs for 32-count yarn rose nearly 2% in 1956, even though the cotton yarn utilization rate rose from 77 to 94% and raw cotton prices were steady; the amount of wood used in making wood pulp rose in 1956 by 1 or 2% after falling steadily from 1953 through 1955; and raw materials used per unit of output in five types of edible oils, with one exception, increased in 1956 after falling between 1953 and 1955. In the producer goods sector, excess consumption of raw materials was largely responsible for the failure of the Ministry of Heavy Industry to meet its cost reduction and profits targets in the first quarter of 1956.[33] Although it is not possible to make a precise estimate,

[33] For the sources of these cost data see Perkins, 1966, (pp. 132–133). Rising average cost, of course, does not always indicate inefficiency. In some cases, for example, the long-run average cost curve may be rising for technological reasons completely unconnected with inefficiencies. It is doubtful that an economic justification for the performance described above can be found, however. Even if it were possible, and I doubt that it is, to demonstrate that average costs rose in these industries simply because they were approaching capacity levels of output, and not because of inefficient performance, they still would have been

it is reasonable to assume that this waste in 1956 accounted in part for the slow 1957 rate of growth in industrial output.[34] Unfortunately, data of comparable quality and relevance cannot be found for 1958 and after, but there is little doubt that the effects of lax discipline on costs of production were similar, only more extreme.

It is not going too far, therefore, to say that the nature of Communist Party control in China was such as to make an efficient allocation of resources difficult to achieve. Significant factors encouraged the use of decentralized economic controls, but ideology and lack of sophistication made the most highly developed of all decentralized controls, the market, of only limited use. At times, as during the Great Leap, these same factors undermined all controls, even the most centralized ones, causing high costs of production, low quality of output, and general disorganization. Two possible escapes from these difficulties would have been (1) to turn over more economic authority to non-Party economists and technicians (as in 1957 and since 1960) or (2) to emphasize technical and economic training for the cadres themselves. The former, however, endangers the basic political position of the Party and is bound to be resisted. Furthermore, too much relaxation in this direction might weaken the discipline necessary to enforce any plan direction (centralized or decentralized) in state-owned industries. The latter alternative, on the other hand, would eventually transform the Party itself from a revolutionary body to a party of technical bureaucrats, a transformation that has, in fact, progressed quite far in the Soviet Union and for which the Chinese Communists have shown considerable distaste. There is no obvious path out of this dilemma, and one has certainly not been found on the mainland of China.

IV. Conclusion

Industrial planning and management in Communist China would have run into fewer difficulties if Soviet economic goals and the Soviet system of

---

better off (had a greater total output of yarn, oils, etc.) if some of the raw materials had been used in the next year when the more usual condition of excess capacity returned to these industries.

[34]The near-stagnation in agricultural output was a more important reason.

centralized planning, emphasizing output targets, had proved as suitable for China as they did for Russia in the 1930s. (This is not to argue that this system was particularly suitable even for the Soviet Union.) In some respects, of course, the system worked quite well for China. The relatively small number of commodities involved, the weak links between different industrial sectors, and the opportunity to rely heavily on importation of complete industrial plants from the Soviet Union, all tended to ease the problem of centralized planning with respect to both the coordination of existing output and the planning of investment in new plant capacity. On the positive side, central planning provided Peking with sufficient authority to bring about a rapid change in the basic structure of Chinese industry.

It can be argued that it was a mistake to try to wrench Chinese industry into the modern world of heavy industry and large-scale plants so quickly, but this decision was based primarily on considerations beyond the narrow purview of economics, principally on the desire for military power and autarky. Beginning in 1961 (and to some extent earlier), there was a shift away from such heavy emphasis on machine tools and steel. However, this did not result from failures of central planning and management, but from the effects of neglect and reorganization on agriculture.

Although failures in central planning and centralized methods of implementation were not the principal cause of the regime's decision to shift emphasis after 1961 toward agriculture and the consumer goods industry, one still cannot conclude that the system had worked very well. As early as 1956, the regime began to realize the shortcomings of overcentralization. The backwardness of Chinese industry, the large number of firms involved, and the desire to develop and exploit more labor-intensive technologies all encouraged the Chinese Communists to give consideration to various decentralized methods of planning and plan implementation. Although central planning remained the most important of the various controls utilized, partial decentralization was carried out both through the market and through administrative reorganizations. The former involved enhancing the profits target and relaxing the rules that prevented firms from dealing directly with each other in the purchase and sale of non-key commodities. Profits, however, were not the principal success criterion, and they never were a major criterion for deciding what products were to be produced and where plant capacity was to be expanded, no matter whether that decision was made by the central planners or by the enterprise itself. Administrative decentralization was usually accomplished by transferring authority down to provincial and lower level authorities; large-scale enterprises generally remained under centralized control.

When decentralization measures were put into effect, however, it was usually in conjunction with a transfer of power to Communist Party units within the enterprise, or, in effect, political centralization. Any alternative would have been considered undesirable because it would have threatened the paramount role of the Party, which is fundamental to the existence of Chinese Communism, at least in its present form. Party influence, however, meant control by cadres inexperienced in economic matters and imbued with an ideology that was, to a degree, incompatible with market forms of decentralization and was not sensitive to problems of allocation in general. When these influences were combined with the bias against financial targets inherent in material balances planning, the cadres' tendency was to ignore or try to evade all varieties of financial constraints on their decisions, even though those constraints would have enhanced the efficiency of the decisions. It was not just financial constraints that were ignored. In fact, during periods of extreme political control, as during the Great Leap Forward, the system degenerated into economic anarchy.

Conceptually, it is possible to divorce the problem of maintaining ideological purity and political reliability from economic rationality. The Chinese Communists' reemphasis on political influence within the enterprise in 1964 and 1965 was apparently not accompanied by a downgrading of economic controls, financial or otherwise. Pressures against long-run maintenance of an effective divorce between politics and economics, however, are great. One cannot get around the problem of giving politically and ideologically reliable personnel the requisite technical training, because that training does itself tend to undermine ideology.

Thus, the costs of overcentralization in Chinese industry were high, but the costs of decentralization as it was actually carried out were even higher. The costs of both overcentralization and inappropriate decentralization could be overcome, to a degree, by a higher rate of investment, but events since 1959 have demonstrated that there are strict limitations on how high investment in industry can be without materially affecting incentives and, through incentives, production, particularly in agriculture.

Acknowledgment

The author wishes to thank the discussants at the Carmel conference, Joseph Berliner, Gardner Clark, Jung-Chao Liu, and Chu-yuan Cheng, for their helpful comments, as well as Abram Bergson and Simon Kuznets, who read an early draft. There were also a number of helpful comments from other conference participants, particularly Gregory Grossman and Ta-Chung Liu.

References

Bergson, A (1961). *The Real National Income of Soviet Russia Since 1928*. Boston, MA: Harvard University Press.

Chandrasekhar, S (1961). *Red China, An Asian View*. New York.

Chang, C-S (1958). The Anshan Financial Office on how to strengthen enterprise financial overseeing work, *Ts'ai-cheng* (January 5, 1958), 1, pp. 25–27.

Ch'en, H-Y (1959). "The 1958 Banking Work and the 1959 Tasks," *Chung-kuo Chin-jung*, May 25, 1959, translated in *Extracts from China Mainland Magazines*, No. 178, pp. 28–39.

Chenery, HB, and PG Clark (1959). *Interindustry Economics*. New York.

CHCC (*Chi-hua ching-chi*) (1956). Editorial, "Prepare Properly the National Economic Plan for 1957," December 23, 1956, translated in *Extracts from China Mainland Magazines*, No. 69, pp. 36-42.

CHCC (1958). "Problems to Merit Attention in Carrying Out the 1958 Capital Construction Plans," February 9, 1958, translated in *Extracts from China Mainland Magazines*, No. 124, pp. 37–41.

Chinese Communist Party (1957). Central Committee and State Council, "Regulation Reforming Plan Management Rules." *Fa-kuei hui-pien*, No. 8, pp. 96–99; "Several Regulations for Reforming the Commodity Distribution System," *Fa-kuei hui-pien*, No. 8, pp. 100–101.

Chu, J-C (1956). "Full Utilization of Coastal Industry," *Chi-hau ching-chi*, June 23, 1956, translated in *Extracts from China Mainland Magazines*, 50, pp. 20–24.

Fan, J-Y (1957). "More on the Price Policy for Heavy Industry Products," *Ching-chi yen-chiu*, June 17, 1957, translated in *Extracts from China Mainland Magazines*, No. 98, pp. 14–31.

Fang, C (1963). "All-Round Improvement in China's Economy," *Peking Review* (August 23, 1963), 34, pp. 38–43.

Fang, F (1956). "Some Common Knowledge of the National Economic Plan," *Hsueh-hsi*, October 2, 1956, translated in *Extracts from China Mainland Magazines*, 65, pp. 38–41.

Financial and Economic Committee (1950). "Methods of Enforcing Currency Management and Compiling Currency Income and Outgo Plans," December 25, 1950. Published in *Hsin-hua yueh-pao* (January 25, 1951), 15, pp. 610–615.

(*FFYP*) *First Five-Year Plan for Development of the National Economy of the People's Republic of China in 1953–1957*. Peking, 1956.

Ho, C (1956). "What Does Further Development of Light Industry Demand of Agriculture," *Cheng-chih, hsueh-hsi* (August 12, 1956), 8.

Holzman, F (1955). *Soviet Taxation*. Boston, MA: Harvard University Press.

Hsia, Y (1959). *K'ao-yen* (*The Test*). Peking.

Hsiao, L (1962). "Mindful of the General Good and Strict Execution of Policies and State Plans," *Kung-jen jih-pao*, Februrary 11, 1962, translated in *Survey of China Mainland Press*, 2690, pp. 1–4.

Hsueh, M-C (1957). "A Preliminary View of the Current Plan Management System," *Chi-hua Ching-chi*, 9, pp. 24–27.

Ishikawa, S (1960). *Chugoku Ni Okeru Shihon Chikuseki Kiko* ("Capital Formation in China"). Tokyo.

JMJP (*Jen-min jih-pao*), May 5, 1957 (*People's Daily*, Peking.)

JMJP (1958). Columnist, "The Correct Way of Settling Industrial Circulating Capital Problems," reprinted in *Hsin-hua Pan-yueh-k'an* (September 10, 1958), 17, pp. 122–123.

Kao, C-T (1957). "Make Coal Mining Construction More Economical and Rational," *Chien-she yueh-k'an*, July 3, 1957, translated in *Extracts from China Mainland Magazines*, 99, pp. 35–37.

Kao, K-C (1964). "Chemical Fertilized Industry Flourishes," *Peking Review* (September 18, 1964), 38, pp. 25–26.

Kornai, J (1959). *Overcentralization in Industry*. London.

K'uang, JA (1963). "Tentative Views on the Question of the Practice of Strict Economic Accounting by State-Owned Industrial Enterprises," *Ching-chi Yen-chiu*, August 17, 1963, translated in *Extracts from China Mainland Magazines*. 388, pp. 30–42.

(*KJJP*) *Kung-jen jih-pao*, May 9, 1956, translated in *Union Research Institute*, Ill (17).

Kung-tso T'ung-hsun (1961). "Report on Work of the Rear Services Department in the Entire Army" (August 4, 1961), 30.

Li, CM (1962). *The Statistical System of Communist China*. Berkeley and Los Angeles.

Li, FC (1960). "Report on the Draft 1960 National Economic Plan," March 30, 1960, *Second Session of the Second National People's Congress of the People's Republic of China*, pp. 1–48.

Li, HF (1956). Speech, *Eighth National Congress of the Communist Party of China*. II, pp. 304–317.

Liu, TC and KC Yeh (1965). *The Economy of the Chinese Mainland: National Income and Economic Development, 1933–1959*. Princeton, NJ: Princeton University Press.

Ma, WK (1964). "China's State-Owned Industrial Enterprises — Their Nature and Tasks," *Peking Review* (June 26, 1964), 26, pp. 23–27.

Ministry of Finance (1955). "Methods of Dividing and Using Profits of State Enterprises in Excess of the Plan in 1954," *Fa-kuei hui-pien* (October 18, 1955), 2, pp. 523–524.

Ministry of Finance (1956). "Regulation on the Distribution and Use of 1956 State Enterprise Profits in Excess of Plan," *Fa-kuei hui-pien* (October 11, 1956), 4, pp. 267–268.

Ministry of Finance (1958). "Notification of Several Regulations on Dividing Local Financial Income in 1958," *Fa-kuei hui-pien* (January 23, 1958), 7, pp. 221–223.

Nan, P and S Chen (1957). "The Value of the Means of Production and the Function of the Law of Value Under the Socialist System," *Ching-chi yen-chiu* (February 17, 1957), 1, pp. 38–51.

New York Times, December 30, 1964, p. 1.

People's Bank of China (1955). "Report on Eliminating the Use of Commercial Credit Between State Industries and Between State Industries and Other State Enterprises as a Substitute for Bank Balances," *Fa-kuei hui-pien* (March 30, 1955), 1, pp. 270–273.

Perkins, DH (1966). *Market Control and Planning in Communist China*. Cambridge, MA: Harvard University Press.

Pfeffer, RM (1963). "The Institution of Contracts in the Chinese People's Republic," *China Quarterly*, Part I (April–June), pp. 153–177; Part II (July–September), pp. 115–139.

Pilmin, AM (1955). "The Role of Public Finance in the Enforcement of the Economy and Austerity Program," *Ching-chi yen-chiu*, October 17, 1955, translated in *Extracts from China Mainland Magazines*, 21, pp. 33–42.

Po, IP (1956). Speech, *Eighth National Congress of the Chinese Communist Party*. II. 45–62.

Po, IP (1958). "Report on the Draft 1958 National Economic Plan," *Hsin-hua Pan-yueh-k'an* (March 10, 1958), 5, pp. 12–23.

Po, IP (1963). "The Socialist Industrialization of China," *Peking Review* (October 11, 1963), 41, in *Extracts from China Mainland Magazines*, 388, pp. 20–29.

Rostow, WW (1954). *The Prospects for Communist China*. Cambridge, Mass.

Schurmann, HF (1964). "China's 'New Economic Policy' — Transition or Beginning," *China Quarterly*, 17 (January–March), pp. 65–91.

Schurmann, HF "Industrial Management in China" (unpublished manuscript), Chapter II. B.

Secretariat of the National Conference for Small Scale Ore Dressing Plants (1959). "A Small Copper Dressing Plant Built and Put into Operation in Only 21 Days," *Yu-se chin-shu*, February 18, 1959, translated in *Joint Publications Research Service*, 1080D, pp. 1–9.

Shanghai chieh-fang ch'ien-hou wu-chia tzu-liao hui-pien (*A Compilation of Pre- and Post-Liberation Prices in Shanghai*). Shanghai, 1958.

Shih, C-H, H-L Yeh and H-L Ch'en (1963). "On Aid to Agriculture by Light Industry," *Ching-chi yen chiu*, November 17, 1963, translated in *Extracts from China Mainland Magazines*, 396, pp. 1–11.

CIA (1963). "The Short-lived Liberal Phase in Economic Thinking in Communist China." Washington.

State Council (1958). "Regulation Putting into Effect the Enterprise Retained Profits System," *Fa-kuei hui-pien* (May 22, 1958), 7, pp. 239–242.

State Statistical Bureau (SSB) (1960). *Ten Great Years*. Peking.

Sun, YF (1957). "A Discussion of 'Gross Value of Output,'" *Tung-chi kung-tso* (July 14, 1957), 13, pp. 8–14.

Sung, HC (1961). "The System of Retaining a Percentage of Profits by Our Enterprises," *Peking Ta-kung pao*, May 12, 1961, translated in *Survey of the China Mainland Press*, 2543, pp. 7–8.

Sung, P (1957). "The Problem of Employment," *Lao-tung*, October 4, 1957, translated in *Extracts from China Mainland Magazines*, 117, pp. 19–23.

Ta-kung pao (1961). Editorial, "Satisfactorily Control and Use the Circulating Funds of Industry," Peking, June 20, 1961, translated in *Survey of the China Mainland Press*, 2543, pp. 5–6.

TCKT (*T'ung-chi kung-tso*) (1957). "A Brief Description of the State Distribution of Commodities During the Past Year," July 14, 1957, translated in *Extracts from China Mainland Magazines*, 97, pp. 21–27.

TCKTTH (*T'ung-chi kung-tso t'ung-hsun*) (1957). Data Office, "The Breakdown and Organization of the Number of Workers and Employees in Our Country in 1955," *Hsin-hua pan-yueh-k'an* (January 25, 1957), 2, pp. 87–89.

T'ung-chi yen-chiu (1958). February 23, 1958, 2, p. 18.

Wang, T-S (1957). "To Understand Better the Relationship between Light Industry and Capital Accumulation," *Hsueh-hsi*, March 18, 1957, translated in *Extracts from China Mainland Magazines*, 86, pp. 20–22.

Wiles, PJD (1962). *The Political Economy of Communism*. Cambridge, Mass.

Wo kuo kang-t'ieh, tien-li, mei-tan, chi-chieh, fang-chieh, tsao-chih kung-yeh-te chin-hsi (*Our Country's Iron and Steel, Electric Power, Coal, Machinery, Textile, and Paper Industries*). Peking, 1958.

Wu, A (1961). *Steel and Tempered.* Peking.

Yin, H "The Reporting of Industrial Statistics in Communist China." (Draft, unpublished Ph.D. thesis, Columbia University.)

Yun, C (1956). Speech, *Eighth National Congress of the Communist Party of China.* II, pp. 157–176.

CHAPTER 5

CHINA'S ECONOMIC POLICY AND PERFORMANCE

I. Introduction

Few really new economic ideas or policies were put forward during the Cultural Revolution decade (1966–1976). There were economic debates leading up to and during the Cultural Revolution, but these debates had their roots in an earlier period, specifically in the Great Leap Forward and its immediate aftermath, when Chinese high and low attempted to understand what had gone wrong.

By 1956, the Chinese state had completed the takeover of private industry and commerce, and agriculture had been collectivized. The tools of planning and control over this socialized economy had been borrowed wholesale from the Soviet Union. China's economic strategy emphasizing machinery and steel was virtually a carbon copy of Stalin's development strategy for Russia in the 1930s.

This choice of planning tools and development strategy in part reflected a view among the leaders of many developing countries at the time that the Soviet Union represented the one real alternative to capitalist economic development, and a very successful alternative at that. China's leaders shared this view of Soviet accomplishments, but from the beginning they were uneasy with many features of the Soviet economic system. The sources of this uneasiness varied among the senior Chinese leaders. Some were concerned with the rigidities of the highly centralized system of planning and control, and others knew that China could not afford to follow the Soviet lead in neglecting agriculture. At some point, Mao Tse-tung and those close to him became bothered by the implications the Soviet system held out for the increasing bureaucratization of society and its emphasis on values more consistent with capitalism than with the future communist ideal.

Virtually as soon as socialization was completed, therefore, Chinese leaders began tinkering with the system to make it better fit their perception of China's needs. In 1957, efforts were made to loosen the impact of overcentralization by reducing controls on certain private markets and by decentralizing some decisions to the province and below. In 1958 and 1959, there was the dramatic experiment of the Great Leap Forward and the people's communes. And with the collapse of the Great Leap in 1960, there was a return to centralized planning, combined with efforts to enhance the role of the market and to enhance private initiative, particularly in agriculture and also to a degree in industry.

Throughout much of the second half of the 1950s, the lines between what later came to be labeled "right" and "left," or "radicals" and "pragmatists," were not clearly drawn. On the one hand, there were leaders, such as Ch'en Yun, who concerned themselves with economic matters. On the other were Mao Tse-tung and much of the senior Party leadership, whose concern was with political consolidation of the revolution. The concerns of the people with these portfolios did overlap because major issues, such as the pace of collectivization, involved both politics and economics. But Mao, in particular, did not concern himself with the central issues of economic development. His 1956 speech "On the ten great relationships" was probably more of a collective effort using his signature to give it authority than it was an attempt to articulate deeply held personal views.

Then, in 1958, Mao injected himself into economic decision-making in a way that was to have a profound influence over the next two decades. In Mao's own words:

> Before August of last year [1958], my main energies were concentrated on revolution. I am a complete outsider when it comes to economic construction, and I understand nothing about industrial planning. ... But comrades, in 1958 and 1959 the main responsibility was mine, and you should take me to task. In the past the responsibility was other peoples'. ... Who was responsible for the idea of the mass smelting of steel? K'o Ch'ing-Shih or me? I say it was me.[1]

---

[1]Mao (1959).

As the above passage indicates, Mao not only intervened in economic decision-making in 1958 and 1959, but did so on the basis of a very modest understanding of economic development. The efforts of the Great Leap, in fact, owed more to political ideas than to anyone's concept of economics. The Great Leap was one long mass campaign designed to move China into the ranks of industrialized nations in a hurry. The key input was to be human effort — effort to make steel in backyard furnaces, effort to move millions of tons of dirt and rock so as to irrigate the parched fields of North China.

The quantitative dimensions of the disaster that followed this mass campaign are discussed elsewhere in this chapter. The key point of relevance here is that individual members of the leadership drew very different conclusions about the nature of the disaster. Analysis of what had happened was complicated by the fact that the weather was bad in the 1959–1961 period and even more by the Soviet Union's decision to withdraw its technicians from China in 1960. Thus, those who shared Mao's vision could argue that the basic ideas of the Great Leap were sound, but poor implementation, bad luck (weather), and Soviet perfidy led to temporary failure. On the other side were those leaders who saw the very conception of the Great Leap as the main source of the disaster.

In the early 1960s, these differences in viewpoint had only a modest impact on economic policy because all agreed that recovery was the number-one priority. But in 1962, evidence of disagreement was apparent from Mao's opposition to the agricultural responsibility system that he saw as undermining the rural collective economy. The more extreme forms of the responsibility system were, in fact, halted or reversed and did not appear again until the 1980s. Aside from efforts to contain the retreat from collectivism, however, Mao turned his attention to what he considered the root of the problem, the still unreformed values and attitudes of the great majority of the people, including much of the membership of the Chinese Communist Party (CCP). The result was, first, the effort to reform the army, followed by the launching of the Socialist Education Campaign.

If Mao also spent the early 1960s rethinking or refining his ideas about economic development, there is little evidence to that effect. There is little economic content of any but the most casual kind in Mao's speeches from that period. Nor were those close to Mao busy working out a development strategy that would retain the essence but eliminate the shortcomings of the Great Leap.

When the Cultural Revolution got under way in 1965–1966, therefore, there were few guidelines for those who might want to promote a new, more radical path for the economy. The effort in the early 1960s to increase the role of financial targets and controls could be attacked as "putting profits in command," and Sun Yeh-fang, an advocate of financial controls, could be vilified. But there was little in the way of economic strategy that could be put in the place of the policies worked out under the leadership of Liu Shao-ch'i and Teng Hsiao-p'ing, except for the experiments of the Great Leap. But no one wanted an undiluted repeat of the Great Leap, either.

The strategy pursued from 1966 on, therefore, was an amalgam of policies from the 1950s as modified in the early 1960s plus pieces of the Great Leap formulas of 1958–1959. The nature of that strategy can best be understood not by reading the speeches of the leadership, left or right, but by dissecting the actual performance of the economy in the decade that followed. It may be that few leaders attempted to articulate a strategy because it was politically easier and safer to act from day to day in an ad hoc manner. But even policies designed to do little more than respond to short-run considerations can over time add up to a long-run strategy of a sort.

II. Disruption in the Economy, 1966–1969

Before turning to China's development strategy in the Cultural Revolution period, however, one must first deal with the argument that China had no coherent strategy in the period because the country was in continual chaos. Politics, of course, was frequently chaotic, but the question here is whether politics regularly spilled over into the economy, causing work stoppages and worse.

The principal data on which this analysis is based are presented in Tables 1–3. The basic message in these tables is clear and consistent. First, the disruption was largely confined to three years, 1967, 1968, and 1969. Industry and transport were hit the hardest, but only in 1967 and 1968. By 1969, most industries had reached and surpassed the peak levels of 1966. Furthermore, even during the years of chaos, industrial output often did not fall farther than levels achieved in the "normal" year of 1965 and

Table 1. Indexes of industrial output during the Cultural Revolution (1966 = 100).

	1957	1962	1965	1966	1967	1968	1969	1970	1975
Electric power	23	56	82	100	94	87	114	140	237
Steel	35	44	80	100	67	59	87	116	156
Coal	52	87	92	100	82	87	106	140	191
Petroleum	10	40	78	100	95	110	149	211	530
Cement	34	30	81	100	73	63	91	128	230
Chemical fertilizer	6	19	72	100	68	46	73	101	218
Machine tools	51	41	74	100	74	85	156	253	319
Cloth	69	35	86	100	90	88	112	125	129
Bicycles	39	67	90	100	86	97	142	180	304

Source: State Statistical Bureau, *Statistical Yearbook of China, 1981*, 225–231.

Table 2. Agricultural outputs and inputs during the Cultural Revolution (m. = million).

	1957	1962	1965	1966	1967	1968	1969	1970	1975
Grain (m. tons)	195	160	194.5	214	218	209	211	240	284.5
Index	91	75	91	100	102	98	99	112	133
Cotton (m. tons)	1.64	0.75	2.10	2.34	2.35	2.35	2.08	2.28	2.38
Index	70	32	90	100	101	101	89	97	102
Hogs (m. head)	145.9	100.0	166.9	193.4	190.1	178.6	172.5	206.1	281.2
Index	75	52	86	100	98	92	89	107	145
Chemical fertilizer (m. tons)									
production	0.15	0.46	1.73	2.41	1.64	1.11	1.75	2.44	5.25
imports	1.22	1.24	2.73	3.15	4.88	5.21	5.55	6.42	4.94
supplied to farmers[a]	1.79	3.11	8.81	12.58	13.63	10.13	13.61	115.35	26.58
supply index	14	25	70	100	108	81	108	122	211

[a] These figures are given in terms of gross weight, whereas the production and import figures are in terms of nutrient.

Sources: State Statistical Bureau, *Statistical Yearbook of China, 1981*, 229, 386; *Chung-kuo nung-yeb nien-chien, 1980*, 34, 40.

Table 3. Transport and commerce during the Cultural Revolution.

	1957	1962	1965	1966	1967	1968	1969	1970	1975
Freight traffic (billion ton/ km)	181.0	223.6	346.3	390.1	305.0	310.9	375.3	456.5	729.7
Railroad traffic (billion ton/ km)	134.6	172.1	269.8	301.9	226.9	223.9	278.3	349.6	423.6
Retail sales (billion yuan)									
Urban	23.84	31.85	33.89	36.28	38.20	37.32	39.35	40.00	60.69
Rural	23.58	28.55	33.14	37.00	38.85	36.41	40.80	45.80	66.42
Farm products purchases (billion yuan)	21.75	21.11	30.71	34.59	34.48	33.82	32.40	34.78	47.86
Grain purchases (million tons)	45.97	32.42	39.22	41.42	41.38	40.41	38.45	46.49	52.62
Foreign trade (billion US$5)									
Exports	1.60	1.49	2.23	2.37	2.14	2.10	2.20	2.26	7.26
Imports	1.51	1.17	2.02	2.25	2.02	1.95	1.83	2.33	7.49

Source: State Statistical Bureau, *Statistical Yearbook of China, 1981*, 283, 333, 345, 357.

remained far above the depression figures of 1962. Although the degree of disruption varied between provinces, most provinces suffered severe disruptions in both 1967 and 1968. A notable exception to this pattern was Shanghai, where industrial production was disrupted in a major way in only one year, 1967. By 1968, Shanghai industry had recovered and passed the previous peak level of 1966.[2] Given that Shanghai was the base of the Cultural Revolution leadership, a more experimental and potentially disruptive set of economic policies could have been anticipated. What little we know about Shanghai's economic experience during the 1966–1976 decade, however, suggests that it was much like that of the rest of the country. Overall industrial growth in Shanghai during this period was slower than the national average growth rate (8.3% versus 10.2% between

[2]Regional data for the 1966–1970 period must be reconstructed from scattered sources. The statement here is based on data in R. Michael Field, Nicholas Lardy, and John Philip Emerson, A reconstruction of the gross value of industrial output by provinces in the People's Republic of China: 1949–1973.

1965 and 1978), but this performance reflected policies started in the 1950s designed to relocate Chinese industry away from the coast.

Agriculture nationwide was less affected than industry. Grain output fell in 1968 and 1969 and cotton in 1969 and 1970. The number of hogs, usually a sensitive indicator of the status of private plots and the free market, was down significantly in 1968 and 1969. Some of this decline in agricultural output may have been because of bad weather, but in 1968, the principal problem was shortfalls in the availability of chemical fertilizer, supplies of which fell by more than 39%. The shortfall would have been worse if the sharp drop in domestic chemical fertilizer production had not been matched by a 65% rise in imports between 1966 and 1968. Somebody took responsibility to see that farmers did not suffer too severely from the disruption of industry.

By 1970, industry and agriculture had not only recovered to previous peak levels achieved in 1966 or 1967 but had surpassed those levels and regained the long-term trend line. In short, all of the worker strikes, the battles between workers and Red Guards, and the use of the railroads to transport Red Guards around the country had cost China two years of reduced output but little more, at least in the short run. Over the longer run, as the discussion in the next section makes clear, the ability of China's planners to respond to new problems and opportunities was severely constrained by fears of political reprisals, although the difficulties these constraints created were not fully apparent until the late 1970s. Overall, the growth rate of national product in the 3rd Five Year Plan (FYP) period (1966–1970) may have averaged as much as 6% per year.[3]

The contrast between the disruption caused by the Cultural Revolution and that resulting from the Great Leap Forward of 1958–1960 is striking. After the Great Leap, grain output fell 26% and cotton output by 38% from the 1958 peak.[4] The number of hogs in 1961 after private agricultural activity had been virtually eliminated was only 52% of the 1957 peak.

---

[3]For example, grain output, which accounts for a substantial part of agricultural production, grew at an annual average rate of 4% in the 1966–1970 period. Electric power output, a crude indicator of what was happening in the industrial sector, in 1970 was 71% above 1965, indicating an annual average rate of growth over the FYP of 11%.

[4]These figures on agriculture are all taken from *Chung-kuo nung-yeh nien-chien, 1980* (Chinese Agricultural Yearbook), 34–36, 38.

The industrial data for the Great Leap period and its aftermath are more difficult to interpret. In all cases, output in the 1961–1962 period was sharply below the peaks of 1958–1959. But the 1958–1959 peaks were inflated by price increases and by outright falsification of data. On the other hand, if there had been no Great Leap, industrial production would still have risen sharply in 1958 and 1959 because of all the new plant and equipment that was started earlier in the 1st FYP period (1953–1957), but whose production was just coming on line at the beginning of the 2nd FYP (1958–1962). In addition, many new complete plants were bought and delivered from the Soviet Union in 1958 and 1959, so that industrial production in the early 1960s should have continued to grow rapidly. In fact, industrial output declined sharply in 1961 and 1962 and had fully recovered by 1965 at the earliest.[5] The Soviet withdrawal of technical assistance in 1960 with only two weeks notice, of course, had more than a little to do with the slowness of this recovery.

In many respects, the best comparisons of the degree of disruption in the Great Leap and the Cultural Revolution period are the figures for the productivity of investment (capital–output ratios) in Tables 4 and 5 in the following section. As these figures indicate, enormous amounts of investment produced only modest increases in production or none at all. The growth rate of national income for the entire 1958–1965 period was less than half that of the 1966–1978 period, and it took almost twice the level of investment to produce a given increase in output in the former period as in the latter. In short, the Great Leap was a very expensive disaster. The Cultural Revolution at its peak (1967–1968) was a severe but essentially temporary interruption of a magnitude experienced by most countries at one time or another.

The most damaging effects of the Cultural Revolution were not the result of the chaos of the Red Guard years. They were the result of the long-term impact of following a particular strategy of development and the quality of planning and management that accompanied that strategy. Thus, China's long-term economic problems could not be solved simply by bringing in the army to quell the Red Guards. More fundamental

[5]The industrial data on which this discussion is based are taken from State Statistical Bureau, *Statistical Yearbook of China, 1981,* 255–231.

Table 4. Investment-output ratios in selected industries.

	1953–1957	1958–1965	1966–1970	1971–1975	1976–1980
Electric power					
Investment	2.978	11.095	6.860	12.939	21.874
Increase in output (billion kwh)	32.24	34.1	75.3	75.2	77.25
Ratio	0.092	0.325	0.091	0.172	0.283
Metallurgical industry					
Investment	4.661	20.317	9.879	17.308	18.969
Increase in rolled steel output (million tons)	6.88	–7.66	7.55	2.24	9.24
Ratio	0.677	—	1.308	7.716	2.05
Machine building					
Investment	3.847	14.129	7.409	21.676	17.846
Increase in machine tool output (thousands)	99.6	–69.0	116.4	15.9	–61.5
Ratio	0.039	—	0.064	1.36	—
Coal					
Investment	2.968	11.213	4.665	9.074	13.625
Increase in output (million tons)	0.011	0.0	0.026	0.063	0.192
Transport					
Investment	9.015	21.708	15.001	31.759	30.245
Increase in freight volume (billion tons/ km)	196.0	22.0	236.0	252.0	333.0
Ratio	0.046	0.987	0.064	0.126	0.091
Petroleum					
Investment	1.198	4.154	3.884	8.900	13.142
Increase in petroleum output (million tons)	2.94	11.08	31.42	46.72	10.64
Ratio	0.407	0.375	0.124	0.190	1.24

Source: State Statistical Bureau, *Statistical Yearbook of China, 1984*, 227–231, 283, 300–302.

Notes: (1) All investment figures are in billions of yuan. (2) Output figures assume a lag of two years between investment and outputs. To eliminate some of the atypical year-to-year fluctuations, three-year averages have been used. Thus, the output increase for 1953–1957 is actually the increase in the annual average of 1958–1960 over 1953–1955, etc. The 1976–1980 increase is 1980–1981 over 1976–1978. (3) The ratio was obtained by dividing the investment row by the increase in output.

Table 5. The marginal capital–output ratio.

	(1) Accumulation (as % of net material product)	(2) Growth rate of real net material product in 1980 prices	(3) Implied capital–output ration (1) ÷ (2)
1953–1957	24.2	6.62	3.66
1958–1962	30.8	−4.30	—
1963–1965	22.7	8.05	2.82
1966–1970	26.3	6.50	4.05
1971–1975	33.0	5.26	6.27
1976–1980	33.2	5.57	5.96
1981–1985	30.8	9.95	3.10

Source: State Statistical Bureau, *Statistical Yearbook of China, 1986,* 40, 41, 49.
Note: The estimates of the growth rate of net material product (national income in Chinese terminology) were estimated by first deriving the sectoral deflation indexes and then using those deflation indexes to convert net material product in current prices into net material product in constant prices.

changes in strategy were required, but Chinese planners did not fully realize this until a decade later.

III. Industrial Development Strategy, 1966–1976

China's basic industrial development strategy was set in the 1st FYP, of 1953–1957. Inspired by the experience of the Soviet Union in building a modern industrial sector on a crash basis, China hoped to accomplish a similar transformation from an even more backward industrial foundation. The first phases of this process were described in *CHOC,* Volume 14. The question here is whether the Cultural Revolution altered this strategy in any significant way. Did the Cultural Revolution lead to a significant change in sectoral emphasis — a shift away from heavy industry, for example?

The short answer to these questions is no; the basic industrial strategy laid down in the 1950s continued unabated right through the late 1960s and early 1970s. Certain major changes in direction, in fact, did not come before 1979, others, not before 1977. It is interesting to speculate whether

Table 6. Realization of plan targets (actual output as percentage of plan target).

	1967	1969	1972	1977	1979	1980
Gross value of industrial output (% increase)	—	—	65.3	178.8	106.3	145.0
Light industry	—	—	—	—	115.7	—
Heavy industry	—	—	—	—	101.3	—
Steel	60.5	83.3	101.7	103.2	107.8	112.5
Coal	76.3	96.7	106.2	112.2	102.4	93.9
Petroleum	81.6	117.5	101.5	100.7	96.5	100.0
Electric power	81.5	95.9	101.6	107.1	—	103.7
Cement	67.1	—	—	—	—	—
Chemical fertiliser	99.5	—	—	—	—	—
Cotton yarn	76.9	75.9	103.9	106.9	—	110.5
Basic construction investment (within budget)	64.5	86.2	94.0	124.9	116.3	144.9

Sources: The actual output data were taken from State Statistical Bureau, *Statistical Yearbook of China, 1981*, 225–231, and *ibid., 1986*, 246–248. The plan data are from Fang Wei-chung, ed., *Chung-hua jen-min kung-ho-kuo ching-chi ta-shih-chi (1949–1980)* (A record of the major economic events of the Chinese People's Republic [1949–1980]), 430–431, 451–452, 488–489, 578, 606, 624.

this consistency in policy was deliberate or the result of paralysis among economic planners during the Cultural Revolution. Some outside observers have gone so far as to suggest that little planning of any kind took place in the late 1960s and early 1970s, but as the data in Table 6 indicate, plans were drawn up and, except for the years when disruption was severe, these plans had some relationship to economic results. Given the weakness of the bureaucracy and particularly the planners during the Cultural Revolution, the explanation that there was planning but that planners' paralysis prevented serious consideration of changes in priorities is the more plausible one. If most new ideas are going to be attacked, the safest course is to continue doing whatever you were doing before.

This emphasis on caution was reinforced by the fact that much of the top economic leadership was purged or at least disappeared from view during the late 1960s, often not to reappear until many years later.

According to one estimate, of the 316 top economic officials, roughly one-third are known to have been purged and only one-quarter appeared in public or in some other way gave evidence of still being in office. Furthermore, the higher the position held, the more likely was the person to have been purged.

An in-depth history of how the economic ministries and commissions were run during the Cultural Revolution has yet to be written, and this chapter is not the place to attempt to do so. Clearly, however, the economic organs of government were deprived of experienced leadership. Few, if any, experienced replacements existed within the ranks of the Political supporters of the Cultural Revolution. The decimated ranks of the economic ministries and commissions, therefore, were left to carry on as best they could. Lacking the strong leadership needed if major changes were to be made, the safest and only practical course was to continue on the preexisting course in determining what to produce and where to allocate investment.

If this view of how lower-level economic administrators kept the system running is correct, it may also help explain why Lin Piao's death in 1971 had little discernible impact on economic performance. The output of most industrial products grew through 1972 and 1973, and capital construction investment stayed at a high level, roughly double the level of 1966–1969. Even farm income grew slightly despite a severe drought in 1972 that did reduce grain output. There were declines in certain key industrial products in 1974 and 1976, notably in steel and machine tools, but energy output and many other products grew even in those politically disruptive years. Thus, even the turmoil of a year such as 1976, which saw the deaths of Chou En-lai and Mao Tse-tung plus the T'ang-shan earthquake, did not have a lasting impact on economic performance comparable to that of 1967–1968 and even less to that of the Great Leap Forward.

What was the industrial strategy that Chinese planners pursued so consistently? The core ideas are simple and can be described in a formal mathematical model without doing violence to reality. The model, usually called the Feldman-Mahalanobis model after the Soviet and Indian economists who independently developed it, makes several key assumptions.[6]

[6]A good and reasonably simple discussion of this model can be found in Hywell G. Jones, *An Introduction to Modern Theories of Economic Growth,* 110–119.

The full model will not be presented here, but the assumptions will be described because Chinese planners, like their Soviet counterparts, at least implicitly operated under similar principles.

The key to the model is the belief that the most important choice facing planners is whether to invest in producer goods or in consumer goods — in items such as machinery and electric power, which can be used to manufacture other products, or in items such as clothing and food to be consumed. Two assumptions are necessary if one is to trace out the implications of this choice:

(1) That the capital–output ratio is fixed: that is, that a given amount of investment will produce the same increase in output year after year.
(2) That foreign trade is small relative to the size of the economy and to the size of total investment: If foreign trade is large relative to investment, planners can invest in consumer industries, then export these products in exchange for producer goods. If foreign trade is small, those producer goods must be manufactured at home or the country will run out of what is needed to construct new plant and equipment, and economic growth will come to a halt.

If these assumptions are valid, then it follows that economic growth will be more rapid as a greater share of investment goes to producer goods. If the share of investment in producer goods is raised, consumption will suffer in the short run, but over time consumption as well will grow more rapidly and will eventually reach levels above what would have occurred if investment had been directed more to consumption in the first place. The only reason why planners would not channel most investment into producer goods is that in the short run consumption may be so low that people will starve (or revolt).

How valid were the key assumptions of this model in China in the 1960s and 1970s? The low foreign trade ratio or closed economy assumption, for one, was a reasonable approximation of reality. Chinese foreign trade and national income figures are presented in Table 7. Before the late 1970s, imports as a percentage of national income generally fluctuated between 5 and 7%. If all imports had been investment goods, China would still have provided less than 20% of its investment needs through such purchases abroad since investment in the late 1960s

Table 7. Foreign trade ratios.

	(1) National income	(2) Exports	(3) Imports	Foreign trade ratios (4) (2) ÷ (1)	(5) (3) ÷ (1)
	(billions of current JMP)				
1952	58.9	2.71	3.75	0.046	0.064
1957	90.8	5.45	5.00	0.060	0.055
1962	92.4	4.71	3.38	0.051	0.037
1965	138.7	6.31	5.53	0.045	0.040
1970	192.6	5.68	5.61	0.029	0.029
1975	250.3	14.30	14.74	0.057	0.059
1978	301.0	16.77	18.74	0.056	0.062
1980	366.7	27.24	29.14	0.074	0.079
1982	426.1	41.43	35.77	0.097	0.084
1986	779.0	108.20	149.86	0.139	0.192

Sources: State Statistical Bureau, *Statistical Yearbook of China, 1981,* 20, 357; *ibid., 1986,* 40, 481; and State Statistical Bureau, *Chung-kuo t'ung-chi chai-yao, 1987* (Chinese statistical summary, 1987), 4, 89.

and 1970s was running at 30% of national income.[7] Four-fifths of all investment goods would have had to be manufactured in China. In fact, one-third or more of imports were either consumer goods or intermediate products, leaving the equivalent of only 3% of national income for imports of investment goods.[8]

This low foreign trade ratio was in part a reflection of China's large size and in part the result of deliberate policy choices. For reasons only partially understood, countries with large populations trade less (relative to their national product) than do small countries. India in the mid-1960s, for example, also imported an amount equivalent to 6% of its national

[7]If imports are 5% of national income and investment is 30%, then, if all imports were made up of investment goods, 16.7% of investment would have been provided by imports (5/30) and the rest from domestic production.

[8]Chinese figures indicate that 80% of all imports were "means of production," but the Chinese include many intermediate products such as textile fibers, rubber, etc.

product, and for Japan the figure was 9%. Smaller countries, such as Malaysia and Thailand, in contrast, had import ratios of 41% and 20% respectively.[9]

But as it will become clear when policy changes in 1977 and 1979 and their impact are discussed, China's trade ratio could have been higher if planners had so desired. Chinese planners instead, like their Soviet counterparts, set out to minimize the nation's dependence on foreign trade, not just in the Cultural Revolution period, but beginning in the 1950s. As the figures in Table 7 indicate, the trade ratio fluctuated from one period to the next, but there was no discernible trend. The lowest import ratios were in the early 1960s in the immediate aftermath of the severe disruption and bad harvests of 1959–1961 and again in 1967–1970 as a result of the disruptions of 1967–1969.

What was the impact of all the Cultural Revolution rhetoric against slavish dependence on foreign products and technology? Steel, copper, chemical fertilizer, and many other imports reached record highs in the late 1960s. Grain and other consumer goods declined, but mainly as a result of better domestic harvests. Imports of machinery and equipment did fall sharply in 1968 and 1969, probably in part as a result of the hostility of the "left" to foreign technology, but the general disruption of industry in 1967 and 1968 presumably was also a factor.[10] Overall, the nominal value of total imports in 1966–1970 was roughly the same as in 1953–1957, and 1971–1975 imports, again in nominal terms, were roughly double the level of 1953–1957. When inflation and the rise in real national income are taken into account, the foreign trade ratio of 1966–1970 was well below that of 1953–1957, but had recovered to that earlier level by 1975. In short, even in the sphere of foreign trade the Cultural Revolution was more a continuation of than a departure from the closed economy strategy initiated during the 1st FYP.

Given a closed economy, China, like the Soviet Union before it, followed the main prescription for high growth laid out in the

[9]These figures are from Hollis Chenery and Moises Syrquin, *Patterns of Development, 1950–1970,* 192–195.

[10]Imports of machinery, equipment, and scientific instruments fell from $348.7 million in 1966 to $136 million and $131.8 million in 1968 and 1969 before bouncing back to $276.6 million in 1970 (United States, Central Intelligence Agency, *People's Republic of China: International Trade Handbook,* December 1972, 25).

Table 8. Investment in capital construction by sector (in %).

	1953–1957	1958–1962	1963–1965	1966–1970	1971–1975	1976–1980
Heavy industry	38.7	54.9	48.0	54.5	52.1	48.0
Construction	3.9	1.4	2.2	1.9	1.7	1.9
Geological prospecting	2.6	1.2	0.4	0.5	0.7	1.3
Transport	16.4	13.8	13.3	16.4	18.9	13.5
Subtotal	61.6	71.3	63.9	73.3	73.4	64.7
Light industry	6.8	6.5	4.1	4.7	6.1	6.9
Agriculture	7.6	11.4	18.4	11.4	10.3	11.0
Commerce	3.9	2.0	2.6	2.3	3.0	3.9
Education, health, etc.	8.1	3.9	6.0	3.0	3.3	5.7
Civil public utilities	2.6	2.3	3.0	1.9	2.0	4.2
Other	9.4	2.6	2.0	3.4	1.9	3.7
Subtotal	38.4	28.7	36.1	26.7	26.6	35.4
Total	100.0	100.0	100.0	100.0	100.0	100.0

Source: State Statistical Bureau, *Statistical Yearbook of China, 1981,* 300–301.

Feldman–Mahalanobis model. The lion's share of investment was directed toward the producer goods sector, not toward plants that would turn out more products for consumption. The classification of items in Table 8 is not precise, but the basic message is clear. Three-quarters of all investment went to make machines to make more machines or to provide the infrastructure required by that sector. The share of producer goods in 1963–1965 was down, but more because of the immediate requirements of recovery from the 1959–1961 crisis than from any long-term change in strategy. It made little sense to put most investment into new heavy industry plants when existing ones were underutilized and the population was barely meeting its minimum subsistence needs. Once the recovery was over, the share going to producer goods jumped back to Great Leap Forward levels.

This strategy, according to the model on which it was based, should have led to a high growth rate not only in national income and the producer goods industry but also in consumer goods and the standard of living of the people. In fact, the only prediction that the model forecast correctly was that the rate of investment would rise as a share of national income. The growth rate of national income did not rise — it fell; and the rate of increase in consumption fell as well. Data on consumption will be presented later, but the first task is to explain why events did not work out as Chinese planners hoped and the model forecast.

As is so often the case, the model itself was sound, but the assumptions needed to make it work were invalid in the Chinese context. The key wrong assumption was that the capital–output ratio was fixed — that given levels of investment would produce the same level of output year after year. In fact, China's capital–output ratio began climbing in the late 1960s and early 1970s so that given levels of investment led to smaller and smaller increases in output.

The data needed to make this point are flawed, but certain relevant figures are presented in Tables 4 and 5. The statistics in Table 4 are not capital–output ratios in the strict sense, but the behavior of these ratios should be roughly similar to the behavior of the true capital–output ratios in these industries. Together the sectors represented in Table 4 accounted for 60% of all capital construction investment and most of the investment relevant to the producer goods sector.

What do the ratios show? In the 5th FYP (1976–1980) period, it took three times as much investment to produce a kilowatt hour of electricity as it did in the 3rd FYP (1966–1970), nearly twice as much investment to produce a ton of steel, and 40% more investment per ton kilometer of transport. Discounting for inflation, different assumptions about the underlying lags between the time investment funds are spent and the beginning of production would alter these results, but not the overall conclusion.[11] China was getting less and less for its money. The impact on a nationwide basis is reflected in the data in Table 5.

We will speculate later in this chapter about the causes of this rapidly rising ratio. Declining worker incentives and bad planning are part of the story. Newer petroleum fields may have been in more difficult areas to develop, and new railroad lines may have been through particularly

[11]The inflation rate in Chinese prices was very modest in these periods.

Table 9. Real and nominal wages and rural collective incomes (in yuan per year).

	Average annual wage in state sector		Rural collective distributed income per capita	
	Nominal	Real (1952 prices)	Nominal	Real
1952	446	446	—	—
1953–1957	559	522	41.75[a]	38.8
1958–1962	546	461	42.9	35.8
1963–1965	651	530	48.7	39.2
1966–1970	623	525	59.5[a]	50.1
1971–1975	614	513	63.8	54.4
1976–1980	672	529	74.2	60.2

[a] Data are for 1956–1957 and 1970 only.

Sources: *Chung-kuo nung-jeh nien-chien, 1980*, 41; State Statistical Bureau, *Statistical Yearbook of China, 1981*, 411–412, 435–436.

Note: Real wages were obtained by dividing nominal wages by the cost-of-living index for workers and staff. There is no appropriate price index for rural areas that would eliminate both changes in prices of purchased industrial goods and changes in accounting prices of goods distributed in kind. For lack of a better alternative, the general retail price index was used.

unfavorable terrain. Whatever the reasons, the national income growth rate was clearly falling, and because the investment rate was rising, the amount left over for consumption had little room for growth.

Consumption was further squeezed in the late 1960s by a rapid increase in defense spending, which according to Western estimates, rose from 24 billion yuan in 1965 to more than 40 billion yuan by 1971. This rise in defense spending may also have contributed to the increase in the capital–output ratio if much of this expenditure was for investment in the production of military equipment. Whatever the case, Lin Piao's fall brought this expansion to a halt. The military budget fell by several billion yuan in 1972 and then stabilized around 40 billion yuan until China's 1979 invasion of Vietnam.

Some indication of what was happening to consumption can be observed in the wage and rural income data in Table 9. Real wages did not rise at all between the 1st and 5th FYP periods. Rural collective income per capita per year did rise, but at a rate just under 2% per annum.

Actually, urban income also increased because the ratio of employed workers to family members rose. Overall, between 1957 and 1978 national consumption rose at an annual rate of 4.5% a year or 2.5% per capita given a population growth rate of 2%.[12] At 2.5% per year, the material living standard of the Chinese people would double every 28 years, a not insignificant accomplishment by the standards of the 19th century experience of the United States or the United Kingdom. But 2.5% is a far cry from the promises of 5% a year and more that the Soviet model of growth seemed to hold out to China in the 1950s. At a 5% growth rate, consumption per capita would have risen fourfold between 1952 and 1980, and real wages would not have stagnated.

IV. Changing Industrial Strategies, 1977–1980

Industrial strategy during the first two years after Mao's death in late 1976 represented only a limited departure from the industrial policies of the past. The key changes from the standpoint of industrial strategy were the increased emphasis on going abroad for foreign technology and the renewed reliance on material incentives to motivate greater and more efficient effort on the part of workers and farmers.

Planners in 1977 and 1978, however, do not seem to have recognized fully the significance for industrial investment policies of this shift in emphasis. Their thinking at the time was represented by the attempt to dust off and implement the Ten-Year Plan (1976–1985) originally developed prior to Mao's death.[13] Steel output was more than double by 1985 to 60 million tons and was still seen as the "key link" in industrial

[12]These consumption estimates were obtained by taking the Chinese estimates of indexes of real national income and by removing the share in accumulation, leaving an index of consumption. China's method of linking its national incomc indexes may slightly overstate the growth rate and hence the consumption growth rate would also be overstated.

[13]The Ten-Year Plan was discussed by the State Council in the summer of 1975, and this was followed by a draft plan that was approved by the Political Bureau but attacked by the Gang of Four. After Mao's death the plan was revised and presented to the National People's Congress in February 1978 for approval. See Hua Kuo-feng's "Report on the Work of the Government" at the First Session of the Fifth National People's Congress, 26 February 1978, *PR,* 10 (10 March 1978), 19.

development. Of the 120 large-scale projects planned, 10 were iron and steel complexes; 9, nonferrous metal complexes; 8, coal mines; 10, oil and gas fields; 30, power stations; 6, new trunk railways; and 5, key harbors. Investment over the eight years remaining in the ten was to "far exceed" the total of the previous 28 years combined. In short, the Ten-Year Plan was a high investment–heavy industry plan of the Soviet type par excellence.

It is doubtful that much careful thought went into preparing this plan. Many important planners had yet to be rehabilitated and given positions of responsibility. Statistics were still being collected at the local level, but these figures were not being cross-checked, and in many cases were not even being compiled at the national level.[14]

One indication of the quality of the plan is the target of 10 new oil fields, "10 new Ta-ch'ings," as the goal was referred to. Ten new Tach'ings would have meant an increase in petroleum production from 100 million tons a year to around 400 million tons. In fact, these new oil fields were a pipe dream. Offshore exploration had not even been started. Onshore exploration was inadequate and had not come up with one new Ta-ch'ing, let alone 10, that was ripe for development. The reality in early 1978 was that Chinese petroleum output was peaking and it would take a major effort at least through 1982 to keep production from falling, but the plan was based on a severalfold rise. Instead of enjoying a large energy surplus available for export, China was about to enter a prolonged period of severe energy shortage. Planning for the steel sector was not much better than that for petroleum. One Western estimate indicated that the Chinese might have to spend as much as $40 billion in foreign exchange to accomplish the 6o million ton target,[15] or $5 billion a year when total annual export earnings in 1978 were only $9.75 billion.

It was not just that planning was sloppy and based on poor data; planners, as already indicated, had not yet come to grips with the implications of the decisions to buy foreign technology in much greater amounts and

[14] This statement is based on, among other sources, a briefing given to an American Economic Delegation in Nanking in the fall of 1979 by Kiangsu statistical authorities.

[15] United States, National Foreign Assessment Center, *China: the Steel Industry in the 1970s and 1980s.*

to raise wages and the purchase prices of farm production in order to improve incentives. To increase imports significantly, China had either to increase exports significantly or to borrow abroad in large quantities. In practice, borrowing was never likely to provide more than a small fraction of China's foreign exchange needs, and so that left exports. But what kinds of exports could China hope to expand rapidly?

Agriculture, the traditional source of China's exports, directly or indirectly still provided more than half of China's foreign exchange in 1977 and 1978. But agricultural development was China's lagging sector, and the government was having trouble extracting enough food for its cities, let alone an increased surplus for sale abroad. Furthermore, with rising wages and farm incomes under the new incentive plan, the domestic demand for food would rise even more rapidly than in the past. Declining population growth would work the other way, but overall, China could not pay for its import requirements by exporting much larger amounts of food.

The drafters of the Ten-Year Plan may have hoped that petroleum would take up the slack, but that, as already indicated, was a vain hope. The only other possibility was to export manufactures, but what kind of manufactures? The plan called for more steel and machinery, but was China to become a major exporter of the products of heavy industry? To a degree, perhaps, but the efficient producers of these items are typically the more advanced industrial nations, not poor developing nations like China. That left consumer goods manufactures. Consumer manufactures were what fueled the export drives of China's neighbors: Japan in the 1920s and 1930s and South Korea, Taiwan, Hong Kong, and Singapore in the 1960s and 1970s.

China's emphasis on material incentives also drove the country in the direction of a greater emphasis on consumer goods, both industrial and agricultural. Increases in wages and farm prices would mean little if the new money could not buy anything. In fact, increased money incomes in the absence of expanded consumer goods production would be counterproductive. Not only would individual consumption not increase, but rationing of what goods were available would have to be tightened either formally (ration coupons) or informally (long queues).

There was, therefore, a basic contradiction between the goals of the Ten-Year Plan and the emerging outward-looking incentive-based strategy. As the year 1978 progressed, either existing planners became aware of this contradiction, or others who understood it all along regained influence, or both. Whatever the case, in December 1978 a decision was made to reorder industrial development priorities, at least temporarily.

The communiqué issued December 22, 1978 by the 11th CC's Third Plenum gave an indication of what was to come. More than half of the discussion of economic measures in the communiqué was devoted to the problems of raising agricultural output and the living standard of the people.[16] Of even greater significance was the election of Ch'en Yun as a CC vice-chairman and a member of the Politburo Standing Committee. Ch'en had been the behind-the-scenes architect of the recovery policies of the 1961–1965 period; earlier, at the CCP's 8th Congress in 1956, he had made a major speech advocating a greater use of the market and limitations on excessive centralization.[17] Although he had been one of the central economic figures in the 1950s when the Soviet-type industrial strategy had been introduced, Ch'en was known as someone who had a keen appreciation of the dangers of overemphasis on heavy industry.

The public unveiling of the new priorities came at the meeting of the NPC in June 1979. Yü Ch'iu-li, head of the State Planning Commission, called for an emphasis on agriculture, light industry, and foreign trade development as top priorities. Planned heavy industry growth in 1979 at 7.6% was, for a change, to be below the planned light industry growth rate of 8.3%.[18] Investment in heavy industry was to be cut back from 54.7% of the total in 1978 to 46.8% in 1979, and the overall investment amount was to be held at the same level as 1978.

Plan targets are not always a good guide to what in fact to expect from actual performance. The Soviet Union's plans frequently call for greater emphasis on consumer goods, but when the year is over, heavy industry has retained its priority position in the actual allocation of funds and key inputs. In China, however, the shift in priorities was real.

---

[16] "Communiqué of the Third Plenary Session of the 11th Central Committee of the Communist Party of China" (adopted December 22, 1978), *PR*, 52 (December 29, 1978), 11–13.

[17] Chen Yun [Ch'en Yun], *Eighth National Congress of the Communist Party of China*, 2. 157–176.

[18] These figures are from Yü Ch'iu-li, "Report on the 1979 draft national economic plan," *JMJP*, 29 June 1979, 1, 3.

Table 10. Economic indicators during the first phase of the readjustment period, 1979–1981.

Growth rates (%)	1979	1980	1981
Heavy industry	7.7	1.4	–4.7
Light industry	9.6	18.4	14.1
All industry	8.5	8.7	4.1
Agriculture	8.6	2.7	5.7
Investment in capital construction[a]	4.2	7.9	–20.7
Export[a]			
Nominal	26.2	28.7	35.0
Real	25.6	20.3	10.6
Import[a]			
Nominal	29.6	20.0	26.2
Real	15.7	6.5	–6.7

[a] Data for capital construction, exports, and imports are in current prices. All other percentages were derived from data in constant prices.
Source: State Statistical Bureau, *Statistical Yearbook of China, 1981,* 136, 210, 299, 357, 390.

Data for the first three years of what is called the "period of readjustment" are presented in Table 10. The indicated changes in priorities are dramatic. Not only did light industry grow faster in each of the three years; in 1981, the output of heavy industry actually fell. Perhaps, the most significant change was the rapid growth of exports. Between 1952 and 1978, export growth averaged only 7% a year and the growth in real terms was even lower. In the 1979–1981 period, the growth in nominal terms was at four times that rate (29% a year), and the difference in real terms was nearly threefold (18.6% a year).[19] Most of this increase in exports came from the sale abroad of manufactured products of which textiles was the largest but by no means the only item. The share of "industrial and mineral products" in exports, a figure that excludes textiles, rose from 37.4 to

[19]We do not have as yet an appropriate price index that can be used to deflate Chinese foreign trade data for this entire period. The 1979–1981 figures in real terms are from *Chung-kuo tui-wai mao-i nien-chien, 1984* China's foreign trade yearbook, 1984, 4, 5.

51.8% of total exports between 1978 and 1980, owing in part to the rise in petroleum prices in 1979, but also because of the rapid expansion of exports such as bicycles, sewing machines, chinaware, and even machine tools.[20] By 1981, exports had climbed to 9.5% of national income or nearly double the ratio of the previous quarter century.[21] In addition, the PRC had access to large subsidized credits from Japan and Western Europe and from its decision to take over China's seat in the International Monetary Fund and the World Bank. China no longer had a "closed" economy, and by opening up, China had greatly increased the options available to those setting future development strategy.

Military expenditures were also to be held down. The war with Vietnam did lead to a temporary burst of military spending in 1978 and 1979, but expenditures were cut back to mid-1970s levels by 1980. Military modernization was one of the "four modernizations," but there was little point in massive outlays to expand the number of obsolete tanks and aircraft. True modernization required first the upgrading of Chinese technology that could then form the base for the design and manufacture of advanced weapons systems.

This dramatic shift in priorities may in part have been a conscious move in the direction of the growth strategies of China's East Asian neighbors, but it was also in part making a virtue out of necessity. It was not just that investment was becoming less and less productive — that conceivably could have been tackled through managerial reforms without an accompanying change in industrial priorities. But managerial reforms could not overcome the fact that China did not have enough energy output to sustain a high-growth heavy industry strategy.

Total energy production between 1952 and 1978 grew at an average annual rate of 10.3%. The slower growth rate of coal production was more than offset in the 1960s and early 1970s by the rapid development of the Ta-ch'ing, Sheng-li, and other oil fields. Between 1978 and 1981, the

---

[20]In 1981, the Chinese changed the way they categorize foreign trade items, and available current data make comparisons of comparable categories between 1981 and earlier years impossible.

[21]"State Statistical Bureau report on the results of the 1981 National Economic Plan," *Chung-kuo ching-chi nien-chien, 1982*, 8, 79, 82–83.

increase in total energy output came virtually to a halt, rising at a minuscule 0.2% a year over the three-year period. Neglect in exploration efforts in earlier years, in the development of new coal mines, and in building the railroads to move the coal to where it could be used, had all taken their toll. If Chinese planners had continued the inefficient heavy industry strategy of the past, overall growth in national income would also have ground to a halt. Continued growth after 1978 was possible only if China shifted to industries in the consumer goods sector that required much less electric power per unit of output and began investing in energy-efficient equipment. Planners also began a major investment program to develop new sources of petroleum and coal and a supporting transport network, but these investments, even with the participation of the major international energy corporations, would not begin paying off in a major way until the mid-1980s. The readjustment period, therefore, was really the final outcome of the mistakes and inefficiencies of the Cultural Revolution industrial strategy and performance.

V. Accelerating Industrial Growth, 1982–1987

The readjustment period in industry was expected to last through much of the 1980s. As it turned out, however, 1981 was the only year when overall growth slowed to the levels set by the readjustment targets in the 6th FYP of industrial growth of only 4% per year.[22] By 1982, China was in the early stages of an economic boom that was to continue throughout much of the 1980s.

Several events intervened to make the readjustment plan obsolete soon after it was introduced. To begin with, total energy production, which had fallen in 1980 and 1981, resumed growth in 1982, and by 1984, the growth rate of energy output had surpassed 9% a year, a figure comparable to the rates achieved in the early 1970s, before falling back in 1986 to growth of only 3%. No dramatic offshore oil discoveries or other breakthroughs accounted for renewed energy growth. These increases resulted instead from a broad effort to expand coal production, to use imported

[22] *Sixth Five-Year Plan of the People's Republic of China for Economic and Social Development (1981–1985)*, 23.

technology to extract more petroleum than had previously proved possible from existing fields, and a modest expansion in hydroelectric power, notably the completion of the first phase of the Ko-chou dam. Demands for energy by Chinese industry still exceeded supply by a wide margin, but excess demand is a characteristic of the Soviet-style bureaucratic-command economy.

Of equal or greater significance was the loosening of the foreign exchange constraint on Chinese industry. China's initial efforts to expand exports proved remarkably successful. Exports in the three years after 1978 more than doubled in nominal terms, wiping out the trade deficit by 1981 and generating a sizable surplus in 1982 despite a rapid increase in imports (Tables 11 and 12). The increase in exports was the result of an expansion in manufactured exports and the 1979 run-up in the price of oil. Petroleum exports briefly accounted for a quarter of all Chinese exports before falling off as the price of oil declined (see Table 13).

On top of this expansion of exports, China began to borrow significant amounts of money from abroad and to open the gates to large-scale

Table 11. Growth of foreign trade.

	1970	1975	1978	1980	1983	1986
		(in million US dollars)				
Total exports	2,260	7,260	9,750	18,120	22,230	30,940
Total imports	2,330	7,490	10,890	20,020	21,390	42,920
Balance of trade	−70	−230	−1,140	−1,900	840	−11,980
		1971–1978		1979–1983		1984–1986
		(in % per year)				
Growth rate of exports:						
Value		20.0		17.9		11.7
Quantity		7.8		16.9		n.a.
Growth rate of imports:						
Value		21.3		11.2		26.1
Quantity		12.9		6.7		n.a.

Source: State Statistical Bureau, *Statistical Yearbook of China, 1986,* 481; State Statistical Bureau, *Chung- kuo t'ung-chi chai-yao, 1987*, 89; *Chung-kuo tui-wai ching-chi mao-i nien-chien, 1984*, 4–5.

Table 12. Financing China's trade deficit (all figures in million US dollars).

	1978	1979–1982	1983	1984	1985	1986
		(average per year)				
Balance of trade Deficit (–) or Surplus (+)	–1,140	–55	+840	–1,270	–14,890	–11,980
Foreign exchange from tourism	263	662	941	1,131	1,250	1,530
Foreign loans utilised	n.a.	2,718	1,065	1,286	2,688	5,015
Foreign direct investment utilised	n.a.	442	916	1,419	1,959	2,244
Foreign exchange Reserves — end of year (excluding gold)	2,154[a]	5,079	14,342	14,420	11,913	10,514

[a] This figure is for 1979.

Sources: State Statistical Bureau, *Statistical Yearbook of China, 1986*, 499, 530; State Statistical Bureau, *Chung-kuo t'ung-chichai-yao, 1987*, 80, 93.

Table 13. Structure of Chinese exports.

	Total exports (million US$)	Manufactured exports (% of total)	Of which: heavy and chemical (% of total)	Primary exports (% of total)	Of which: petroleum and mining products (% of total)
1953	1,022	20.6	8.3	79.4	0.8
1957	1,597	36.4	10.1	63.6	1.1
1965	2,228	48.8	17.8	51.2	3.1
1970	2,260	46.5	12.8	53.5	2.8
1975	7,264	43.6	12.5	56.4	15.0
1978	9,745	46.5	10.4	53.5	13.8
1980	18,272	46.6	12.9	53.4	25.1
1983	22,197	53.8	22.0	46.2	21.2
1986	30,942	63.6	n.a.	36.4	11.9

Sources: *Chung-kuo tui-wai ching-chi mao-yi nien-chien, 1984*, 4, 9; State Statistical Bureau, *Chung-kuo t'ung-chi chai-yao, 1987*, 89.

tourism. Initially this borrowing took the form of subsidized credits from China's major trading partners. In 1980, China took its seat in the International Monetary Fund and the World Bank, and the first World Bank loan to China was approved in 1981.[23] Decisions were also made to allow direct foreign investment in the form of joint ventures and other arrangements. The decision to allow joint ventures meant that China had to codify this system formally with a joint venture law, new tax laws, and other laws that would introduce some predictability and stability into relations between foreign investors and the Chinese government. No amount of codification, however, could fully protect foreign investors from the uncertainties connected with an economic system where most inputs were allocated by the state rather than being freely available through a market. Nevertheless, companies in Japan and the United States began to invest sizable amounts in the hope of future profits. By far, the largest amount of direct investment, however, came from Hong Kong and went into Kwangtung province next door to the colony. In the early 1980s personal connections based on cultural, linguistic, and family ties were probably a surer protection against the uncertainties of dealing with the Chinese government than was the country's fledgling legal system.

As the figures in Table 12 indicate, China was receiving $3 billion to $4 billion a year from tourism, loans, and direct investment at a time when the country had either a trade surplus or a small deficit. The result was a rapid run-up in China's foreign exchange reserves. These reserves passed $11 billion in 1982 and $14 billion in 1983. Despite increases in borrowing, China became a net lender on international financial markets. The combination of an investment slowdown caused by readjustment policies and this rapid increase in foreign exchange resources meant that China was accumulating more foreign exchange than it could effectively utilize. To continue the low-growth-rate targets of the readjustment period with this accumulating surplus made little economic sense.

Finally, the Chinese leadership, somewhat to its surprise, found itself in the middle of an agricultural boom in the early 1980s. The year 1980 itself experienced a poor harvest after two very good years, but output

---

[23] Harold K. Jacobson and Michel Oksenberg, "China and the keystone international economic organizations."

bounced back in 1981 and then soared in 1982 and 1983. The reasons for this accelerated growth will be discussed later in this chapter. The point of mentioning it here is that slow agricultural growth in China places limits on the pace of development of industries. Agriculture is a major source of inputs to consumer goods industry. Agricultural exports are a source of foreign exchange, and agricultural imports were important users of foreign exchange. Chinese grain imports, for example, grew from 8.8 million tons in 1978 to 16.1 million tons in 1982, but fell back to only 6 million tons by 1985.[24] This fall in grain imports alone saved more than a billion dollars in foreign exchange.

The loosening of these three constraints on the economy coincided with policies introduced that had been designed to decentralize control over economic decision making further, including the allocation of investment.[25] In the 1971–1979 period, for example, investment in state-owned enterprises that was carried out within the state budget was twice as large as investment in state-owned enterprises outside of the control of the budget. In the 1980–1984 period, in contrast, investment in state enterprises outside the budget was 40% higher than that made through the budget.[26] Efforts to reassert central control over investment beginning as early as 1981, therefore, were not successful.

If the central government had been more successful in reasserting its control, it is far from clear that this would have led to measurable net benefits to the Chinese economy. What China achieved, partly as a result of earlier decentralization policies, was an industrial boom. Furthermore, the boom was concentrated to a large degree outside the state sector with its large-scale enterprises. More than half of the rise in the gross value of industrial output in the five years from 1982 through 1986 was accounted for by small- and medium-scale enterprises under collective rather than state ownership. A third of the total increase in industrial output was accounted for by enterprises in rural areas (see Table 14).

---

[24] *Chung-kuo tui-wai ching-chi mao-i nien-chien, 1984,* 4. 118; and State Statistical Bureau, *Chung-kuo t'ung-chi chai-yao, 1987,* 91.

[25] Barry Naughton, "Finance and planning reforms in industry," in US Congress, Joint Economic Committee, *China's Economy Looks Toward the Year 2000,* 1.604–629.

[26] Dwight H. Perkins, "Reforming China's economic system," *Journal of Economic Literature,* 26 (June 1988), Table 2.

Table 14. Industrial growth, 1981–1986.

	State industry	Rural collective industry	Urban collective industry and other	All industry
	(Gross value of output) (billion yuan in 1980 prices)			
1981	405.44	60.10	80.04	545.58
1982	434.03	65.90	88.24	588.17
1983	474.78	78.91	100.29	653.68
1984	517.12	111.31	132.02	760.51
1985	584.02	170.28	171.28	925.58
1986	620.13	223.06	187.54	1,030.73
	Annual growth rates (in %)			
1982	7.1	9.7	10.2	7.8
1983	9.4	19.7	13.7	11.2
1984	8.9	41.1	31.6	16.3
1985	12.9	53.0	29.7	21.7
1986	6.2	31.0	9.5	11.4
1982–1986	8.9	30.0	18.6	13.6

Sources: State Statistical Bureau, *Chung-kuo t'ung-chi chai-yao. 1987,* 24, 38; State Statistical Bureau, *Statistical Yearbook of China. 1986,* 130, 227; *ibid., 1984,* 194–195; *ibid., 1983,* 215.
Note: The figures for "Rural collective industry" and for "Total industry" include "village-run industrial enterprise output." Chinese data normally include village-run industrial output in gross agricultural output.

Rural industrialization in China began in the 1950s, but its development was aborted by the mistakes of the Great Leap Forward (1958–1960). A renewed effort to develop rural industries to provide agriculture with key inputs such as fertilizer and cement was carried out in the late 1960s and early 1970s; and it is discussed at length in the section on rural development. Rural industrialization in the early 1980s, however, was different in character from these previous efforts. Much of this new rural industrial investment was concentrated in rural areas near some of China's major cities. The largest single concentration was in southern Kiangsu province around Shanghai, Wu-hsi, Nanking, and the other large cities of that region. Many of these new rural industries had subcontracting relationships with large state

Table 15. Heavy and light industry: output and investment (%).

	1966–1978	1979–1981	1982–1986
Gross value output of industry: total	10.2	7.1	11.8
Heavy industry GVO	11.8	1.3	12.5
Light industry	8.3	14.0	9.1
Share in capital construction:			
Heavy industry	50.0	40.8	38.3
Light industry	5.5	8.2	6.4
Housing	5.7	19.7	19.3

Sources: State Statistical Bureau, *Statistical Yearbook of China, 1986,* 373, 375; and State Statistical Bureau, *Chung-kuo t'ung-chi chai-yao, 1987*, 65–66.

enterprises in the cities. Emphasis on small-scale output did not mean a continuation of the readjustment period's emphasis on consumer goods. Investment in heavy industry remained below previous levels, but heavy industry output growth leapt ahead whereas the growth rate of light industry fell back to levels similar to those in the years 1966–1978. (see Table 15).

This boom nearly doubled Chinese industrial output between 1981 and 1986, but it was a development pace that could not be sustained. The major constraint on the especially rapid rate of industrial growth in 1984 and 1985, as it turned out, was foreign exchange. In 1985, China's foreign exchange reserves, especially that portion under the control of the central government, began to drop sharply. Only a major effort to expand borrowing abroad kept reserves from falling back to levels not seen since the 1970s. China's total external debt as a result grew, and may have reached $20 billion by 1987.

Accelerated industrial growth by stimulating a large annual increase in imports was the demand side of the problem. The supply-side part of the problem was caused by the slowdown in the growth of Chinese exports after 1981. The fall in petroleum prices did not have a major impact until 1986. The main difficulty was China's inability to maintain earlier growth rates of the export of manufactures. The barrier was not so much rising protectionism or the world recession abroad as it was a price system (including the exchange rate) that favored domestic over foreign sales. Enterprises could make larger profits selling on the domestic market.

Devaluations of the Chinese currency beginning in 1985 together with other price adjustments helped correct this situation, and in 1986 manufactured exports rose by 45% making it possible for total exports to rise by 13% despite the sharp drop in petroleum prices. In 1987, Chinese manufactured exports leapt up again and imports were curtailed and China once again came close to a balance on its trade account despite an increase in the industrial growth rate.

It is not unusual during periods of rapid growth for the pace of industrial development to fluctuate widely. In Taiwan in the 1970s, the annual growth rate of manufacturing was as low as minus 6.3% (in 1974) and as high as 25.6% (in 1976).[27] In the Republic of Korea in the same period the range was between 11.6% (in 1970) and 35.7% (in 1973).[28] Japan in the 1950s and 1960s before it acquired a chronic balance-of-payments surplus used to experience industrial booms followed by brief periods of slow growth caused by balance-of-payments constraints. The ups and downs of Chinese industrial growth rates, therefore, should be seen as a fairly typical accompaniment of rapid development. Analogies to China's own Great Leap Forward, when industrial output rose 110% over two years (1958–1959) in a completely unplanned and uncoordinated way with disastrous consequences, are not relevant to the cycles in industrial performance in China in the late 1970s and 1980s. China's 7th FYP (1986–1990) called for an annual average increase for industry of 7.5% per year,[29] more realistic than the 6th FYP (1981–1985) target. Whether China would just make this target or surpass it would depend on the severity of the foreign exchange constraint and the overall progress of economic reform.

Reforming the industrial system

China's efforts to overcome energy and foreign exchange bottlenecks in order to achieve accelerated industrial growth are only part of the industrial-policy story of the 1980s. The changes with the most long-run

[27]Council for Economic Planning and Development, *Taiwan Statistical Data Book, 1986,* 83.

[28]Economic Planning Board, *Major Statistics of Korean Economy, 1986,* 83.

[29]*Chung-hua jen-min kung-ho-kuo ching-chi he she-hui fa-chan ti-ch'i ko wu-nien chi-hua, 1986–1990* (The 7th five-year plan for the economic and social development of the People's Republic of China, 1986–1990), 23.

significance are those involving efforts to change the system used to coordinate and manage industrial enterprises.

The urban industrial system China possessed in the 1970s was in many respects a carbon copy of the bureaucratic-command system in Soviet industry. Central planners decided what was to be produced and the inputs to be used in production. Enterprises received these inputs directly from state agencies responsible for such allocations. If more inputs were required, the enterprise either had to go back to the planners for an additional allocation or work out an informal (and often illegal) trade with some other enterprise that had a surplus of that particular item. The option of buying additional inputs on the market was not open because such markets did not exist.

Investment decisions were even more centralized. Special enterprises were set up to carry out major construction of new plant capacity that was then turned over to the producing enterprise when completed. The funding came directly from the government budget with no charge to the producing enterprise. The prime role of the banking system was not to be a major source of funds to finance investment, but was mainly to monitor compliance with the plan.

The rigidity of this Soviet-style system bothered Chinese economists from the beginning. Overcentralization of decision making was seen as one cause of the rising inefficiency of Chinese industry described earlier in this chapter. The main solution attempted before the 1980s was to decentralize decision making to the province and even to the county. The principal features of the bureaucratic-command system, however, remained intact. Allocations of key inputs were made by government agencies in accordance with the plan. Markets played little or no role in these decisions.

In 1979, Chinese planners were already beginning experiments with reform of this bureaucratic-command system. These early efforts at reform involved such steps as allowing enterprises to compete with enterprises in other regions of the country where before each enterprise had a monopoly of its own region's market.[30] There were also attempts to

---

[30]William Byrd *et al.*, *Recent Chinese Economic Reforms: Studies of Two Industrial Enterprises.*

improve the internal efficiency of the enterprise by reintroducing bonuses for workers and managers and by placing greater emphasis on the profits target in the government's plan rather than the gross value output target.

None of these early changes fundamentally altered the predominant role of central planning and the bureaucratic-command system. The role of market forces increased but was clearly subordinate to the plan. Efforts to increase the role of the market were resisted strongly by some members of the Politburo and they were reasonably successful in blocking radical reform in 1982 and 1983. Once again a central figure in the debate was Ch'en Yun, only now he was on the side of those resisting further change. Ch'en Yun saw a role for the market but firmly believed that planning and the bureaucratic-command system should predominate.[31]

It was not that Ch'en Yun's views had changed. What had happened instead was that a group of younger, much more radical reformers had acquired positions of power and influence. Foremost among this group was Chao Tzu-yang, who became premier in 1980. These more radical reformers were primarily responsible for the October 1984 document "On the reform of economic structure."[32] This document, written in language that somewhat obscured its full intent, was in practice, a call for a major move away from the bureaucratic-command system and toward the use of market forces in all sectors of the economy.

The political battle over the appropriate role for market forces waxed and waned in the following three years (1985–1987). Those favoring the market appeared to be gaining the upper hand in 1986, only to suffer a setback when Hu Yao-pang was demoted and reformers outside the economic sphere were purged in early 1987. By the 13th CCP Congress in the fall of 1987, however, the market-oriented reforms were back on track, despite the presence of two members of the new Standing Committee of the Politburo who were seen as supporters of a continued role for the bureaucratic-command system.

[31] See, for example, Ch'en Yun's statement of 8 March 1979, reprinted as "Planning and the market," *Beijing Review,* 29.29 (July 21, 1986), 14–15.

[32] "Decision of the Central Committee of the Communist Party of China on reform of the economic structure" October 20, 1984, *Beijing Review,* 27.44 (October 29, 1984), I–XVI.

Whatever the political base of support for such reforms, the years after the October 1984 document witnessed a major expansion in the role of market forces, but an expansion that left elements of central planning and the command system intact.

There are five key elements in any attempt to make markets work in a way that will promote economic efficiency:

(1) First, inputs and outputs of industry must be made available for purchase and sale on the market. As early as the first half of 1985 market sales by a sample of 429 enterprises had risen to 43.8% of total sales from 32.1% in 1984. Material inputs supplied by the market to these same firms had risen from 16.4 to 27.3%.[33] Those percentages have risen considerably since, but concrete statistics are not available.

(2) Enterprise managers must behave in accordance with the rules of the market, or market forces will not lead enterprises toward efficient outcomes. There is little doubt that Chinese enterprise managers by the mid-1980s no longer attempted to maximize gross value output, as is typical in the Soviet command system but is completely inappropriate in a market system. Enterprises were concerned primarily with profits that could be used to pay bonuses, build housing, or otherwise provide for worker welfare.[34] But the key to an efficient market is to have enterprises raising profits by lowering their costs or raising sales, not by finding ways of extracting more subsidies from the government.

Chinese enterprises, however, still depend heavily on the bureaucracy for subsidies of various kinds. Tax rates, for example, are supposed to be calculated at a fixed rate according to one recent reform, but are still in practice negotiated rates set so that the enterprise can avoid making losses.[35] Bank loans are still too readily available at highly subsidized interest rates, despite efforts to harden up the terms on which bank loans are made.

[33] *Kai-ko: wo-men mien-lin ti t'iao-chan yü hsuan-tzu* (Reform: we face challenge and alternative), 45.

[34] William Byrd and Gene Tidrick, "Factor allocation in Chinese industry."

[35] See, for example, Andrew G. Walder, "The informal dimensions of enterprise financial reforms," in United States Congress, Joint Economic Committee, *China's economy looks toward the year 2000,* 1, 630–645.

An effort has been made to pass a bankruptcy law, but in 1987 it was still being used on only a trial basis. Only one state firm in Shenyang had actually been allowed to go bankrupt, although small collective firms were often allowed to go out of business with or without a bankruptcy law.

In the mid-1980s, therefore, Chinese enterprise managers were responding to a mix of signals. Concern with profits led them to pay attention to market forces much more than was the case in the 1970s or earlier. But success for these managers still depended critically on their ability to cater to the desires of higher-level economic bureaucrats.

(3) Getting prices to reflect the true relative scarcities in the economy is the third critical element in reform. If prices are distorted, inputs and outputs will not get to where they are most needed. But price reform is extremely difficult to implement in a system where the state sets most prices, as it did in China. Every time the state changes a price, there is a winner (the producers who receive a higher price for their product) and a loser (those who must pay the higher price). The losers will do everything in their power to resist such changes. Because many of the losers in the Chinese case would be managers of large enterprises paying higher prices for energy and other inputs, their capacity to bring influence to bear on the price-setting bureaucracy was considerable. A few state prices were changed in the early 1980s, but most remained fixed at levels often set as many as twenty years earlier.

As more and more industrial inputs and outputs became available on the market, however, the Chinese discovered that there was much less resistance to fluctuating prices on these markets. What evolved, as a result, was a dual-price system. Goods allocated by the bureaucracy were paid for at the old prices fixed by the state. The same kind of product sold on the market was paid for at prices determined by supply and demand on the market. The key to price reform, therefore, was to expand the scope of goods available on this secondary market where prices were not fixed, and that was what in fact was happening in 1986 and 1987. Whether the market would eventually be allowed to set all prices or whether the state would retain a major price-setting role was still a subject for considerable debate.

(4) A major reason for expanding the role of the market is to promote accelerated productivity growth. But markets enhance productivity in

large part because of the forces of competition felt through the market. If each enterprise has a monopoly of its own market, there is little pressure to improve performance. In China, in the early 1970s, even county enterprises were given monopoly control over the local county market. Competition between enterprises was not over markets but took the form of contests to surpass norms set by the state, with the winner receiving a red flag or a trip to Peking.

State enforcement of enterprise monopolies began to disappear in the early 1980s. In the commercial sphere where collective and private traders competed directly with state retailers, the impact on improved performance (longer hours, more service-oriented sales personnel) was readily apparent. Industrial enterprises producing items that were in oversupply also had to cut their price, improve quality, or increase their sales effort. The problem was that many industrial enterprises faced markets where demand greatly exceeded supply. For those enterprises, there was little competitive pressure to improve performance. Sales were automatic even where quality was low and service poor. Increasing competition involves more than simply abolishing state-enforced monopoly rights. Reform must also remove the sources of excess demand by getting managers to behave according to the rules of the market as described under (2) above.

(5) Finally, an effectively operating market requires that the government maintain an acceptable level of price stability. Politics determines what is acceptable. In China, consumers were used to long periods when prices did not rise at all or at most at 1 or 2% a year. Such stability was in part a reaction against the hyperinflation of the 1940s that had played an important role in undermining the Kuomintang government and bringing the CCP to power. Chinese politicians therefore had a low tolerance for price increases. When prices began to rise in the 1980s, their natural instinct was to reimpose price controls. But price controls in the face of excess demand lead to queuing and other forms of rationing, setting the economy on a path back toward the bureaucratic-command system. The problem in China was particularly acute in 1985 and 1986, when the official urban cost-of-living index rose by 12% and 7% respectively. Unofficially, it was widely believed that the rate of price increase was considerably higher. Urban residents in particular were disturbed by these increases, and their

criticisms were an important force slowing the pace of market-oriented reform. The only solution for the reformers was to learn to do a better job of using macroeconomic controls to restrict excess demand and hence the rate of increase in prices. But the task was a difficult one, in part because the reformers had no prior experience with control of inflation through the indirect levers of macroeconomic policy.

By the end of 1987, China had made real progress on all five fronts in moving toward a more market-oriented system in the industrial sector. But bureaucratic controls over enterprise behavior, particularly the large-scale state enterprises, were still pervasive. Probably, no one among the reformers envisaged moving all the way to a free market system such as the one prevailing in Hong Kong. But many saw the possibility of a mixed bureaucratic-command and market system with features in common with what existed in Japan in the 1950s or South Korea in the 1960s. The principal remaining difference between China and its East Asian neighbors would be in the area of public versus private ownership. In Japan, South Korea, and the province of Taiwan, private ownership predominated in industry, although there were many state-owned enterprises. In China, virtually all large-scale firms other than joint ventures with foreign firms were owned by the state, and there were no plans to sell off any of them to the private sector.

The future of market-oriented reforms in China did not depend only on politics and the makeup of the Politburo. Of equal or perhaps even greater significance was what was happening with small- and medium-scale enterprises. In 1986, there were 400,000 such enterprises producing 40% of China's industrial output. There was no way that the center could hope to control these enterprises through the techniques of central planning. In practice in the mid-1980s, most of these enterprises bought their inputs and sold their outputs on the market. The great majority of such firms were collectively owned, but private ownership of a sort was playing an increasing role.[36] As long as this small-scale sector continued to grow

[36]The most systematic studies of rural industrialization that bring the story up to 1987 are in the papers prepared for the Chinese Academy of Social Science — World Bank Conference on Township Village and Private Enterprises held in Peking in November 1987.

so rapidly, there was little prospect of the state's going back to a full Soviet-style command system as in 1956–1957 or 1963–1965. The efforts to promote rural and other collective industries in the mid-1980s, therefore, had the effect of reinforcing pressures to move toward more market-oriented reforms.

VI. Rural Development Strategy

Chinese leaders could rationally decide to neglect investment in consumer goods before 1978–1979 because of their belief in some version of the Stalinist or Feldman–Mahalanobis model of development. But Chinese planners had an additional reason for not being concerned in earlier years by the consequences of this neglect. Somewhere between two-thirds and three-quarters of all consumer goods were supplied by the agricultural sector.[37] And for agriculture China had a development strategy that did not require large-scale state investment in rural infrastructure.

The core idea of this rural development strategy was that farmers could accomplish most of what was needed without much outside help. The term "self-reliance" has meant different things over the past three decades in China, but in the 1960s and 1970s in rural areas it meant a strategy whereby farmers provided most of their own inputs, whether labor, capital, or current inputs, such as fertilizer.

Like so much else in the Cultural Revolution period, the ideas underlying this self-reliant strategy had their origins in earlier years — specifically, in the first phase of the nationwide collectivization campaign of 1955–1956 and even more clearly in the Great Leap Forward years of 1958–1959. What were the characteristic features of this strategy? There were variations in emphasis over time, but the main components were there throughout until the change in policies in

[37] In the late 1970s and early 1980s, food constituted about 65% of rural household budgets and 60% and more of urban household budgets. In addition, clothing, much of whose value comes from cotton, accounted for another 12–15% (*State Statistical Bureau, Statistical Yearbook of China, 1981,* 439, 443).

1978–1979 and some components even survived these changes. The main features were:

(1) There was belief that China's large rural labor force was an asset that could be mobilized for development. If properly motivated and led, this labor force could provide its own infrastructure of irrigation systems, roads, and leveled fields. The key was how to provide the necessary motivation, and the "solutions" ranged from efforts through "socialist education" to encourage people to work altruistically for the good of society, to restructuring agricultural cooperatives (APCs) and communes to ensure that rural construction would serve peasants' material self-interest.
(2) Particularly after the bad harvests of 1959–1961, it became clear that agriculture had to have more modern inputs, such as chemical fertilizer and machinery, but the issue remained as to who was to provide those inputs. The solution during much of the 1966–1976 period was to turn to small-scale enterprises in rural areas rather than to larger plants often imported from abroad and located in urban industrial centers.

These two main features had a clear relation to what actually happened in rural areas before the late 1970s. There were several other characteristic elements that often appeared in public rhetoric, but whose relation to what was actually happening was less clear. There was emphasis on reducing inequality both within the rural areas and between farm and city. There was the slogan "Take grain as the key link" that led to neglect of cash crops, but not as consistently as sometimes has been argued. The slogan "Take agriculture as the foundation" was interpreted by some analysts as indicating that agriculture had the number one priority in investment and in the allocation of key inputs, but, as the discussion above of investment priorities makes clear, this was far from the case. We shall return to issues of income distribution and overemphasis on grain, but first we need a clearer understanding of the central features of the self-reliant strategy and an appraisal of their actual impact on production and income.

Labor mobilization for infrastructure

The single most important economic justification for the nationwide formation of APCs in 1955–1956 and rural people's communes in 1958 was the belief that their formation would make it possible to mobilize millions of "surplus" farm laborers to build the rural infrastructure of irrigation systems and roads that China lacked. The idea was not a new one. Economists in the West (Nurkse, Myrdal, and many others) had long argued that the rural areas of developing countries had a large, untapped resource in the form of farmers who were less than fully occupied raising crops on tiny plots of land. These farmers, the argument went, could make their own capital equipment (shovels, baskets for carrying dirt) and use their spare time to dig ditches, transform hilly wasteland into arable land, and much else. If properly organized, this work could be done at no cost to the central government budget and with no decline in agricultural output even in the short run. Community development schemes in India and rural public works programs around the world were founded on the belief that surplus labor could be mobilized in this way. As it turned out, many of these schemes were outright failures, and others existed only as long as they received large subsidies from the central government or international aid agencies.

China, however, was different because it had abolished private ownership on most agricultural land. Private ownership made it difficult to get rural labor to volunteer for public works schemes because the people who did the work were often not those who reaped the main rewards. With a new irrigation canal, for example, the main beneficiaries were those who owned land near the canal and had the most ready access to the water. But those who did the work often had to be drawn from some distance away, and many would be landless laborers or tenants. Either they saw no increase in productivity at all, or they lived near enough to the canal to experience increased yields only to see those increases eaten up by higher rents.

The formation of APCs and later communes made it possible to relate effort to reward. An entire village could be mobilized to build a canal that increased yields on only one-quarter of the village land. The villagers (commune members) would be paid in "work points," the number varying according to the amount of work done. The increased output would not go to those who farmed the more productive quarter, but to the entire village. All output, including the increased portion, would be divided up among the villagers in proportion to the number of work points earned.[38]

Following these principles, the Chinese mobilized tens of millions of farmers in 1956–1957 and even more in 1958–1959. Enormous quantities of dirt and rock were moved, but there followed in 1959–1961 the most serious crop failures of the post-1949 period. As with regard to so much else in the Great Leap Forward, it was difficult to sort out how much of the subsequent disaster could be attributed to bad weather, to bad management, and to the fact that the whole idea of labor mobilization may have been based on false assumptions in the first place. Lacking any clear basis for judgment, those who still felt labor mobilization was the key to rural development were in a position to reassert their position once recovery from the Great Leap crop failures had been achieved. Such models as the Ta-chai brigade and Lin county became famous throughout China for their achievements in turning uneven, parched land into large, level, well-irrigated fields. We have no good data on the amount of labor mobilized and construction completed in the late 1960s and early 1970s, but it was substantial. The question, however, is whether this construction had much of an impact on agricultural production.

Basic data on agricultural output in China are presented in Table 16. These indicate that production grew at a rate well above the population growth rate of 2% throughout the 1966–1976 period. The issue is whether this rise in output was achieved through labor mobilization or as a result of increased amounts of such modern inputs as chemical fertilizer and

---

[38]More precisely, the cooperative or production team, whichever was the basic accounting unit, calculated its gross output and then deducted certain amounts for taxes, investment, current costs, and the welfare fund. The amount remaining was divided by the total number of work points to determine the value of a single point, and family collective incomes were set by multiplying this amount times the total number of family work points.

Table 16. Growth rates of agricultural output (in % per year).

	1953–1957	1958–1965	1966–1978	1979–1982	1983–1986
Grain	3.5	0	3.5	3.9	2.5
Cotton	4.7	3.1	0.2	13.5	−0.4
Oil-bearing crops	0	−1.8	2.8	22.7	5.7
Sugar cane	7.9	3.2	3.6	15.0	8.1
Meat	3.3	4.1	3.4	12.1	9.2
Gross value of agricultural output (minus sideline output)	5.2	0.9	3.1	6.4	5.8

Sources: State Statistical Bureau, *Statistical Yearbook of China, 1986,* 130; and State Statistical Bureau, *Chung-kuo t'ung-chi chai-yao, 1987*, 28–31.
Note: Sideline output, most of which is rural industry, was subtracted from total gross value of output and then all figures were converted into 1980 prices using price indexes derived from Chinese gross agricultural output figures in 1971 given in both 1957 and 1970 prices, and for 1980 given in both 1970 and 1980 prices.

improved plant varieties. Some relevant figures on agricultural inputs are presented in Table 17.

The main purpose of labor mobilization for rural construction is to increase the amount or raise the quality of land used to grow crops. But the figures in Table 17 indicate that the amount of arable land actually declined slightly between 1965 and 1975, whereas the amount of irrigated acreage rose by 10 million hectares and accounted for 43% of all acreage, up from 32% in 1965. Because the arable land data are widely believed to be underreported,[39] it may be that there was a net increase in arable land during the Cultural Revolution period. On the other hand, most of the increase in irrigated acreage was due to the introduction of tube wells on the North China Plain, and tube wells have little if anything to do with labor mobilization.

[39] *Chung-kuo ching-chi nien-chien, 1981,* 6.9, states that "cultivated acreage figures are biased downward, subject to future verification."

Table 17. Agricultural inputs.

	1957	1962	1965	1970	1978	1982	1986
Rural labor force (millions)	205.7	213.7	235.3	281.2	303.4	332.8	379.9
Labor force in agriculture[a]	n.a.	n.a.	233.0	n.a.	294.2	320.1	313.1
Arable land[b] (million ha)	112.0	102.3	103.9	101.2	99.4	99.6	96.85[d]
Irrigated area (million ha)	27.34	30.48	33.06	36.04	44.97	44.18	44.23
Power irrigated area (million ha)	1.20	6.07	8.09	14.99	24.90	25.15	25.03
Agriculture use machinery (million hp)	1.65	10.29	14.94	29.44	159.75	225.89	284.33[d]
Rural use of electric power (kwh per ha)	1.25	15.7	35.8	94.5	253.1	396.9	606.0
Consumption of chemical fertilizer (million tons of nutrient)	0.373	0.630	1.942	3.21[c]	8.84	15.13	19.35

[a] Figures are actually for the labor force in the primary sector and therefore include a small number of nonagricultural laborers.

[b] Land data were derived in part from data on mechanically plowed or irrigated acreage and the percentage of mechanically plowed or irrigated to total. Land data are widely believed to be underreported.

[c] Figures were derived from "standard weight" fertilizer assuming a nutrient content of 0.202 (the actual nutrient content in 1978).

[d] Figures are for the year 1985.

Sources: *Chung-kuo nung-yeh nien-chien, 1980,* 4.342–345; State Statistical Bureau, *Statistical Yearbook of China, 1981*, 185; State Statistical Bureau, *Chung-kuo t'ung-chi chai-yao, 1987*, 17, 19, 36; State Statistical Bureau, *Statistical Yearbook of China, 1986*, 4.111.

It may be that the main impact of rural construction was to protect farmers from drought and flood in bad years rather than to raise average yields in good years. But the area directly affected by flood and drought disasters in 1972, 1978, and 1980 was 17.2, 21.8, and 22.3 million hectares respectively. Only in the terrible years of 1960 and 1961, when the affected area was 25.0 and 28.8 million hectares, can one find higher figures in the post-1949 period.[40] No doubt the impact of these disasters on yields was less in the 1970s than in earlier periods, so some significant gains can be attributed to rural construction efforts, but the gains seem modest when put up against the enormous amounts of labor time involved over the two decades, 1956–1976.

An alternative way of approaching the question of the contribution of labor mobilization to increases in agricultural output is to attempt first to estimate the contribution of modern inputs to that increase and then estimate the impact of labor mobilization by calculating the residual not explained by modern inputs. The method is known as "growth accounting" or "sources of growth" analysis and is usually used to estimate improvements in productivity.[41] The data needed to make these calculations are, in the Chinese case, crude and must be derived using assumptions that are arguable. Still, the results as presented in Table 18 are instructive. Taking the two decades of labor mobilization as a whole (1957–1979), the biological package involving increases in chemical fertilizer, pesticides, and improved plant varieties accounts for nearly two-thirds of the total increase in crop output. Increased labor used directly on crops and augmented by labor-saving machinery[42] plus expansion of the irrigated acreage accounts

---

[40]These figures are from State Statistical Bureau, *Statistical Yearbook of China, 1981*, 205–206.

[41]Formally, growth accounting assumes a production function of the following form, $Q = F(L, Ld, K, C, t)$ where Q is output, L is labor, Ld is land, K is fixed capital, C is current inputs, and t is time. The specific form used here involves assuming constant returns to scale and differentiating a simplified version of this equation with respect to time, arriving at the following: $dQ/dt = F/t + F/C \times dC/dt + F/L \times dL/dt + F/Ld \times dLd/dt,$ where chemical fertilizer is a proxy for current inputs and irrigated acreage increases represent the only significant changes in Ld.

[42]The question of mechanization was a major issue during the Cultural Revolution period and before. Mechanization was in part done to break labor shortages, such as in a two- or three-crop-a year economy when one must harvest one crop and transplant another in a relatively short period. Mechanization, however, was also seen as serving sociopolitical ends, such as reducing the differences in work style between city and countryside and consolidating the collective economy. (Tractors, particularly when owned by the

Table 18. Accounting for China's agricultural growth (in billion 1970 yuan).

Contributing inputs	1965–1975	1957–1979
Biological package (chemical fertilizer, improved plant varieties)[a]	8.35	22.7
Labor and labor augmenting machinery used in raising crops[b]	3.9	6.6
Expansion of irrigated acreage[c]	4.4	7.7
Change in gross value of crop output (1970) prices[d]	22.0	35.2
Residual-contribution of all other factors and increases in productivity [4 – (1 + 2 + 3)][e]	5.35	–1.8

[a] Although there are variations depending on local conditions, a ton of chemical fertilizer measured in terms of nutrient (NPK) usually produces about 10 tons of increases in grain output. The increases in fertilizer output were obtained from data in Table 19, were multiplied by 10 to obtain the increases in grain output, and further multiplied by 216.4 yuan, the average purchase price of grain in 1970 (*Chung-kuo nung-jeh nien-chien, 1980*, 381). If we had assumed that some of the fertilizer was used on cash crops, a slightly higher total would have been reached.

[b] This labor estimate involves the most assumptions based on the least reliable data. The rural labor force figures are from Table 17. We have assumed that each laborer devoted 130 days a year to raising crops. This figure is for 1957 and is from *T'ung-chi yen-chiu*, 8 (August 23, 1958), 8. The most difficult problem is to estimate the marginal product of that labor without first estimating an agricultural production function. One Chinese survey indicated that the average value (income) of collective labor per day was 0.56 yuan in 1976, down from 0.70 yuan in 1956 and 0.68 yuan in 1957 (*KMJP* December 7, 1978). These are average product figures, and since they are falling, the marginal product was presumably below the average. Used here is an estimate of 0.5 yuan for the marginal product of a day spent laboring to raise crops.

[c] Data on the expansion of irrigated acreage are derived from Table 19. Irrigated land is assumed to produce two tons more grain per year than unirrigated land, and grain in 1970 prices is worth 216.4 yuan.

[d] The gross value of agricultural output (GVAO) figures for 1957 and 1965 in 1957 prices and 1970, 1975, and 1979 in 1970 prices are from *Chung-kuo nung-yeh nien-chien, 1980*, 41. Data on 1980 crop output in 1970 and 1957 prices indicates a deflater for crop output of 1.35, which is roughly the same as the farm purchase price index for 1970 over 1957 of 1.33. I converted the 1957 data into 1970 prices using 1.35. The 1975 crop output figure was obtained by assuming that 70% of GVAO was accounted for by crops.

[e] This figure is obtained by subtracting identified input contributions (1, 2, 3) from the change in gross value of crop output (4).

for all the remaining increase in output and more. And most of this increase in irrigated acreage, as already indicated, was due to capital

---

collective, helped reinforce the need to labor collectively.) See Benedict Stavis, *The politics of agricultural mechanization in China*.

investment in modern power-driven tube wells, not to irrigation systems built by large labor corvées. The data for 1965–1975 are less reliable but tell only a slightly different story. For that period, the residual is at least positive, meaning that there is some part of the rise in crop output left over to be explained by factors other than the increase in modern inputs or the direct application of more labor and machinery to crops.

Slightly different assumptions would lead to somewhat different results, but only radical changes could alter the main conclusion. Either the massive effort to mobilize rural labor had a quite small impact on crop output directly or indirectly, or the impact was great but led to such inefficiency in the use of modern inputs that most of the gains were lost by this inefficiency. Put more concretely, chemical fertilizer and related inputs accounted for half or more of the rise in output if it was used efficiently and produced the expected yield response of 10 kg of grain for 1 kg of nutrient. Or fertilizer was used inefficiently and produced a much lower yield response, in which case land improvements through labor mobilization may have accounted for a larger share of the rise in production. The technique of growth accounting as used here does not allow differentiation between these two alternative explanations.

Neither explanation leads one to conclude that labor mobilization for rural construction proved to be a successful way of achieving rapid increases in Chinese agricultural output. At best, it was a supplementary contributor. The reason why the impact was not greater was partly because of management and incentive problems connected with the commune structure that was an essential part of the labor mobilization strategy. But it was also the case that rural construction projects of this type were not the appropriate technology to bring improved irrigation systems to those parts of China that lacked them. South China had begun building such systems a thousand years earlier, and, although these systems could be improved, the gains from such improvements were modest. North China desperately needed a more reliable source of water, but only in a few areas, such as on the edge of the T'ai-hang mountains where both Ta-chai and Lin counties are located, was it possible to achieve significant expansion of the irrigated acreage by labor mobilization alone. Elsewhere, one had to make more use of the water of the Yellow River, which meant first removing much of its silt, and that could be done only with a massive program of dam building and grassland development on the upper reaches of the river.[43] Or, as has been considered from time to time, one must find a way of diverting the waters flowing down the Yangtze northward, no mean trick under any circumstances and certainly not the job for a few million farmers working on their own with pickaxes and shovels.

Rural small-scale industry

Although modern inputs probably accounted for much of the rise in farm output, in the 1966–1976 period, at least many of these inputs were provided by quite small plants located in the countryside. As mentioned earlier, in the discussion of industrial strategy, like so much else during the Cultural Revolution period the basic idea for rural industrialization originated during the Great Leap Forward. But the design of the Great Leap small-scale-industry program was badly flawed. Backyard iron and steel furnaces that popped up all over were the prime example of the inappropriateness of the industries chosen for emphasis. These furnaces, like most other commune-run enterprises, wasted materials and time and produced little of value. By 1963, their numbers had been reduced to 11,000 from a 1960 level of 117,000 commune enterprises, and by 1966, there were still only 12,000.[44]

Between 1966 and 1970, however, commune industrial enterprises were once again on the rise and were joined by many new county-level state plants that fit within the small-scale category. But unlike the earlier effort in the Great Leap, this program was based on something other than the utopian wishes of the leadership. The key ideas in this period were straightforward. Agriculture required modern inputs, but it would divert a large share of the state investment and foreign exchange budget if these inputs were to be supplied by large-scale and imported turnkey enterprises. Furthermore, high rural transport costs made it sensible to locate enterprises near both their sources of raw material and the users of their

---

[43]For discussions of North China's water problems, see James E. Nickum, *Hydraulic Engineering and Water Resources in the People's Republic of China*; Alva Lewis Erisman, "Potential costs of and benefits from diverting river flow for irrigation in the North China plain"; and Dwight H. Perkins, *Agricultural Development in China, 1368–1968*, 4.
[44]State Statistical Bureau, *Statistical Yearbook of China, 1981*, 207.

product. Cement, which uses limestone and coal as inputs, illustrates the point. Because small outcroppings of limestone and coal can be found in many of China's rural areas, it is possible to locate cement plants near these outcroppings in order to produce cement for lining of canals, as well as for other purposes. If the plant is small, local people can build the plant themselves with only a limited amount of technical supervision from outside. The alternative of building a large 1 or 2 million ton cement plant would have led to the production of higher-quality cement, but most communes would have spent double and triple the original cost of production to transport the cement to where they could use it.

Farm machinery illustrates another advantage of small plants located near the users of their products. Tractors and other machines break down frequently. In industrial countries a farmer can go to the repair shop of a nearby distributor for a replacement part. But developing countries have few distributors and inadequate or no inventories of spare parts. A farmer could send his tractor off to Shanghai or Peking for repairs, but that might take months or years. The solution is to have repair facilities located near users in the commune. But a major overhaul capacity involves many kinds of skills and equipment needed to manufacture the item in the first place, so it is not difficult to convert a major repair facility into a manufacturing enterprise, and that is what the Chinese did.[45]

Between 1965 and 1970, the number of small, commune-run enterprises had risen to 45,000, and by 1976, the number was 106,000, nearly back to Great Leap levels. Five industries received special emphasis — cement, farm machinery, chemical fertilizer, iron and steel, and electric power. By the early 1970s, half of China's total cement output and nearly all of the cement reaching the countryside were produced in small-scale plants (see Table 19). Roughly half of all chemical fertilizer also came from small-scale plants, mainly in the form of low-quality ammonium bicarbonate. In the late 1970s, China began closing down many

[45]There are a number of useful works on small-scale industry in the Great Leap and Cultural Revolution periods. See, for example, Jon Sigurdson, *Rural Industrialization in China*; Carl Riskin, "Small industry and the Chinese model of development," *CQ*, 46 (April–June 1971); and Dwight H. Perkins, ed., *Rural Small-Scale Industry in the People's Republic of China*, report of the American Rural Small-Scale Industry Delegation.

Table 19. Small-scale cement plants.

	No. of small-scale cement plants[a]	Annual growth rate of small-scale cement plants	Share of small-scale cement plants in total production (%)
1949	—	—	7.6
1953–1957	—	—	2.6
1958–1962	—	38.0	19.8
1963–1965	—	77.1	26.8
1965	200	—	—
1966–1970		14.9	39.0
1972	2,400	—	—
1971–1975	—	20.8	53.0
1975	2,800	—	—
1976–1980	—	14.8	65.9
1980	4,533	—	—

[a] Small-scale includes county as well as commune-run cement enterprises.

Sources: Kao Wen-hsi, "China's cement industry," *Chung-kuo ching-chi nien-chien, 1982*, 5.205; Jon Sigurdson, *Rural Industrialisation in China*, 153: and American Rural Small-Scale Industry Delegation, *Rural small-scale industry in the People's Republic of China*, 86.

small-scale enterprises on the grounds that they wasted materials and generally were run at prohibitively high cost. Not surprisingly, many of the decisions to build plants in the 1966–1976 decade were made without adequate consideration of their economic efficiency. The surprising thing is that there were not many more plant closings for inefficiency given the highly politicized atmosphere in which decisions were made in the Cultural Revolution.[46]

One sector that was hard hit by the closing was the small-scale iron and steel industry, where 300 of 500 plants (mainly the smallest) were closed. Small chemical fertilizer plants also came in for much criticism, but output in such plants after many of the least efficient had been closed

[46] A useful study of the post-1976 period is by Christine Wong, "Rural industrialization in the People's Republic of China: Lessons from the Cultural Revolution decade," in US Congress, Joint Economic Committee, *China under the four modernizations*, 394–418.

may have been three-quarters of its peak level.[47] Overall, however, small-scale industry kept growing at a rapid pace. By 1980, there were 187,000 commune-run enterprises, 80,000 more than in 1976.

Some of the original five small industries, notably cement, continued to grow in the late 1970s (Table 21). In 1979, machinery and construction materials (bricks as well as cement) still accounted for more than half of the rising gross value of output of commune-run enterprises, and chemicals and coal another 13%.[48] But at least in communes near urban industrial centers, there was an increasing effort to use commune industries as subcontractors to larger-scale, city-based enterprises. These and other changes led to the already described rapid expansion in small-scale collective industry that occurred in the 1980s. The developments in the 1980s, however, were a part of China's industrialization strategy and only secondarily related to issues of rural development. As such they were discussed earlier, in the section on industrial strategies, and that discussion will not be repeated here.

VII. Rural Policy Changes After 1979

In certain respects, notably in the continued development of small-scale industry, the post-Cultural Revolution period continued trends under way since 1966. In other respects, however, there were dramatic changes. The Ta-chai brigade was publicly pilloried for making false claims. Large labor corvées for rural construction may still exist, but their use has been sharply deemphasized.

In the minds of the Chinese leadership of the early 1980s, China's agricultural performance through 1977 had been inadequate to the country's needs, and the fault lay mainly with bad planning and management and with farmers who had little incentive to work hard or to take any initiative. Where Mao and his colleagues had relied on changes in organization to accomplish agricultural miracles through mass labor mobilization, Teng and his colleagues also relied on reorganization, albeit of a very different kind, to increase agricultural productivity.

---

[47] This, at least, was the case in Shantung province (Wong, "Rural industrialization in the People's Republic of China," 413).

[48] These figures are from *Chung-kuo nung-yeh nien-chien, 1980,* 368.

The first step was to free up the market for rural subsidiary products and to encourage farmers to maximize both their collective and their private incomes. In principle, free markets and private household subsidiary production were restored in 1960 and 1961 and existed uninterrupted thereafter. Private household plots were also restored in 1960 and actually increased modestly in size in the early 1960s[49] and continued in existence throughout the Cultural Revolution period. In practice, private activities of all kinds were constantly under pressure from rural cadres responsible for collective production. These cadres were responsible both for seeing that grain and other collectively raised crop output and delivery targets were met and for ensuring that peasants acquired socialist values and styles of work. Private activities took time away from collective effort and encouraged values that were felt to be "capitalistic." Before 1979, therefore, private trading was on a small scale, and private household activity was probably mainly for one's own use, although no published data exist with which to verify this statement. By 1979, however, private activities, rather than being seen as an unfortunate necessity, were being actively encouraged, with results readily visible to the naked eye. Rural trade fairs blossomed, and farmers by the hundreds of thousands entered cities daily to sell the produce of their private plots. In 1964, private income accounted for about 19% of family income, in the 1966–1976 period the figure was probably lower; but by 1982, private income, according to one survey, may have accounted for 38% of family income.[50]

By 1979, an even more profound change was under way in the organization of collective agricultural activity. In the poorest provinces of China, notably in Anhwei, China's leadership had begun to experiment with something called the "production responsibility system." From 1962 through the 1970s, the basic accounting unit of the collective system was

[49] In 1964, in 10 communes surveyed by a Pakistani delegation, for example, private plots accounted for 7.55% of the total arable land as contrasted to the 5% figure that was the declared government objective. Shahid Javed Burki, *A Study of Chinese Communes, 1965*, 35–36.

[50] The 1960s figure is from *ibid.*, 40. The 1982 figure is from State Statistical Bureau, *Statistical Yearbook of China, 1984*, 471.

based on the production team with an average of 25 families each.[51] The raising of collective crops was organized by the team and the collective income of team members was based mainly on the output of that team. In some cases, representing less than 10% of the rural population, the brigade, the next level up in the commune organizational structure with an average of 200 families, was the basic accounting unit.[52] For the most part, however, the brigade and commune levels dealt with marketing and rural small-scale enterprises, not with the raising of crops. The main agricultural production unit, therefore, was small but its form still collective.

The production responsibility system retained collective or group farming in some cases, but in others responsibility devolved down to the household. In the poorest provinces, by 1981 or 1982, more than 90% of the households were responsible for farming formerly collective land on a household rather than a team basis, and the system was increasingly prevalent in the richer provinces as well. Income in some cases still depended on overall team results, but in other cases even income was determined by what the household itself produced.[53]

By the end of 1983, even these vestiges of collective agriculture had largely disappeared from the Chinese countryside. It no longer made sense to divide income between collective and private sources because almost all farm production was on a household basis. Even the names "commune" and "production brigade" were replaced with the older terms "township" *(hsiang)* and "village" (*ts'un*). Farming, after a quarter century of collective experiments, was once again based on the household as the main producing unit.[54]

---

[51] The figure fluctuates a bit from year to year. This figure is for 1965 (*Chung-kuo nung-yeh nien-chien, 1980*), 5.

[52] *Ibid*.

[53] For a discussion of the various kinds of responsibility systems as of 1981, see Liu Shu-mao, "An introduction to the several types of production responsibility systems currently in use in our rural areas," *Ching-chi guan-li,* 9 (September 15, 1981), 9.12–14. These systems are discussed at greater length in Kathleen Hartford, "Socialist agriculture is dead; long live socialist agriculture!: organizational transformations in rural China," in Elizabeth J. Perry and Christine Wong, eds., *The Political Economy of Reform in Post-Mao China*, 31–62.

[54] The process of transition to household farming has been described and analyzed by a number of authors. The early part of the process is ably described, in part based on first-hand village studies, in William L. Parish, ed., *Chinese Rural Development: The Great*

The role of market forces in the rural areas was also expanded further. Conversion to a market-oriented system of coordination and distribution was inherently simpler in the rural areas than it was for the urban industrial sector. To begin with, a fledgling market for many agricultural products already existed and had been allowed to grow significantly, beginning in 1979, as already mentioned. Even for major crops under collective management before 1979, the market played some role. As a result, crop prices were occasionally changed even during the Cultural Revolution years, and these prices probably did not diverge from true relative scarcities as much as was the case in urban areas.[55] Perhaps most important, farm households as producing units naturally behaved in ways consistent with what the market required. Farm households were natural income or profit maximizers because higher profits meant a higher standard of living for household members. Furthermore, the only way to maximize profits was to increase output or cut production costs. There were no state subsidy schemes or friendly bankers standing by to bail out farm households that consistently ran losses, as there were in industry. The state stepped in only when starvation threatened. Finally, monopoly rights over particular markets were infeasible when one was dealing with several hundred million farm households. Competition was inevitable whether the bureaucracy approved of it or not.

The underlying conditions required by well-functioning markets, therefore, existed in the Chinese countryside. This fact, however, did not mean that all members of the state bureaucracy were comfortable with steps designed to let changes in relative prices govern what was produced and sold. Still, movement toward a market system made much greater progress in agriculture than in industry, and by the mid-1980s, there was a decision in principle to have all farm output bought and sold through the market. Compulsory state purchase quotas for farmers were to be abolished and replaced with voluntary contracts. In practice, however, the state

---

Transformation. See also David Zweig, "Opposition to change in rural China: the system of responsibility and the people's communes," *Asian Survey*, 23.7 (July 1983); Frederick W. Crook, "The reform of the commune system and the rise of the township-collective-household system," in US Congress, Joint Economic Committee, *China's Economy Looks Toward the Year 2000*, 1.354–75.

[55] There were still substantial departures from true scarcity prices, however. See, for example, Nicholas Lardy, "Agricultural prices in China."

bureaucracy was reluctant to surrender that much control. Contracts, at least through 1987, were not completely voluntary.

The nature of the problem as seen through the eyes of the more reluctant reformers can be illustrated with the market for grain. By the mid-1980s, the Chinese government was under great pressure to reduce its role in grain marketing because of the high cost of maintaining the subsidies involved. Urban sales prices for grain were well below the prices paid to farmers, particularly when transport and marketing costs were involved. The resulting losses were a major drain on the resources of the central government.

Simply freeing up grain prices was not a solution that could be taken easily. Urban food prices would have shot up immediately with consequences for political stability that could have been profound. This short-term danger was eased in part by the big grain harvests of 1982–1984, about which more will be said later. With such large surpluses overhanging the market, grain price increases should have been moderated. Still, urban market prices for grain in 1985 were 88% higher than the state list prices so that abolition of all state grain sales would have led to a large price increase, although nothing so large as 88%.[56]

Even if the immediate political problem could have been managed, from the point of view of Party conservatives there was another, more basic, long-term problem connected with reliance on the market for basic foodstuffs. The danger, from the conservatives' perspective, was what would happen if the market failed to stimulate adequate levels of grain output. A serious shortfall in supply could lead to sharp increases in prices or worse, even serious malnutrition, as occurred in parts of the country in 1960 and 1961. That 1960–1961 crisis was a major element in causing the split within the CCP that culminated in the excesses of the Cultural Revolution. This danger did not seem very great in 1985 after three record harvests in a row, but by the end of 1987, the grain harvest for three years

[56] Secondary market prices often will not reflect what would happen if dual markets (one controlled) were replaced by one single uncontrolled market. Prices would rise on this unified market above state control levels of the past, but higher prices would cut back consumption of grain so that demand and supply would normally reach equilibrium at prices below the full secondary market price. Determining the specific price reached, however, involves a variety of assumptions much too complex to deal with in this footnote.

Table 20. Grain imports and exports (annual averages in million metric tons).

	Imports	Exports	Net imports
1950–1960	0.082	2.273	–2.191[a]
1961–1965	5.932	1.623	4.309
1966–1976	5.015	2.772	2.243
1977–1978	8.089	1.767	6.322
1979–1981	13.203	1.419	11.784
1982–1984	13.321	2.135	11.186
1985–1986	6.867	9.372	–2.505

[a] A minus sign indicates net exports.

Source: State Statistical Bureau, *Statistical Yearbook of China, 1981*, 372, 388, 394, 398; *ibid., 1984*, 397; State Staristical Bureau, *Chung-kuo t'ung-chi chai-yao, 1987*, 90–91.

Table 21. Urban and rural consumption per capita (yuan in current prices).

	(1) Rural consumption	(2) Nonrural consumption	(3) Ratio (2) ÷ (1)
1952	62	148	2.39
1957	79	205	2.59
1965	100	237	2.37
1978	132	383	2.90
1980	173	468	2.71
1982	212	500	2.36
1986	352	865	2.46

Source: *Chung-kuo ching-chi nien-chien, 1982*, 7.28; and State Statistical Bureau, *Chung-kuo t'ung-chi chai-yao, 1987*, 98.

running had failed to match the 1984 peak and conservative fears seemed more plausible.

The reality was that in the mid-1980s, China had ample supplies of grain and in 1985–1986 was actually a net exporter despite increases in domestic consumption per capita (see Table 20). Furthermore, China was earning $30 billion a year from its exports as contrasted to less than $2 billion in 1960–1961. In 1987, it was possible to import 10 million tons of grain for a price of around $1 billion. If China had experienced a major harvest failure in 1987 and had been forced to import, say, 50 million tons of grain at then existing world prices, the cost would have been under $6 billion, or less than 20% of China's foreign exchange earnings. Even if world prices of grain had risen sharply, as is possible if Chinese purchases had been so large, China had the foreign exchange to weather the shortfall without a fall in consumption. In any case, direct government intervention in what farmers were allowed to plant, the conservatives' answer to the danger, was a weak foundation on which to build an effective grain security policy. Government-set grain delivery quotas were no protection against bad weather. They did in the past limit farmers' ability to shift out of grain to cash crops, but almost certainly at the cost of a lower level of overall agricultural output than would have been the case in the absence of controls.

The real problem in Chinese agriculture was not the danger of a cyclical downturn caused by bad weather or a sudden decline in grain prices leading to an undesirably large shift of land out of grain. The central issue for Chinese agricultural and food policy was how to meet the nation's rapidly rising demand for food, given an arable-land endowment comparable to that found in Japan, Taiwan, or South Korea. China's East Asian neighbors dealt with this land problem by relying increasingly on food imports. South Korea in 1979, for example, was importing 145 kgs of grain per year for each person in the country. An equivalent level of imports for China would have been 145 million tons of grain purchases from abroad. In the 1980s that level of imports would have been well beyond China's capacity to pay for in foreign exchange.

This longer-term problem was obscured in the early 1980s by the bumper harvests that followed the downturn in crop output in 1980. The reasons for these bumper harvests were varied. Good weather played some role. Freeing up farmers to decide themselves what to produce on their land led to a reallocation of inputs toward cash crops that raised overall agricultural productivity. But grain output also leapt ahead in 1982–1984, suggesting that the relaxation of controls over farmer incentives had a positive impact that went beyond the shift out of grain to cash crops. Key inputs such as chemical fertilizer, farm machinery, and electric power also continued to increase in the 1980s. This chapter is not the place to attempt to measure the precise contribution to output growth of each of these components. The effect of one component no doubt reinforced the impact of the others. Without the introduction of household agricultural production under the responsibility system, however, there is little doubt that farm output growth would have been substantially lower than what in fact occurred in the early 1980.

China's spurt in agricultural growth in the 1980s, when farm output increases (excluding rural industry) averaged more than 9% annually, could not possibly have been sustained for long. The experience appears to have been a one-shot acceleration brought about by the removal of barriers to efficient production. Once higher levels of efficiency had been achieved, the Chinese agricultural growth rate fell back to a more sustainable level in 1985–1987, although poorer weather may also have been a factor. Five percent annual increases in farm output are considered high by world standards, and anything higher is extraordinary. In the East Asian context with its limited land endowment and rapid industrialization, much lower rates are the norm. In Japan, for example, agricultural output in the early 1980s was essentially the same as in the mid-1960s. Per capita grain production was only half as high as in the mid-1960s.[57] In South Korea, a more relevant comparison, agriculture averaged 4.3% per annum between 1965 and 1984, but grain grew at only 1.2% a year.[58] The comparable figures for Taiwan over the same period are 2.4% and minus 0.3%.[59] For China, therefore, a growth rate of total agricultural output of 4% a year and of grain of 2 to 3% a year would be an achievement.

China's long-term problem is that the demand for agricultural products, and for grain in particular, is growing faster than 3 to 4%. In 1980–1984, Chinese demand for grain, for example, must have grown at more

---

[57] United Nations, *Statistical yearbook for Asia and the Pacific, 1984*, 277.

[58] Economic Planning Board, *Major Statistics of Korean Economy, 1986*, 75.

[59] Council for Economic Planning and Development, *Taiwan Statistical Data Book, 1986,* 65, 67.

than 5% a year,[60] but production grew at more than 6% a year, generating a surplus that made it possible for China to become a net exporter in 1985–1986. If grain output were to grow on a sustained basis at 3% a year, demand at current rates of industrialization and national income growth will increase by at least 4% a year if not higher, and China will revert to being a major grain importer like its East Asian neighbors.

The responsibility system and the resulting spurt in agricultural development, therefore, gave China a brief respite from the country's long-term agricultural problem. Industrialization could surge ahead and per capita incomes in the rural areas could double without demand for food outstripping the domestic supply. By 1987, however, China may have gotten back on a more normal trend consistent with the country's having only 0.1 hectare per capita of arable land. The agricultural choices for the future, therefore, were more likely to resemble those faced in the late 1970s. Accelerated growth in real per capita income was possible provided that China invested enough in agriculture to ensure a growth rate in that sector sufficient to keep agricultural imports from growing more rapidly than China's ability to earn foreign exchange to pay for them. For investment in agriculture to have this desired impact, it was also essential for farmers to be given incentives to use this investment and other inputs to maximum effect, as occurred in the early 1980s.

A reversion to controls over farm output would have solved China's long-term excess demand for grain, mainly if it succeeded in lowering incentives by enough to slow markedly the growth in incomes and hence of demand. A turn inward away from an export promotion strategy would have had much the same result. By slowing national income growth overall because of slow import growth for all products, not just grain, demand for grain could be held down. Alternatively, the state could have reimposed a rigorous rationing system that would have held down grain consumption despite a rapid rise in income. Given those kinds of choices, it

[60]Chinese income was growing at about 9% per year. A conservative estimate of the income elasticity of demand for grain (including grain fed to animals) would be 0.6, which would mean that demand for grain would grow at 5.4% a year. Different assumptions give different results, but it is difficult to come up with plausible assumptions that result in a growth rate in demand of below 5% for this period.

is hardly surprising that some reformers, at least, preferred a more market-oriented policy to encourage farmer incentives combined with vigorous export promotion to meet the foreign exchange requirements of anticipated increases in food imports.[61]

Income distribution

Whatever the virtues and drawbacks for production of the way agriculture was organized in the 1966–1976 period, it was widely believed that the system at least reduced inequalities within the rural sector and between urban and rural residents. Policy changes after 1978, it was feared, would lead to increasing inequality. Data published in the early 1980s raise questions about both of these hypotheses. Land reform in the late 1940s and early 1950s, as Roll's estimates have shown, led to a major increase in income of the poorest 20% of the rural population, mostly at the expense of landlords, who lost most of their possessions without compensation.[62] Inequalities that remained in the 1953–1955 period were those between rich and poor peasants in a given region and between rich and poor regions. The formation of APCs in 1955–1956 eliminated differences in the amount of land owned. Inequality remaining within the cooperative (and later the production team) was due to variations between families in the ratio of healthy adult workers to nonworking dependents (children, aged parents, and the sick). Although these differences could be substantial, they were a far cry from inequalities caused by variations in the amount of land owned.

What impressed visitors to the Chinese countryside was this relatively egalitarian structure within any given collective unit. What visitors could not or did not see were the large disparities in income between regions. Collectivization could have no impact on these disparities at all. Farmers

[61] Tu Jen-sheng, in a talk to a conference on township and village enterprises in Peking in November 1987, for example, made an explicit connection between export promotion policies and solutions to the grain problem.

[62] C. R. Roll, "The distribution of rural income in China: comparison of the 1930s and the 1950s."

in poor mountainous regions banded together in a team with other poor farmers in the same region, as did rich suburban farmers. The better-off farmers in the mountainous region, whose income was still well below the national rural average, experienced a decline in income, whereas the less well-off suburban farmers, whose income was often double the national average, experienced a rise.

Data necessary for a definitive calculation are not available, but a manipulation of Roll's data suggests that inequality declined little if at all in 1956–1957 as a result of collectivization.[63] Regional differences were great enough to dominate any decrease in inequality within collective units. The question of central relevance to this chapter is whether measures taken after 1965 in any way changed this outcome.

A decline in rural inequality could have been achieved in any of four ways: Progressive taxes on the rural communes could have reduced inequality, but there was little if any progressivity in the Chinese tax system. Welfare payments to the poorest regions would also have helped. Although there is much we do not know about the Chinese rural welfare system, transfers between regions appear to be quite small. Communes faced with serious malnutrition apparently got support, but most other communes were expected to fend for themselves. A third measure would have been to move peasants from the poorest regions into richer ones, but in a nation with little new land to open up this is a method guaranteed to produce severe rural conflict. Finally, the state could have directed investment and current inputs toward the poorest rural areas, and may on occasion have done so. But such a policy will frequently be at the cost of slower increases in productivity because the rate of return on investment in many poor areas is going to be low. It is often the richer areas that have the adequate supplies of water that make it possible to use more chemical fertilizer and improved plant varieties.

---

[63] Roll's data give the income of rich, middle, and poor peasants by region. If one assumes that all rich and poor peasants in a given region had the same income as middle peasants after collectivization, one can derive a gini coefficient for this simulated distribution of 0.211, only marginally less than the 0.227 figure for the precollectivization (and post-land reform) periods.

There is little reason, therefore, to expect that rural inequality, albeit low compared with that in most other developing countries, declined much in the 1960s and 1970s, and the few figures available appear to support this view. A standard measure of inequality is the gini coefficient whose value can range from "0" (perfect equality) to "1" (perfect inequality). Data on the distribution of brigade collective income in 1980, for example, suggest a gini coefficient of 0.232, which is virtually identical with the 0.227 coefficient obtained from Roll's data for the period after land reform and preceding collectivization.[64] This conclusion is reinforced by provincial data that suggest that 70% of the differences in per capita rural income between provinces can be accounted for by differences in the quantity and quality of land per capita.[65] Because the relative quality and quantity of land per capita between regions changed little over the 1960s and 1970s, relative incomes changed little as well.

Did changes after 1978 alter this picture? Generally, it is difficult to discern trends in income distribution over short periods, and available Chinese data are not suitable for such precise calculations in any case. It is possible, however, that already rich communes near cities and major transport lines benefited disproportionately from opportunities to expand cash crops and subsidiary activities. Poor mountainous regions, after all, cannot deliver vegetables to urban residents, nor are they usually in a position to do subcontracting work for urban enterprises. Liberalized economic controls, therefore, may have led to some rise in inequality in the early 1980s.

When we turn to the question of what happened to rural–urban differences in income, however, the connection between liberalized controls and greater inequality is much less clear. Liberalization, under certain conditions, in fact, could lead to a significant decline in inequality.

A central feature of the entire 1960s and 1970s period was the virtual prohibition on rural-to-urban migration. In addition, urban youth were shipped off to rural communes and state farms by the millions. At the same time, as described earlier in the chapter, the state continued to pour investment into urban-based industry. While this investment became increasingly capital intensive, there was still a steadily rising demand for

---

[64] Roll, "The distribution of rural income in China," 72.

[65] Dwight Perkins and Shahid Yusuf, *Rural development in China,* 115–119.

labor in the urban areas, a demand that had to be met either by people who were already urban residents or by those who lived in nearby communes from which they could commute into the city and thus avoid the need for an urban residence permit. The result in the cities was a steady rise in the ratio of workers to dependents within the city population, and an increase in urban job opportunities for those communes that were already the richest in the nation. Wages did not rise, but urban per capita consumption, as a result, did rise much faster in the cities than in the countryside, as the data in Table 21 indicate. Comparable data on suburban communes are not available, but they would probably indicate a similar trend.

What happened after 1978? Part of the answer is that rural-to-urban migration was not one of the liberalization measures introduced in that period. Many urban youth sent off to the countryside were allowed to return or returned on their own accord, and some rural people were allowed to move into the smaller towns by the mid-1980s, but rural residents still could not move to the cities easily. Large increases in purchase prices for farm produce did improve the rural residents' relative position, but because urban food sales prices were not raised, the cost of this measure to the central government budget was large and not likely to be repeated.[66] Large-scale investments in urban housing and general urban wage increases have helped urban residents keep their relative position vis-à-vis the rural areas. In any case, as long as farmers in the poorer regions of China are restrained from leaving those areas and moving to the cities or even to the county towns, rapid industrialization is likely to be accompanied by a large and possibly widening rural–urban income gap. The narrowing in 1980 and 1982 over 1978, therefore, should not be seen as the beginning of a long-term trend. The gap did in fact widen in 1986, although the quality of the data in Table 21 are such that strong conclusions cannot be drawn from small differences in the estimates.

VIII. Conclusions

Clearly, it is wrong to say that there was no economic strategy at all during the Cultural Revolution period. The investment plan was an unmodified

[66]This issue is discussed at greater length in Lardy, "Agricultural prices in China."

version of a Stalinist emphasis on machinery and steel. Self-reliance or minimizing dependence on foreign imports and foreign technology had a Maoist ring when included in the rhetoric of the 1966–1976 decade, but in practice self-reliance was not dramatically different from the Chinese autarkic policies of the 1950s or Russian policies toward foreign trade in the 1930s.

In rural China, policies owed much less to Soviet experience. To begin with, there was recognition that stagnation in agricultural output could be fatal. The question was how to achieve agricultural growth, not whether to do so, and China had a two-pronged strategy that combined the ideas of both "pragmatists" and "radicals" in an uneasy juxtaposition. The "pragmatists" pushed the rapid development of a chemical fertilizer industry plus increases in fertilizer imports. Those closer to Mao promoted the mass mobilization of labor and the Ta-chai model. They also insisted that a large portion of the modern inputs required by agriculture be provided by small-scale plants in rural areas.

In form, the system of planning and control over the economy remained true to the centralized Soviet model, modified only slightly by reforms instituted in the early 1960s. Five-year plans may have been problematic, but annual plans still governed what an enterprise was to produce. And key commodities and equipment were allocated by administrative means rather than through a market. Wages were paid in accordance with the Soviet eight-grade system, and rural collective incomes were based on the number of work points earned just as in the 1950s (except for the Great Leap) and the early 1960s.

If the form was the same, the actual implementation of policies within that form changed considerably in the late 1960s and early 1970s. The Soviet eight-grade wage system was designed to provide material incentives for more productive effort, but the Chinese removed these incentives by freezing promotions and eliminating bonuses. In the rural areas, political attitudes often counted for as much as effort in allocating work points. At the management level, enterprises continued to receive targets for cost and input reduction, but these targets did not have to be taken seriously if output targets were met. In addition, political considerations regularly interfered with judgments made in other countries on more technical grounds.

During the Cultural Revolution period itself, political interference and efforts to curtail the use of material incentives do not appear to have slowed growth. In fact, now that data are available with which to analyze growth in the late 1960s and early 1970s, development in the period, to the surprise of many analysts, was quite rapid except for the two years, 1967 and 1968, when political chaos was at a peak. But growth was built on ever higher levels of investment and inputs of energy that were being used more and more inefficiently with the passage of time. As long as the investment could continue to be raised and the Ta-ch'ing field poured out more and more petroleum, this was a viable means of maintaining growth, although a less effective means of raising the living standards of the population.

By the mid-1970s, however, labor discipline was breaking down after two decades of stagnant real wages, and production from the Ta-ch'ing and other oil fields peaked and threatened to decline. The rate of investment continued to rise, but the capital–output ratio may have been rising even faster. The years of steady growth based on the profligate use of human and material resources were coming to an end, whoever held the reins of political power.

Following Mao's death and the purge of the Gang of Four, in an attempt to accelerate development the interim leadership of China in 1977–1978 made a dramatic turn outward, encouraging enterprises to import foreign technology in great quantity, and made an equally dramatic reversal of Cultural Revolution incentive policies by restoring bonuses, raising farm purchase prices, and implementing general wage increases and promotions. But the emphasis on machinery and steel continued, and this emphasis was not consistent with the new incentive and foreign trade policies.

In late 1978 and early 1979, Chinese planners finally abandoned Stalinist economics, at least temporarily. For the first time, consumer goods received priority over producer goods both for home consumption and for export. China's development strategy had made a significant step toward the pattern pursued so successfully by its East Asian neighbors.

Some features of the first phases of the reform period did not last long. The effort to slow the overall growth rate so as to "readjust" the economic structure did not extend beyond 1981, when the growth rate in both industry and agriculture shot up. The deemphasis on heavy industry also proved to be temporary. In the 1982–1986 period, the ratio of heavy to light industry growth reverted back to levels similar to those prevailing during the Cultural Revolution. Stagnation in the supply of energy gave way to renewed growth in that crucial sector, making it possible once again to push the energy-using heavy industry sectors.

China's sectoral development strategy did not revert completely to earlier patterns, however. The turn outward, with an emphasis on expanded exports, borrowing abroad, and foreign direct investment in China, not only continued but grew and took on ever more diverse dimensions. The deemphasis on light industry and consumer goods was more apparent than real. The surge in agricultural production meant that consumer products to match the higher wages and other incentive payments were available.

In terms of sectoral growth strategies, China had made a significant move in the direction of the strategy that had proved so successful among its East Asian neighbors. Exports did not play as large a role in the development strategy of China as they did for, say, South Korea, but that was more a reflection of China's large size and the fact that trade is typically a smaller share of gross national product (GNP) in large countries than in small ones. China's trade ratios, though much smaller than those of South Korea or Taiwan, were similar to the ratios that prevailed in Japan in the 1960s. This Chinese trade ratio in comparison with the country's smaller neighbors was also an important reason why China had to pay more attention to the growth of heavy industry at this early stage of development as compared to South Korea, which in the 1960s could concentrate on light industry and meet its heavy industrial product needs through imports.

Changes in sectoral strategies were only one part of the reforms introduced after Mao's death in 1976 and the Third Plenum in December 1978. Of potentially greater significance were the moves fundamentally to change the system used to manage the economy.

Loosening of central management over foreign trade began as early as 1977, but centralized control had to be restored when enterprises took advantage of the situation to begin signing contracts for imports far in excess of China's ability to pay for them. The first reforms that lasted involved the removal of controls over the operation of rural markets. These were followed in the early 1980s by the introduction of the responsibility system that culminated in 1983 with the effective abandonment of collective agriculture. In five short years, 1979–1983, China had gone from a collectivized agricultural system tightly controlled from above by a combination of state-set quotas and more informal slogans enforced by party cadres, to individual household agriculture controlled mainly through the indirect mechanisms of the market. A few marketing quotas remained, but steps were taken in the mid-1980s to begin removing these as well.

Removal of the Soviet-style system of planning and management in industry moved at a slower pace, in part because the changes required were much more complex than was the case with agriculture. Experiments with industrial systems reform began as early as 1979. These first efforts were in essence attempts to make the Soviet-style bureaucratic-command system work better. Changes were made in the way firms were managed internally, monopoly control over regional markets was relaxed in favor of competition, and the priority given to various plan targets was adjusted to give greater emphasis to efficiency-oriented targets and less emphasis to output targets.

By October 1984, in part because of the dramatic success of the rural reforms, the Party called for much more sweeping reforms in the industrial sector. Over the next three years, important steps were taken toward changing China's industrial management and control system away from the centralized bureaucratic-command system of the past in the direction of a system combining market methods of control and coordination with continued bureaucratic control in key sectors. The goal, for some of the reformers at least, was a socialist version of the mix of market and state controls found in Japan or South Korea in the 1960s. The reality by the end of 1987, however, fell far short of this goal. Some members of the Politburo elected at the CCP's 13th Congress in October 1987 probably still opposed changes of this magnitude in the economic system. Of equal or greater importance, bureaucratic systems of control were deeply entrenched and even the most determined reformers faced many obstacles in attempting to root them out.

In many ways, China's changes in sectoral strategy and efforts to reform its economic system represented a long-delayed recognition of the country's underlying economic resources. The problem in agriculture was how to get the most food out of a very limited land endowment and an excess of labor power. Efforts to accomplish this goal through mass labor mobilization had failed. More chemical fertilizer and improved plant varieties were part of the answer, but equally important was the need to use these inputs more efficiently. Household-based agriculture had proved to be an efficient user of resources elsewhere in Asia and proved after 1981 that it could do equally well in China.

Similarly, a highly centralized system of planning and control was bound to be an inefficient method for controlling and coordinating several hundred thousand small-scale enterprises producing under widely varying conditions. Attempts to assert central control had led to local monopolies and other measures that seriously interfered with the growth and efficiency of the small-scale enterprise sector. When these controls were dismantled, the sector boomed.

With the boom in both agriculture and industry, China's GNP rose at a rate nearly comparable to that experienced in the earlier booms of South Korea, Taiwan, and Japan. For 11 straight years from 1977 through 1987, China's net material product averaged a growth rate of over 8% a year. In per capita terms, GNP doubled. Even with growth of this magnitude, however, China's economy in per capita terms was probably only comparable to that of Korea in the mid-1960s and to Taiwan's a few years earlier. The majority of China's labor force was still in agriculture, and an even larger percentage of the population still lived in rural areas. These percentages were falling rapidly in the 1980s, but it would take an additional decade or more of comparably rapid growth before most of China's population and work force would be urban and industrial.

The benefits of this first phase of accelerated growth were widely shared by the people of China. In fact, because the rural areas experienced the economic boom first, there even may have been some reduction in inequality nationwide in the early 1980s. The urban areas did less well, but their incomes did rise and most urban families began to purchase such consumer durables as refrigerators and television sets. Conceivably, continued rapid growth based on market principles could lead to increasing inequality. But in the late 1980s, China still had a highly egalitarian distribution of the benefits of growth.

China by the end of 1987, therefore, was not a carbon copy of its East Asian neighbors on a mammoth scale. A socialist system evolving out of

Soviet-style central planning was bound to end up somewhat differently from the mixed planning and market systems based on private ownership found elsewhere in East Asia no matter how hard Chinese reformers pushed for greater use of the market. China was also still some distance from the urban prosperity found in the rest of East Asia in the late 1980s. But China by the late 1980s had taken several giant steps away from the rural peasant economy steeped in poverty that had existed for millennia and that was still in evidence in modified form in the early 1970s.

CHINA'S ECONOMIC REFORMS, 1978–2013

CHAPTER 6

REFORMING CHINA'S ECONOMIC SYSTEM*

I. Introduction

Following the death of Mao Zedong in 1976, China's leadership put revolutionary politics and class struggle aside and set out to make the nation wealthy and powerful. Economic development became the number one priority, even more than was the case in the 1950s. Equally important, those who took over the levers of economic policy after 1978 were reform minded. Most of these new leaders had been treated badly during the Cultural Revolution period (1966–1976) and had a strong distaste for many of the policies and values that played so large a role during that decade. Many were also aware that China's economic performance over more than two decades suffered in comparison to that of the country's East Asian neighbors.

It is unlikely that China's leaders had a worked out blueprint in mind when they set out to reform the economic system. One reform led on to another until China by 1987 had moved a considerable distance from the Soviet-style command system it had introduced in the 1950s.

This reform process was still under way in 1987 and appears likely to continue for some time. Where it will all end is not known to anyone either inside or outside of China. But enough is known about what has occurred to date to step back and take stock of these reforms in midstream.

**Note regarding Chinese names:* Chinese authors are cited in text in accord with their practice of putting the family name before the given name; so, for example, a name that appears in the discussion as "Dong Furen' will be found in the reference list under "Dong." Some exceptions occur in the case of authors with Chinese names who have written articles for Western publications.

The first part of this essay is devoted to a description of the rural and urban reforms introduced between 1977 and 1987 and an analysis of the rationale, implicit as well as explicit, behind these reforms. The latter half of the essay looks at the impact of reform on economic performance. Did productivity increase and economic structure change as a result of the reforms? Did the standard of living of urban and rural consumers rise and were the benefits of accelerated growth distributed equitably, or was inequality on the rise as market mechanisms became more and more important?

The analysis in this chapter draws on many sources. The perspective of this essay is that of a Western economist observing China's economy from the outside, and the chapter draws heavily on the works of other Western economists who approach China's economy from a similar perspective. This essay also makes extensive use of official Chinese statistics, occasionally modifying these figures in an attempt to eliminate known biases. The major Chinese statistical handbook of the relatively open publication period of the 1950s contained only 200 pages of tables, and publication of all statistics by China virtually ceased between 1960 and 1980. Since 1980, however, the Chinese have been publishing economic data at an accelerating rate. The official 1986 statistical yearbook, for example, contains over 800 pages of data, each page containing much more data than its 1950s equivalent. In addition, many individual provinces and economic sectors have published their own statistical handbooks that are full of data not in the national handbook.[1]

There is also a rapidly burgeoning literature in China's numerous economics journals some of which deal with issues discussed in this essay, particularly issues connected with the reform of the economic system. Only sporadic references will be made to this literature. Any

[1] In addition to the general handbooks, for example, there are yearbooks that include data and much other relevant information on the iron and steel industry (Ministry of Ferrous Metals Compilation Committee, 1985), coal (Ministry of Coal Industry Compiling Committee, 1982), agriculture (China Agricultural Yearbook Compilation Committee, every year since 1980), the urban sector (State Statistical Bureau, 1985a), and commerce (Trade and Price Office of the State Statistical Bureau, 1984). Provincial statistical handbooks include ones for poor provinces rarely visited by foreigners such as Guizhou (Guizhou Yearbook Compilation Committee, 1985) as well as the richer coastal provinces.

attempt to do justice to the various discussions and debates in Chinese journals would require a separate essay or essays devoted to that purpose alone.

II. Economic System Reform

The key to making China wealthy and powerful was to raise total factor productivity. The idea was understood clearly enough even if the Chinese did not use the term. The Soviet-style system of centralized bureaucratic control over the economy had proved effective in mobilizing capital and labor inputs, but the amount mobilized had to rise continually and rapidly simply to maintain a gross national product (GNP) growth rate between 4 and 5% per year, corresponding to a per capita growth rate of 2 to 3%.

Debate over the course of economic reform has been vigorous, but most participants appear to share a common perception of the nature of the problem. Central planning led to a misallocation of both investment goods and of current inputs and outputs. Excessive control from the center, together with restrictions on the use of material incentives of any kind, dampened the energies and enthusiasm of workers, managers, and farmers alike. In the terminology of modern economics, there was both allocative inefficiency and X inefficiency on a grand scale.

Among debate participants there was also some agreement on what was required to improve efficiency and raise productivity growth. Production units in industry and agriculture needed to be given greater autonomy to make decisions on the basis of their superior understanding of local circumstances. And rewards, whether in the form of wages, bonuses, or payments to farmers, should be closely tied to economic performance. Moral as contrasted to material work incentives, to the extent they were given any attention at all, were to play a secondary role.[2]

---

[2]One way of partially understanding the campaigns against "spiritual pollution" and corruption is to see them as an indirect way of attacking what was perceived by some as an excessive emphasis on material incentives. The focus of attacks has been on cadres who take bribes to commit illegal acts, but the line between what is legal and illegal is often a fuzzy one in the Chinese economic system. An attack on corruption thus can become a generalized attack on an "excessive" pursuit of profits or other "capitalist" values, hence on material incentives.

Where consensus broke down in China was over how to achieve greater enterprise and farmer autonomy and how to tie reward more closely to performance. Opinions ranged from those who would retain a dominant role for central planning and bureaucratic control to those who would move to full-fledged market socialism. By 1985, the balance of power had shifted toward advocates of a major or even a dominant role for the market, but many features of central planning remained entrenched in the system and there were considerable differences even among advocates of the market on how much further to go and at what speed.

China's efforts to increase enterprise autonomy and raise productivity are in many respects similar in nature to efforts at liberalization under way in the 1970s and 1980s in a number of developing countries ranging from India to Brazil. The essence of liberalization is to reduce the hold of the government bureaucracy over the economy and to replace bureaucratic direction with the impersonal forces of the market. Enterprise managers in the bureaucratic system are simply lower-level bureaucrats fighting with each other and with higher-level bureaucrats to get a larger share of the goods and other forms of support that are in the higher-level bureaucrats' hands to give out. In a true market system, on the other hand, enterprise managers must succeed or fail on the basis of their ability to lower their own production costs or to market more of what they produce at a higher price.[3]

Defining liberalization in this way, China differs from other developing countries mainly in the distance it must travel to reach some form of a market system. Soviet-style central planning involves more or less complete bureaucratic control over industry and even much of agriculture, while most developing countries have a mixture of centralized planning, bureaucratically manipulated markets, and markets that are free of bureaucratic manipulation.

The more government bureaucracies attempt to intervene in markets, the more the system slides back toward one of bureaucratic planning even if it is in a slightly disguised form. If China were formally to abolish centrally determined compulsory plan targets for enterprises as, for example,

[3]This part of the analysis owes much to discussions with János Kornai. See particularly János Kornai (1986).

has been done in Hungary, it does not follow that enterprise managers would give up behaving in accordance with bureaucratic principles. More is required.

What are the essential features of a well-functioning market system that the Chinese would have to duplicate if they are to achieve something approaching full-fledged market socialism? These features are discussed first in the abstract and then compared with what is actually happening in China in both the rural and urban areas. There are four essential features:

(1) Inputs and outputs must be available for purchase and sale on the market. Some goods and factors may be centrally allocated, but the marginal decisions of managers should mainly involve whether to purchase more or less on the market, not whether to go back to the government bureaucracy for a larger administrative allocation.

(2) Enterprise or farm decision makers must behave in accordance with the rules of well-functioning markets — that is, they must approximate some form of profit-maximizing behavior. Few enterprise managers anywhere in the world are pure profit maximizers, but a well-functioning market requires that they give primary attention to raising profits.

This criterion seems at first glance to be easy to meet. It might be thought that in a Soviet-style system of planning such as that in China, all one need do is to change manager success criteria from fulfillment and overfulfillment of the gross value output target to overfulfillment of a profits target. In practice, much more is involved. The planners and other elements of the bureaucracy will always have objectives that involve more than profit maximization, so the question becomes one of whether enterprise managers will have to pay attention to those objectives or can safely ignore them. They cannot safely ignore them if,

(a) the selection of enterprise managers is done by the bureaucracy as contrasted to some kind of board of directors that is concerned with profit;

(b) inputs are in chronic short supply so that some form of rationed allocation by the bureaucracy results even if formal central allocation has been abolished;

(c) entry of new firms into an industry or exit of firms from an industry is determined by the bureaucracy. Entry, for example, may require a government license. Exit of firms in difficulty can be and frequently is prevented by government intervention in the form of bail out loans and other similar measures.

The features (b) and (c) are closely related to a common feature of most socialist countries, the "soft budget constraint." If enterprises have access to almost unlimited credit and subsidies as long as they stay in favor with the bureaucracy, the incentive to be concerned with profits will be weak.

The issues of enterprise success criteria, enterprise autonomy, and the soft budget constraint are also tied in with the question of ownership. It is sometimes naively assumed that private ownership guarantees enterprise autonomy, but bureaucracies can interfere with privately owned firms as well as public ones. In any case, China has very little of what could be termed private ownership except in agriculture and the service sector. Most enterprises are either fully public, owned by the state, or collective, owned by their workers but subject to state direction. The Chinese have clearly rejected selling off large state enterprises to private owners or encouraging new large private firms except where foreign investment is involved. But there has been much talk about alternative forms of public and collective ownership that might contribute, among other things, to making enterprises more independent of the bureaucracy. So far, however, the experiments along this line have been modest.[4]

(3) The markets faced by enterprise managers must be competitive. Perfect competition in a world of oligopoly, of course, is not feasible. But in many developing countries, monopolistic situations are more often the creations of government interventions than of underlying "natural" economic conditions. Quotas and other instruments of trade policy in particular are often used to give a favored enterprise shelter

---

[4]There is a lively discussion in the Chinese literature on issues of ownership and an interest in such systems as the "share economy" and "capital markets" among other things. See, for example, Dong Furen (1985) and Shi Yousheng (1986).

from international competition. Licensing can accomplish much the same ends within the domestic market. The Chinese in the early 1970s even went so far as to give most small-scale enterprises monopolies over their local markets and to prohibit sales beyond that market.

(4) Prices on a well-functioning market must reflect long-run relative scarcities in the economy. Prices that depart from this principle give the wrong signals to producers and consumers. The result is misallocation and inefficiency.

Liberalization is often seen by economists as a question of "getting the prices right." In nations where all of the other features of a market system are working reasonably well, all that may remain is the task of letting prices adjust to reflect relative scarcities. Some of the early discussion of reform in China stressed the central importance of price reform once inputs and outputs became available on the market.[5] The theme is still an important one and deservedly so, but there is increasing awareness that there is more to making a market work efficiently than "getting the prices right." Indeed, if the other requirements of well-functioning markets are present, the "prices" will be right if they are not controlled.

The prereform economic system

What was the nature of the economic system that China's leadership set out to reform?[6]

Agriculture in China was collectivized in the winter of 1955–1956 by the formation of agricultural producers' cooperatives with an average size

---

[5]Since the 1950s, there has been a vigorous debate in Chinese over the appropriate role of prices and how prices should be determined. In the early 1960s, Sun Yefang was one of the major advocates of greater use of the market and of price reform. He was severely criticized and the Institute of Economics was abolished for a time partly as a result. The debate over the reform of prices continues to attract the attention of economists. In the journal *Jingji yanjiu* (Economic Research), for example, in the two and a half years following the issuing of the urban reform directive in October 1984, there were a dozen or more articles dealing with aspects of price reform and the role of prices in the Chinese system. See, for example, Xue Muqiao (1985); Wang Zhenzhong (1985); and Yu Guangyuan (1986).

[6]For those interested in the English language literature on China's economy in the prereform period, see Dwight H. Perkins (1983).

of about 200 families. Most crop production was done on a collective basis with individuals receiving work points based on the amount of time, effort, skill, and political attitude brought to their collective work. Collective income at the end of the year was determined by the number of work points accumulated plus the value of each work point. The latter was calculated from the net income of the cooperative after deducting taxes, investment expenditures, and a welfare fund. Farm household members also worked in their spare time at home and on small "private plots" that constituted about 5% of all arable land. Household production could be sold on free markets that were allowed to exist for that purpose. Collective product was sold to the state marketing system. The state set quotas for the deliveries of the main crops and fixed prices for those deliveries at levels below what would have been required to elicit voluntary sales.

This cooperative system went through convulsive changes during the Great Leap Forward of 1958–1959 with the formation of Rural People's Communes, but by 1962 the system had reverted to being much like what had existed in 1956–1957, although the names were changed. At the height of the Commune movement in 1958 and 1959, the basic collective unit had around 5,000 families and food was being distributed as much on the basis of need as on the basis of the number of work points earned. Private plots and free markets were abolished and peasants were left with little time for household production. By 1962, the basic collective unit for organizing labor and determining the value of the work points (the basic accounting unit) had become the production team, a subunit of the Commune with only 20 to 30 families. Private plots equivalent to about 7% of arable land had been restored and free markets or rural trade fares were once again allowed to exist on a restricted basis. The marketing of collectively produced crops continued to be done through the state system on the basis of state set quotas.

This collective agricultural system remained intact with only modest changes until the end of the 1970s. There were variations in how work points were determined and a few brigades, subunits of the commune with several hundred families, were made basic accounting units. But these changes left the key features of the system of the early 1960s intact.

In industry in the 1950s, the Chinese leadership set out to create a system consciously patterned on that of the Soviet Union. Thousands of

Soviet technicians came to China to help install the system, and Chinese regulations governing the way the system worked were often direct translations of Soviet regulations. The first step in the early 1950s was for the state to take over all enterprises, whether public or private, controlled by the Kuomintang government or by the Japanese. By 1956, virtually all industry and large-scale commerce had been socialized. Even what were called joint public-private enterprises were really enterprises owned and controlled by the state.

Along with ownership went the installation of a Soviet-style system of central planning and control. The first five-year plan in principle governing major investment projects for the 1953–1957 period was not published until 1955, but had some influence on investment in the latter part of the plan period. Annual plans set output targets that enterprises were obligated to try to surpass and input targets that governed the state's allocation of most important inputs. Inputs and outputs were generally not available on any market but only through the state's material allocation system. For the most part enterprises tried to maximize gross value output subject to these planned input constraints. Financial variables such as profits played only a secondary role backing up the plans' physical targets. The banking system was also little more than a unit designed to use financial controls to help enforce the physical targets. Investment in major new plant and equipment was carried out by separate enterprises in accordance with the plan and the new capacity was turned over to the producing enterprise on completion.

Almost from the beginning, the Chinese were dissatisfied with the degree of centralization of decision-making implied by this Soviet-style system. During the Great Leap Forward they virtually abandoned central planning and decentralized decision making to the enterprise. But decentralization was not accompanied by any method for coordinating inputs and outputs and the result was chaos.

As in agriculture, the state in the early 1960s attempted to restore many of the features of the pre-Great Leap system, but with one important modification. Planning based on physical input and output targets and the state-run material allocation system was restored, but no longer was all planning and allocation to be done by Beijing. Instead, many planning and allocation decisions were decentralized to the province and later even to the county. Provinces in China have an average population of 30 to 40 million and some approach 100 million or more. In many cases, enterprises obtained most of their inputs from within the province and most of their output was sold to others in the same province; hence, there was no need to coordinate these inputs and outputs on a nationwide basis. By the 1970s, a large proportion of Chinese enterprises were under the authority of the provinces rather than Beijing. In most cases, particularly with larger enterprises in strategic sectors, Beijing retained effective control even if planning formally was at the provincial level.

Trade between provinces in this decentralized system was handled in a way analogous to foreign trade. State trading firms in the provinces determined what was required from outside the province and the resources available to export in exchange. Unlike the situation with foreign trade, however, Beijing then balanced the various provincial demands and supplies and allocated financial subsidies to those provinces running a deficit.

Formally, five-year plans and annual plans at both the national and provincial level continued to be drawn up and to govern performance throughout the 1960s and 1970s. In practice, in the Cultural Revolution period (1966–1976), there were many forces interfering with any attempt at systematic planning. Scholars continue to debate whether a system of central planning existed in this period. One thing is certain, however. By some mechanism, inputs and outputs and their allocation between enterprises were coordinated in a way that avoided the chaos of the Great Leap Forward, and this coordination was in no sense achieved through a revived market mechanism. China in the industrial sphere remained a nearly complete bureaucratic command system. It is not clear just who in the bureaucracy did much of the planning and control of enterprises, but planning and control through the bureaucracy did take place. Prices were set by this bureaucracy as was the case prior to the Cultural Revolution. The level of savings and investment outside the rural sector was largely determined by the state budget. Enterprises had almost no autonomy and were, in effect, simply the bottom layer in a bureaucratic hierarchy.

Rural reform

Reform of the economic system in rural areas preceded that in urban areas in part because the task in rural areas was easier and in part because many of the previously described conditions necessary for a well-functioning market were already in place before the reform effort began.

It is likely that no one in the Chinese government realized how far the process would take them when they started out on the task of rural reform after the Third Plenum held in December 1978. The objective was simply to raise the material rewards going to farmers and to relate those rewards as firmly as possible to the effort expended.

The first step was to free up the rural trade fairs or "free markets," a step implemented in 1979. Limited free markets, as pointed out above, had existed in China throughout the period of collective farming (1956–1982) except for a year or two following the initial formation of the People's Communes. Their main function was to provide an outlet for the goods produced by the farm household working in its spare time and on its private plot. The private plots, with 7% of the arable land of the collective, were themselves a compromise with full collectivization designed to give farmers an incentive to work in their spare time. Grain and the major cash crops, with few exceptions, were raised on collective land and sold to the state partly because the task of raising and harvesting grain lent itself to collective management and supervision. State control over the supply and marketing of grain was also seen as critical for maintaining the urban food supply. Supervising and planning household spare-time activities, in contrast, was completely beyond the capacity of rural cadres. Hogs and vegetables, for example, were largely spare time products, and when attempts were made to restrict private hog and vegetable farming, the result was invariably a sharp drop in the output and marketing of these products. Such drops occurred in 1955–1956 and again in 1958–1960.

While private plots and rural trade fairs had existed throughout the decade of the Cultural Revolution (1966–1976), they were tightly controlled and their scope severely limited by rural cadres who opposed them on both ideological and practical grounds. The "practical" grounds were that private plots and free markets made the cadre's task of getting farmers to work on collective land more difficult. The marginal rate of return to peasants on private land was much higher than on collective land.

There is no reliable measure of the extent that rural markets were freed up in 1979, although the results were readily apparent to any traveler who visited the Chinese countryside in both the early 1970s and 1979. The impact on household incomes is also measurable. Income from raising poultry, livestock, and other small animals, primarily a private activity, jumped 58% in 1979 and another 35% in 1980 (State Statistical Bureau, 1984). These increases are in current prices but inflation was less than 5% a year. Poultry and livestock were only one particularly dynamic component of private activity, but overall, according to one carefully reconstructed estimate, private sideline income rose by 10% in 1979 and 11% in 1980 as contrasted to 2.8 and 6.9% for rural collective income in those same two years (Lee Travers, 1984).

Reform of Chinese agriculture's collective sector also began in 1979 but proceeded slowly until 1981 when the replacement of Hua Guofeng by Hu Yaobang as Communist party chairman removed the most reluctant reformer from a leadership position.[7] The name given to the new ways of organizing agriculture was the "responsibility system," and its spread was the result both of spontaneous actions at the local level and of facilitating actions in Beijing. In its early stages, the responsibility system encompassed a variety of organizational forms. The objective of all of the new forms was to tie the reward received more closely to the work actually performed.

In principle, the existing commune system with the production team of 30 families as the basic accounting and labor management unit was a system that tied reward to work effort. Farmers, as indicated earlier, received "work points" based on the amount of work they performed measured in both quantitative and qualitative terms. At the end of the year, the total work points of all team members would be added up and divided into the net income of the team to determine the actual value of each point. Income was then distributed on the basis of the number of work points earned multiplied by the average value of each point.

In practice, it was difficult to tie income to performance under this work point system. Self-assessment of the quantity and quality of work done was not likely to produce an accurate measure of actual effort.

[7]Recently published data have made it possible to reconstruct many of China's economic policy debates. See, for example, Michael D. Swaine (1986). Among other sources Swaine makes good use of the unpublished but widely available version of a book compiling a record of major economic events and decisions. The published version is People's Republic of China Record of Major Economic Events Publishing Committee (1985).

But mutual assessment by all members of the team was also difficult. It could take up enormous amounts of time and lead to great tension among village families because some would inevitably feel they were unfairly treated. Left to their own devices, therefore, production teams tended to favor more egalitarian forms of distribution. "Leftist" ideology could reinforce these egalitarian tendencies, but they were present even in its absence. A third alternative was to have work points set by team cadres acting as supervisors of the various production activities. Effective supervision of small peasant agriculture, however, is a much more difficult and costly task than supervision of a factory production line. Farm work often involves shifting back and forth among many different tasks on a highly irregular basis.[8]

The responsibility system's methods of relating reward to effort ranged from paying work points to small groups in exchange for completing specific tasks (for example, the transplanting of one hectare of rice seedlings) to the allocation of a certain amount of land to an individual family on a long-term basis with the family to receive all income from the land after meeting certain obligations to the collective and the state.

By 1983, most of the more collective forms of the responsibility system had given way to what amounted to individual household farming.[9] Nuclear farm families were allocated a portion of the formerly collective land for a period of 15 years in exchange for meeting certain tax and crop delivery obligations to the state. The commune and the production team no longer existed in any operational sense and this reality was recognized soon thereafter with the removal of the term *rural people's commune* from the names of rural governmental and production units. Except for issues connected with the distribution of income within individual families, reward was unequivocally tied to effort.[10]

---

[8]For an empirical attempt to test this proposition on the basis of a theoretical model, see Justin Lin (1985).

[9]For more detailed studies of the politics of rural reform in this period, see David Zweig (1983).

[10]One of the best collections of studies of the process of decollectivization, much of it based on scholars who did field work in China, is by William L. Parish (1985). Other useful articles include Kathleen Hartford (1985) and Yak-Yeow Kueh (1984).

With the demise of team farming, the major remaining issue was how the state was to go about ensuring that farm families produced what society and the state required. Under the collective system, the state signed contracts with collective units requiring them to deliver a certain amount of a given crop to the state at a fixed price, a price generally well below what would have been required to elicit comparable deliveries on a purely voluntary basis. From time to time, the state did adjust the relative prices of particular cash crops to encourage greater production of cotton or sugar, but price adjustments were rare during the decade of the Cultural Revolution. The emphasis during that period was on grain and regional self-sufficiency. In effect, provinces and even smaller subregions were expected to provide for most of their own needs and to purchase as little as possible from outside their boundaries.[11]

Beginning in 1979, the state increased the premium paid for above-quota deliveries of grain and raised farm purchase prices in general, but with the large increases in grain and total agricultural output, the state budget soon found itself heavily burdened by the huge subsidies required by the organizations involved in marketing agricultural products. The main problem was that grain was sold in urban areas at prices fixed at a low level 20 years earlier. Increases in urban grain prices were blocked by fear of the political repercussions. By 1981, the cereals subsidy had reached 12.9 billion yuan or the equivalent of 10% of total government expenditures (Lardy 1983b, p. 194).[12] Total grain purchases had risen from 50.7 million tons in 1978 to 60.1 million tons in 1980 to 117.2 million tons in 1984.[13] Because the government had fixed grain delivery quotas for five years, above-quota purchases at premium prices rose particularly rapidly.

[11]The major works on Chinese price policy in the 1970s and the impact of the grain self-sufficiency policy are by Nicholas Lardy (1983a, 1983b). See also interesting papers by Terry Sicular (1986a, 1986b). For an analysis of price policy in the 1950s and early 1960s, see Dwight H. Perkins (1966), Chs. III–IV.

[12]This percentage is derived by adding the cereals' subsidy to reported government expenditures to get a figure for government expenditure including the subsidy.

[13]These figures are in terms of "trade" or milled grain and are from State Statistical Bureau (1985b, p. 480).

The government, therefore, had a powerful fiscal incentive to get rid of grain purchase quotas and their accompanying subsidies. At the same time, the household responsibility system had made it much more difficult to set crop quotas in a way that did not interfere with allocative efficiency even more than was the case with collective units. There had been 4.6 million production teams but there were 185 million farm families in 1983 (China Agricultural Yearbook Compilation Committee, 1984, pp. 67–68). Clearly, it made sense to use the indirect methods of the market rather than the direct allocation of physical quotas to stimulate output of desired products.

The bumper harvest of 1984 which followed on several bumper harvests in previous years also increased the feasibility of moving to a market system. There was little danger that severe shortages would cause food prices to spiral upward. With storage facilities overflowing with grain, grain prices on the open market in 1984 fell by 10% from 1983 and rose only 1.8% in 1985 despite the poorer grain harvest (State Statistical Bureau 1985b, p. 535; 1986b, p. 100). In 1985, the state felt able to cut back sharply on the use of compulsory state quotas for agricultural crops including grain with the goal of their complete elimination within a short but unspecified period.

What was the impact of these reforms in the rural areas? Abstract reasoning alone cannot provide an answer because such reasoning can make a case for the productive superiority of either the collective or the private household form of agricultural organization. In fact, some models of collective farm behavior demonstrate under certain assumptions that farmers in a collective system will work more rather than less than under an individual household system. In addition, if there are economies of scale, the collective farm may have further advantages. Problems of monitoring work effort, incomplete information, and uncertainty will tend to offset these advantages of the collective under some but not all circumstances.[14]

In certain respects, the demise of the collective system may have had a negative impact on rural welfare. The communes were involved in much

[14] For an interesting attempt to explore these issues in the context of formal models of team and household behavior, see Louis Putterman (1985).

more than the cultivation of crops. They were also the main vehicle for the provision of rural education and health care. For a decade and more, for example, China's barefoot doctors had organized preventive health campaigns and dispensed remedies for minor illnesses and preliminary diagnoses of more serious illnesses requiring referral to more qualified doctors. Partly as a result of this system, life expectancy in the Chinese countryside was much longer than in any other nation at a comparable level of per capita income. But barefoot doctors were part of the commune work point system and, with its elimination, they had to charge a fee for service and many of them found they could do better by abandoning health work and concentrating on agricultural production. Preventive campaigns in particular must have been difficult to organize on a fee basis because of the free rider problem.[15] The problem may have been more severe in poorer areas where the need for primary health care was greatest, but the ability to organize alternatives to the collective health care system was weakest.

Labor mobilization for construction of irrigation systems and rural roads was also made more difficult by the return to household agriculture. Such labor mobilization had been at the core of the Maoist vision of how to raise farm output in China with its massive quantities of underemployed labor. But 20 years of labor mobilization had produced results in terms of increased output that were disappointing. A few areas of North China enjoyed large increases in productivity as a result, but the gains in much of the rest of China proved illusory. The idea of mobilizing labor to build irrigation systems, after all, was one that went back 2000 years and most of the areas where this form of labor-intensive construction was feasible had completed such systems often hundreds of years earlier. In such areas, gains from a renewed mobilization effort were modest.[16]

Whatever the costs of the decline in these collective efforts, the overall performance of agriculture during this period of reform has amply

[15]The number of barefoot doctors fell from 1.35 million in 1982 to 1.25 million in 1984 and one suspects that the amount of time spent on health activities by barefoot doctors declined even more sharply. See a discussion of these issues in William Hsiao (1984) and Perkins and Shahid Yusuf (1984), Ch. 7.

[16]For an elaboration of this argument, see Perkins (1969, Ch. IV).

justified the reformers' diagnosis of agriculture's slow growth rate. A general appraisal of the rate of growth of output and productivity in the Chinese economy is the subject of the next section. The question here is whether one can attribute what has happened to the reforms.

Data on the increase in agricultural output and its components during the 1970s and 1980s are presented in Table 1. Figures for rates of growth and for the composition of the increase in output are given for the period immediately preceding reform (1972–1978), the first stage of reform when collective farming was still the dominant form of agricultural organization (1979–1982), and the second stage of reform when farm management and accounting were on a household basis (1983–1986). Because farm output fluctuates from year to year as a result of weather and other causes, growth rates for short periods such as those in the table are quite sensitive to which years are selected in defining a period. The decline in the grain output growth rate in 1983–1986, for example, is due to the fact that 1985 and 1986 were poor years for grain, in part, but only in part, because of weather. The total area sown to grain in 1985 and 1986, for example, was respectively 3.6% and 1.7% below 1984 and other inputs may have been shifted to nongrain crops as well. Still, with this qualification, the data in Table 1 are useful indicators of the principal sources of growth of Chinese farm output. A more systematic analysis will have to wait until the Chinese collect and release large micro data sets that can be used to estimate national and regional agricultural production functions.

In the period prior to reform, the main contributions to agricultural output growth were increases in grain and in subsidiary output, mainly rural small-scale industrial output which the Chinese include in their gross agricultural production figures. After the freeing up of rural markets in 1979, all components of farm output grew more rapidly including grain despite the de-emphasis on "taking grain as the key link." The largest increases in output growth, however, were in cash (nongrain) crops and animal husbandry. After decollectivization, cash crops and animal husbandry continued to grow rapidly, but the most dramatic contribution to accelerated growth was by rural industry. Nearly 60% of the increases in output in the three years, 1983–1986, was accounted for by village industry.

Table 1. The composition of agricultural output growth (based on 1980 constant prices).

	1971–1978	1980–1982	1982–1986
A. Growth rates (in percentage per year)			
Gross value of agricultural output	4.3	7.5	13.0
Crops	2.7	5.6	4.2
Grain	2.9	3.9	2.5
Nongrain	2.1	13.2	9.4
Animal husbandry	2.6	10.1	10.1
Subsidiary output	17.9	13.7	40.0
Village industry	23.5	14.8	43.1
B. Share in total output growth (in percentage)			
Gross value of agricultural output	100.0	100.0	100.0
Crops	45.8	49.2	17.8
Grain	39.6	27.1	7.9
Nongrain	6.3	22.1	9.8
Animal husbandry	9.1	19.7	11.5
Subsidiary	34.5	25.5	66.3
Village industry	27.2	19.5	58.7
Forestry and fisheries	10.6	5.6	4.4

Sources: Data for this table were derived from figures in State Statistical Bureau (1986b, pp. 32, 37); State Statistical Bureau (1984, pp. 133, 141, 448); and State Statistical Bureau (1987, pp. 24, 28).

The value of grain output in 1980 was derived by multiplying grain output in tons in each year by the average purchase price for all grains in 1980 of 360.6 yuan per ton. The value of nongrain crop output was derived by subtracting the value of grain output from the reported figure for total crop output.

The increase in grain output despite a decline in the acreage sown to grain of 10% between 1978 and 1985 can be seen as a rise in X efficiency together with a rise in inputs other than land. The increase in cash crops and animal husbandry was due to both improved allocative efficiency as regions paid more attention to their comparative advantage to increases in inputs such as chemical fertilizer and improved plant varieties, and to improved total factor productivity or X efficiency, particularly the release of energies connected with private household output.[17] The dramatic rise in rural industry, particularly after 1982, cannot be readily explained in these terms without more information and research on the policy changes that affected rural industry. Certainly, there is more to the story than the impact of decollectivization and the freeing up of rural markets. In fact, a plausible case can be made that decollectivization should have made it more difficult to raise capital and labor for rural industry. Clearly, however, that was not the case.

The transformation of rural China from a system riddled with bureaucratic controls to one based increasingly on market forces thus was a clear success in raising output and productivity and was perceived as such by much of China's leadership and probably by most farmers. In fact, it was this success with agriculture that provided much of the momentum for those desirous of reforming industry.

The task of reforming agriculture, however, was inherently easier than that of industry. Many of the ingredients of a successful market system were already in place prior to reform or could be readily created. Many agricultural products were sold on markets prior to the beginning of reforms, so rural markets, if only in embryonic form, already existed. Factor markets, to be sure, did not exist and they do not really exist today and their absence may become a more serious problem with time. Perhaps most important, households are natural profit or income maximizers. They have little choice, because the state is not likely to bail them out if they run at a loss. In China, the state's only obligation to rural households has been to step in when they are threatened by starvation. Transfer of decision-making authority from commune cadres to heads of households thus automatically created decision-making units that behaved in accordance with market rules. Finally, farm households are so numerous that

[17]One cannot really measure the contribution of better allocative and X efficiency without a more systematic attempt to estimate agricultural production functions. No such attempt is made in this essay. One can say that the growth of such key inputs as mechanical and electric power and chemical fertilizer all increased at rates no higher and in most cases lower in the 1979–1985 period as contrasted to the 1965–1978 period. Thus the rise in output growth rates combined with a decline in input growth rates might imply a rise in productivity of some kind, but these facts do not constitute conclusive proof that such was the case. Variation in weather conditions further complicates the analysis.

atomistic competition is the norm. Major crop prices, however, are not generally set by the market in China. As in many other countries, they are set by the state. China has long experience in adjusting relative agricultural prices to stimulate lagging sectors so, while relative price distortions still existed in China in the mid-1980s, they were not the source of major resource misallocations.[18] The major problem for setters of farm purchase and sales prices was how to eliminate the huge state subsidies that contributed to the deficit in the government's budget. Eliminating these subsidies, however, had profound implications for the distribution of income and hence for political support for the reforms. Bumper harvests in the 1980s did not by themselves solve this problem, but they did make the task of eliminating subsidies easier.

Urban–industrial reforms

On October 20, 1984, the Chinese government released a document on urban reform. The document was meant to signal the beginning of a major push to alter significantly the system of Soviet-style central planning that China had established in the 1950s and had more or less maintained throughout the 1960s and 1970s. A careful reader of this document, however, could be excused for being puzzled by what this document portended for China's urban-industrial reforms. There was no clarion call for the introduction of market socialism. Instead there was talk of increasing the role of economic levers (read the market) combined with continued central planning for goods of particular importance to the economy and an expanded role for something called "guidance planning" which different people defined in dissimilar ways.

In fact, the October 1984 statement, "On the Reform of Economic Structure," represented an important step toward major changes in the system. Experiments with urban reform had begun immediately after the Third Plenum of December 1978 and continued throughout the early 1980s. But

---

[18]Relative price distortions, of course, were far from being completely eliminated. Grain prices, for example, are probably too low with the elimination of premium payments for above-quota sales, and feed grain prices may have been low relative to other grains. See Thomas Wiens (1987).

there was powerful opposition to the more market-oriented reforms in the person of Chen Yun, a member of the Standing Committee of the Politburo and a dominant economic policy maker in the 1950s and again in the early 1960s after the failure of the "Great Leap Forward" of 1958–1959.

Chen Yun's views were expressed in a number of speeches but the essential point was contained in a March 8, 1979, statement:

> There must be two types of economy, *throughout* [emphasis added] the socialist period:
>
> (1) The planned economy (the type that needs to be developed in a planned and proportionate way).
> (2) The market-regulated economy (the type that is not subject to planning but is conducted in accordance with the changing market supply and demand, i.e., regulated in an unplanned way).
>
> The first type is fundamental and predominant; the second, though supplementary and secondary in nature, is indispensable.[19]

In the 1950s and particularly during the decade of the Cultural Revolution, this statement would have (and did) put Chen Yun solidly in the ranks of those opposed to the radicals around Mao who saw no role for the market at all. But by 1982, this view represented those most opposed to far-reaching change in the industrial system. Debate between this view and those who wanted to move ahead rapidly slowed reform for two years, but by 1984, the pace of reform once again accelerated (Wu Jinglian and Zhao Renwei, 1987).

How far had China in fact gone toward reform by 1985–1986? To lend clarity to an inherently complex topic, the issues involved will be grouped around the four essential features involved in making a market system work outlined above.

(1) *Creating Markets for Inputs and Outputs.* In the 1960s and 1970s, most Chinese industrial products were distributed through administrative channels in accordance with the dictates of central and provincial plans.

---

[19] This statement was reprinted in Chen Yun (1986, pp. 14–15). For a more complete exposition of Chen Yun's views in earlier periods, see Lardy and Kenneth Lieberthal (1983).

By 1984–1985, a considerable share of these inputs and outputs were being purchased and sold on the market at prices largely set by market forces. The products involved included steel, machinery, and raw materials and not just minor inputs and a few consumer goods. A survey of 429 enterprises indicated that market sales by these enterprises had reached 32% of their total sales by 1984 and rose further to 44% in the first half of 1985. Material inputs supplied by the market over the same period rose from 16% to 27% (General Survey Group of the Chinese Institute for Economic Systems Reform, 1986, p. 45).

Percentages such as these, however, are only a rough guide to whether distribution is dominated by market or bureaucratic forces. Most enterprises, for example, acquire inputs both through administrative channels and through purchases on the market. Administrative allocation, as already indicated, is governed by annual plans set by the central or provincial government. Most enterprises, however, will require more inputs than are provided for in the original plan. Under the system as it existed prior to reform, these additional inputs were obtained either by going back to the planners for supplementary allocations or by informal trades with other enterprises. After reform many of these additional inputs were instead purchased on the newly created markets. If all inputs had been available for purchase on the market, one could argue that market forces governed most enterprise decisions because the marginal choices were being made on the basis of prices on the market, not the prices of goods allocated administratively. But where key inputs were not available through the market, for example, electricity, it was planners' decisions about how much to allocate rather than market forces that governed enterprise behavior. In other cases, inputs may have been available on the market, but plan allocations at lower prices met all of an enterprise's requirements. In such cases it was also planners' decisions that determined enterprise behavior. The key question is which of these two kinds of systems, market or bureaucratic, dominated decision-making in most Chinese enterprises. Evidence on that score is not really available. There is no doubt that market forces play a greater role than in the past, but the administrative allocation of certain key inputs ensures that enterprises must still pay close attention to the wishes of the planning bureaucracy.

Factor markets, as contrasted with product markets, have not been freed up to any significant degree. Urban land is in very short supply relative to demand for it, and acquisition of new land usually involves complex negotiations with suburban communes or townships in which the township or other rural unit gives up part of its land in exchange for guaranteed jobs for some of its members. The labor market is also highly restricted. Regular workers in enterprises have permanent employment, the famous "iron rice bowl," and workers are allocated by administrative means to enterprises and are not free to change jobs. Enterprises can and do hire "temporary" workers who are easier to dismiss in slack times, but there are numerous restrictions on a firm's right to hire new workers, temporary or permanent.[20]

Reform groups in the government have advocated the freeing up of the urban labor market. They have taken polls to show that a large share of enterprise employees would like to change jobs and would be willing to take the responsibility for themselves for finding a new job (General Survey Group of the Chinese Institute for Economic Systems Reform, 1986, Ch. 5). Labor in much of the urban collective and individual service sector[21] is able to move from job to job. But in the mid-1980s regular (as contrasted to temporary) employment in state enterprises was still permanent and governed by administrative rather than market rules. Many enterprise jobs could in fact be inherited by the children of workers who retired.

Capital markets involve issues that are best left to the next section.

(2) *Making Enterprise Managers Behave in Accordance with the Rules of the Market.* The primary target in the objective function of managers in a Soviet-style centrally planned economy is maximization of gross value of enterprise output. Many of the characteristic features of the Soviet economic system derive in part from this objective function, notably the excessive buildup of inventories and the neglect of product quality.

---

[20]The urban labor allocation and wage system by the mid-1980s was still much like what it was in the 1950s and 1960s. For an analysis of the system in that earlier period, see Christopher Howe (1973).

[21]"Urban collective and individual service sector" employment refers to people who work in restaurants, shops, and small factories that are owned on an individual or cooperative basis. The contrast is with people who work in state enterprises that are owned by "all the people" of the nation.

The objective function of Chinese enterprises by the first half of the 1980s, in contrast, paid little attention to gross value of output. Questionnaires sent to 359 enterprises came back with "improvement of efficiency and benefits" as the number one objective with "fulfillment of production quotas" listed in the eleventh position (General Survey Group of the Chinese Institute for Economic Systems Reform, 1986). Attempts to get behind these shorthand answers to questions about objectives suggest that enterprise managers are driven by a desire to increase benefits to enterprise employees through higher bonuses, better housing, and more employment opportunities for their children (William Byrd *et al.*, 1984; Byrd and Gene Tidrick, 1985). The main avenue for pursuit of these ultimate objectives was increased profits. The portion of profits that enterprises have been allowed to retain has risen steadily in the 1980s, and profits have become the main source of funds spendable according to an enterprise's own determination of its needs, as contrasted to funds whose use is specified in detail by the planning bureaucracy.

This pursuit of profits, however, does not prove that enterprises are driven by market as contrasted to bureaucratic forces. The issue is one of how enterprises pursue profits. If profits are raised primarily through bargaining with the bureaucracy for lower tax rates or by getting hold of larger allocations of low-priced raw materials from the central planners, Chinese enterprises would still be operating in a bureaucratic rather than a market environment.

With respect to tax policy, the objective is clearly to abandon the pre-1970s Soviet-style system where all profits after paying turnover taxes and subtracting a small retained portion for the enterprise are simply turned over to the state. In this kind of system there is in effect a 90 plus % corporate profits tax. The Chinese, in contrast, are attempting to move toward a corporate profits tax that allows substantial retained earnings and is the same for all enterprises. In the practice of the mid-1980s, however, the rates varied enormously between enterprises and were set through individual bargains made with the state. The main obstacle to adopting a single rate was the wide variation in enterprise profit rates, including many enterprises operating at a loss, together with the state's reluctance to allow these loss makers to fail.

The existence of loss-making enterprises propped up by subsidies is symptomatic of what János Kornai calls the "soft budget constraint." It is a pivotal obstacle to moving from a bureaucratic to a market system. The problem has several dimensions, but the essential question is whether enterprises must live within a budget set by the profitability of the firm, where profitability is determined by market forces rather than bureaucratic manipulation. One dimension is whether enterprises that run losses for long periods will be allowed to fail. If, instead, losing enterprises can always turn to the state to bail them out, the incentive to live within the enterprise's own resources is a weak one. The Chinese have introduced a bankruptcy law designed to move away from the guaranteed bail-out, and in 1986, the first bankruptcy was announced with great fanfare in Shenyang. But there was considerable resistance to the bankruptcy law when it was first introduced and little or no evidence as of 1987 that bankruptcy in any form would become common.[22]

Another key dimension of the soft budget constraint involves the availability of bank credit and grants from the central governmental budget. The Chinese in the 1980s have been moving steadily away from provision of investment funds on a grant basis from the government budget. Both working capital and investment financing now come mainly from the enterprise's own funds or from the banking system at government-determined rates of interest. The magnitude of these changes with respect to investment is given by the data in Table 2. By the 1980s, only 27.5% of total accumulation (roughly equivalent to gross domestic investment) went through the state budget.

Turning funding over to the banks, however, does not necessarily harden the budget constraint. The fundamental question is who decides whether or not a loan is to be given. If interest rates are below market-clearing rates, as is apparently the case in China, there is credit rationing rather than market allocation.[23]

---

[22] There is a growing literature in Chinese on the appropriate role of the bankruptcy law. See for example, Zhu Yongyi (1986) and Wu Ming (1986).

[23] If one could assume that enterprises maximized profits subject to output and input prices and subsidies and taxes were outside of enterprise control, then the excess demand for credit would be prima facie evidence that the interest rate did not reflect the true scarcity price of capital. Because one cannot fully make these assumptions, there could be excess demand even if interest rates were set at rates that would equilibrate a financial market if all participants were playing according to market rules.

Table 2. Investment in and outside of state budget (annual averages in billions of yuan).

	Investment in state-owned enterprises				Investment by collective enterprises in individual housing and for other purposes		Total accumulation (investment)	
	Within state budget		Outside of state budget					
Period	Amount (1)	% (2)	Amount (3)	% (4)	Amount (5)	% (6)	Amount (7)	% (8)
1953–1957	10.87	54.5	1.36	6.8	7.73	38.7	19.96	100.0
1958–1962	19.14	55.2	7.00	20.2	8.50	24.5	34.64	100.0
1963–1970	16.86	47.2	4.50	12.6	14.37	40.2	35.73	100.0
1971–1979	34.23	41.2	18.17	21.9	30.61	36.9	83.02	100.0
1980–1984	36.54	27.5	51.19	38.5	45.37	34.1	133.10	100.0

Sources: State Statistical Bureau (1985, pp. 36, 413, 420, 450). See also Barry Naughton (1986).
Explanation of table:

(1), (3) State enterprise investment includes both "capital construction" and "investment in technical updating, transformation."

(5) These figures are derived as a residual [(7)–(1)–(3)]. The Chinese have published estimates for these categories only for the 1980s.

(7) Total accumulation includes all investment in material-producing sectors including housing minus depreciation.

The issue then becomes one of who determines which clients of the bank receive the funds available and what criteria they use to make these allocations. In China government authorities, both central and local, play a major role in these decisions. Thus, enterprise managers in need of funds must still deal with the government bureaucracy and their allocation criteria. Still, the situation is a far cry from the lax financial policies of the Great Leap Forward (1958–1959) or the system of the 1960s when the banking system existed mainly to monitor the plan and had little authority of any kind to allocate funds. In that period, any enterprise that wanted credit could usually get it if it could show that the proposed uses had some connection with the plan. Enterprises were often awash with credit, but these funds were of limited use because inputs were available only through administrative allocation determined by the plan.

The constraint on enterprise behavior, therefore, was the plan, not the enterprise budget.[24] Even the shift to greater emphasis on enterprise-retained profits did not necessarily harden the budget constraint as long as the level of taxes payable to the state remained an item for negotiation between the enterprise and the bureaucracy. The state, as mentioned above, is attempting to move to fixed tax rates, which would harden the constraint, but as of 1986 it was still possible for an enterprise in financial difficulty to negotiate a lower rate.

Finally, there is the question of who hires, fires, and promotes enterprise managers. Even with a hard budget constraint, managers may pay special attention to the interests of the planning bureaucracy if they hope someday to be a part of that bureaucracy. If, on the other hand, they care most about their share of profit-based bonuses or the goodwill of their workers who want bonuses and jobs, they will behave more in accordance with the rules of the market. In an effort to reduce this element of bureaucratic control, there is even some talk in China of creating independent boards of directors for enterprises and allowing the boards to select the managers. Little has been done to implement this proposal, however, and it has vigorous opponents (Xu Jingan, 1987; Ma Bin and Hong Junyan, 1987).

Clearly in the mid-1980s, both bureaucratic and market forces governed enterprise behavior. Unfortunately, there is no systematic way to measure the relative strength of these opposing forces with the data now available, but there is indirect evidence. Foreign trade liberalization in 1984–1985, for example, led to a substantial run on foreign exchange reserves and a reintroduction of tight central exchange controls, suggesting that there was considerable excess demand for imports. But was this excess demand due to a soft enterprise budget constraint, an overvalued exchange rate, or simply the expectation that foreign exchange liberalization would not last long? Whatever the source of this excess demand, it was far less than the excess import demand that appeared when trade was

[24]There is a good deal written about the operation of the banking system prior to the recent reforms. See, for example, Katherine Huang Hsiao (1971); William Byrd (1983); and Perkins (1966). Articles that take the story up through 1984 or early 1985 include Barry Naughton (1986) and Andrew G. Walder (1986).

liberalized in 1977–1978 prior to the reforms. At that time, Chinese firms are reported to have signed contracts or letters of intent to purchase some US$600 billion worth of foreign imports, a formidable excess given that exports at that time were running at US$10 billion a year.[25] By comparison with this experience in 1977–1978, the budget constraint had been hardened considerably in the mid-1980s.

Another relevant indicator is the "Kornai index," which measures the ratio of input inventories to output inventories. High ratios are indirect evidence of a seller's market created by bureaucratically controlled shortages of inputs, while a low ratio indicates the demand-constrained buyer's market that is typically found in a market economy. The Kornai ratio for a sample of Chinese enterprises fell from 4.4 in 1984 to 3.8 in the first half of 1985. Comparable figures for the Soviet Union are 9.2–12.3, for Hungary 7.3–8.5, and for the United States 0.9–1.2 (General Survey Group of the Chinese Institute for Economic Systems Reform, 1986, p. 18).

Neither of these tests is conclusive, but when put together with more impressionistic material, there is little question that China had made strides toward creating enterprises that behave according to market rules. It is equally the case, however, that government bureaucratic involvement in enterprise decisions remains pervasive if less strong and direct than in the past.

(3) *The Introduction of Competition and the Abolition of Monopoly Power.* There was little direct competition in China's centrally planned system of the prereform era. There were few markets on which to compete. Markets made the job of central planners more difficult by directing inputs from designations set by the plan to alternative unplanned uses.

When China decentralized the allocation of inputs and outputs in the 1960s and 1970s, it did so, not by increasing the role of the market, but by setting up planning and materials allocation systems at provincial and even county levels. Typically, a provincial-level firm would acquire most of its inputs from within the province and would have a monopoly over the provincial market for its output. County-level firms similarly would

[25]These figures come from a private communication to the author and were estimated by a firm in Hong Kong.

have a monopoly of the market within their county for such products as cement or farm machinery. If the demand for threshers within the county was exhausted, the enterprise did not attempt to find a market for its threshers in a neighboring county. Instead, it shifted to producing some other type of machinery where the county's demand had not yet been met (American Rural Small-Scale Industry Delegation, 1977).

At the national level, competition was further restricted by isolating domestic enterprises from foreign competition. Special corporations under the Ministry of Foreign Trade had a complete monopoly of imports and exports within their sphere of product specialization. Generally, these corporations would not import items that were being produced within China even if the Chinese products cost more and were of lower quality. Domestic firms thus did not have to worry about losing their markets to superior foreign products.

It is not that the Chinese saw no virtues in competition. Emulation campaigns, where one enterprise attempts to surpass another in producing a new product or more of an old one, were a regular feature of enterprise life. But competition was indirect and not allowed to interfere with the orderly allocation of inputs and outputs through the plan.

In the early 1980s, however, the Chinese made a major effort to increase direct competition for markets. Competition was most readily apparent in urban services when the government abolished the regulations that had prevented private and collective traders from operating. State-run department stores, repair shops, and food distribution outlets then suddenly found themselves in a head-to-head battle for customers with individual traders and small collective shops. To keep up with the competition, state stores had to stay open later and pay more attention to serving their customers.

Industries also lost their monopoly control of regional markets. Where buyer's markets existed because products were in excess supply, enterprise behavior had to be modified, often substantially, to meet the new competition. The Chongqing Clock and Watch Factory, for example, found itself in 1981 facing a saturated market for clocks in part because the southwest China market has been opened up to competition from high-quality efficient producers in Shanghai and Tianjin. The Chongqing Factory, having failed to reintroduce effective bureaucratic limits on competition, was forced to cut prices, launch a serious market effort, and develop new products more in line with consumer preferences (Byrd *et al.*, 1984).

Where excess demand prevailed, however, competition was more hypothetical than real. There was little market pressure to pay more attention to marketing, lower prices and costs, and raise quality Excess demand for foreign imports combined with tight controls over foreign exchange meant that competition from foreign producers also was largely absent. Chinese exporters of manufactures, in contrast, did have to meet foreign competition in markets outside of China, but it was foreign trade corporations which did most of the exporting, so that competitive pressures were filtered through these corporations and may or may not have been felt by the manufacturer of the goods exported.

(4) *Setting Prices in Accordance with Relative Scarcities.* Chinese prices fluctuated in accordance with market conditions in the early 1950s, but with the introduction of central planning and the abolition of the private sector, industrial input and output prices were frozen at existing levels. For all but a few products, industrial prices remained frozen at mid-1950s levels for the next quarter century. China did not even institute the periodic price reforms found in the Soviet Union designed to make prices bear some relation to costs.

During these two and a half decades of frozen prices, Chinese industry grew from 16% of net material product in 1955 to 50% in 1978 (both in 1980 prices). Relative conditions and hence prices in the world outside of China also changed during this period most notably as a result of the OPEC oil price rise of 1973. Chinese prices in the mid-1950s may have been a reasonable reflection of relative scarcities of that time, but they bore little relation to the relative scarcities of the 1980s.

Chinese reformers recognized early on that an increased role for market forces required major changes in relative prices. The question was when and how to introduce these changes and according to what criteria. There were hesitant steps in 1979–1982 to raise or lower state-set prices for particular industrial products such as coal and iron ore. This effort picked up momentum in 1983 with price changes for certain consumer durables, textiles, chemical products, and railroad freight, but the state prices of most industrial products remained frozen (Naughton, 1986, p. 626).

The real breakthrough came in 1985–1986 with the recognition that, if prices on the portion of enterprise inputs and outputs available through the market were allowed to fluctuate, the state could avoid the arduous task of changing prices by administrative means. Prices would reflect scarcities of these unregulated markets. China thus created a dual price system. More than half of all industrial inputs and outputs continued to be distributed at administered prices, but it appears that many marginal enterprise decisions were made on the basis of uncontrolled market prices. The question in 1986 was whether to retain this dual price system indefinitely or move toward a single market determined set of relative prices either quickly or slowly (Cyril Zhiren Lin, 1986). Advocates of a return to administered prices also existed but included mainly those who wished to stick with a centrally planned economy.

A move toward the greater use of market prices opens up the issue of which market prices to use, those of the uncontrolled market of the dual price system, of a single unified national market, or of the world market.[26] If world market prices are desired at least for traded goods, a mechanism is needed to bring Chinese domestic relative scarcities in line with relative scarcities in the outside world. In the absence of more foreign trade liberalization than is currently contemplated, however, it will be difficult to create the pressures required to bring domestic market prices for tradeable goods in line with world prices.

Opening up the economy

The subject of foreign trade deserves greater emphasis in this context than is given by the passing references made in the preceding discussion. One of the most dramatic elements in China's urban reform movement was the decision to reject the autarkic policies of the previous two decades and to

---

[26]The coexistence of two sets of prices for the same products was made possible by the fact that enterprises were not free to sell on whichever market gave them the highest price. Instead, enterprises had first to meet their delivery quotas set by the plan. Only the surplus over and above those quotas could then be sold at higher prices on the market. Discussions of the dual price system and its implications for efficiency and other issues can be found in various sources including Wu Jinglian and Zhao Renwei (1987) and Byrd (1987).

open up the economy. Opening up actually began earlier than most other urban reforms and is a major reason why the years 1977 and 1978 should be viewed as part of the reform period.

It is a widely held view that the rapid expansion of foreign trade, particularly the fast-paced development of the export of manufactures, had much to do with the high level of economic performance experienced elsewhere in East Asia (Japan, South Korea, Taiwan, Hong Kong, and Singapore). Between 1977 and 1981, Chinese exports as well rose from US$7.6 billion to US$22.0 billion, or at 30% a year, a very high rate even when the relatively high world inflation rates of that period are taken into account. In addition, the government took other steps to open up the economy. China returned to its seats at the World Bank and the IMF and began to borrow from those institutions. A Joint Venture Law was passed and foreign direct investment, formerly prohibited, was actively encouraged. Special economic zones, in effect export-processing zones, were created in Guangdong and Fujian Provinces. By 1985, foreign credits and direct investment commitments reached US$9.87 billion before falling off in 1986, although foreign capital actually used in 1985 was US$4.46 billion (State Statistical Bureau 1986a, p. 581). The cumulative total of actually utilized foreign investment and credits over the 1979–1985 period was US$21.8 billion.

How did this opening up further the urban reform process? Exporters of manufactures, to begin with, operated in a highly competitive market. Chinese bureaucratic planners had no control over consumers in Hong Kong, the United States, or Japan. Chinese exporters, however, were usually foreign trade corporations, not the manufacturers of the goods exported. With the advent of reforms, the number of these foreign trade corporations proliferated and such firms did to some degree compete with each other. But competitive pressure on the manufacturers themselves was indirect. Chinese enterprises may also have felt competitive pressures on the import side, but high excess demand for imports kept bureaucratic controls over imports tight. It is unlikely, therefore, that competitive pressure from imports operated through the market mechanism by reducing the profits of domestic firms producing import substitutes. Imports, however, may have had a positive "demonstration effect" on domestic enterprises. The more Chinese purchasers became aware of the quality differences between a Sony and Chinese-brand television set, or between a Toyota and a Shanghai automobile, the more pressure there was on Chinese producers to raise their quality.

It is impossible to measure the quantitative impact of these competitive pressures, but it is likely that their magnitude was much less than that among China's East Asian neighbors. To begin with, even after opening up, trade was still a small share of China's GNP or of its industrial output. Exports of goods and services from South Korea in 1975, for example, were 22% of GDP in 1975 and rose to 39% in 1985, and the share of imports was even higher (Economic Planning Board, 1986). China's export share in GDP, presented in a later part of this paper, was only about a third the level of Korea in 1975 (see Figure 1, which appears in Section IV). A lower export ratio is to be expected given China's large size and the fact that there is a strong negative relationship between trade share and country size. The fact remains, however, that a lower trade ratio means less competitive pressure from abroad.

Imports were not freely available through the market in either China or South Korea. The bureaucracy set and allocated quotas in both countries, thus sharply restricting competitive pressures from this source. The degree of bureaucratic control in China, however, was more pervasive than in Korea, even the Korea of the tight import controls of the 1960s. China did attempt to loosen controls by decentralizing the authority to import to provinces and even on occasion to enterprises, but the process remained a highly bureaucratic one.

Will bureaucratic controls over foreign trade be loosened further in coming years, and will such a loosening move China's foreign trade most of the way toward a market system? There are formidable obstacles in the way. In a bureaucratic system with a soft budget constraint there is an almost insatiable demand for imports. Nearly anything imported can be sold at a large profit, particularly when it comes to high technology investment goods. Conceivably, the exchange rate could be devalued to a point low enough to bring import demand in line with the availability of foreign exchange, but the resulting exchange rate would have to fall a long way as long as the soft budget constraint continued to persist in Chinese industry. China's currency has been devalued several times in recent years without achieving an equilibrium in the demand and supply of imports or anything close to it.

The bureaucratic command system is also an obstacle to the expansion of exports of manufactures. It is difficult for enterprises used to supplying goods of poor quality to a captive market to convert to meeting the constantly shifting demands for high-quality stylish products required by export markets in the West and Japan. Despite this handicap, however, Chinese exports rose by over 20% a year between 1976 and 1986 (in nominal US dollar terms) from US$6.9 billion in 1976 to US$30.9 billion in 1986 and manufactures made up over 60% of total exports in 1986. The question for the future is whether exports will continue to grow rapidly and whether import demand can be held back through hardening the budget constraint, devaluation, and other similar measures to a point where the supply and demand for traded goods will be in equilibrium and bureaucratic controls will be unnecessary. China still has a long way to go.

Macro economic controls

In principle, the question of functioning markets and appropriate relative prices is separable from the question of the overall price level. In practice, it is difficult for reformers to keep these two questions apart. Inflation in the general price level usually leads to attempts to control inflation that typically have profound implications for relative prices and the orderly functioning of markets. Nowhere is this more true than in China where political sensitivity to inflation is keenly felt. The Communist party came to power in part because of the hyperinflation of the 1940s, and 30 years of a nominal price level that hardly rose at all have made the Chinese population averse to even small annual increases in the general price level.

Official indexes of Chinese retail, worker cost of living, and free market (trade market) prices are presented in Table 3. As these figures indicate, China had little or no overt inflation prior to the 1980s except for the famine harvest years of 1960–1962, when output for consumers fell much faster than money income and purchasing power. Prices between 1966 and 1979 were in essence frozen, but in 1980, China got its first burst of overt inflation since 1962 followed by another jump in 1985. In fact, inflation may have been higher than these figures indicate because the retail cost of living indexes reflect state list prices better than they reflect what consumers actually paid for goods purchased.

Table 3. Annual increase in prices (in percent).

Period	General retail prices	Worker cost of living	Trade market prices
1950–1959	2.3	2.6	n.a.
1959–1962	7.5	7.3	n.a.
1962–1965	–4.1	–3.6	n.a.
1965–1979	0.2	0.4	n.a.
1980	6.0	7.5	3.3[a]
1981	2.4	2.5	4.9[b]
1982	3.3	2.0	3.5
1983	1.5	2.0	4.1
1984	2.8	2.7	0.3
1985	8.8	11.9	17.2
1986	6.0	7.0	8.1

[a] 1980 figure is the average rate of increase for the two years, 1979 and 1980.
[b]The 1981 figure was derived from an index for 1980–1985.

Sources: State Statistical Bureau (1984, p. 433); State Statistical Bureau (1985b, pp. 530, 535); State Statistical Bureau (1986b, pp. 100–101); State Statistical Bureau (1987).

Controlling inflation on consumer markets was a comparatively simple task prior to reform. Controlling inflation on industrial investment and intermediate goods markets was even easier and in fact trivial because prices were frozen and had little influence on allocation as pointed out above. Excess demand on the investment and intermediate goods markets did not spill onto the consumer market because the wage bill was tightly controlled by the central planners, not the individual enterprises.

The control of inflation was thus a problem of matching the planned increase in state-marketed consumer goods at fixed retail prices with the increase in the wage bill and the value of state purchases of farm products minus the increase in individual bank savings deposits. All these variables except perhaps savings deposits (and private hoarding) were under the direct control of the planners.

Inflation is still possible in this system, usually because the wage bill may grow more rapidly than the availability of consumer goods.

Inflation may be either overt or repressed. In the latter case, it manifests itself in the form of an involuntary increase in savings deposits. Such inflationary pressure is likely to be the case if employment in the producer goods sector is growing more rapidly than in the consumer sector or if there is a shortage of labor and weak control over wage rates leading enterprises to bid against each other for workers. Both of these conditions existed in the Soviet Union in the 1930s. But in China in the 1960s and 1970s, labor surplus conditions made control of the wage rate by the center comparatively easy, and strict controls on hiring and rural-to-urban migration limited the ability of enterprises to increase the number of workers on their payroll. The main motivation behind the restriction on rural-to-urban migration was a desire to avoid additional expenditures on urban infrastructure and housing, but the policy had the additional role of making it easier to control the size of the wage bill.

In statistical terms, China's experience with inflation since the 1950s fits a monetarist or quantity theory view of the process. Gregory Chow, for example, estimates an equation that explains the increase in the logarithm of retail prices with the increase in the logarithm of the money supply divided by real national income available,[27] but one gets comparable results with quite different assumptions about the relevant variables and the nature of the relationship between them.[28] Much more work is required before we have a reliable model for analyzing China's inflationary experience.

In general what was happening in China was that money (defined as currency in circulation, because bank demand deposits played no consumer role) was used almost exclusively by consumers. There were strict and very low limits on the use of currency by enterprises. The demand for currency was thus highly correlated with cash income, hence with the wage bill and farm purchases, which are the main sources of cash income.

---

[27] Gregory Chow, forthcoming, gets the following results:

$$\Delta \ln P = \underset{(0.0461)}{0.0075} + \underset{(0.025)}{0.127}\, \Delta \ln (M/y)$$

$$R^2 = 0.465$$

See also Chow (1985, pp. 228–227).

[28] A useful analytic survey of many of the issues involved is in Hang-Sheng Cheng (1987).

The task for planners, therefore, was to control money incomes and the money supply would take care of itself.[29]

This straightforward method of controlling inflation, however, began to break down with the reforms of 1979 and after. The problem in 1980 in part was simply a result of excessive increases in the wage bill and in prices paid to farmers in 1979 and 1980. The state in effect attempted to solve pent-up frustrations due to long-stagnant wages and farm incomes a bit too quickly.

But more was going on than a small miscalculation. The segmentation between the consumer and producer investment and intermediate goods markets had begun to break down.

(a) Retained profits were rising and could be used to raise worker bonuses, and state control of enterprise hiring was weaker.
(b) The large collective enterprise sector made up of hundreds of thousands of small industrial and commercial firms was not subject to central control, and local authorities had little interest in or ability to aid the anti-inflation effort. These collective enterprises could hire labor subject to few if any central controls.
(c) The decline in state compulsory purchases of farm products and the floating of many purchase prices meant the government had much less direct control over the amount of cash income received by farmers.
(d) Certain important products such as cement (used by individuals for rural housing) and coal (used for home heating) were sold on both consumer and producer markets neither of which were directly controlled. Thus excess enterprise demand could directly impact on consumer prices.

In short, the system with its many new leakages between consumer and producer markets was much more complex. Government macro economic planners attempted to maintain control over aggregate demand, but

[29] This assertion may overstate the direction of causation, particularly in recent years when Chinese economists have talked more about the need to control the money supply as a principal form of macro economic control. See, for example, Li Chengrui (1986); Lin Jiken (1985); and Zhao Haikuan (1985).

in this new environment they had only a vague idea of how to go about it. There was an effort to balance the government budget, but no clear understanding of what connection, if any, there was between a government deficit and rising consumer prices.

In 1986, the process of achieving a better understanding of China's post-reform macro economic system had only just begun. How well policy makers succeed in achieving this understanding will influence the future course of reform in general. Some societies could tolerate 10 or even 20% inflation each year without undue strain or temptation to resort to price controls and other similar methods that create suppressed inflationary pressures and a return to forms of bureaucratic control. But China is not likely to be able to tolerate price increases of this magnitude, mainly for political reasons.

Surplus labor in the countryside may do as much for holding inflation in check as any increase in the government's skills in the manipulation of macro economic controls. The impact of surplus labor on wages, however, will be muted if the government continues to create artificial urban labor shortages through its strict control over rural-to-urban migration. These controls on migration were relaxed a bit in the mid-1980s, but very real restrictions on the ability of enterprises to hire new workers were retained.

The future of reform

In 1986, China's rural reform process had largely run its course, but urban reforms were still in midstream. While it is conceivable that the urban reforms could stabilize at this midpoint, it is more likely that the reform effort will continue on toward a greater role for the market or will slide back toward tinkering with a restrengthened system of planning and bureaucratic control. The current mix of market forces and bureaucratic control is not a stable one.

The direction of change will depend in part on whether the reforms have achieved their goals of raising productivity and the Chinese standard of living. As the discussion in the next section will indicate, the first eight to ten years of reform (1977–1986) were marked by conspicuous success in meeting these goals and this success gave clear impetus to further reform. But much of this early success was due to the performance of agriculture. As agriculture settles back into a slower growth path as is likely, will industry pick up the slack? Future periods of slow growth and inflation could be logically used to make a case for further reform, but the more likely result would be a retreat to more bureaucratic control. Perceptions of why economic growth has been fast or slow thus will play an important role in deciding whether to push ahead or fall back. Except among a handful of reform activists and Western-trained economists, few among the Chinese leadership believe instinctively in the superiority of market forces. Most people in developing countries are suspicious of market forces, and in China this suspicion is reinforced by Marxist ideology that views market forces as chaotic.

The exercise of power is also involved in decisions to expand the role of the market. A decline in bureaucratic control means a decline in bureaucrats' power. If the new system makes bureaucratic skills built up over decades of practice obsolete, those being made obsolete will fight reform for that reason as well. It is no accident that much of the impetus behind reform in 1985–1986 came after virtually all of China's ministers, enterprise managers, and institute directors had been replaced by individuals typically two decades younger than those who had run China's economy up to that point.

The relationship between reform and power is important at a more fundamental level. All political power in China is monopolized by the Chinese Communist party, a party that is organized along Leninist lines. In Leninist parties, power is centralized at the top and not easily challenged from below. On the one hand, this centralization of power facilitates major changes in policy direction once a few top leaders are convinced change is required. Bureaucratic resistance can slow implementation of such changes, but it cannot overrule them. If power had been diffused among the planning commission, the ministries, and lower-level party committees, the pace of the 1979–1986 reform efforts would have been much slower. The ability to change policy quickly can, of course, affect reform negatively as well as positively. A change in thinking at the top could lead to an equally rapid retreat at least with respect to urban reforms.

The Chinese Communist party is not only organized along Leninist lines. It is a party made up of people who share or profess to share a common set of values and modes of analysis based on Marxism. It is these shared values as much as the desire to retain power that is the glue holding the party together in much the same way that shared Confucian values held together China's imperial bureaucracy for a thousand years.

How do these shared values predispose China's leadership toward reforms involving an expanded role for the market? Reformers have argued that central control and planning have little to do with Marxism. It is simply the way the Soviet Union set out to implement Marxist principles and other national goals in a particular historical context. But will a party steeped in the Marxist classics be comfortable with a system in which enterprises are allowed to go bankrupt and workers allowed to become unemployed? In addition to Marx, there are Mao Zedong's own values that he tried so hard to inculcate into the population. Much of Mao's effort, most notably the Cultural Revolution, had an effect opposite to his intentions. But are Maoist values and the values of Yenan and the Long March completely a thing of the past?

There are no conclusive answers to any of these questions. Much of what had occurred by 1986 was not inconsistent with an optimistic outlook for reform. Rural reforms involved a major surrender of party and bureaucratic power in the countryside, albeit one falling far short of total abdication. Mao's strictures against material incentives did not outlast him by more than a year. And, at a less cosmic level, a small sign of the times was the effort by the State Education Commission to revamp the economics curriculum of China's universities to include a strong dose of "Western" economics. Western theories of how markets work were to be placed alongside traditional courses on Marxist political economy.

No one, including the Chinese, knows when or how this reform process will end. Momentum in the fall of 1986 appeared clearly on the side of those pushing for reform, but by January 1987 Hu Yaobang was out of office as party secretary and conservatives associated with Chen Yun and Peng Zhen appeared to be gaining strength. By the 13th Party Congress in October 1987 reformers appeared once again to have the upper hand. These swings in the relative fortunes of the reformers and the conservatives will no doubt continue, but the wild swings in policy of the Cultural Revolution period and before are not very likely.

III. Measuring Economic Performance

What is the evidence that China's reforms have had a positive impact on the performance of the economy? The most convincing figures are those for the growth rate of what the Chinese call national income but which Western economists usually refer to as net material product (NMP). Net material product differs from the more familiar concept of GNP because it excludes a large part of the service sector.[30]

As the data in Table 4 indicate, the growth rate of net material product (in 1980 prices) fell from an impressive 6.2% during the first five-year plan period (1953–1957) to a more modest average of 3.9% a year during the 19 years (1958–1976) that encompassed the Great Leap Forward and the Cultural Revolution. In the nine years following the death of Mao Zedong, in contrast, the growth rate accelerated to nearly 9% a year.[31]

What accounted for this accelerated growth? As the growth accounting calculations in Table 4 suggest, after 1976 there was both an increase in the growth rate of the capital stock and in the rate of growth of total factor productivity, but it was productivity growth that registered the more significant change. Throughout the 19 years prior to 1977, total factor productivity growth was zero or even slightly negative. From 1977 on, productivity growth accounted for over 40% of total growth.

These estimates, to be sure, are derived from very crude data. The capital stock data in particular are based on assumptions about the initial capital stock and on the appropriate deflator for figures expressed originally in current prices. The NMP estimates in 1980 prices are based on more solid data, but are still subject to error and the 1980 prices only vaguely reflect "true" relative scarcities in the Chinese economy. Finally, the methodology used to separate the contributions of increases in factor

---

[30]The Chinese have begun to calculate gross domestic product (GDP) estimates in accordance with standard international methodology (Albert Keidel, September 8, 1986, and October 20, 1986). For work on this and related price issues, see Kung-chia Yeh (1986).

[31]In making these calculations, I have treated the entire 1977–1985 period as a reform period rather than the more conventional choice of the year 1979–1985. In 1977 and 1978, the Chinese government took a number of important steps to open up the economy and to restore material incentives.

Table 4. Sources of growth (percentage increase per year).

Period	Growth rate of net material product (1980 prices) (G_Y)	Contribution of increase in capital stock ($W_K \cdot G_K$)	Contribution of increase in labor force ($W_L \cdot G_L$)	Productivity increase contribution (a)
1953–1957	6.61	0.84	1.67	4.10
1957–1965	2.09	1.87	1.63	−1.41
1965–1976	5.11	2.81	1.68	0.62
1976–1985	8.78	3.30	1.69	3.79

Sources: State Statistical Bureau (1984, pp. 29–32, 107, 425); State Statistical Bureau (1985b, pp. 33–36, 213); and State Statistical Bureau (1986b, pp. 7, 27).

Methodology: These figures are derived from an aggregate production converted into the standard growth accounting form:

$$G_Y = a + (W_K \cdot G_K) + (W_L \cdot G_L),$$

where G = the growth rate of the variable in question,

Y = net material product or national income as the Chinese define that term,

K = the capital stock,

L = the total labor force,

W_K = elasticity of output with respect to capital,

W_L = elasticity of output with respect to labor,

a = productivity growth or the residual derived by subtracting the contribution of labor and capital inputs.

Data Estimation: The official indexes for real national income (net material product) are linked indexes in which sectoral value added for the 1980s is calculated in constant prices for subperiods. Output for 1952–1957, for example, is calculated in 1952 constant prices, while that for 1981–1985 is calculated in constant 1980 prices. The subperiod indexes so derived are then linked to get an index in "comparable prices" for the whole period. This procedure tends to bias early year growth rates upward because of the very high industrial and low agricultural prices of those earlier periods. These high industrial and low agricultural prices reflect relative scarcities in the recovery period from wartime destruction (1949–1952) and do not reflect relative scarcities in other periods including the latter half of the 1950s. To remove this source of bias, I have recalculated each sector's net value added into 1980 prices for all periods. The procedure followed was first to derive the deflator used by the Chinese for their linked index (index in current prices/index in comparable prices) and then use that deflator to estimate sectoral value added in 1980 prices. The result is a quantity index of net material product based on 1980 price weights. The method is crude but it has the virtue of recalculating net material product using prices that give a more realistic weight to agriculture and industry than do prices from the 1950s. Many other sources of bias in the data remain, however. High prices for certain fast-growing industrial products such as petroleum and low prices for slower-growing industries such as coal, for example, may bias upward the constant price industrial price index. Agricultural value added is deflated by an index based mainly on the purchase prices of farm products, but we know that farm input prices behaved very differently from output prices and value added should have been derived by first deflating gross output and inputs separately. For a discussion of those and other sources of bias, see Yeh (1986).

Table 4. (*Continued*)

Labor force growth rates are based on official data on the size of the labor force. Capital stock data were estimated from official data on annual "accumulation" in current prices deflated by the same index used for industry. This index may understate inflation in the investment goods industry in the 1980s, in which case the true capital stock growth rate in the 1980s would be lower than the figures used in this table, and productivity growth would be higher (K. Chen *et al.*, 1987). It was assumed that the capital stock depreciated at 5% a year and that the initial capital stock in 1980 prices was 214.5 billion yuan (3 times net material product in that year). Capital stock figures for later years were obtained by adding deflated annual accumulation minus depreciation to the initial capital stock estimate.

The capital and labor output elasticities (W_K and W_L) were assumed to be 0.4 and 0.6 respectively. Estimates of these elasticities for other countries have used differing methodologies and have come up with widely varying results. The estimates for China in this study are similar to those of L. R. Cummings, D. Cummings, and D. W. Jorgenson for various countries, but are substantially different from the elasticity estimates of Edward Denison (W_L typically is around 0.75) or Robinson (W_L is about 0.35). Given that the incomes of factors of production are not determined by market forces in China, Chinese income data are not a reliable basis for estimating what income shares would be under market conditions. All one can really do, therefore, is to use some plausible estimate of the shares or a range of plausible estimates. Only an implausibly high estimate for the share in income of capital, a capital elasticity of say 0.7 or 0.8, would require alteration of the conclusions reached in the text of this essay. In fact, even such a high elasticity, if it existed earlier as well, would not change the conclusion that the rate of growth in productivity was higher after the reform than before.

inputs and rising productivity in the use of those inputs remains a controversial topic on theoretical as well as measurement grounds. However, one comes down on these data and methodological issues, no plausible estimates are likely to upset the principal conclusion that productivity growth after 1976 was much higher than it was in the years prior to that date.

Did an increase in the growth rate of the capital stock lead to a rise in the rate of productivity increase or was it the productivity increase that pulled up the rate of growth of the capital stock? If the reforms were responsible for the higher NMP growth rate, then causation would have been from productivity growth to higher rates of capital formation rather than the reverse and this appears to have been the case. In the first half of the 1970s, the Chinese gross domestic capital formation rate was around 30% of GDP, an extremely high rate for a poor country. If Chinese planners had tried to push the rate even higher, say to 40%, the likely result would have been even more pressure on consumption and resulting negative influences on worker and farmer incentives and productivity. A higher rate of capital formation would have made it possible to introduce more new technology embodied in that additional capital, but the amount of embodied new technology in the absence of reform was greatly reduced. Reform was particularly critical to increasing the amount of new technology imported from abroad. It was reform, therefore, that made possible a rise in productivity and growth of net material product which in turn allowed for an increase in both consumption and the absolute amount (but not the share) of capital formation. After peaking in 1978, however, the rate of capital formation actually fell by 8% points by 1981 before rising slightly again in subsequent years.

Reform and productivity growth thus led the way to higher overall growth, but which reforms were most instrumental and where was productivity growth highest? Unfortunately, it is not possible to disaggregate product, capital stock, and labor force data by sector or by industry in a way that would allow a systematic identification of those sectors that accounted for most of the rise in productivity. The discussion that follows, therefore, is based on impressionistic evidence and is in no sense definitive.

Agriculture clearly played an important role in the accelerated productivity growth of the reform periods. As demonstrated in Table 1, the growth rates of grain and cash crop output and of animal husbandry accelerated markedly after rural reform got under way in 1979. Growth rates of major agricultural inputs, however, did not rise significantly in the late 1970s and early 1980s. Growth in chemical fertilizer and farm machinery accompanied the reform effort but growth rates were lower than in previous years.[32]

Another possible contributor to productivity growth was the small-scale industrial sector. Data on the number of small- and large-scale enterprises and on their gross value of output are presented in Tables 5 and 6. The output of collectively organized small-scale industries actually grew faster than that of the large- and medium-scale sector and by 1984

[32]Conceivably, the growth rate of the total fixed and working capital stock in agriculture could have risen even though the growth rate of specific components such as chemical fertilizer fell. It does not seem likely that this was the case in China in the 1980s, however. While the growth rate in the use of chemical fertilizer fell, the amount of chemical fertilizer used doubled between 1978 and 1985, and was a large share of current input.

Table 5. The scale of industrial enterprises (number of enterprises).

	Total	Large- and medium-scale	Small-scale	Of which: collective	Of which: rural collective
1957	169,500	n.a.	n.a.	119,900	n.a.
1959	318,000	n.a.	n.a.	219,000	n.a.
1962	197,400	n.a.	n.a.	144,400	24,600
1965	157,700	n.a.	n.a.	111,800	12,200
1970	195,000	4,000	191,000	138,000	45,000
1975	262,900	5,700	257,200	187,900	77,400
1977	322,700	6,600	316,100	240,600	133,000
1979	355,000	4,500[a]	350,500	271,200	171,500
1982	388,600	5,400[a]	383,200	301,900	185,800
1984	437,200	6,400[a]	430,800	351,100	217,200
1985	463,200	7,900[a]	455,300	367,800	217,100
1986	499,300	8,790[a]	490,500	400,100	246,000

[a]The definition of "large- and medium-scale" is based on data on physical production capacity (tons of steel produced per unit, etc.). The definition was made more restrictive after 1977, thus reducing the number of enterprises in this category.

Sources: State Statistical Bureau (1981, p. 207); State Statistical Bureau (1985b, pp. 305, 315); State Statistical Bureau (1986a, pp. 234, 276); State Statistical Bureau (1987, p. 38).

Table 6. Gross value of industrial output by enterprise scale (billion yuan).

Year	Total	Large- and medium-scale	Small-scale	Of which: collective
1952	34.3	—	—	1.2
1957	78.4	—	—	14.92
1965	139.4	—	—	13.84
1975	321.9	—	—	54.02
1979	459.1	—	—	87.09
1980	499.2	215.56	283.69	103.44
1982	557.7	248.38	309.37	119.28
1984	703.0	315.32	387.67	175.78
1985	829.5	382.87	446.58	230.08
1986	902.8	421.88	480.92	263.80

Source: See Table 5.

accounted for a quarter of all industrial output. A standard criticism of these small-scale industries as they performed in the early 1970s was that they made inefficient use of key inputs such as steel and electric power and thus were a drag on growth in the large-scale enterprises. One recent econometric estimate using county cross-section data, however, suggests that the rate of return on capital in the small-scale sector was significantly higher than in the large-scale sector. Total productivity and the marginal product of labor, on the other hand, were lower in small-scale industries.[33] A related consideration is that small enterprises, particularly those located in rural areas, could mobilize local supplies of labor, small coal mines, and other local resources that would otherwise lie idle. Small enterprises in the early 1970s were also criticized for overemphasis on regional self-reliance leading to a proliferation of farm machinery and other plants of inefficient scale (Christine Wong, 1982).

In the late 1970s and 1980s, however, the state took steps to consolidate plants where there were obvious economies of scale and to restrict or close down those enterprises that made wasteful use of key inputs. There was a greater emphasis on subcontracting relationships between small and large enterprises. There is no hard evidence, but the likely result of these measures was a marked improvement in productivity in this sector.

The one sector that may not have experienced major gains in total factor productivity is large- and medium-scale industry. The evidence, however, is somewhat contradictory. As mentioned above, cross-section data suggest that total factor productivity in Chinese large-scale industry is much higher than in the small-scale sector even though capital is used less efficiently in the former. Time series data for the state-owned industrial sector which includes most large- and medium-scale plants suggest that total factor productivity did not rise at all during the first years of the 1980s (The World Bank 1985, p. 157). There are numerous problems with the data including, for example, the lack of any reliable price index for deflating the industrial capital stock figures given in current prices (Thomas G. Rawski, 1986). Until these data issues are resolved, it is difficult to say anything very conclusive about whether

[33]These are preliminary results reported in Gary H. Jefferson (1986).

reforms in the 1980s did or did not have a positive impact on state industry's productivity.

Finally, some mention should be made of the service sector. Because more than half of all services are excluded from the Chinese definition of net material product, changes in the performance of the service sector do not account for a significant portion of the changes in productivity estimated in Table 4. Services grew rapidly during the first five-year plan and then were actively suppressed for the next two plus decades. All but a few restaurants were closed down, for example. The state had a monopoly of most commerce and did little to develop commercial networks beyond ensuring the delivery of basic supplies to a limited number of retail outlets. This negative attitude toward services began to change with the freeing up of rural markets in 1979, and the change gathered momentum in the early 1980s. By the mid-1980s, Chinese cities were teeming with new collective shops and restaurants and hundreds of thousands of individuals providing personal services of various kinds. As a result, the service sector in 1984 and 1985 may have grown by as much as 26% a year.[34] Whether or not such a high growth rate occurred, data and methodological limitations make it impossible to say anything about the contribution of productivity growth in the service sector.

There is little doubt, therefore, that productivity growth in China accelerated during the late 1970s and first half of the 1980s and it is plausible to assume that reforms had something to do with this acceleration. But, as the above discussion indicates, it is difficult to identify the measures that had the largest productivity impact.[35] If these sources of growth could be more precisely identified, that knowledge would contribute to an understanding of what needed to be done to sustain high growth in China in the future.

[34] The service sector, according to preliminary data, measured in accordance with the definition used in calculating GDP, rose by 14.8% in 1953–1957, but only 2.1% per year in 1958–1978 and 3.9% per year in 1979–1982 or at just over half the rate of GDP in the latter two periods. In 1984–1985 services grew at a rate 60% above the overall GDP growth rate (Keidel, 1986b, p. 2). In 1986 that part of services included in GNP but excluded from NMP grew by 21.1% in nominal terms (State Statistical Bureau, 1987, p. 4).

[35] For a further discussion of the complexity of relating performance to specific reforms see Robert F. Dernberger (1986, pp. 15–48).

IV. Structural Change

China's per capita product rose threefold between 1953 and 1985. Rises in per capita income of that magnitude are usually accompanied by important changes in the structure of national product and China is no exception to that rule. But were the structural changes in China similar to those of other nations at comparable levels of per capita income?

To answer this question requires an estimate of Chinese per capita GDP in US dollars or some other currency that makes comparison across countries possible. But how does one convert Chinese GDP into dollars? Official exchange rates are an unreliable basis for such a conversion under the best of circumstances and China's exchange rate bears no relationship to a free trade equilibrium exchange rate. And there are a variety of official exchange rates to pick from in any case. The rate was 1.98 yuan to the US dollar in 1983, 2.33 in 1984, 2.94 in 1985, and reached 3.7 in 1986.

There have been a number of attempts to convert Chinese product into US dollars on a product-by-product basis, but these have yielded widely varying results because of the difficulty in getting prices for goods that are truly comparable in type and quality across countries.[36]

The assumption used here is that Chinese per capita GDP in 1985 was about US$500. This estimate would imply that Chinese per capita GDP in 1952 was under US$170 (in 1980s prices). China in 1952, by that estimate, was comparable to Burma and only slightly above the 1980 GDP per capita levels of Nepal, Bangladesh, and Ethiopia. I am skeptical that China was in fact that poor in 1952, but it certainly was not poorer than these countries, which are among the poorest in the world.[37]

---

[36] Attempts to calculate Chinese GDP in US. dollars range from an estimate that puts China at a per capita level near that of the Philippines ($700 in 1980) (Irving Kravis, 1980, pp. 64–86) to $205 per capita (Keidel, 1986a, pp. 1–3). The problems in making reliable comparisons of China's prices with those of other countries are described in Jeffrey R. Taylor (1986).

[37] Agricultural output per capita, for example, was much higher in China than in these countries and the Chinese industrial sector was also more developed. One scholar estimates that China in 1952 was at a level of per capita income roughly comparable to India in the early 1950s (Subramanian Swamy, forthcoming, Ch. 2). This study is controversial, however, and is not used as the basis for the estimate of per capita GDP used here.

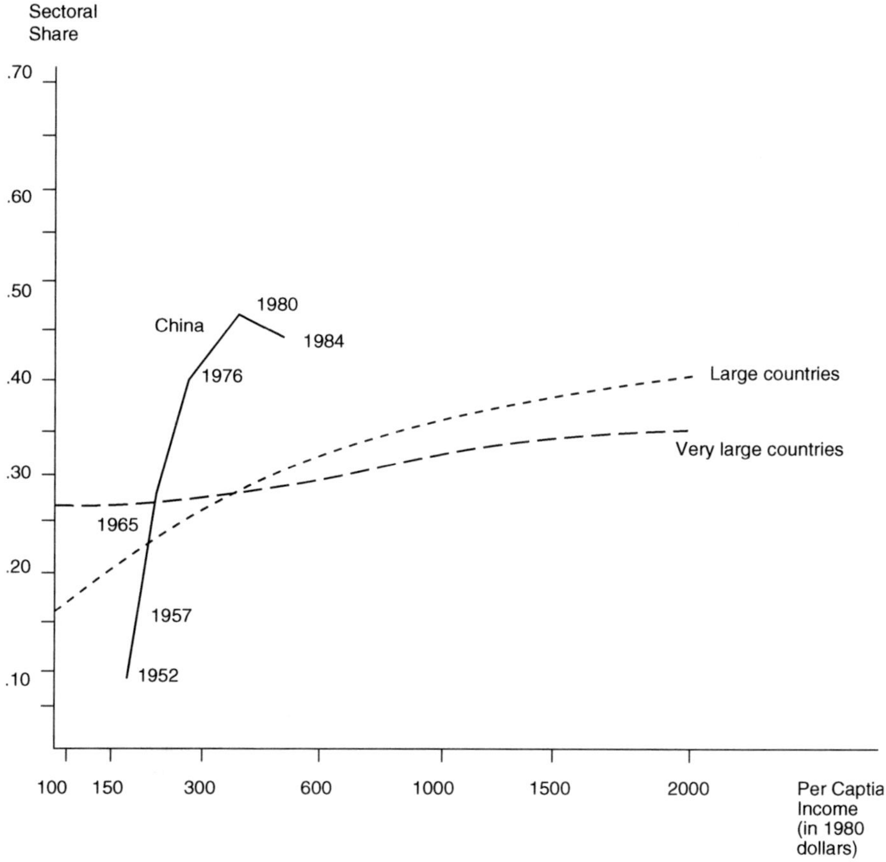

Figure 1. Share of Industry in GDP.

In Figs. 1–3 structural changes in Chinese GDP are compared with the patterns of large (over 15 million population) and very large (over 50 million population in 1965) countries.[38] Because space is limited, the

[38] *Sources*: The data in Figures 1–3 are for 108 countries for the years 1960–1982. Among socialist countries, only China and Hungary are included in the sample. Very large countries were those with a population of more than 50 million in 1965. The data are from a data bank made available to me by Hollis Chenery and Moshe Syrquin as part of research for a joint paper on large countries (Dwight Perkins and Moshe Syrquin, forthcoming). The Chinese data were derived by taking the net material product figures and building them up to GDP so that these figures would be comparable to those for other developing countries.

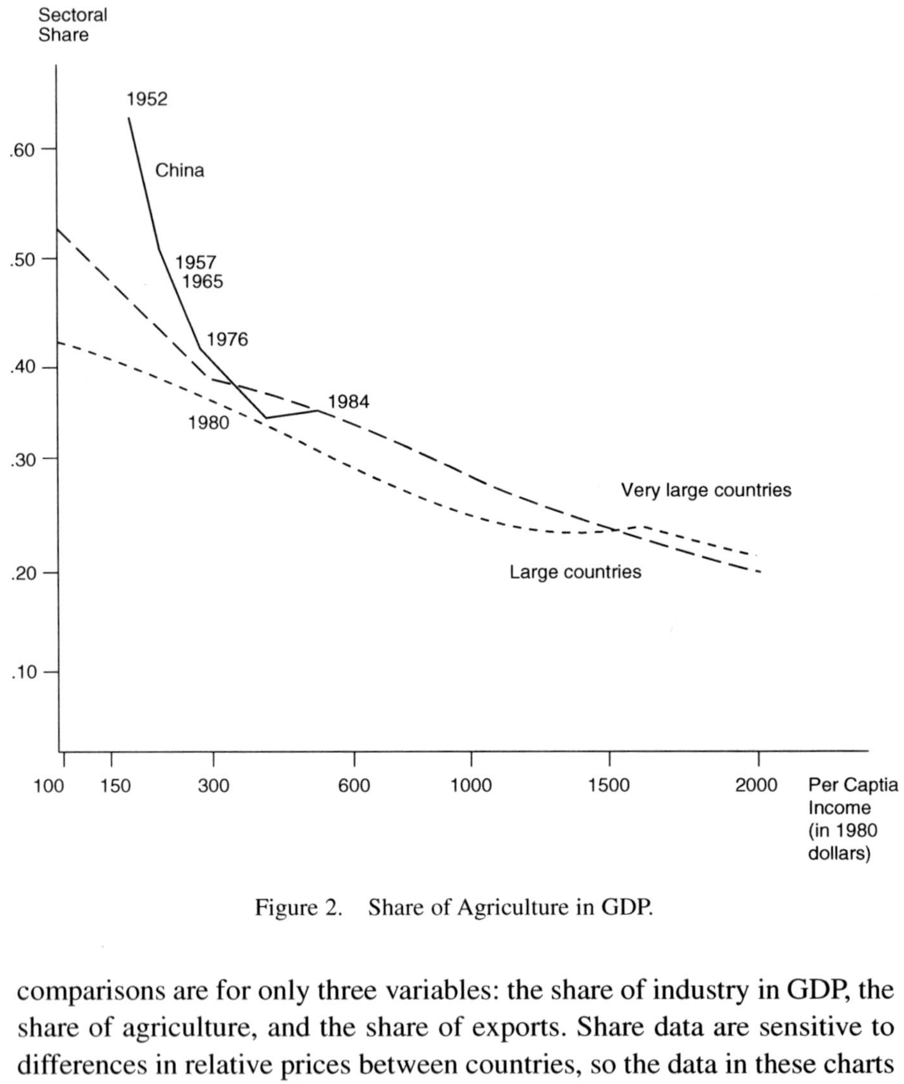

Figure 2. Share of Agriculture in GDP.

comparisons are for only three variables: the share of industry in GDP, the share of agriculture, and the share of exports. Share data are sensitive to differences in relative prices between countries, so the data in these charts should be interpreted with caution. The Chinese share data are based on 1980 relative prices, which are much closer to the relative sector prices of other developing countries than 1952 or 1957 prices, which weight the industrial sector much more heavily.

As the patterns in these figures indicate, China prior to 1976 experienced a pattern of growth strikingly different from that of other large nations. Industry's share in GDP grew much more rapidly, agriculture's

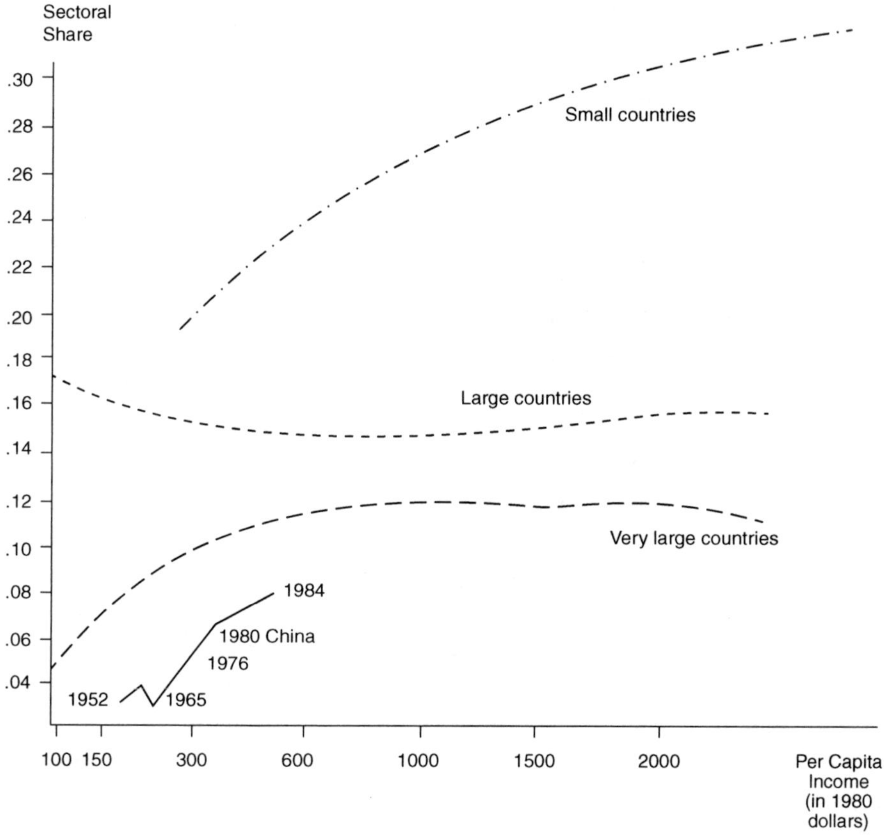

Figure 3. Share of Exports in GDP.

share fell faster, from a very high level to be sure, and the foreign trade share fluctuated around a very low level. These patterns, of course, reflect the Stalinist growth strategy pursued by China throughout the 1950s and into the early 1970s. The emphasis was on industry and autarky. Within industry, the focus was on the heavy industry sector, particularly machinery and steel. Between 1952 and 1976, the share of heavy industry rose from 36% of the gross value of industrial output to 56%.

Since 1976, however, and particularly in the 1980s, China's growth pattern has moved in the direction of the pattern of other large nations at a comparable level of per capita income. In part, this change results from a rethinking of China's long-term development strategy, but short-term probably temporary influences are also involved. The doubling of the foreign trade ratio, for example, is the direct result of China's turn outward in order to better exploit the potential for gains from trade. The decline in the share of industry, on the other hand, reflected the bumper harvests that followed on the introduction of agricultural reforms plus the fact that rapidly growing rural industry was classified as being a part of agriculture. When rural industry is reclassified and the growth of grain and other crops settles back onto a more sustainable path, the share of industry may resume its rise.[39]

In a similar vein, the share of heavy industry fell from 56% in 1976 and 57% in 1978 to 48.5% in 1981, in part because of a long-term effort to achieve a better balance between heavy and light industry. But it is also the case that the severe energy shortage of 1980–1981 necessitated a cutback in industries that were major users of energy inputs. With the easing of the energy shortage, the share of heavy industry began creeping up again and reached 53% in 1985.

If the data were available, it also would have been desirable to include a figure portraying the changing share of the service sector in Chinese GDP. Like most socialist countries, China neglected its service sector throughout the 1950s and 1960s and well into the 1970s. In the 1980s, as already discussed, in an effort to ameliorate the urban employment problem, the state removed many of the restrictions on the urban service sector, and as a result, restaurants, small traders, and many personal services blossomed. The state also began putting large amounts of investment into housing. In the 1960s only 5% of all capital construction investment went into residential buildings. In the 1980s this figure had risen to 21%. The data, however, are not yet in a form that allows for systematic comparisons of the Chinese service sector with patterns of service sector development elsewhere.

[39] Chinese relative prices may still exaggerate the share of industry. Thus, a renewed upward trend in the share of industry would not necessarily take Chinese industry to an unprecedented share of GDP if the value of industry were measured in relative prices similar to those in large countries.

Chinese planners are still groping for an appropriate sectoral development strategy. The greater emphasis on material incentives necessitates greater attention to providing the consumer goods to back up the increases in incomes. Export promotion has a similar influence, because China's comparative advantage lies mainly with consumer manufactures. On the other hand, China's low foreign trade ratio and its large investment budget combine to encourage the continued rapid growth of construction materials, steel, and machinery. The demand for steel, for example, continues to grow rapidly as does the demand for energy, and China does not have sufficient foreign exchange earnings to meet these needs entirely with imports.

V. Income Distribution and Welfare

In most societies, the ultimate purpose of economic growth is to raise the consumption and welfare of the people. Did growth in China lead to a rise in the standard of living of the Chinese people? Was the rise that occurred faster or slower after the introduction of reforms?

Data on the rise in per capita consumption in real terms are presented in Table 7. Alternative data sets and deflaters give results that differ from those in this table, but the basic trends remain much the same. As the estimates in the table make clear, the impact of the reforms on the standard of living of the Chinese people was dramatic, particularly in agriculture. The rise in real per capita consumption of the average Chinese farmer was greater during the 7 years after 1978 than in the entire previous 26 years (91% versus 76%). The change was less dramatic in urban areas but the average annual growth rate still doubled, although the quality of these urban figures is open to question.[40]

[40]The figures on urban consumption in Table 7 and the income data in Table 8 need to be treated with great caution because there are important differences in these two series that are difficult to explain. The reported urban population, for example, actually grew faster than the total urban wage bill (measured in real terms), which implies a decline in average per capita real income in the 1980s. The urban population figures, however, significantly overstate the rise in urban population in the 1979–1985 period because the definition of what was urban was changed for the 1984 and 1985 estimates. Until we have better urban population data, it will be difficult to know whether the urban consumption data are consistent with urban income data (net of savings).

Table 7. Urban and rural consumption per capita (yuan in 1985 prices).

	(1) Rural	(2) Urban	(3) Ratio (1) ÷ (2)
1952	96.6	248.9	0.388
1957	113.4	314.6	0.360
1965	129.4	331.4	0.390
1978	169.1	514.1	0.329
1985	324.0	754.0	0.430
	Growth rates (percent per year)		
1951–1978	2.2	2.8	
1978–1985	9.7	5.6	

Note: The data in this table were originally given in terms of current prices for the "farm" and "nonfarm" population. They have been converted into real income by deflating the urban figures by the worker cost of living index and the rural figures by the nationwide retail price index. The use of the nationwide retail price index to deflate rural consumption may overstate the growth of rural consumption, mainly because rural consumers do not have easy access to goods sold at the official retail prices that dominate the national retail price index. Thus peasants buy more on uncontrolled markets where prices have risen faster than on controlled markets. How much of a difference this would make in the above estimates cannot be known until we have a better deflator and we know more about how the consumption figure in current prices was calculated.

Were these increased benefits equitably distributed? In this section, we shall look at the distribution of benefits defined to include money income and goods and services distributed through the market. In the next section, we shall deal briefly with how the state allocated one particularly critical social service, health care, and will mention briefly other benefits not distributed through the market. A common assumption both inside and outside of China is that the expanding role of the market would to some degree reverse the presumed trend toward reduced inequality of the previous three decades. The Chinese press, for example, has frequently proclaimed in recent years that it is all right for a few to get rich first and pull the others along with them later. These proclamations have generally followed incidents in which successful small entrepreneurs have been criticized or subjected to extortion by local cadres and their neighbors. The perception among many, therefore, is that inequality is on the rise and in politics perceptions often matter more than the reality. The reality in China in the early 1980s was in fact quite in contradiction to these perceptions.

Nationwide income inequality in China is driven by what has happened to the distribution of income within the urban and rural sectors and to the ratio of income between these two sectors. Data on the within-sector distribution of income are based on small sample surveys and are not reliable. These figures, however, do not support the view that inequality has changed significantly in recent years. Within the rural sector, there was a major decrease in inequality in the early 1950s when landlord land was confiscated and turned over to the poorest elements in the villages.[41] Surprisingly, collectivization of agriculture had little impact on the size distribution of income in rural areas. Regional differences in the distribution of rural income accounted for most of the inequality before and after collectivization. Because regional inequalities did not narrow significantly if at all in the 1960s and 1970s, the rural income differences also did not narrow significantly. Attempts to estimate Lorenz curves or Gini coefficients from rural household income surveys suggest that the rural distribution of income in China in the 1970s and 1980s may have been little changed from the mid-1950s.[42]

Similarly, in the urban sector, inequality was reduced significantly in the first half of the 1950s by the confiscation (sometimes with modest compensation) of most privately held urban property. The within-urban inequality that remained after this state takeover of urban property was due to wage and salary differentials in state enterprises. These differentials were set by the central government and there was little regional

[41] The one study of the income distribution implications of land reform is by C. Robert Roll (1974).

[42] There is a growing literature on the distribution of income in rural China based on data released over the past few years by the Chinese government. See, for example, E. B. Vermeer (1982); Perkins and Yusuf (1984, Ch. 6); and Lardy (1983b, Chap. 4).

variation in either the average urban wage or the differentials between one grade and another. Furthermore, neither the average real wage nor the size of these differentials changed much from the time they were first introduced in the 1950s to the late 1970s. In the early 1970s and perhaps earlier, new entrants to the labor force came in at the lower end of the scale and there were few promotions. When wages were unfrozen in the late 1970s, the initial increases were concentrated in the lower wage grades, which should have reduced inequality further. The large increase in collective and individual service workers in the 1980s may also have had an impact on inequality, but the direction of that impact cannot be determined by a priori reasoning. For what it is worth, an urban household survey for 1984 indicates that inequality in that year was slightly less than in the 1981 survey.[43]

Wages and bonuses constitute only a part of the real income of the urban population and we know even less about the distribution of non-wage benefits over time such as highly subsidized housing and health care. For the urban elite, there are the added privileges of access to automobiles, telephones, and stores where high-quality imported goods are available. These privileges existed before 1976 and they have continued to exist since, but it is not possible to say whether their share in total real income has risen or fallen. The real significance of these special privileges, however, does not rest with their impact on formal measures of income inequality. It is people's perceptions of these privileges and whether they are increasing or decreasing that will have the greatest influence on the future of reforms. If it is widely felt that a small elite is enriching itself by manipulating the system to their personal benefit whether by soliciting bribes or through conspicuous consumption of imported goods, opposition to the system that made this possible will build.

Trends in the rural–urban income and consumption differentials are easier to trace and to explain than the within-urban differences. As the data

---

[43]The standard deviation of urban household income divided by the mean of that income was 0.31, down from 0.345 in 1981. An estimate for 1964 suggests a ratio of 0.35, but this latter figure is based on data that required assumptions by the analyst that could significantly bias the results. These figures are from State Statistical Bureau (1985b, pp. 561, 565) and State Statistical Bureau (1981, p. 438).

in Table 7 indicate, the ratio of rural to urban consumption per capita changed little between 1952 and 1965, declined perceptibly by 1978, and then rose sharply after 1978. Even when one takes into account the uncertainties connected with the estimates of rural consumption (see note to Table 7), there is little doubt that rural consumption grew faster than that in urban areas. In the urban areas, real wages per worker were frozen throughout the 1960s and much of the 1970s but real wages per urban resident rose at around 3% a year. Heavy urban investments combined with tight restrictions on rural-to-urban migration led urban enterprises to employ a higher percentage of the members of urban households. Thus, the real income per household rose even though the wage rate remained unchanged.

Rural income and consumption also grew over the pre-1978 period but at a slower rate. Value-added per farm worker increased little (see Table 8), but improvement in the rural-urban terms of trade meant that rural purchasing power did rise at nearly 2% a year. The rise in rural

Table 8. Growth rates in real per capita income (in percentage per year).

	1951–1978	1978–1984
Agricultural sector		
Value added per capita deflated by farm purchase prices	0.4	9.4
Value added per capita deflated by retail prices	1.9	14.3
Urban state wages		
Average wage of state workers	0.5	—[a]
Total state wage bill divided by total urban population	3.2	—[a]

[a] Because of the large increase in the collective sector wage bill and in the number of workers in that sector plus the redefinition of urban areas in 1984, it is misleading to divide the state wage bill by total urban population. The growth rates so derived are negative but meaningless.

Note on methodology: Agricultural value-added deflated by prices paid to farmers for their output is a measure of the real net output of the agricultural sector. Agricultural value added, however, is also a measure of the income in current prices of farmers. But the real value of this income to the farmers is determined by how much in terms of consumption goods this net value can purchase. Money income (or value added) in current prices deflated by the retail price index of goods sold to farmers is the appropriate measure of changes in real farmer purchasing power. If the prices paid to farmers for their output rise faster than the prices paid by farmers for consumption goods, the real purchasing power of farmers will rise faster than their real production. The retail price index used here to deflate agricultural value added is subject to some of the same limitations discussed in the note to Table 7.

income relative to that in the urban areas after 1978, of course, is the result of both the agricultural boom brought about by the rural reforms plus a continued improvement in the rural–urban terms of trade. There was no comparable boom in the urban areas in the 1980s.

Despite the closing rural–urban gap after 1978, a nationwide measure of inequality such as a Gini coefficient could still show rising inequality if the percentage of population in the urban areas was rising fast enough to offset the effect of the declining gap in average incomes.[44] Between 1957 and 1978, official data suggest that the urban share in total population rose only modestly, but data published in 1984 and 1985 indicate a big jump in the share of people in urban areas (Table 9). But this jump resulted from a change in definition of what constituted an urban area and the formal designation of many new cities and towns. Some of the new "urban" residents are in fact still farmers. More to the point, while an increase in the urban share in total population has occurred and may be of the order of magnitude indicated in Table 9, that increase may have occurred over the previous decade or even two decades. It is not possible, therefore, to estimate how this changing share in total population affects nationwide measures of inequality in particular periods such as the seven years following the institution of reforms.[45]

Despite the poor quality of the data, there is no support for the view that inequality in China fell significantly during periods such as that of the Cultural Revolution or rose as a result of market-oriented reforms. Conceivably, the trends were the reverse because of what happened in these two periods to the rural–urban income gap, but the data simply are not good enough to tell for certain. Whatever the precise trends in inequality turn out to be as a result of further research using better data, there is no doubt that the economic benefits of the reforms in the 1979–1987 period were widely shared.

---

[44] If urban incomes are higher than those in rural areas, then national inequality rises as the percentage of population in urban areas rises up to the point where half the population is in the urban areas, after which further rises in the urban share will lead to a decline in inequality. All of this assumes that the rural-urban differential itself does not change.

[45] For a useful attempt to construct nationwide Lorenz curves over a longer period, see Irma Adelman and David Sunding (1987).

Table 9. Urban and rural population data.

	Within cities and towns		Within rural villages (communes)	
	(Millions)	(Percentage)	(Millions)	(Percentage)
1952	71.6	12.5	503.2	87.5
1957	99.5	15.4	547.0	84.6
1960	130.7	19.7	531.3	80.3
1965	130.5	18.0	594.9	82.0
1976	163.4	17.4	773.8	82.6
1978	172.5	17.9	790.1	82.1
1983	241.3	23.5	783.7	76.5
1985	382.4[a]	38.0	662.9[a]	62.0

[a] In 1984, the Chinese redefined the population designated to be in urban areas by including newly formed townships and the like. Definitional changes have also occurred in earlier years, although none had the impact on the totals as did that of 1984. See Kam Wing Chan and Xueqiang Xu (1985).

Note on urban population data: Chinese population figures include all people within an area designated as urban even if many of those people are farmers. People living in rural villages or communes are classified as rural even if those people work in industrial or commercial enterprises. Given these and other uncertainties and conceptual problems connected with China's urban statistics, they are crude indicators at best of the level and pace of urbanization in China.

VI. Health and Population

This discussion of income and inequality would not be complete without mention of the fact that many goods and services destined for consumers in China are distributed outside the market mechanism and are not included in data on either consumption or income. Rents for urban housing, for example, include only part of the basic maintenance and utility charges, and none of the cost of capital embodied in the dwelling.

One of the most important of these nonmarket goods and services was health care. In fact, the case for greater equity in China in the 1960s and 1970s rests in substantial part on the view that certain "basic needs" such as health care were more equitably distributed than income. Health care in the 1960s and 1970s shifted from an urban-based emphasis on curative medicine to a focus on the rural areas and preventive medicine. "Barefoot doctors" or rural paramedics were trained and rural clinics and hospitals built. The commune system provided selected members with the time to acquire training and with income support when they returned to the commune to practice what they had learned.

As is the case with income distribution data, statistics on health in China such as life expectancy and infant mortality are not very reliable. Various analysts have tried to piece together plausible series from scattered data using formal demographic models. The story these estimates appear to tell is a dramatic one. Infant mortality in China in 1965 may still have been as high as 165 per 1,000. Twelve years later in 1977, it had fallen to 64 per thousand despite only modest increases in per capita income. Life expectancy at birth in 1965 is estimated to have been 44 years. By 1977, it had risen to 64 years (Dean T. Jamison *et al.*, 1984). If these figures give a rough picture of what occurred in this period as appears likely, the improvement in health care in rural areas was unprecedented either in China or anywhere else where per capita incomes were comparable. Another Western estimate also supports the view that infant mortality fell substantially (from 84 to 45 per 1,000) and that life expectancy rose (from 57.8 to 64.2 years) between 1965 and 1976, although these changes are not so large (Judith Banister, 1986). On either estimate, these health measures suggest that there was a great deal more than rhetoric to China's basic needs strategy. Declines in mortality of these magnitudes could only have occurred if the benefits of better nutrition, better curative care, and organized preventive health programs were widely available throughout China. Programs concentrated in urban and a few rich rural areas could not have yielded these results.

Have the reforms of the 1980s undermined these health care and nutrition efforts? The demise of the commune system withdrew one important base of support for rural nutrition and preventive health programs (Athar Hussain, forthcoming). The number of barefoot doctors declined significantly. On the other hand, the number of people with more formal training increased. It may be that the barefoot doctor system had done its job by the 1980s and needed to give way to a system based on longer, higher-quality medical training. It is too early, however, to know whether this is the case.

Mention should also be made of China's population policies which were intimately tied to both the health programs and the rural political and

Table 10. Population and vital rates

	Population (millions)	Crude birth rate (per 1,000)			Crude death rate (per 1,000)			Rate of natural increase (per 1,000)
			Reconstructed			Reconstructed		
		Official	(a)	(b)	Official	(a)	(b)	Official
1953	587.96	37.0	42.2	45.5	14.0	25.8	30.7	23.0
1957	646.53	34.0	43.3	45.0	10.8	18.1	23.4	23.2
1960	662.07	20.9	26.8	24.5	25.4	44.6	36.0	−4.6
1962	672.95	37.0	41.0	41.0	10.0	14.0	19.5	27.0
1965	725.38	37.9	39.0	41.5	9.5	11.6	17.5	28.4
1970	829.92	33.4	37.0	34.0	7.6	9.5	10.1	25.8
1976	937.17	19.9	23.1	20.1	7.25	7.8	9.3	12.7
1978	962.59	18.25	20.7	18.7	6.25	7.5	8.0	12.0
1980	987.05	18.2	17.6	18.5	6.3	7.7	7.8	11.9
1982	1015.41	21.1	21.1	—	6.6	7.9	—	14.5
1985	1045.32	17.8	—	—	6.6	—	—	11.2
1986	1060.08	20.8	—	—	6.7	—	—	14.1

Sources: The official data are from State Statistical Bureau (1984, p. 83); State Statistical Bureau (1986b, p. 21); and State Statistical Bureau (1987, p. 16). The reconstructed figures under (a) are from Judith Banister (1986, pp. 165–166). The reconstructed figures under (b) are from Jamison *et al.* (1984, p. 113).

economic control system of which the commune was the core element. The official estimates of China's population and vital rates together with two Western estimates of China's vital rates are presented in Table 10. The Western reconstructions suggest that the 1960–1961 famine may have been worse than even the grim official figures suggest. Differences between the two Western reconstructions and between them and the official series also raise questions about when and how rapidly the crude death rate began to fall.

All three series, however, tell much the same story about China's rate of population growth. China's demographic transition began with a sharp fall in the crude death rate between the early 1950s and 1970. During that same period, birth rates fell modestly, if at all, and China's population growth rate rose about 2.5% a year. After 1970, however, the crude birth rate declined sharply by 15 or 16 per thousand in only six years and then leveled off. China's population growth rate, as a result, fell to an average of 1.2% per year in the 10 years after 1976.

What could explain such a rapid fall in the crude birth rate? To begin with, the national rate was driven by the fall in birth rates in rural areas. The urban birth rate decline began much earlier, but the urban share in total population was too small to have a major impact on the national averages. Because rural real income per capita grew by only 4% between 1970 and 1976 or 8% between 1965 and 1976, it is difficult to see how rising per capita incomes could explain much of the change.

There is little reason to doubt that most of the explanation for China's birth rate decline in the 1970s rests with the country's family planning program, particularly given the fact that China's changing age structure, other things being equal, would have led to a rise in the crude birth rate. Education about family planning was backed up by both material incentives and some degree of coercion (John Aird, 1986). Political relaxation and a consequent reduction in the coercive power of rural cadres might have had something to do with the rise in the birth rate in 1981 and 1982 and again in 1986, but we do not really know. The advent of household agriculture under the responsibility system, which should have provided peasants with an incentive to increase family size, was initially accompanied by a renewed decline in the crude birth rate. This decline possibly can be explained in part by the vigorous campaign to limit family size to one child per couple. When enforcement of the one child family policy was relaxed slightly in 1985 and 1986, the crude birth rate did rise. Until more data are made available and until more analysis is done on the data that are available, however, no firm conclusions are possible about which measures explain the fertility decline.

VII. Conclusion

No short article can do justice to the magnitude of China's economic reform efforts in the decade following Mao's death in 1976. The task of simply describing the diversity of initiatives is made doubly difficult by the fact that reform as of the mid-1980s was an ongoing process. Major strides toward expanding the role of the market in both rural and urban areas had been made, but many features of central planning and bureaucratic control remained. The direction was toward further expansion of the market's role, but there was also resistance, most of it political in nature.

Fueling the momentum of reform was its impact on economic performance. The improvement in performance was particularly marked in rural areas, but there were urban successes as well. Nationally, total factor productivity rose dramatically after 1976 only in part due to agriculture. China also moved away significantly from its earlier Stalinist emphasis on machinery and steel and on autarky. Foreign trade expanded rapidly and consumer goods and services were much more plentiful in the 1980s.

Nor does this first phase of reform appear to have led to a significant worsening in the size distribution of income. The farm output boom of the late 1970s and early 1980s actually reduced inequality by narrowing the rural–urban income gap, although other forces may have been at work that widened within-sector inequality. The rural–urban gap had clearly widened during the previous decade of the Cultural Revolution (1966–1976). On the other hand, the pre-1976 decade coincided with a period of pronounced and widely shared improvements in rural health and other "basic needs," so it would be incorrect to picture that decade as one of rising inequality.

If the future of market-oriented reforms in China was indicated by its success to date measured in economic terms alone, that future would seem to be assured. Except for the inflation rate, all measures of performance favor the post-1976 period over what went before, usually by a wide margin. But in China, politics have more often driven economics than the reverse. A slowdown in growth in the future could feed political discontent and generate opposition to reform, and even the most rapidly growing developing nations experience periods of slow growth and stagnation. Whether those who oppose reforms are capable of mobilizing sufficient support to slow or reverse the reform process during periods of lowered growth only time will tell.

What is required is not movement all the way to an unfettered market system with or without private ownership of industry and commerce. Expansion of the role of the market is an essential part of the reform package, but large areas of bureaucratic control and direction will remain. Of equal or greater importance than expanding the scope of market forces are efforts to improve the functioning of the market forces that are allowed to operate. To achieve that goal, enterprise managers need to gain more autonomy from China's economic bureaucrats and to pay attention to cutting enterprise costs, increasing sales, and raising product quality. The budget constraint needs to be hardened substantially. Price reform is also important and that involves further restrictions on the quantity of goods distributed through the state allocation system at fixed prices. Finally, the hope for productivity gains from continued reform depend critically on maintaining an open economy and rapidly growing exports of manufactures. Without rapidly growing exports, the foreign exchange bottleneck will be a chronic drag on rapid growth. Whether or not China will be able to expand exports rapidly, however, is not in China's hands alone.

Acknowledgment

I am indebted directly and indirectly to many people for help and encouragement in writing this essay. I particularly wish to mention Moses Abramovitz, whose idea it was in the first place and who contributed many comments on the initial draft. Others who contributed extensive comments include Abram Bergson, Gregory Chow, Robert Dernberger, Janos Kornai, Nicholas Lardy, Thomas Rawski, and an anonymous reader. Gretchen O'Connor was responsible for the production of the manuscript itself. It is hoped that those readers will see many of their ideas reflected in the revised manuscript. Most scholarship is a collective effort and this chapter is certainly no exception, even if I alone am responsible for any errors.

References

Adelman, I and D Sunding (1987). "Economic policy and income distribution in China". *Journal Comparative Economics*, September, 11(3), pp. 444–461.

Aird, JS (1986). Coercion in family planning: Causes, methods and consequences. In U.S. Congress; Joint Economic Committee, pp. 184–221.

American Rural Small-Scale Industry Delegation (1977). *Rural Small-Scale Industry in the People's Republic of China*. Berkeley, CA: University of California Press.

Banister, J (1986). Implications of China's 1982 Census Results. In U.S. Congress; Joint Economic Committee, pp. 160–183.

——— *China's Pattern of Population Growth*. Stanford, CA: Stanford University Press.

Byrd, W (1983). *China's Financial System: The Changing Role of Banks*. Boulder: Westview Press.

Byrd, W (1987). "The atrophy of central planning in Chinese industry: Impact of the two-tier plan/market system." *Journal of Comparative Economy*, September, 11(3), pp. 295–308.

Byrd, W and T Gene (1985). "Factor allocation in Chinese industry." Paper prepared for conference on Chinese enterprise management. Beijing, August.

Byrd, W (1984). *Recent Chinese economic reforms: Studies of two industrial enterprises*. World Bank Staff Working Papers No. 652, 1984.

Chan, KW and X-Q Xu (1985). "Urban population growth and urbanization in China since 1949." *China Quarterly*, December, 104, pp. 583–613.

Chen, K (1987). "New estimates of fixed investment and capital stock for Chinese state industry." Un-pub. Manuscript.

Chen, Y (1986). "Planning and the market." *Beijing Review*, July 21, 29(29), pp. 14–15.

Cheng, H-S (1987). "Monetary policy and inflation in China." Paper presented to conference on Challenges to Monetary Policy in Pacific Basin Countries, Federal Reserve Bank of San Francisco, September.

China Agricultural Yearbook Completion Committee (1984). *Zhongguo nongye nianjian*. Beijing: Agricultural Press.

Chow, G (1985). *The Chinese Economy*. NY: Harper & Row.

Chow, G (1987). Money and Price Level Determination in China. *Journal of Comparative Economics*. September, 11(3), pp. 319–333.

Dernberger, RF (1986). "Economic policy and performance." In U.S. Congress; Joint Economic Committee, pp. 15–48.

Dong, F (1985). "More on the Forms of China's Socialist Ownership." *Jingji yanjiu*, April 20, 4, pp. 3–11.

Economic Planning Board (1986). *Major Statistics of Korean Economy*. Seoul: Economic Planning Board.

General Survey Group of the Chinese Institute for Economic Systems Reform (1986). *Gaige*: *Women mianlin de tiaozhan yu xuanze*.

Guizhou Yearbook Compilation Committee (1985). *Guizhou Nianjian*. Guiyang: Guizhou People's Press.

Hartford, K (1985). Socialist agriculture is dead: Long live socialist agriculture! organizational transformation in rural China. In *The Political Economy of Reform in Post-Mao China*. Eds.: Elizabeth Perry and Christine Wong (eds.), Cambridge, MA: Council on East Asian Studies, Harvard University, pp. 31–61.

Howe, C (1973). *Wage Patterns and Wage Policy in Modern China*. Cambridge: Cambridge University Press.

Hsiao, KH (1971). *Money and Monetary Policy in Communist China*. NY: Columbia University Press.

Hsiao, WC (1984). "The transformation of health care in China." *New England Journal of Medicine*, April, 310, pp. 932–936.

Hussain, A. "Nutrition and nutritional insurance in China, 1949–1984." Forthcoming.

Jamison, DT (1984). *China: The Health Sector*. Washington, DC: The World Bank.

Jefferson, GH (1986). "Allocative Efficiency and the Sources of Productivity Growth Within Chinese Industry." Unpublished manuscript, Brandeis University.

Keidel, A (1986a). "How poor is China?" *China Macroeconomic Newsletter*. Washington, DC: Rock Creek Research, May 19.

Keidel, A (1986b). "China Economic Letter." Washington, DC: Rock Creek Research, September 8, (revised).

Keidel, A (1986c). "China Economic Letter." Washington, DC: Rock Creek Research, October 20.

Kornai, J (1986). "The Hungarian reform process: Visions, hopes and reality." *Journal of Economic Literature*, December 24(4), pp. 1687–1737.

Kravis, I (1980). An Approximation of the Relative Real Per Capita GDP of the People's Republic of China," in *Report of the CSCPRC economics delegation to the People's Republic of China*. Washington, DC: National Academy of Sciences, pp. 64–86.

Kueh, Y-Y (1984). China's new agricultural policy program: Major economic consequences, 1979–1983. *Journal of Compartive Economics*. December, 8(4), pp. 353–375.

Lardy, N (1983a). Agricultural Prices in China. World Bank Staff Working Papers, No. 606, Washington, DC.

Lardy, N (1983b). *Agriculture in Chinas Modern Economic Development*. Cambridge: Cambridge University Press.

Lardy, N and K Lieberthal (1983). *Chen Yun's Strategy for China's Development: A non-Maoist Alternative*. Armonk NY: M. E. Sharpe.

Li, C (1986). "Money, supply and macroeconomic controls." *Social Sciences in China*, September, 7(3), pp. 51–62.

Lin, CZ (1986). "Some issues in Chinese price reform implementation." Paper presented to the ACLS-SSRC Conference on Price and Wage Reform in the People's Republic of China, Washington, DC, June.

Lin, J (1985). "A method for forecasting the demand for money." *Jingji yanjiu*, August 20, 8, pp. 11–15.

Ma, B and H Zhunyan (1987). "Enlivening large state enterprises: Where is the motive force?" *Journal Comparative Economics*, September, pp. 503–508.

Ministry of Coal Industry Compilation Committee (1982). *China Coal Industry Yearbook*. Hong Kong: Economic Information and Agency.

Ministry of Ferrous Metals Compilation Committee (1985). *Zhongguo gangtie gongye nianjian*. Ferrous Metals Industry Publishers.

Naughton, B (1986). "Finance and planning reforms in industry." In U.S. Congress Joint Economic Committee.

Parish, WL (1985). *Chinese Rural Development: The Great Transformation*. Armonk, NY: M. E. Sharpe.

People's Republic of China Record of Major Economic Events Publishing Committee (1985). *Zhonghua renmingonghequo jingji dashiji (1949–1984)*. Beijing: Beijing Press.

Perkins, DH (1966). *Market Control and Planning in Communist China*. Cambridge, MA: Harvard University Press.

Perkins, DH (1968). *Agricultural Development in China, 1368–1968.* Chicago: Aldine Press.

Perkins, DH (1983). "Research on the economy of the People's Republic of China. A survey of the field." *Journal of Asian Studies*, February, 42(2), pp. 345–372.

Perkins, DH and S Moshe. "The development of large countries: The influence of size." In *Handbook of development economics*. H. Chenery and T. N. Srinivasan (eds.), Forthcoming.

Perkins, DH and Y Shahid (1984). *Rural Development in China*. Baltimore: Johns Hopkins University Press.

Perry, E and C Wong (1985). *The Political Economy of Reform in Post-Mao China*. Cambridge, MA: Council on East Asian Studies, Harvard University Press.

Putterman, L (1985). "Theoretical considerations regarding the demise of team farming in China." Working Paper No. 85–86, Dept. of Economics, Brown U., March.

Rawski, TG (1986). "Productivity change in Chinese industry: Problems of measurement." Paper presented to conference on price and wage reform in the People's Republic of China, Washington, DC, June 17–18.

Reynolds, B (1987). *Journal of Comparative Economics* [Special Issue: *Chinese Economic Reform: How Far, How Fast?*], September, 11(3).

Robinson, S (1971). "Sources of growth in less developed countries: A cross-section study." *Quarterly Journal of Economics*. August, 85(3), pp. 391–408.

Roll, CR (1974). "The Distribution of Rural Income in China: A Comparison of the 1930s and 1950s." PhD dissertation, Harvard University.

Shi, Y (1986). "An exploration of a model for China's stock financing." *Jingji yanjiu*, January 20, 1, pp. 23–28, 34.

Sicular, T (1986a). "Recent agricultural price policies and their effects: The case of Shandong." *China's Economy Looks Toward the Year 2000*. Washington, DC: U.S. GPO, pp. 407–430.

Sicular, T (1986b). Agricultural Planning in China: The Case of Lee Willow Team No. 4. *Food Research Institute Studies*, 20(1), pp. 1–24.

State Statistical Bureau (1981). *Statistical yearbook of China*.

State Statistical Bureau (1984). *Statistical Yearbook of China*.

State Statistical Bureau (1985a). *Zhongguo chengshi tongji nianjian, 1985*. Beijing: New World Pub.

State Statistical Bureau (1985b). *Zhongguo tongji nianjian*.

State Statistical Bureau (1986a). *Zhongguo tongji nianjian*.

State Statistical Bureau (1986b). *Zhongguo tongji zhaiyao*.

State Statistical Bureau (1987). *Zhongguo tongji zhaiyao*.

Swaine, MD (1986). "Heavy Industrial Dominance Under Hua Guofeng: Bureaucracy and the Policy Process." PhD dissertation. Harvard University.

Swamy, Subramanian. "A comparative perspective of the economic growth in China and India: 1870–1985." Forthcoming.

Taylor, JR (1986). "China's price structure in international perspective." Paper presented to the ACLS-SSRC Conference on Price and Wage Reform in the People's Republic of China, Washington, DC, June.

Trade and Price Office of the State Statistical Bureau (1984). *Zhongguo maoi wujia tongji ciliao, 1952–1983*. Beijing: China Statistical Pub.

Travers, L (1984). "Post-1978 rural economic policy and peasant income in China." *China Quarterly,* June 98, pp. 241–259.

U.S. Congress; Joint Economic Committee (1986). *China's Economy Looks Toward the Year 2000*. Washington, DC: U.S. GPO.

Vermeer, EB (1982). "Income differentials in rural China." *China Quarterly*, March, 89, pp. 1–33.

Walder, AG (1986). "The informal Dimension of Enterprise Financial Reforms." In *China's Economy Looks Toward the Year 2000*. Washington, DC: U.S. GPO.

Wang, Z (1985). "The relations between domestic and international prices." *Jingji yanjiu*, September 20, 9, pp. 38–45.

Wiens, T (1987). "Issues in structural reform of the agricultural sector." *Journal Comparative Economics*, September, 11(3), pp. 372–384.

Wong, CPW (1982). Rural Industrialization in the People's Republic of China: Lessons from the Cultural Revolution Decade. In *China Under the Four Modernizations. Joint Economic Committee of the U.S. Congress*, Washington, DC.

The World Bank (1985). *China: Long Term Issues and Options*.

Wu, J and R Zhao (1987). On the dual pricing system in China's industry. *Journal of Comparative Economics*, September, 11(3), pp. 309–318.

Wu, M (1986). "Economic uncertainty and the bankruptcy of socialist enterprises." *Jingji yanjiu*, July 20, 7, pp. 40–45.

Xu, Jing'an (1987). "The stock-share system: A new avenue for China's economic reform." *Journal of Comparative Economics*, September, 11(3), pp. 509–514.

Xue, M (1985). "Readjust prices and transform the price control system". *Jingji yanjiu*, January 20, 1, pp. 3–7.

Yeh, KC (1986). "China's price structure and the measurement of economic growth." Unpublished manuscript.

Yu, G (1986). "Put the price ahead of the value." *Jingji yanjiu*, May 20, (5), pp. 25–35.

Zhao, H (1985). "On some problems in adjusting the supply of money." *Jingji yanjiu*, August 20, 8, pp. 16–19.

Zhu, Y (1986). "Carrying out the bankruptcy law: Its suitability and limitations." *Jingji yanjiu*, September 20, 9, pp. 50–52, 11.

Zweig, D (1983). "Opposition to change in rural China: The system of responsibility and People's communes." *Asian Survey*, July, 23(7), pp. 879–900.

CHAPTER 7

CHINA'S "GRADUAL" APPROACH TO MARKET REFORMS

China's market-oriented economic reform efforts began earlier than in most other former Soviet-type economies except Hungary, have progressed further, and have been carried out despite the absence of radical political reform. Furthermore, by any reasonable yardstick, China's economic reforms have been a success. There ought to be, therefore, lessons for others that can be learned from China's experience — unless, of course, the underdeveloped nature of China's economy, its location in East Asia, and other special characteristics make the Chinese experience unique.

Some former Soviet-type economies, notably Vietnam, have observed what has been transpiring in China and have learned from it; occasional references will be made in this chapter to Vietnamese economic reform efforts. There is also some interest in China's reform experience in such Central Asian republics as Uzbekistan. But are there any lessons for the more industrialized nations of Eastern Europe, Russia, or the Ukraine?

The economic success of China's reforms cannot be seriously challenged by anyone with any kind of comparative perspective. The gross national product (GNP) growth rate data in Table 1 are a part of the story. Since 1978, China's GNP has averaged a growth rate of 8.5% per year. There has been no 15% or 20%, decline in output during the transition period. Even in the aftermath of the Tiananmen tragedy in 1989 and 1990, China's GNP growth rate averaged 4.5% annually. There are some problems with these figures, to be sure.[1]

[1] China's estimates of the growth rate of township and village enterprises, for example, may include some figures that are in current rather than constant prices, which would bias the GNP growth estimates upward.

Table 1. Growth rate of GNP (billion renminbi, constant 1990 prices.

	GNP	Primary sector	Secondary sector	Tertiary sector
1978	655	252	253	150
1979	703	268	274	162
1980	746	264	311	171
1981	782	282	317	183
1982	852	315	334	203
1983	938	341	369	229
1984	1,075	385	423	267
1985	1,204	392	501	312
1986	1,303	405	552	346
1987	1,456	424	628	404
1988	1,592	434	719	438
1989	1,647	448	748	451
1990	1,738	476	789	473
	Growth rates (percent per year)			
1979–1980	6.7	2.4	10.9	6.8
1981–1983	7.9	8.9	5.9	10.2
1984–1988	11.2	4.9	14.3	13.8
1989–1990	4.5	4.7	4.8	3.9
1991	7.0	—	14.2	—
1978–1990	8.5	5.4	9.9	10.0

Adjustments for overstated small-scale enterprise growth, prices not reflecting market forces, and the like would probably reduce these GNP growth rates slightly, but not by enough to change the basic story.

China's ability to expand exports has been equally notable. Chinese exports rose from US$2.3 billion in 1970 to US$9.8 billion in 1978 to over US$70 billion in 1991. In real terms this amounted to a 12% increase per year over the 18-year period 1970–1988 (see Table 2), and that growth has continued through 1991 at more or less the same rate. Three-quarters of the 1991 exports from China were manufactured

Table 2. The growth of foreign trade.

	Exports		Imports	
	Indexes (1970 = 100)			
	Nominal	Real	Nominal	Real
1970	100.0	100.0	100.0	100.0
1975	321.4	162.2	321.8	170.5
1978	431.2	182.2	468.3	264.4
1980	808.6	275.2	840.5	326.0
1983	982.3	398.2	796.6	366.3
1985	1,146.6	474.7	1,475.9	773.6
1988	1,798.3	735.6	1,712.9	724.7
	Growth rates (percent per year)			
1970–78	20.0	7.8	21.3	12.9
1979–83	17.9	16.9	11.2	6.7
1984–88	12.9	13.1	16.5	14.6
1989–90	14.3	—	−1.8	—

Source: China Foreign Economic Relations and Trade Computation Committee, *Zhongguo duiwai jingji maoi nianjian. 1984.* pp. lv–5 and *1989–1990,* p. 303.

Note: These indexes are based on the trade data of the ministry of foreign economic relations and trade (MOFERT) rather than the more generally published trade data from customs. Before 1981, the state statistical bureau also used MOFERT, data but switched over to customs figures in that year. The growth rates of the customs figures are higher than those of MOFERT after 1983.

products, and a high proportion of these were destined for Western markets. Taiwan Province exports, by way of comparison, grew from US$13.4 billion in 1978 to US$64 billion in 1990, while those of the Republic of Korea grew from US$12.7 billion to US$65.0 billion over the same period.[2] In short, China's foreign debt by September 1991 had

[2]National Statistical Office (1991). *Major Statistics of Korean Economy.* Seoul, p. 203, and Council for Economic Planning and Development (1991). *Taiwan Statistical Data Book, 1991.* Taipei, p. 208.

also risen to US$52.55 billion, but foreign exchange reserves had increased to US$40 billion (not including gold holdings worth another US$4–5 billion).[3] Given the rapid rise in exports together with the (probably excessive) clampdown on import growth, China had no problem whatsoever servicing its foreign debt.

Perceptions are that income distribution became substantially more unequal during the reform period. By 1990, there were apparently a handful of people with a net worth of over 100 million yuan (over US$20 million) and a few hundred more with wealth of over 1 or 2 million yuan (US$200,000 or $400,000).[4] Before 1978, almost no one had a net worth of more than a few tens of thousands of yuan. Politically, this handful of wealthy people may have been significant, but in terms of Gini coefficients or some other objective measure of inequality, these "millionaires" were of little consequence. During the first period of reform through 1984, the size distribution of income almost certainly became less unequal largely because farmer incomes rose much faster than incomes in the richer urban areas.[5] After 1984, agricultural output growth slowed, and those with the greatest gains in income were in suburban areas of large cities where much of the boom in small-scale industry was occurring. Remote rural areas did not share much in the rural industrial growth. Still, a large share of China's people saw major improvements in their standard of living. Housing conditions improved markedly in both urban and rural areas, most urban residents and a large number of rural people had television sets where few existed before 1978, and food was plentiful in all but the poorest mountainous regions.

Despite these accomplishments, there was considerable discontent in the urban areas by 1988 and 1989. Inflation was one of the reasons. The official retail price index rose by 18.5% in 1988 and another 17.8% in 1989, and prices on the free markets rose by 30.3% in 1988 according to

---

[3] *China Daily,* December 31, 1991, p. 1.

[4] There is no hard public evidence of the wealth of these people, but informed people feel that such wealthy people in more or less these numbers exist.

[5] Between 1978 and 1984, per capita consumption among the agricultural population according to survey data rose by 68%, while that among the nonagricultural population rose by 30%. State Statistical Bureau (SSB) (1990). *Zhongguo tongji nianjian, 1990.* Beijing: Statistical Publishers, p. 291.

official estimates, which may understate the true rate of increase.[6] These figures will seem modest to those familiar with East Europe or the republics of the former Soviet Union, but the Chinese were used to rates of under 1% a year. The hyperinflation of the 1940s had undermined the political strength of the Guomindang government and sensitized a generation of Chinese leaders to the dangers of rapid price increases. Corruption was also perceived as a major problem by 1988 and 1989, and the reforms were seen as one of the causes. Connections (*guanxi*) and outright bribes became the common route used to bypass officials. The dual price system, described below, provided opportunities for easy profits for those who could get allocations of goods at state prices and then resell them at the much higher market prices. Objectively, it would be more accurate to say that corruption resulted from the continuation of unreformed government regulations and state-set prices rather than from the reforms themselves. If the dual price system had been replaced by a single market-determined price system, that source of corruption, at least, would have disappeared. But the widely held perception was that corruption had risen sharply during the reforms, and so the reforms got the blame. Student demonstrators in the spring of 1989 were able to tap into this well of discontent.

One lesson from the Chinese economic reform effort therefore is that a rising standard of living does not guarantee support for the government in power during the period of ascent. One could learn this lesson from a variety of other historical episodes, however, such as the experience of South Korea in the 1980s. The more interesting lessons from China's experience lie elsewhere.

I. The Sequencing of Reforms

There is a growing body of literature on which reforms should be tried before others.[7] The Chinese, however, did not start out with any particular

[6]The weights for the construction of the price indexes, for example, may be biased toward goods sold at state prices, but the degree of bias would not fundamentally alter the picture of inflation portrayed by the official indexes.

[7]For a review of some of the literature, see Michael Roemer and Stephen C. Radelet (1991). "Macroeconomic reform in developing countries." In *Reforming Economic Systems in Developing Countries,* Dwight Perkins and Michael Roemer (eds), pp. 56–80. Cambridge: Harvard Institute for International Development.

sequence in mind. Most Chinese leaders did not even have a clear reform objective. Those leaders who may have had a concrete plan — Chen Yun is a case in point — mainly wanted to make the system of central planning and state ownership work more efficiently by increasing the role of market forces in peripheral areas where central planning worked poorly. The market for household-produced goods and private plot crops, for example, was the first area to be liberalized after the December 1978 Party Plenum.

No one realized it at the time, but reforms in China started with certain important advantages over the kind of situation that was later to face Eastern Europe, the republics of the former USSR, and Vietnam. First, China's effort to increase the role of the market domestically was not intertwined with the breakup of the country's international trading arrangements. China had once been a part of the Soviet trading system, but that had come to an end with the Sino-Soviet breakup of 1960. As the data in Table 3 indicate, China had to sharply curtail imports beginning in 1961, and recovery of the previous capacity to import was not achieved until the mid-to-late 1960s. Not only did it take time for China to convert its exports to convertible-currency countries as the share of total exports to the USSR fell from 49% in 1959 to 2% in 1964;[8] China also faced an American embargo that extended to most of America's allies. In addition, China had a debt to the USSR, which it paid off during the 1960s by running a trade surplus with the USSR through 1965. For both similar and different reasons, Vietnam faces an equally daunting task today, more daunting because of the American embargo than that faced by Eastern Europe or Russia.

By the time the worst excesses of China's Cultural Revolution were finished in 1970, and the embargo had begun to lift, China had fully converted to a trading system oriented toward Japan and Western Europe. Beginning in 1970, in fact, China began an export drive, albeit one of more modest proportions than what was to occur after reforms began in earnest in 1978.

China also had no foreign debt of any consequence in 1978. Chinese leaders had made a virtue of necessity by refusing to borrow from abroad,

---

[8]SSB (1983). *Statistical Yearbook of China, 1981*. Hong Kong: Economic Information and Agency, p. 363.

Table 3. The foreign trade transition.

	China (million US dollars)					
	1957	1959	1961	1963	1965	1967
Exports	1,600	2,260	1,490	1,650	2,230	2,140
with USSR	747	1,118	536	407	222	55
Imports	1,500	2,120	1,450	1,260	2,020	2,020
with USSR	618	979	292	194	186	56

	Vietnam (millions of dollars or rubles)				
	1986	1987	1988	1989	1990
Ruble exports	438.9	487.9	590.7	807.5	1,019.5
Ruble imports	1,659.4	1,953.8	2,028.5	1,725.9	1,353.7
Balance	−1,220.5	−1,465.9	−1,437.8	−918.4	−334.2
Dollar exports	384.0	361.5	434.7	1,138.2	1,169.7
Dollar imports	495.7	501.3	728.5	839.9	1,241.7
Balance	−111.7	−139.8	−293.8	298.3	−72.0

Sources: General Statistical Office, Ministry of Trade. *Economy and Trade of Vietnam. 1986–1990.* p. 141. and SSB. *Statistical Yearbook of China.* 1981, pp. 357 and 363.

unlike several Eastern European states, among others, which sustained growth in domestic consumption with foreign loans. China therefore started its domestic economic reforms from a relatively strong balance-of-payments position. China's first trade deficit of over US$1 billion was in 1978. In most previous years, China had run modest trade surpluses.

Second, China began its reform period without any significant degree of inflationary pressure, other than that which is inherent in the Soviet-type command economy because of such phenomena as "investment hunger."[9] There was no government budget deficit equivalent to 10% or more of GNP hemorrhaging new money into the system. In 1978, there was actually a very modest budget surplus. Nor was the banking system

[9]The term is used here in the way Janos Komai uses it in *Economics of Shortage* (Amsterdam: North Holland, 1980).

issuing credit in an uncontrolled manner. As reforms proceeded, this situation would change, but on the eve of efforts to free up prices China's consumers were not standing in long lines waiting for state-supplied goods that more often than not were simply unavailable.

China therefore did not have to begin reforms with an across-the-board stabilization effort, unlike Vietnam, the former Soviet Union, and much of Eastern Europe. That stabilization effort is not the only reason for the decline in GNP that is occurring in these other former Soviet-type economies except for Vietnam, but it is an important reason. If China had had rampant inflation plus a large current account deficit and a sizable foreign debt, it would have had little choice but to start with stabilization. For historical reasons, it did not have to make that decision.

Where, in fact, did China begin the reform process? It began principally on two fronts, agriculture and foreign trade. In certain respects, foreign trade reform began first with efforts going back well into the 1970s to expand the exports of manufactures and petroleum. But these measures largely took place within a Soviet-type foreign trade system dominated by state corporations with monopolies over particular products. An attempt to free up imports in 1977 and 1978 came to naught when state enterprises went on a buying spree, signing letters of intent to purchase hundreds of billions of dollars worth of foreign imports. The letters had to be torn up and the control of imports recentralized. From that point on, the government began to revamp the foreign trading system in a step-by-step process that will be described below.

It was in agriculture that China's reformers first began to fundamentally overhaul the Soviet-type system and move toward a market economy. The action began with the freeing up of rural markets for most rural produce except grain and a few other key commodities. These rural markets existed in the early 1970s, but operated under the tight strictures of local cadres. In 1979 these strictures were removed and the local markets blossomed.

The end of the commune-production team collective system did not begin until 1981, and it was not a systematically planned effort. Initially, certain poor areas were allowed to experiment with household farms. The motive, as in the case of all the early rural reforms, was to find a way to overcome persistent rural poverty. Per capita agricultural output in 1978 was essentially the same as in 1955–1957, and there were large areas containing over 100 million people where malnutrition was a chronic problem. What started as a special program to alleviate difficulties in pockets of poverty, however, began spreading to other areas. Local cadres often tried to halt the movement to household agriculture, but at critical times Beijing, with the backing of Deng Xiaoping, endorsed the changes. By the end of 1983 collective agriculture had ceased to exist. Within teams land had been divided up on an egalitarian basis, although no attempt was made to redistribute land among communes or teams.

Redistribution of the land did not involve going back to some older way of raising crops. Labor-intensive Asian-style agriculture had been the method under the collective teams as under the precollective household system. Nor did previous owners of the land lay claim to it. After 26 years in a collective, too much had changed for that to be even considered, unlike in the southern half of Vietnam, where the collectives existed for only a few years before the country returned to household farming. And new organizations for the supply of agricultural inputs, notably chemical fertilizer, were not required. The old organizations continued, only now they sold to households rather than teams.

The return to household agriculture laid the foundation for a further expansion of market forces in rural areas. The state had always used prices to a limited extent to influence which crops were planted, but the key device was a contract signed with the team and with higher levels of the commune. The contract was in turn based on the central plan. There was some flexibility, but the contracts were not voluntary. The team was required to plant so much land in a particular crop or to deliver a certain amount of that crop to the state in exchange for cash and key inputs. The contract system was cumbersome enough with 50,000 communes and 5 million teams; with over 170 million households, the contract system was not only cumbersome but unnecessary.

Contracts were not done away with, but they did become progressively more voluntary as more and more agricultural prices were freed up and allowed to reach market-clearing levels. After 1984, the government was even talking about freeing up grain prices. The primary motivation was the fact that government subsidies designed to keep urban sales prices low and farm purchase prices high were growing at a rate that threatened fiscal stability. From a modest 3.9 billion yuan in 1978, state grain subsidies ballooned to 11.9 billion yuan in 1980 and 23.4 billion yuan in 1984.[10] Successive bumper harvests in 1982, 1983, and 1984 also created favorable conditions for reliance on market forces, and increasing amounts of grain as well as most lesser crops were sold at market-clearing prices. But China's leaders could not quite bring themselves to go all the way to a pure market system for the rural areas. As grain output stagnated after 1984, and with the increasing strength of conservative forces within the top leadership in 1988 and 1989, price controls over state grain purchases and sales were retained.

By the latter half of the 1980s, therefore, China had an agricultural economic system much like that found in other parts of Asia. Farm households managed most of agricultural production and sold their produce at market-clearing prices except for a few key commodities such as grain, for which the state continued to set prices below market-clearing levels on a portion of the crop. Over a period of roughly five years, China had converted the agricultural sector from a bureaucratic command system to a market system. While this conversion was taking place, value-added in agriculture rose in real terms at the extraordinarily high rate of 7% a year (see Table 1). Analysts have not yet sorted out all of the elements that went into this 1979–1984 agricultural growth spurt. Improved farmer incentives to work harder and manage better were part of the story, as was movement toward better allocative efficiency in the choice of which crops to plant where. Chemical fertilizer use rose from 8.8 million tons (88 kg of nutrient per hectare) to 17.4 million tons (174 kg per hectare), and the rural use of electric power in 1984 also rose by 83% over 1978.[11] This increase in inputs would have accelerated agricultural growth even if collective agriculture in the form of production teams had been retained. Using a similar line of reasoning, the slowdown in the agricultural growth rate in the subsequent six years, 1985–1990, from 7.6 to 4.5% per year, can be seen in part as a modest slowing down in the growth rate of inputs, but mostly

---

[10]Qiao Rongzhang (1990). *Jiage butie*. Beijing: China Price Publishers, p. 28.

[11]China had roughly 100 million hectares of land under cultivation. In addition to chemical fertilizer, Chinese farmers used great quantities of organic fertilizer, so the amount of fertilizer nutrient per hectare was comparable to that found in other East Asian heavy users of fertilizer.

the exhaustion by 1984 of what could be accomplished with harder work, better management, and improved allocative efficiency.[12] The stagnation in grain output until the bumper harvests of 1990 and 1991 was also caused in part by the state's efforts to keep state purchase prices below market-clearing levels.

The boom in agricultural output and incomes that accompanied the 1979–1984 rural reform efforts gave great credibility to those who, in the Chinese context, were considered radical reformers. The urban reforms that accelerated beginning in late 1984 would have taken on a different and less market-oriented tone if agricultural output in general, and grain in particular, had not done well prior to 1984.

What made the conversion to a market system in rural China such a smooth and crisis-free process? A large part of the answer is that it is much easier to make a market system work in agriculture than it is in an industrial sector dominated by large firms. There are five elements required by a well-functioning market system:

(1) Prices must be stable, in the sense that inflation must be low enough to avoid politically induced state price fixing and to encourage farmers and traders to make money by producing and marketing, not by speculating on price changes. As indicated above, China did not have to worry that much about price stability in the early 1980s, in part because prices prior to 1979 were stable and in part because fiscal and monetary policy in the period from 1981 through 1983 was relatively conservative.

---

[12]One requires reliable estimates of an agricultural production function to properly sort out the contribution of productivity versus increased inputs to growth. However, a crude estimate of the contribution of fertilizer (and complimentary inputs) to grain output can be obtained by assuming a yield response of 8 kg of grain for one kilogram of fertilizer nutrient, and that 80% of fertilizer was used on grain. Fertilizer using these figures would have been responsible for an increase in grain output of 54 million tons between 1978 and 1984 (out of a total increase in grain output of 102.5 million tons, or 53% of the total), and an increase in grain output of another 54 million tons between 1984 and 1990 (out of a total increase in grain output of 28 million tons, or 193% of the total). Either weather was substantially worse in 1990 than in 1984, or yield responses to fertilizer fell because of heavy use, or there is some third explanation for the drop in the grain output growth rate after 1984, despite the large increase in fertilizer use.

(2) Goods must be made available through the market rather than allocated through the channels of the government bureaucracy. Many agricultural inputs were sold rather than allocated to farmers even prior to 1979–1984. Part of agricultural output was sold on markets in earlier periods as well, and it was a straightforward process to expand the scope of goods allowed onto these markets.

(3) Prices must reflect relative scarcities in the economy. Chinese agricultural output and input prices were distorted by state interventions, but state price setting had always had to take into account that severely distorted prices led to undesirable production responses, even when farmers were organized into production teams and brigades. Thus prices, while distorted, were not as far out of line as those in industry. Furthermore, the direction of the distortion was clear, certain crop prices were too low, and hence the solution was to allow these prices to rise. The political dangers of passing on higher grain prices to urban consumers did lead to increasingly costly state subsidies, but these distortions affected only a few crops and only a portion of the marketed output of those crops.

(4) There must be competition, or there is little point in moving to a market system; competition drives the productivity gains that are the object of reform. Farmers, however, are the textbook example of the perfectly competitive producer. Whether as individual households or production teams, they are price takers.

(5) Decisionmakers in producing units must behave according to the rules of the market; that is, they must maximize profits by cutting their costs or increasing sales, not by inducing the state to provide them with subsidies or monopoly prices. This condition is sometimes described as being a question of property rights or privatization. Property rights changes and privatization are often part of the solution to the absence of appropriate behavior by producing units, but the key problem is to change that behavior by whatever means will bring it into line with the requirements of the market. The early literature on market socialism assumed that this change in behavior could be accomplished by the government issuing an order. Privatization advocates assume everyone will behave properly once they are owners of the property in question. Reality in the urban industrial sector is

considerably more complex, but not in agriculture. Once farming has been turned back to individual households, agriculture is in the hands of natural profit or net income maximizers. The connection between effort and reward is direct. Even in the 20- to 30-family production teams that existed prior to 1981, there was a substantial connection between effort and reward, but social pressures within the team plus outside state and party pressures on leadership cadres diluted the connection. The return to household farming reestablished it.

Because agriculture in China was so readily convertible back to a market system, the reforms worked as advocates of marketization hoped they would. Because the reforms worked in this critical consumer goods sector, the quantity, quality, and variety of food products available in the shops and markets improved dramatically and prices remained fairly stable. As food made up over half of the expenditures of urban consumers, and clothes (where much of the value added came from cotton) made up another 13%, the quality of life in urban areas improved in a way that all could see.[13] In the rural areas, where three-quarters of the population lived, the improvement in living conditions was even more pronounced. According to household survey data, real consumption levels in rural China by 1985 were 81% above the per capita levels of 1978.[14]

These reforms were not accomplished in a year or 500 days. They were accomplished in the relatively brief period of five years, but some issues remained to be tackled. Long-term household rights to the land, for example, were not defined with sufficient clarity to encourage adequate levels of investment in the land. And the absence of a land market meant families held on to their plots even when most members left for urban jobs. Despite these limitations, farm consumption per capita continued to rise after 1984 at around 4% per year through 1990.

[13] SSB, *Zhongguo tongji nianjian, 1990,* p. 300.

[14] These figures were derived by taking the increase in per capita consumption in current prices for rural areas and dividing by the rural retail price index. Incomes and consumption rose faster than agricultural output in part because of an improvement in the rural-urban terms of trade, and in part because of increased income from rural nonagricultural enterprises.

II. Opening to the Outside World

The rapid expansion of Chinese exports during the reform period has already been mentioned, but what role did the reforms play in this process? And what made possible the imports of large amounts of foreign capital in the form of loans and private direct investment? Early on, prior to 1979, Chinese leaders thought they could solve their foreign exchange needs through the rapid expansion of petroleum exports at high OPEC prices. Ten new Daqing oilfields were anticipated both offshore and onshore, and the one existing Daqing field produced 1 million barrels a day of crude oil.[15] Even large state monopoly corporations have little difficulty exporting basic commodities such as petroleum, and several million barrels a day available for export at US$30 a barrel would indeed have met most of China's immediate foreign exchange needs. As it turned out, China did not discover even one new giant field, and petroleum exports rose only slowly to a quarter of a million barrels a day and later to half a million barrels a day, but at the much lower prices of the latter half of the 1980s. Agricultural exports were also not the solution, mainly because with only 100 million hectares of land, or 0.1 hectare per capita, China — like most of East Asia — was probably destined to be a net importer of agricultural crops, although the balance of agricultural trade in the late 1980s was modestly positive (exports exceeded imports by about US$5 billion). If exports were going to meet China's foreign exchange needs, growth had to come primarily from the export of manufactures. But China's foreign trade corporations under the ministry of foreign trade were not known for their skill in marketing Chinese manufactures or in getting Chinese industrial enterprises to produce what the more discerning foreign markets required. Many of China's export contracts were negotiated at the semiannual Canton Trade Fair, and there was virtually no contact between the Chinese manufacturer and the foreign purchaser.

China had one big advantage in its initial efforts to expand exports of manufactures: the example of its East Asian neighbors, which had already

[15]The ten-year plan was first discussed in 1975, then attacked by the "Gang of Four," and then revived by Hua Guofeng and others in February 1978. Hua Guofeng (1978). "Report on the Work of the Government," February 26, in *Beijing Review*, March 10, 1978.

demonstrated what a resource-poor, labor- and skill-rich people could accomplish. Hong Kong, the Republic of Korea, and Taiwan had shown that the markets existed. The problem for China was how to get into the competition for those markets. The Chinese groped their way to a solution on a trial-and-error basis. There was no well worked-out plan at any stage, but there was also never a retreat from the basic objective. Even during the height of the conservative reaction to the events in Tiananmen in June 1989, the opening up of the economy to foreign trade was not seriously questioned.

The initial steps taken after 1978 involved the partial breakup of the monopoly control of foreign trade by the state trading corporations and the creation of rules designed to promote foreign direct investment. Later, as world prices were increasingly passed through to the Chinese domestic market, the government gradually became aware of the importance of avoiding an overvalued exchange rate.

The end of Beijing's trade monopolies was accomplished by decentralizing authority to hundreds of provincial and lower-level foreign trade organizations. Although many of these organizations were in a sense the subordinate units of the central corporations, provinces in China in the 1980s — and to some degree even earlier — acquired a substantial degree of autonomy from Beijing. As the provincial leadership achieved freedom of action from central dictates, so did these regional organizations.[16]

Foreign direct investment also began to play some role in exports. Special economic zones (basically export processing zones) were created in three areas of Guangdong and one in Fujian Province. Initially, these zones were seen as something of a failure, involving large Chinese infrastructure investments but relatively little foreign investment or production for export markets. By 1988, however, Shenzhen, the largest of the zones and located in a former rural area next to Hong Kong, had exports of US$1.85 billion, up from US$11 million in 1980 and still only US$250 million in 1985.[17] Many of the rules that initially only applied to these

---

[16]China's trade reforms are discussed at length in Nicholas Lardy (1992). *Foreign Trade and Economic Reform in China, 1978–1990*, Cambridge: Cambridge University Press.

[17]China Foreign Trade and Economic Relations Compilation Committee (1989). *Zhongguo duiwai jingji maoi nianjian, 1989/1990.* Beijing, p. 247; and Guangdong statistical office (1987). *Guangdongsheng tongji nianjian, 1987.* Hangzhou: China Statistical Publishers, p. 332.

special zones were then applied to other cities with foreign trade potential. Guangdong exports for the whole province, for example, rose from US$1.4 billion in 1978 to US$8.2 billion in 1989, the latter figure accounting for 15.5% of national exports.

The first steps designed to promote foreign direct investment involved writing a joint-venture law. The initial rather unspecific joint-venture law was followed by numerous other commercial laws, many of which were applied to domestic as well as foreign firms. China, it should be noted, had for all practical purposes eliminated most commercial law during the Cultural Revolution period, along with all of the lawyers. A legal system suitable for an international trading country had to be rebuilt from scratch, and that did not happen overnight.

Data on foreign investment in China are presented in Table 4. As the table indicates, foreign direct investment was quite modest during the first four years of reform, averaging only US$291.5 million per year, but rose to over US$3 billion a year in the 1988–1990 period, despite the Tiananmen tragedy. What the table does not show is the central role of Hong Kong in this growth. In 1988 and 1989, Hong Kong alone accounted for 63% of all foreign direct investment utilized. Japan and the United States, the next two largest sources, together accounted for only

Table 4. Foreign capital utilized (million US dollars).

	Total foreign capital	Foreign loans		Foreign direct investment	Other foreign commercial investment
		Total	Official		
1979–1982[a]	3,114.3	2,672.5	603.3	291.5	150.3
1983–1986[a]	4,147.8	2,513.3	—	1,199.9	277.3
1987	8,452.0	5,805.0	—	2,314.0	333.0
1988	10,226.0	6,487.0	5,074.3	3,193.0	546.0
1989	10,059.0	6,286.0	2,327.0	3,392.0	381.0
1990	10,289.0	6,534.0	2,612.0	3,755.0[b]	—

[a]Annual average.

[b]This figure includes "other foreign commercial investment."

Sources: SSB, *Zhongguo tongji nian jian, 1990,* p. 653, and SSB. *Zhongguo tongji zhaiyao, 1991,* p. 102.

21%.[18] By 1990 and 1991, the other significant trend was the rapid increase in investment from Taiwan. In effect, Hong Kong and Taiwan were moving their labor-intensive industries such as shoes and toys out of their own increasingly high-wage territory to the low-wage areas of Guangdong and Fujian Provinces, where the local people were not only still Chinese, but in some cases even relatives.

No understanding of China's trade performance is possible without bringing in the special role of Hong Kong. That role went well beyond the provision of foreign direct investment or supporting infrastructure for the Shenzhen Special Economic Zone. Prior to the reform period, about 20% of China's exports were sent to Hong Kong, and most of these exports were retained and consumed in the colony. In 1970 and 1975, for example, only 4% of China's total exports were reexported through Hong Kong. That figure later rose to 11% in 1984 and to an extraordinary 40% in 1990.[19] Hong Kong had become the primary trade intermediary between China and Taiwan Province, and it was a major player in China's trade with much of the rest of the world. There is no way of estimating what the growth of China's foreign trade would have been in the absence of Hong Kong, but it would certainly have been slower. Shanghai, for example, the most logical competitor for Hong Kong, saw its exports peak in 1980 and then stagnate for the next six years and more, while the share of Shanghai exports in China's total exports fell from 29.7% in 1978 to 11.6% in 1986.[20] It was Hong Kong that knew how to market products in the United States, Europe, and Japan, Shanghai was learning, but slowly.

More difficult to assess is the role of the spreading marketization in the Chinese economy on the growth of exports. In 1991, the exports of rural industries and foreign investment enterprise were over US$10 billion

---

[18]These figures are based on data whose coverage is not as broad as that for the official estimates of total foreign direct investment. SSB, *Zhongguo tongji nianjian, 1990*, p. 654.
[19]Yun-wing Sung (forthcoming). The economic integration of Hong Kong, Taiwan, South Korea and Mainland China. In *Economic Reform and Internationalization: China and the Pacific Region*, p. 31. Ross Garnaut and Liu Guoguang (eds).
[20]Shanghai Statistical Office (1987). *Shanghai tongji nianjian, 1987*. Shanghai: Shanghai People's Press, p. 295.

each,[21] and neither of these two sectors would have experienced dynamic growth if across-the-board central planning had been retained. They would not have been able to get the necessary inputs, nor would they have had much incentive to export. In the early stages of reform, the incentive to export was in fact quite weak. There was what has been called an "air lock" between foreign and domestic prices. The Chinese currency was overvalued, but that did not matter to the producing enterprises because they neither purchased nor sold goods at world prices. The trading corporations lost money on exports, but they made money on their imports, and profits were not that important anyway.

By the late 1980s not only were profits important, but world prices were increasingly being passed on to producers. In addition, export earners were allowed to retain a portion of their foreign exchange earnings and use them to buy imports. To deal with the complaints from foreign investors that they could not obtain the foreign exchange required to repatriate profits or even to buy imported inputs, the government opened foreign exchange adjustment centers, or "swap markets." Initially, only foreign investors could use them, but then domestic firms began to be allowed into these markets as well. By 1991, these markets accounted for a substantial share of all foreign exchange transactions. Furthermore, the exchange rate on these swap markets in 1991 was less than 10% above the official rate. The official rate was devalued in both 1990 and 1991, and China's large trade surplus combined to bring the two rates into line. All that remained was for the government to take the final step of making the renminbi fully convertible, but that the government could not quite bring itself to do, although moves toward a single exchange rate were under way in 1992. The increasing role of the swap markets is one of a number of examples of a reform measure designed originally only for foreigners that came in time to have a big impact on domestic businesses.

In addition to making the renminbi more nearly convertible, the government also took steps to remove its overvaluation. As the data in Table 5

---

[21] Rural industry exports were expected to reach US$12.8 billion (Wang Dongtai (1992). "Record Output of Rural Firms to Continue," *China Daily,* January 8, p. 1). Foreign-funded firms had exports of US$8 billion in the first nine months of 1991 (Ying Pu (1991). "Foreign Investment Set to Increase with Access to New Areas," *China Daily,* November 25, business section, p. 1).

Table 5. China's foreign exchange rate.

	(1)	(2)	(3)	(4)	(5)	(6)	(7)	(8)
	Foreign exchange rate (US$1 = RMB-)	index	Retail price index (1980 = 100)	Chinese export US$ price index (1980 = 100)	Chinese import US$ price index (1980 = 100)	NMP deflator index (1980 = 100)	(3) ÷ (2)	(6) ÷ (2)
1978	1.68	112.0	92.5	74.3	66.2	93.0	82.6	83.0
1979	1.55	103.3	94.3	85.8	83.0	96.7	91.3	93.6
1980	1.50	100.0	100.0	100.0	100.0	100.0	100.0	100.0
1981	1.71	114.0	102.4	103.1	103.5	101.9	89.8	89.4
1982	1.89	126.0	104.4	96.9	91.1	101.8	82.9	80.8
1983	1.98	132.0	105.9	86.4	77.1	102.9	80.2	80.0
1984	2.33	155.3	108.9	88.3	78.6	108.2	70.1	69.7
1985	2.94	196.0	118.5	82.2	74.0	118.3	60.5	60.4
1986	3.45	230.0	125.6	71.7	73.5	123.0	54.6	53.5
1987	3.72	248.0	134.8	76.1	72.2	132.3	54.4	53.3
1988	3.72	248.0	159.7	83.2	91.7	149.8	64.4	60.4
1989	3.77	251.3	188.2	n.a.	n.a.	162.1	74.9	64.5
1990	4.78	318.7	192.1	n.a.	n.a.	167.9	60.3	52.7
1991	5.30			n.a.	n.a.			

indicate, from 1978 to 1980 Chinese currency actually became more overvalued, but from that point on the government began a process of gradual devaluation that probably by 1985 reached a point where the renminbi could no longer be described as overvalued. At least that is what the indexes in columns 7 and 8 of Table 5 seem to indicate, if one takes the view that the currency was not overvalued in 1991 and work backward from there.[22]

This brief discussion cannot do justice to all of the measures undertaken by China to promote foreign trade. China took its seat in the IMF and World Bank, and beginning in 1981 received its first loans from those sources. China obtained most-favored-nation status from the United States, although it was in danger of losing that rating in 1991 and 1992. China was also gradually bringing its trade practices in line with GATT, so that it would become eligible for membership. In essence, China started its export drive with only modest alterations in the Soviet-type trading system that had been in place for more than two decades. A temporary spurt in the dollar value of oil exports helped out at this early stage, just as it did in Vietnam in 1990 and 1991. But step by step China has altered its trading system to where it now can plausibly argue that it will soon be in compliance with GATT rules, although it had not gotten all the way there by 1992. Not all of the steps were forward. Occasionally China recentralized controls when the foreign exchange situation seemed to be getting out of hand, as in 1985 and 1986 when the cumulative balance-of-trade deficit in those two years reached US $27 billion. But these steps backward were the exception, not the rule.

III. Reforming Industry and Services

Petty urban services such as hawkers and small restaurants were freed up early on, but the major urban reform effort was not announced until October 1984. Prior to that time, the Chinese government had experimented with urban reforms in a number of cities, but not on a nationwide basis.

---

[22] Detailed commodity-by-commodity price comparisons to establish that China's potential exports were priced competitively and didn't require subsidies is not possible, but it is unlikely that China's rapid export growth to more than US$70 billion in 1991 was still being fueled by large subsidies to exporting firms.

If one refers back to the four elements needed to make a market work (in addition to stabilization, which was not a serious problem in the mid-1980s), China made substantial progress on three and some progress on the fourth. Only a few of the key changes will be described here.

(1) An increasing share of intermediate inputs as well as output destined for final demand was made available through market channels rather than through the administrative channels of the central government. There are various ways to measure this increasing role of the market. One measure is the number of products at least partially subject to state allocation. In 1978, for example, 689 kinds of producer goods were distributed through the state plan, and 837 in 1982. By 1990 or 1991 that number was down to only 20.[23] The total number of kinds of materials and equipment under a substantial degree of state control in 1990 was only 72, down from nearly 300 as late as 1988.[24] This process was already well under way by 1984. According to a survey of 424 enterprises, the proportion of raw and semifinished materials obtained on the market or through direct purchase from other enterprises rose from 27% of the total supply at the end of 1984 to 44% by June 1985. The proportion of "planned supply" of state enterprise in 1984 was still 87%, but that of urban and rural collective enterprises was only 6.5% and 3.0% respectively.[25] The relationship between an expanding market and the development of collective enterprises is a subject we shall return to below. The central point here is that the role of the market rose steadily but gradually over a period of at least eight years. As late as 1990, the state still distributed 49% of the steel and 43% of the coal produced, but only 12.6% of the cement, much of which

---

[23]Lu Zheng (forthcoming). China's economic reform and development: Historical review and future prospects. *Economic Reform and Internationalization: China and the Pacific Region.* In Ross Garnaut and Liu Guoguang (eds.) and Tang Zongkun (1987). Supply and marketing. *China's Industrial Reform.* In Gene Tidrick and Chen Jiyuan (eds.), p. 229. (Oxford: Oxford University Press).

[24]Li Hong (1990). "Materials Ministry to Take on Market Role," *China Daily,* December 4, p. 1.

[25]Zhang Shaojie and Zhang Amei (1987). The present management environment in China's industrial enterprises. *Reform in China: Challenges and Choices.* In Bruce Reynolds, (ed.) pp. 48 and 53. (Armonk, NY: M.E. Sharpe).

was produced by small enterprises.[26] There was no sudden decision to abolish state allocation and throw everything onto newly evolving markets. The state system continued to operate, but its scope shrank steadily, and that reduced activity faced ever-increasing competition for goods from the market. By late 1990, Liu Suinian, the minister in charge of the ministry of materials and equipment, was calling on the 1.05 million employees of the state distribution agencies to turn their agencies into "competitive dealers" so that they could hold onto market share.[27]

(2) As intermediate as well as final goods became increasingly channeled through the market, the state had to decide at what prices these goods would be sold. The old state-set prices were, for the most part, far below market-clearing levels, and maintaining these low prices throughout the economy would have made the development of markets impossible. Excess demand would lead immediately to long queues of both consumers and enterprises and to a return to state allocations. But China's leaders were not prepared to let all prices just float up to market levels either. There were too many powerful interests prepared to resist loss of their privileged access to low-priced inputs. The solution chosen in 1985 was a dual price system. The substantial but shrinking portion of goods allocated through government channels would be sold at state-set prices, while those goods sold on the market would be priced closer to market-clearing levels. Over time, this market became more and more like a true market with freely determined prices, but initially the state frequently interfered in price setting.

The dual price system accomplished two things. It did create market prices, and increasing numbers of enterprises were making their marginal decisions on the basis of these prices. In fact, most enterprises purchased substantial quantities of inputs on the market, but a few key inputs, notably electric power, were in chronic short supply and only available at state prices. The second accomplishment of the two-price system was increasing opportunities for corruption. It was not long before those with the political influence to get access to supplies at state prices discovered they could make large amounts of easy money reselling them on the market.

[26]Li Hong, *China Daily*.

[27]Li Hong, *China Daily*.

Companies sprung up to take advantage of this opportunity; some, it should be noted, were trying to help enterprises without political clout — foreign joint ventures, for example — to get around the strictures of the state bureaucracy. It was the corruption in the form of large earnings to well-connected individuals and their children, however, that drew the most notice from the urban population and increased their support for the student demonstrators in 1989.

Immediately after the June 1989 tragedy in Tiananmen, there was support for getting rid of the dual price system in favor of a return to a single state-set price not necessarily related to market forces. By 1991, however, reform measures were mostly oriented toward raising state prices all or part of the way to the market price level, or removing goods from state allocation altogether. On April 1, 1991, for example, the dual price system for cement was abolished in favor of one market-determined price.[28] State coal prices, on the other hand, were raised, but only enough to reduce coal mine losses and relieve pressure on the state budget. But the expansion of market prices by 1991 was no longer under effective state control for a wide range of goods. It was simply too easy for firms to raise prices by claiming that the product in question was new or by working out its own trading arrangements with its customers. By one estimate, 75% of goods were distributed through the market, and that percentage was rising steadily.[29]

(3) Competition was introduced into Chinese industry in the early 1980s as well. Prior to the reform period, virtually every Chinese industrial enterprise had a monopoly of its local market and was not allowed to sell outside of that market. County farm machinery plants, for example, would produce plows for the county market. When the local market for plows was saturated, the plant was converted to the production of some other kind of machinery. These monopolies were formally abolished and enterprises were allowed to sell throughout the country, and began in fact to do so. Where there were buyers' markets, this change had the predictable result. Enterprises such as the Chongqing clock and watch factory found themselves in direct competition with the high-quality products of Shanghai and

[28]Li Hong (1991). "State Narrows Two-Tier Price Gap," *China Daily,* May 17, p. 1.
[29]Chen Xiao (1991). "Price Reform Pacing under Debate," *China Daily,* May 17, p. 1.

had to cut their prices and lower their costs.[30] Where there was excess demand and hence a suppliers' market, the competitive pressures were largely absent. Excess demand or "target planning" is a common feature of centrally planned economies and hence suppliers' markets are common, but China to some uncertain degree appears to have been different. Plans in China even early in the reform period appear to have been considerably less taut (excess demand was less often present) than in the Soviet Union and Eastern Europe, and hence buyers' markets were more common.[31]

As a higher portion of goods was sold on the market, competitive pressures rose. An additional source of competitive stimulus was foreign trade. Manufactured exports by 1990 amounted to over 200 billion yuan, or nearly 10% of the gross value of industrial output, up from about 4% in 1985.[32] On the other hand, some industrial products such as electric power had natural monopolies, and others retained state-determined monopolies (the regional airlines, for example). In still other cases, provinces and even counties often erected trade barriers to the influx of goods from elsewhere in China when they threatened a local enterprise. The central government disapproved, but could not necessarily stop the practice.

(4) Making enterprise decisionmakers behave according to the rules of the market has proved to be the most difficult challenge, as it was in Eastern Europe. Farmer families, as pointed out above, are natural profit maximizers through raising output and sales or by cutting costs. In a Soviet-type system, managers of large industrial enterprises, in contrast, are really lower-level department heads within the government bureaucracy. Success is achieved by following the lead of their bureaucratic superiors within the government ministries, and these superiors are typically interested in many goals in addition to increasing sales or cutting costs. As with state-owned enterprises all over the world, the enterprise objective function is muddled by the inclusion of goals that significantly

[30] William Byrd and Gene Tidrick (1984). "Adjustment and Reform in the Chongqing Clock and Watch Factory," World Bank Staff Working Paper No. 652, Washington, DC.
[31] David Granick (1990). *Chinese State Enterprises.* Chicago: University of Chicago Press.
[32] These figures were derived by taking the percentage share of manufactured exports measured in dollars and applying that percentage to the export total in renminbi, and then comparing that figure with gross value of industrial output in current prices. A more accurate figure based on exports valued in Chinese domestic prices was not available.

inhibit the enterprise from concentrating on profit maximization through its own efforts. The enterprise will be asked to employ far more workers than it needs or to deliver its output to favored customers at low prices. In return, profits are ensured not by efficient production, but by state subsidies ranging from cheap loans to government-guaranteed markets.

The essence of achieving reform in this fourth sphere is to break the umbilical cord that connects enterprise managers to the government bureaucracy. The principle is easy enough. Enterprises should be told to maximize profits, not gross value output or employment, and they should have a free hand in deciding how to do that. If they fail to do well in raising profits, managers should be replaced. If the enterprise as a whole runs losses over a long enough period of time, it should go out of business. Applying these principles in practice, however, is not so easy.

The Chinese, for example, have a bankruptcy law, but there have been only a handful of bankruptcies among the larger enterprises, despite the fact that many of these enterprises have consistently made losses. In 1991, some of these losing enterprises were forced to merge with more successful firms in the same sector, but these mergers may have penalized the successful firms that have been pressured to take on a weak partner rather than penalizing the loss-making firm itself. In practice, governments around the world are reluctant to allow large enterprises employing tens of thousands of people to go under, and this is particularly true of socialist countries. In China, as in a number of socialist countries, the difficulty is compounded by the fact that the urban social welfare system is tied to the enterprise. There is no unemployment insurance, and housing is provided by the enterprise, as is day care for children and many health services. The Chinese are gradually trying to change this system, and large-scale experiments to privatize urban housing are under way, but there is a long way to go before urban workers can lose one job and still have a safety net to tide them over until they find another. Banking reform, which cuts off enterprises' easy access to credit with only a weak obligation to repay, is another element in forcing industrial enterprises to survive on their own.

If allowing a firm to fail is difficult, at least the managers of the enterprise could be made to pay the price of failure. Bonuses tied to performance is the traditional Soviet-style way of dealing with this issue, but this arrangement has never worked very well. A major problem is that managers are appointed and promoted by the government bureaucracies and, not surprisingly, see themselves as mainly responsible to those bureaucracies. In recent years in China they have also seen themselves as responsible to their workers, which creates another set of problems.[33] One solution to the issue of making managers responsible for their performance is to privatize the enterprise. Much of the discussion of privatization takes the simplistic view that this step automatically forces enterprises and their managers to survive on their own. As anyone familiar with import-substituting strategies of industrialization knows, there may be very little diminution in government support when the enterprise becomes private. In China, however, the issue is moot, for the time being at least, because the government is not even considering the privatization of large enterprises.

If privatization of large enterprises in not acceptable, is there a public substitute that accomplishes some of the same ends? China in a very modest way has begun experimenting with selling shares in public enterprises. The owners of these shares can be other enterprises, workers, and individuals who are not workers in the enterprise. There are a number of objectives behind share ownership, but if really applied on a nationwide basis, it would provide a vehicle for creating boards of directors that would be primarily concerned with the profitability of the enterprise. These boards could appoint managers who would focus on that goal rather than on whatever their superiors in the supervising ministry wanted. These share ownership experiments, however, are just that — experiments.[34] In 1989, there was some question as to whether the experiments would even be allowed to continue, but by 1991, they were once again under way and being vigorously debated.[35] Enterprise managers, however, are still appointed by the government bodies they serve.

[33]These and other issues of the nature of the enterprise objective function as of the mid-1980s are discussed in William Byrd and Gene Tidrick. Factor allocation and enterprise incentives, *China's Industrial Reform.* In Gene Tidrick and Chen Jiyuan (eds.), pp. 60–102.

[34]The early debates over these issues are covered in Robert C. Hsu (1991). *Economic Theories in China, 1979–1988.* Cambridge: Cambridge University Press.

[35]A securities market was established in Shenyang in 1986, and subsequent markets were set up in Shanghai, Shenzhen, and elsewhere, but the volume on these markets is small. Yuan Zhou (1991). "Shareholding in Focus," January 7 (business weekly), and Jiang Yiwei (1990). "Further Economic Reforms Urged," *China Daily,* October 26, p. 4. The most prominent advocate of a shareholding system is Li Yining of Beijing University.

The reform picture among industrial enterprises, however, is not as limited in scope as the discussion to this point would lead one to believe. The basis for this statement is the rapid rise of small-scale industrial enterprises, many of them based on collective ownership. In some cases, these small enterprises are privately owned and in others the state is still the formal "owner," but, regardless of the ownership type in a formal sense, these small enterprises come much closer than do large enterprises to behaving according to the rules of the market.

The rising share of collective enterprises in total industrial output are presented in Table 6. If small-scale state enterprises were separated out, the share of large-scale state enterprises would be even smaller. As it is, the share of the state sector fell from three-quarters to less than half in just 12 years.

Table 6. Growth rates of state and collective/private industry.

	Gross value of industrial output	Gross value of state industry	Gross value of collective/ private industry
	Growth rate (% per year)		
1979–1984	9.6	7.0	16.6
1985–1988	16.7	10.0	26.4
1989	8.5	3.9	13.7
1990	7.6	2.9	12.4
1991 (11 months)	13.5	9.0	17.8
	Share (in %)		
1978	100.0	77.6	22.4
1980	100.0	75.0	25.0
1984	100.0	67.5	32.5
1988	100.0	52.6	47.4
1990	100.0	48.2	51.8
1991 (11 months)	100.0	46.3	53.7

Sources: These figures differ slightly from those most commonly published. Official data were first converted into constant prices (for 1978) and the shares and growth rates calculated in terms of these constant prices. The estimates for 1990 and 1991 are based on newspaper reports of SSB announcements and are somewhat less reliable than the earlier data.

None of this declining share was due to privatization. It was all due to the more rapid growth of the small-scale and collective sector, despite the government's preference for the large-scale enterprises. This collective small-scale development was a surprise to the planners. The technical foundation for this boom had been laid in the 1970s with the rise of rural industries designed to provide agriculture with inputs such as farm machinery and cement. When industrial inputs were increasingly made available on the market rather than through state-planned allocation, the entrepreneurial energies of rural and suburban entrepreneurs were unleashed. The inability of urban enterprises to expand their labor force or get access to land also encouraged these large enterprises to subcontract with collective suburban firms.

There is considerable variation in the behavior of these township and village enterprises, as they are now called, but there are important common threads. The government units to which these enterprises relate are not the ministries in Beijing or even the provinces, but the local county and township governments. In some cases, these enterprises are formally owned by the counties — that is, they are state-owned firms in a formal sense. But even if they are collective or even private, they make tax payments and other contributions to their local governments and receive government support in return. Government support, for example, can be instrumental in getting bank loans for these small enterprises. These enterprises, therefore, are sometimes almost as closely tied to their local government units as the larger enterprises are to the national ministries. But the soft budget constraint is not the problem for these small enterprises that it is for the large ones. The reason is simple: the county and township governments do not have the resources to bail out chronic money losers for long. Although the banks are not always repaid, a losing county or township enterprise ultimately must be funded out of the profits of another enterprise in the county or township. Local officials, unable to print money, soon decide to jettison the losing firm through reorganization or putting it out of business. In effect, the local government entity, dependent on local enterprises for much of its revenue, behaves more like a mini-conglomerate than a government bureaucracy. The rules of the market, with many deviations to be sure, are obeyed.[36]

[36]The best studies for getting into the microbehavior of township and village enterprises are in William Byrd and Lin Qingsong (1990). *China's Rural Industry: Structure, Development and Reform.* Oxford: Oxford University Press.

What is true of industry is also true of other sectors such as construction, transport, and wholesale and retail trade. Small collective enterprises play a major and rising role in each of these sectors. They fill niches not covered by the large enterprises, but they also compete directly for market share with those enterprises. If one adds up all of the small-scale producing units in agriculture, industry, and services, they account for nearly three-quarters of total GNP. Put differently, three-quarters of Chinese output is produced by units oriented primarily toward the market. Only one-quarter is closely tied to the central government bureaucracy.

Has this change in the way industry is organized had any impact on performance? On the basis of recent studies of both the state and the collective industry sectors, the answer is clearly in the affirmative. The data for the pre-1978 period are of low quality, but numerous partial indicators suggest that productivity growth in industry was unlikely to have been positive. Studies of the post-reform period based on more reliable figures — particularly figures for the capital stock — show positive and rising total factor productivity. In one important set of estimates, total factor productivity in the state sector rose from 1.8% per year in the 1980–1984 period to 3.0% per year in 1984–1988. Collective industry total factor productivity in the two periods rose from 3.5% annually to 5.9%.[37] Increasing factor inputs still accounted for over two-thirds of industrial output growth, but productivity growth presumably generated by the increasing marketization of the economy accounted for the other third. And increasing marketization may also have made it easier to mobilize factor inputs, the reverse of what one would expect, as a strength of the command economy is its capacity to mobilize inputs. Some of the inputs into collective industry may have been diverted from the large-scale state sector, but some were in the form of local labor and capital that the state system may not have been able to mobilize.

[37]These studies also indicate that returns to factors between the two sectors were converging, suggesting improved allocative efficiency. Gary Jefferson, Thomas Rawski, and Yuxin Zheng (forthcoming), Growth, efficiency and convergence in China's state and collective industry (July 1990), and Gary Jefferson and Xu Wenyi (1990). The impact of reform on socialist enterprises in transition: Structure, conduct and performance in Chinese industry, Brandeis University, No. 242.

IV. Partial Reform and Macro Stability

While the discussion to this point makes clear that industrial reforms in the 1980s had a major positive impact on the growth of industrial output and productivity, the partial nature of those reforms also presented problems for the managers of the Chinese economy. These problems manifested themselves in part through rising inflationary pressures that led the government to brake the economy in 1989 and to call for a more moderate rate of growth in the future.[38]

Inflation began accelerating from the beginning of the urban industrial reforms in late 1984, as the figures in Table 7 indicate. By 1988, price increases had reached a level politically unacceptable to most of the leadership. What accounted for this change?

Data on the government budget deficit are presented in Table 8. As these figures indicate, accelerated inflation in 1980 is correlated with a rising government budget deficit, but that was not the case after 1984. The government deficit as a share of GNP actually fell to a minuscule 0.8% in 1985 and was only 2.5% of GNP in 1988, as contrasted to 5.2% in 1979 and 3.8% in 1980.

Data on the money supply in Table 9 get closer to the nature of the problem. Bank deposits plus currency in circulation between the end of 1984 and the end of 1988 grew at an annual rate of 23% a year. What accounted for this increase, more than any other single factor, were bank loans to state and collective enterprises that were increasingly out of the control of those at the center responsible for price stability. The starting point was the high levels of investment of enterprises large and small. The rate of investment, or accumulation in Chinese terminology, was "held down" to under 30% of net material product in the 1981–1983 adjustment period, but jumped to 35% in 1985 and stayed above 34% thereafter. This high rate was financed by bank loans at interest rates well below any market-clearing interest rate. Subsidies to loss-making enterprises were financed in a similar manner. If the banks were reluctant to lend, political

[38] See, for example, Chen Xiao and Zhang Xiaogang (1990). "Economists Urge Slower Growth Rate," *China Daily*, December 27, p. 4, and Lao Zhang (1991). "Minister Outlines Key Tasks for Development," *China Daily*, March 27, p. 1. The GNP growth rate target for 1991 announced by Planning Commission Chairman Zou Jiahua was 4.5%.

Table 7. Consumer price indexes (% increase over the previous year).

	Retail prices	Collective market prices	Worker cost of living
1978	0.7	–6.6	0.7
1979	2.0	–4.5	1.9
1980	6.0	1.9	7.5
1981	2.4	5.8	2.5
1982	1.9	3.3	2.0
1983	1.5	4.2	2.0
1984	2.8	–0.4	2.7
1985	8.8	17.2	11.9
1986	6.0	8.1	7.0
1987	7.3	16.3	8.8
1988	18.5	30.3	20.7
1989	17.8	10.8	16.3
1990	2.1	–5.7	1.3
1991	2.9	n.a.	5.1

Sources: SSB. *Zhongguo tongji zhaiyao, 1991,* p. 38; SSB, *Zhongguo tongji nianjian, 1990,* pp. 249 and 268; SSB, *Statistical Yearbook of China, 1986,* pp. 535 and 544; and SSB. "Statistical Communique on National Economic and Social Development in 1991," February 28, 1992.

pressure was brought to bear and the banks more often than not gave in. After the commercial banks had been separated from the central bank, the central bank continued to support the commercial banks' demand for funds just as it had when the commercial banks and the central bank were the one and same People's Bank of China.

The central bank had the power to stop the rapid increase in money supply, and it more or less did so by cutting off the supply (reducing the growth rate) in 1989, thereby bringing down the rate of growth of the money supply and inflation. At the user end, quotas were set that cut off credit to efficient and profligate borrowers alike. The result was a sharp drop in the growth of industry and increasing layoffs.

Table 8. Government revenues and expenditures (million yuan).

	Expenditures		Revenue	Deficit		
	Including price subsides	Budgeted price subsidies	(– debt income + deductions for price subsides)	(million yuan)	(as % share of NMP)	(as share of GNP)
1978	112,214	1,114	113,224	+1,010	+0.003	+0.003
1979	135,370	7,920	114,719	–20,591	–0.061	–0.052
1980	133,041	11,771	115,990	–17,051	–0.046	–0.038
1981	127,441	15,941	117,583	–9,858	–0.025	–0.021
1982	132.552	17,222	121,236	–11,316	–0.027	–0.022
1983	148,987	19,737	136,696	–12,184	–0.026	–0.021
1984	176,474	21,834	164,290	–6,825	–0.022	–0.018
1985	210,659	26,179	203,834	–20,875	–0.010	–0.008
1986	233,080	25,748	212,205	–20,875	–0.027	–0.022
1987	244,850	29,460	219,935	–24,915	–0.027	–0.022
1988	270,660	31,682	235,722	–34,938	–0.030	–0.025
1989	304,020	37,034	267,360	–36,660	–0.028	–0.023
1990	339,520	n.a.				

Sources: State Statistical Bureau, *Zhongguo tongji nianjian, 1990*, pp. 229, 232, and 244, and State Statistical Bureau, *Zhongguo tongji zhaiyao, 1991*, p. 33.
Note: Chinese budget statistics subtracted price subsidies on certain commodities, notably grain, from total revenue up through 1985, but then changed and added prices to total expenditures from 1986 on. Chinese revenue figures also include income from foreign and domestic borrowing and these have been removed from the revenue totals in this table.

If a full market system had been in place, the central bank could have raised the cost of borrowing to the commercial banks, and they in turn could have passed on that cost to the enterprises. The enterprises with rates of return on their investments below the cost of capital would have stopped borrowing, while those with higher rates could have continued to borrow. But Chinese enterprises still suffered from what Janos Kornai calls "investment hunger" and the "soft budget constraint." If they made losses on their investments, they were still inclined to invest more, knowing the government would bail them out with low-cost loans, a negotiated

Table 9. State bank deposits plus currency in circulation.

	Currency in circulation		Bank deposits		Urban savings deposits	
	(million yuan)	% increase over previous year	(million yuan)	% increase over previous year	(million yuan)	% increase over previous year
1979	26,771		134,004		20,256	
1980	34,620	29.3	166,107	24.0	28,249	39.5
1981	39,634	14.5	203,540	22.5	35,414	25.4
1982	43,912	10.8	238,622	16.3	44,733	26.3
1983	52,978	20.6	276,159	16.7	57,258	30.0
1984	79,211	49.5	338,613	22.6	77,662	13.6
1985	98,783	24.7	393,648	16.3	105,781	36.2
1986	121,836	23.3	538,187	36.7	147,145	39.1
1987	145,448	19.4	657,205	22.1	206,402	40.3
1988	213,403	46.7	742,562	13.0	265,916	28.8
1989	234,402	9.8	901,385	21.4	373,480	40.5
1990	264,437	12.8	1,164,483	29.2	519,258	39.0

Sources: State statistical Bureau (SSB), *Zhongguo tongji nianjian, 1990*, p. 666; SSB, *Zhongguo tangji nianjian, 1987*, p. 639; SSB, *Zhongguo tongji zhaiyao, 1991*, p. 35; SSB, *Statistical Yearbook of China, 1986*, p. 530.

lower tax rate, or some other kind of subsidy. One way to keep this situation from occurring would be to tighten the budget constraint of the commercial banks themselves, thereby forcing them to tighten their loans to the enterprises. But tightening the budget constraint of a few large banks may be just as hard to accomplish as doing so for the enterprises.

Because rationing credit to all enterprises across the board was such a crude device, it proved difficult to maintain for long. Between 1984 and 1988, the Chinese labor force grew by 61.4 million people. Of that huge number, 48 million (78%) were employed outside of agriculture. In 1989 and 1990, the labor force increased by 24.1 million, and 18.5 million (77%) had to be absorbed by agriculture. One uses the word absorbed rather than employed because 100 million or more members of the agricultural labor force were already in some sense superfluous.[39] By the year 2000 the Chinese labor force will increase by another 150 million people, and China cannot afford politically to add three-quarters of these to the surplus labor pool in the countryside. To avoid this, China's GNP must grow at a rate that is at least 6% to 8% per year. But a high rate of growth in an unreformed economy could retrigger inflation, followed by a renewed round of credit rationing. To avoid this kind of stop-and-go growth, China needs a market-oriented financial system as well as a marketized industry. In 1991, however, China did achieve 7% growth in GNP with inflation of only 4%.

V. Conclusion

China, as this account makes clear, has largely abandoned the Soviet-type command system and has replaced it with a system run more by market forces than administrative controls, but still with a heavy dose of the latter. It achieved this change over more than a decade while maintaining an average GNP growth rate for 13 years of around 8% per year.

The key characteristics of this reform were:

(1) China began by marketizing where the process did not involve a fundamental reorganization and retraining of the producing units, that is, it began with agriculture and services.

(2) Reformers in the more complex urban industrial sphere began with experiments in specific regions, which were then gradually tried on a nationwide basis. Where the rural reforms took three to five years for the essentials to be completed, urban reforms have been in process for seven years, and that process is still ongoing. The interests of the

[39]The 100 million figure is a crude calculation based on the size of the rural work force and an estimate of the number of workdays required to farm a hectare of arable land (375) and a work year per person of 200 to 250 days. The resulting figure of 150–188 million employed farm workers compares with a total agricultural labor force (excluding rural enterprises) of around 300 million. The term surplus labor, as used here, does not imply that the marginal product of that labor is zero, only that the marginal product is extremely low, probably below a subsistence wage. See Chen Xiao and Zhang Xiaogang (1991). "Surplus Workers in the Spotlight," *China Daily,* June 21, p. 4.

government bureaucrats or of other conservative political forces have not succeeded in stopping or reversing the process for long, as some analysts feel happened in Eastern Europe prior to the collapse of the communist parties in that region. Even the 1989 tragedy in Tiananmen stopped the spread of market forces for one year at the most.

(3) Marketization has been achieved to the degree it has been without formal privatization of state-owned enterprises. Much of this success in the industrial sphere was due to the rapid expansion of small-scale industrial enterprises that behaved according to the rules of the market. Large-scale enterprises have consistently lagged behind, but competition in and changes in the way the large-scale sector does business have also been profound.

(4) China followed as best it could the East Asian model for expanding the export of manufactures. The country's strong foreign exchange earnings situation made all other changes easier to manage.

Will this process continue until China has achieved full marketization of its economy — at least to the degree achieved by Japan in the 1950s, or the Republic of Korea in the 1960s and 1970s? It is doubtful that the economic bureaucracy in Beijing has the power to hold back the market incentives now driving hundreds of millions of people. The Communist Party may not be present one or two decades from now, but Marxist–Leninist–Maoist ideology has little discernible influence on economic policy, so it is not apparent that it would make much difference whether China was ruled by the Communist Party, a military government, or some third alternative. Any one of these forms of government could be led either by people who understood the forces that have been unleashed and try to guide them, or by people who resist these forces and divert the process for a time along some unproductive channel. No one is going to try, let alone succeed, in turning back the clock to Soviet-style central planning.

Acknowledgments

I wish to thank Linda M. Koenig for her comments on this paper at the El Escorial conference at which it was presented.

CHAPTER 8

THE CHALLENGES OF CHINA'S GROWTH

For the past 27 years China, according to official estimates, has enjoyed an average gross domestic product (GDP) growth rate of 9.4% per year.[1] GDP per capita in 2005 was eight times what it was in 1978. Some analysts argue that these official growth rates may overstate China's true rate of development, but there is also evidence that in some sectors, they understate the true rate. No serious analyst, however, doubts that the pace of economic change has been rapid and that China has gone from being a very poor and economically weak nation in the 1970s to a still relatively low per capita income economy, but one that is now an aggregate economic force to be reckoned with on the world stage in 2006. If growth rates of this magnitude continue for another two decades to 2025, China will reach the level of per capita income of a South Korea today, but the overall size of the economy will be 25 times that of South Korea today and roughly equivalent to, or slightly larger than, the size of the US economy in 2005. Abject poverty, using either the standard of $1 per day or $2 per day, will have been eliminated from this 20% of the world's population — a population that is twice the size of Europe and North America combined. Rising incomes have made China a major market for exporters of both

[1]There is some debate over whether this officially estimated growth rate overstates China's true rate of GDP growth. Notably, however, when China's National Bureau of Statistics in 2005 adjusted their GDP estimates to better lake into account the growth in the services sector, the result was a small increase in the growth rate. That said, there are certainly reasons for thinking that GDP growth in years such as 1997–1999 may have been overstated (see Thomas Rawski, 2001), but there is also scholarly work supporting the view that GDP growth may have been understated (Kojima, 2002, and Klein et al., 2005). Whatever the precise figure, there is no question that China's GDP growth rate has been very rapid in comparison to that of most other countries.

natural resource products and high technology manufactures. For exporters of labor-intensive and some higher-end manufactures, however, China has become a formidable competitor. On the negative side, another economy the size of that of the United States' that, like the United States uses energy wastefully, will put a large strain on the world's environment. At the moment, China, in terms of energy use per unit of GDP, is even more wasteful than the United States. But China also is making vigorous efforts at present to raise the efficiency of its energy use. Where China will be in this regard two decades from now remains to be seen, but there is little doubt that China will be a major emitter of greenhouse gases and other pollutants by that time. China is also rapidly building up its military capacity, and that buildup is likely to continue as long as the economy keeps growing rapidly. But will this high growth rate of GDP continue and for how long?

Economies that grow rapidly for a time do not always continue along that path until they reach high income status. Argentina is the economy most often cited to illustrate this point. Argentina, in 1910, had a per capita income higher than that of Germany or France, but then growth slowed. From 1948 to 1959 and from 1974 through 1994, there was no growth whatsoever in Argentina's per capita income.[2] The misguided industrial policies of President Juan Peron and many of his successors, together with the 1980s debt crisis, account for the long periods of economic stagnation. But Argentina is one country among many. Between 1913 and 1950, despite two world wars and the Great Depression, average per capita income in 11 major West European countries did grow at a modest 1.4% per year, but in Germany, per capita income in 1949 was virtually the same as in 1913. In France, it was not until 1949 that the per capita income climbed back to the level achieved in 1929.[3] In more recent times, we have the example of the former centrally planned command economies of Eastern Europe and the former Soviet Union. There the transition to market economies came at the price of a deep depression for almost all of them. Ten years after the collapse of the Soviet-style economic system (in 1989) only Poland, the Czech Republic, Slovakia, and

---

[2] Maddison, 1995, 202–203.

[3] Maddison, 1995, 194–195.

Hungary had recovered to or slightly surpassed the per capita income levels of the pre-1989 period.[4]

Thus, there are many ways in which growth can be stopped. Prolonged warfare on one's territory is an obvious example. Misguided policies can achieve similar results. A decision to abandon one economic system for another can lead to years of adjustment before growth is restored. Nations heavily dependent on natural resources such as oil regularly go through cycles of boom followed by bust. But China has managed so far to avoid most of these pitfalls. China has enjoyed peaceful relations with its neighbors since at least 1980. China made the transition from a command economy to a market economy without a recession — to the contrary, growth accelerated immediately once the transition process began. And China is not a natural resource-rich country that experiences boom and bust when mineral prices rise and fall. But China is also a country that has not made a transition to a political system that fosters active citizen participation in the political process. Can rapid economic growth in China continue without comparable changes in the political system? If changes in the political system are likely in the not-too-distant future, will those changes be gradual and peaceful or sudden and violent?

In the remainder of this chapter, we will first review just how profound the economic and social changes of the past 27 years have been. We will then turn to the question of whether the economic forces at work will allow this economic transformation to continue. As the brief discussion above makes clear, however, it is not economic forces that typically bring periods of sustained growth to a halt. The question for China is whether major disruptions in the domestic or international political arena are likely to change what in economic terms appears to be a very positive forecast. We will end with a few remarks about the implications of these likely trends for American policy toward China.

---

[4]This statement is based on World Bank data and excludes the countries that have been formed out of the breakup of Yugoslavia. Estimates of GDP in US dollars or in purchasing power parity for former centrally planned economies are fraught with methodological problems. Thus, the statement in the text here should be taken as a general indicator of performance in these countries. Slightly different methodologies would give somewhat different results, but the basic fact of an economic decline in much of the region is not in doubt.

I. The Past 27 Years

Before assessing the prospects for continued rapid growth in China, it is helpful to have a clearer picture of just what has, and has not, occurred in China over the past 27 years in both economic and political terms. In 1974 and 1975, when I first visited the People's Republic of China, there was little construction going on in China's cities and construction cranes were simply not in evidence. New housing for urban residents was also not in evidence and nationwide even many engineers, professors, and medical doctors were squeezed into a tiny space where typically three people lived in an area of 13.2 m^2 or 140 ft^2 that included the sleeping and living area[5], a tiny kitchen sometimes shared, and a shared bathroom. Farmers had roughly double that amount of space, but they often had to share it with their animals. By 2004, in contrast, China was building 479 million m^2 of new urban residential space a year for an urban population of 543 million, and the average living space for an urban family of three had quintupled to 75 m^2 or nearly 800 ft^2.[6] If one looked out the window of a high-rise building in a city such as Shanghai, virtually every building one could see had been constructed within the past 10 years.

Beginning in 1959 through 1961, because of Mao Zedong's Great Leap Forward and Rural Peoples Commune movements, over 30 million Chinese died prematurely, largely because of the indirect effects of inadequate levels of food. This was due partly to a decline in production and even more so to the poor distribution of the food supplies that did exist. Severe malnutrition came to an end with the recovery of agriculture after 1961, but rationing of grain and other key agricultural commodities continued through the 1970s. By the first years of the 21st century, however, food rationing was long gone and all but the poorest people in the more remote rural areas had enough to eat. The percentage of household income spent on food in the urban areas had fallen from 57% in 1981 to 38% in 2004, and the comparable Engel coefficient for the rural areas had fallen from 60% to 47% as incomes rose.

[5]This figure is for 1978. The figure in the statistical yearbook is given in per capita terms and I have multiplied the number by 3. State Statistical Bureau, 1982, 429.

[6]National Bureau of Statistics, 2005, 333.

In the late 1970s and early 1980s, there were no mobile phones and relatively few landline phones even in the urban areas. A call from Beijing to Shanghai could take hours to put through.[7] By 2004, there were 111 mobile phones per 100 households in urban China and there were 54.5 phones of all kinds per 100 households in the rural areas although there was considerable variation from one province to another. In 1981, hardly anyone in the rural areas had a television set (0.16 sets per 100 families), but by 2004, the great majority of rural residents had a television set and two-thirds of those sets were color.

Rural Chinese in 2004 still mainly rode bicycles, but one-third had motor bikes or used their hand tractors as mini-trucks (there were 19 mini-tractors per 100 households). In the cities, passenger cars in the 1970s were reserved for high-level cadres and for important visitors. Production of motor vehicles other than trucks in 1981 was less than 70,000 per year, mainly of vehicles based on a Soviet design that was itself patterned on a US design of the 1930s. In the first half of 2006, in contrast, passenger automobile production had reached 1.8 million vehicles, with Buick edging out Volkswagen for the top spot in terms of sales. In urban China in 2004, however, there were still only 2 automobiles per 100 households, a figure similar to that of Japan in the early 1960s.[8]

Even a small percentage of automobiles per capita in a country with a population of 1.3 billion, however, can create major traffic jams. Beijing has built one ring road after another and barely keeps up with the need. Nationwide in the 1970s, the main trunk highways linking major cities were typically two-lane paved roads, and truck traffic could be almost bumper to bumper for hundreds of miles on key roads. Feeder roads onto these main roads more often than not were unpaved. Beginning in the 1990s, however, Beijing decided that it needed a modern countrywide highway system, and in the decade that followed, the nation constructed a

---

[7]A Chinese government official with whom I was working in the early 1980s had spent the whole day trying to get through from Beijing to Shanghai to arrange our appointments without success. According to him, the capacity of the phone system for all of China was roughly equal to that of the city of Hong Kong alone.

[8]In 1960, the total number of vehicles on Japanese roads (including trucks and buses) was only 1.35 million but that figure rose rapidly in subsequent years to reach 25 million vehicles in 1973 (Japan Automobile Manufacturers Association web page, 2006).

multi-lane limited access highway system throughout the nation comparable to the American interstate system (although not quite as long as the latter because the main roads of the northwest and Tibet were still mostly two-lane and not particularly crowded with traffic).[9]

In the 1970s, China's one airline used mainly old Soviet planes; purchase of its first 10 Boeing 707s was a major event. By 2004, China had purchased 675 large and medium commercial aircraft from Boeing and Airbus, and its purchase of some smaller passenger planes was approaching 100 a year. Lufthansa, by way of comparison in 2006, had a fleet size (including subsidiary airlines) of 429 aircraft with 52 more on order.[10] American Airlines, the largest airline in the world, had 707 planes in 2005.[11] Virtually, every provincial capital had a new modern airport with state-of-the-art navigation equipment. In 1979, by contrast, even a major city such as Wuhan had an airport that closed down, often for days, when there was a light rain.[12]

Most Chinese shared at least to some degree in this increased prosperity, but there are exceptions, mainly in the rural areas. In 1980, the average expenditure per capita in the rural areas (in 2004 prices) was just under 600 yuan and net income was 7% higher.[13] In 2004, net income (also in 2004 prices) was 2,936 yuan. Only 2.4% of rural households in 2004 had a per capita net income of 600 yuan or less. Another 10.1% had a household per capita income of less than 1,200 yuan. From personal observations made in designated poor counties in China's two poorest provinces (Gansu and Guizhou provinces in 1999), the poorest families in those villages were *very* poor indeed. Some slept under a thatched roof on slats a few feet above their privately owned hog that in turn resided next to the very crude kitchen. The children in these families were poorly clothed and barefoot and, despite compulsory education through eight grades, one saw young girls who were clearly not in school. But even in these designated

[9]Based on personal observation.

[10]Answers.com, "Lufthansa," www.answers.com/Lufthansa.

[11]Wikipedia, "American Airlines," http://en.wikipedia.org/American_airlines.

[12]Based on personal observation.

[13]This figure was obtained by multiplying the expenditure level in 1980 in current prices by the retail price index (the rural consumer price index does not go back to 1980 but the retail price index and consumer price index tend to track each other fairly closely).

poverty counties, however, the roads into them are often paved and many, and possibly most, have electricity. If they have a family member working in the factories on the coast, the children are well dressed and are clearly still in school. Their homes have tile roofs.

Converting these figures into US dollars in order to compare China with the commonly used measures of poverty of $1 and $2 per day introduces some subjectivity, mainly because China has never officially calculated its GDP in purchasing power parity (PPP) dollars. According to World Bank estimates, the PPP exchange rate between the Chinese yuan and the US dollar is 4.8 times the official dollar to yuan exchange rate.[14] Using the PPP exchange rate, therefore, the average net income of Chinese farmers in 1980 was $360, meaning that the average farmer just made the $1 per day poverty level. In 2004, the average PPP net income was $1,762 or well above the higher $2 per day poverty line. In 1980, over half of the rural population was below the $1 poverty line and much of the rest were below the $2 per day poverty line. According to Chen and Ravallion, the number of people in the entire Chinese population below the $1 per day poverty line in 2001 had fallen to 16.6% of the total population and the number below the $2 line in 2001 was 46.7%.[15] By 2005, these percentages would have fallen further. Whatever the validity of these precise numbers, there is no question that poverty in China has fallen dramatically over the past quarter century.

Economic progress in China over the past 27 years, therefore, has been impressive. But the changes in China go well beyond income and infrastructure. China is less and less a nation of peasants, for example. The officially registered urban population has risen from 17.9% of the total to 41.8%. Total employment in the primary sector (which is mostly agriculture) fell from 70.5% in 1978 to 46.9%.[16] Along with this shift out of

---

[14]This ratio was obtained from data in World Bank, 2003, 234. Until the Chinese government officially joins the UN system for calculating purchasing power parity exchange rates, however, any estimate such as the one used here is subject to a larger than normal margin for error.

[15]Chen and Ravallion (2004).

[16]These 2004 data are derived from the census of the year 2000 and sample surveys conducted by the National Bureau of Statistics for subsequent years (National Bureau of Statistics, 2005, 92–93, 115–118). There are significant problems with these data, particularly the employment data, but the basic trend that they reflect is not in doubt.

agriculture have come a number of changes, not all of which have had a positive impact on welfare. The rural health system built up under the communes has fallen apart under free markets, and few rural people have any health insurance. Moving to the cities does not help, because few migrants from the rural areas can afford the cost of urban health care. The household registration system also makes it difficult for rural migrants to put their children in urban schools. We shall explore these problems at greater length below.

Perhaps least appreciated by the world outside of China are the major changes that have already taken place in the political sphere and in the populations' access to information. While Mao Zedong was still alive and his wife Jiang Qing dominated the culture world, even the Chinese elite had very limited access to information about what was happening in the outside world or to what was happening in China itself. The main publication available to a narrow elite was *cankao xiaoxi* (reference news) that had clippings from the Western press among other sources. The open press did little more than published official decrees of the government and reports on important visitors from abroad. Even popular entertainment, such as Beijing operas, was limited by the cultural czars to a handful of performances that gave the "correct" political message. People were afraid to talk frankly about issues with their neighbors and even close friends for fear that they would then be dragged in front of a meeting to confess and self-criticize their behavior — or worse. Suicide not uncommonly followed on the worst of these confrontations.

Contact with foreigners was even more dangerous. Simply having a relative living abroad could be grounds for persecution. Chinese speaking to foreigners made sure that the contact was officially sanctioned and that they were always together with another Chinese who could testify to what they had said to the foreigner. One member of what was then called the US Liaison Office in Beijing found he could only talk to individual Chinese without these strictures if he happened to be riding alongside them on his bicycle and the Chinese citizen involved knew he could always veer off quickly and be gone if he saw he was being observed by someone who might report him. When contact with foreigners was authorized, the conversations seldom veered from officially sanctioned positions on all issues except at the very highest levels. At banquets, the one safe topic was the food.[17] By any reasonable standard, China prior to 1976 was a totalitarian state in the full sense of that term. Using the Frieclrich–Brzezinksi definition of totalitarianism, China was a totalitarian nation par excellence. In particular, China during the first three decades of Communist Party rule was a state that had an official all-encompassing ideology to which "general adherence was demanded." The Chinese people were not allowed to passively adhere to this ideology; they had to actively support it in numerous study (*xuexi*) meetings and more public forums. The demand for adherence was backed up not only by police terror but also by a pervasive community mutual surveillance system.[18]

Fast forward to the 21st century and the situation could not be more different. Millions of Chinese have traveled abroad singly and in groups. Hundreds of thousands have studied at, or been visiting scholars to, universities in North America, Europe, and Japan. One-on-one conversations between Chinese and foreigners are common and most of the time no one representing the security apparatus is trying to listen in (although there are, of course, exceptions). The foreign press is subjected to considerable surveillance by the authorities, but most other foreigners are ignored unless they are involved in particularly sensitive issues.

The number of Chinese with access to the Internet has passed 100 million and is increasing rapidly. Some sites on the Internet are blocked, but the vast majority are not. And even for the blocked sites, there is reason to believe that those who want to get through to the banned sites often can do so.[19] Western books, magazines, and newspapers are available to

---

[17]These remarks are based in part on personal observation during trips to China in 1974 and 1975 and in part on numerous reports verbally and in writing from numerous other visitors to China.

[18]An all-encompassing ideology to which adherence was demanded and police terror to back it up were the first two components of the definition of totalitarianism. The other four components of the Friedrich–Brzezinski definition were a "single mass party hierarchically organized and closely interwoven with the state bureaucracy and typically led by one man, monopolistic control of the armed forces, monopoly of the effective means of communication, and central control and direction of the economy." (Plueger, 2006). China also met these other four criteria for being a totalitarian system.

[19]*New York Times* columnist Nicholas Kristof experimented during a recent visit to China with what could be found easily on the Internet when in China; he was able to reach some blocked sites and was able to tell quite easily in some cases what passages or terms were being blocked (Kristof, 2005).

most who have the money to pay for them, although there is still censorship. There are dozens of television channels available showing thousands of movies, documentaries, news, and a wide variety of entertainment. Whatever one thinks of the quality of what is shown on television, there is a great deal of it.

The main area where there has been very limited change is in the nature of the political system that governs China. The Chinese Communist Party has a complete monopoly on all major government positions and policy decisions. The top leadership of the party is formally selected by the party Central Committee but in practice it is picked by a small group of Politburo members. There are more candidates for membership on the Central Committee than there are positions, so disfavored candidates can be, and are, kept off the Committee, but the number so affected is very small. The party has also broadened the criteria for those allowed to be party members to include private business people. In effect, the Chinese Communist Party has abandoned its belief in maintaining a government monopoly over the economy, a central tenet of the ideology with which it governed China until very recently.

Elections involving the population at large exist mainly at the village level. At that level, there is often real competition for slots to lead the locality, and officials who are incompetent or worse are often defeated. Chinas experiment with village democracy, however, at present appears to be mainly directed at curbing local cadre abuses and is not necessarily a model that will be gradually expanded to include higher level political units and the cities.

Corruption among officials in China is widespread. The Transparency International Index places China tied for No. 78 out of a total of 159 countries ranked with a raw score of 3.2 (with 10 being no corruption and 1 being completely corrupt). The Chinese-majority societies of Singapore and Hong Kong by comparison were ranked Nos. 5 and 15 with raw scores of 9.4 and 8.3.[20] The raw index score in this index may be a better indicator than China's ranking against other countries. China, for example, is only 1.1 higher than countries in the bottom 10% of all those rated but is 3.0 below No. 30 on the list and 6.2 below Singapore. Put differently, China is grouped with a large number of very corrupt nations even if it is near the

[20]Transparency International (2005).

top of the list of the very corrupt. The country has a long way to go to reach a level comparable to that of countries that most outside observers would consider only mildly corrupt (Italy and South Korea at 5.0 for example).

Rather than rely on elections that could "throw the rascals out," China has mainly attacked the problem with severe criminal penalties — including death for the worst cases. China could also ease the corruption problem by ridding itself of the myriad of licenses and permits needed to do business that have caused China to be ranked 91st out of 155 ranked countries in the World Bank's ranking of the "ease of doing business."[21] When it comes to obtaining licenses, for example, out of 155 countries, China ranks No. 146 in terms of the number of procedures necessary, with 30 procedures that take 363 days to complete, and is tied for No. 148 in terms of the time required to secure them. Raising China's ranking in these' areas — mainly by eliminating licenses and similar procedures — would do more to curtail corruption than any realistic number of executions.

Can China sustain this seeming contradiction between having a dynamic economy and an increasingly open society on the one hand and a political system that is slow to change and is widely perceived as being very corrupt on the other? Before trying to answer that question, however, we must first explore whether China's economy will continue on its high growth trajectory.

II. Forecasting China's Future Economic Growth

Forecasting China's long-term growth prospects is a very different exercise from forecasting whether China will grow rapidly next year or will face a hard landing and a recession because of the excessively high growth rate of 2006. All kinds of external shocks and short-term policy mistakes can affect growth from year to year. Since the reform period began, China's annual GDP growth rate has fluctuated between a low of 4.2% (in 1989 and 1990) and a high of 14.1% (in 1993). Forecasting the extent of growth over a decade or longer generally must take into account these short-term influences. To forecast China's long-term economic growth prospects, one needs to begin with an understanding of how the high long-term growth of the past 27 years was achieved. The methodology best

---

[21] World Bank (2006, p. 92).

suited to answer that question is growth accounting or sources of growth analysis mainly from the supply side.

Following Robert Solow, we use the production function:

$$Y = f(K, L, t),$$

where Y is GDP, K is the stock of capital, L is the labor force, and t is the shift in productivity over time. This equation (with certain assumptions), can be differentiated and rearranged into the following form:

$$g_y = w_k \times g_k + w_l x g_l + a,$$

where g_y is the growth rate of GDP, g_k is the growth rate of the capital stock, g_1 is the growth rate of the employed labor force (and in the quality of that labor force as measured by its education level), w_k and w_1 are the shares in national income of the income of capital and labor respectively, and a is the rate of growth of productivity — usually referred to as total factor productivity (TFP). The growth accounting data for China from 1952 through 2005 are presented in Table 1.

Table 1. Sources of China's economic growth.

		Growth rate			Shares of contribution to GDP growth		
Period	GDP	Capital stock	Labor and human capital	TFP*	Capital	Labor and human K	TFP*
1952–2005	6.95	8.28	2.66	1.9	51.2	21.8	27.1
1952–1957	6.52	6.80	1.71	2.6	44.9	15.0	40.1
1957–1965	2.41	6.18	2.11	–1.5	110.4	50.0	–60.3
1965–1978	4.87	7.72	3.15	–0.3	68.2	36.9	–5.2
1978–2005	9.46	9.45	2.75	3.8	43.0	16.6	40.4
1978–1985	9.73	7.97	4.56	3.7	35.2	26.7	38.1
1985–1990	7.70	9.26	2.91	2.1	51.7	21.6	26.7
1990–1995	11.73	9.33	2.20	6.3	35.7	10.7	53.6
1995–2000	8.58	8.52	1.61	4.0	42.7	10.7	46.6
2000–2005	9.48	12.42	1.81	3.1	56.3	10.9	32.8

Sources and methodology: See Perkins and Rawski, 2006, appendix.
Note: TFP = Total Factor Productivity.

The central point of this table is that the major difference between China's slow economic growth prior to 1979 and its rapid growth from that year onward is driven mostly by the shift from negative TFP growth in the 1957–1978 period to strongly positive TFP averaging 3.8% per year from 1979 onward. Formally, the growth rate of the capital stock after 1978 accounts for slightly more of the growth than productivity (43% versus 40.4%), but this is misleading. The reforms that began in late 1978 did not raise the rate of capital formation as a share of GDP. The rate of investment as a share of GDP changed little from the pre- to the post-1978 period. Reforms that caused the jump in productivity by raising the rate of GDP growth thus also raised the rate of growth of capital (since the same share of investment was now applied to a higher level of GDP).

High productivity growth probably also had something to do with why the rate of investment as a share of GDP remained so high after 1978. Before the reform period, the rate of investment was driven by the government's decision to generate a high savings rate mainly through creating high monopoly profits in industry that were then taxed away from the enterprises and subsequently returned in the form of state-led investment. The rate of investment in this earlier period was thus an administrative decision made by the government and was not driven by the rate of return on that investment. After 1978, and particularly by the 1990s and during the first years of the 21st century, however, investment was increasingly in private profit-oriented hands and high productivity produced high profits that led to high rates of investment.

Sustaining high GDP growth rates in China over the next two decades, therefore, is first and foremost a question of continuing to generate high growth in TFP. Forecasting productivity growth, however, is a highly subjective exercise, so we will begin with the somewhat easier part of the story — forecasting the contribution to GDP growth of capital formation and the growth of the labor force and the quality of that labor force (human capital).

In a closed economy without access to foreign capital, the rate of investment is driven in part by the rate of return to that investment but also by the level of domestic savings that can be mobilized to finance that investment. China today is no longer a closed economy in that sense since foreign direct investment (FDI) has reached $60 billion a year in 2004 and

2005. However, as large as that figure is, it is less than 10% of total Chinese investment that, as of 2004, was an extraordinary 44.2% of GDP — which translates in US dollar terms into more than $700 billion at the official exchange rate. Thus, the rate of investment in China still depends to an important degree on whether China's current, very high savings rate remains high in the future.

A nation's savings rate is the product of savings decisions by several distinct groups — those of individual households, of the government, and of industrial and commercial enterprises. Future government savings is likely to be low due primarily to its large unfunded pension liabilities, the fact that commercial banks still require refinancing of an excessive number of nonperforming assets, and because the social welfare system in general, and the health care system in particular, will require large-scale government support. If high growth continues, however, enterprise profits are likely to remain high, and a substantial portion of those profits will be plowed back into investment. At present, enterprise profits tend to be concentrated in the energy sector, but that could change over time.

The most important source of savings in China today, however, is households, and households save for a number of reasons. Many, for example, save in order to accumulate funds to purchase large consumer durables. The privatization of housing has created another reason to save now that families must purchase their homes. Expanding consumer credit and larger and longer-term mortgages could erode these reasons for saving over time. If, as argued below, China must shift aggregate demand from a dependence on rapid export growth to domestic consumption and investment, then an expanded consumer lending program would be a way of accomplishing this shift.

The major motive for saving in households around the world, however, is to prepare for retirement. The model that best captures this effect is the life-cycle model of savings that relates the level of household savings to a country's dependency ratio: the ratio of children and the elderly who are not in the labor force, to those who are in the labor force. The dependency ratio from 1990 to 2025 is presented in Table 2.

The central point in this table is that China's dependency ratio has been low for some time and is likely to remain low for the next two decades. The reason for this low dependency ratio is due partly to the

Table 2. China's dependency ratio, 1990–2025.

	Total population (in millions)	Population aged 16–65 (in millions)	Ratio age 16–65 to total	Dependency ratio
1990	1,143	737	0.64	0.36
2000	1,267	853	0.67	0.33
2005	1,306	909	0.7	0.3
2015	1,387	991	0.715	0.285
2025	1,472	968	0.66	0.34

Sources and methodology: See Perkins and Rawski, 2006.

one-child family policy that began in the 1970s. All new entrants to the labor force over the past decade and a half and over the coming decade and a half are a product of the one-child policy. Only a sharp increase in the birth rate during the next five years would change that picture, and then only for the years 2021 to 2025, when those born today and in the next few years turn 15 years of age (and even those are likely still to be in the education system longer than is the case today).

China's workforce today, in contrast, was mostly born after 1952 through the early 1970s when Mao Zedong and other Chinese leaders thought that the bigger the Chinese population the better. Those born in 1952 are not yet of retirement age, even using the early retirement age applied to the state sector. With most adults in good health staying actively occupied until their mid-60s, retirement of China's "baby boom" generation will not really begin until after 2015. In Table 2, there is in fact a slight rise in the dependency ratio between 2015 and 2025, but only back to the levels of the 1990s. After 2025, the picture begins to change dramatically. Most of the "baby boomers" will be retired by 2035 (the youngest will be 63 years of age) and, with increasing life expectancy in China, more and more of them will be living into their 80s and beyond. The workforce, in contrast, will be made up entirely of products of the one-child policy. Chinas dependency ratio will soar and the household savings rate will no doubt fall, but that is beyond the period with which we are concerned in this essay. For the next two decades, the savings rate is likely to remain high and, if the investment opportunities are there, the investment rate will keep up with the savings rate. Capital formation in China will continue at a rapid pace.

China's labor force, however, will not continue to grow at the past rate. As those born in the 1950s begin to retire and are replaced by the one-child policy generation, the numbers of people in the labor force will stagnate and may even decline slightly. Currently 70%[22] of those of school age (aged 6 to 21) are now in school, and that percentage will rise, perhaps to 75 to 80%, as China moves toward universal high school education and increasing university enrollments. The reduction in the labor force, because of increased time in school, will probably be offset by simultaneous increases in the age of the older-age groups still in the workforce (particularly if the pension systems remain as weak as they are today). In terms of growth accounting, the increase in education will mean that the quality of the labor force is steadily rising, and this will mean that labor will continue to make a positive contribution to growth — but a very modest one.

This analysis of the contribution of the labor force and human capital to growth, however, leaves out one important element that, in the above calculations, shows up as TFP, but is in reality a contribution to growth by labor. In China in 2004, there were still 352.7 million workers in the primary sector, and most were farmers cultivating less than 122 million hectares of arable land.[23] The United States, in contrast, cultivates more than 110 million hectares of land with only 3 million farmers. Over the next two decades, a large share of China's fam workers will leave farming and move to jobs in industry and services, with most of those jobs being in China's cities. Based on the differential in urban and rural wages of unskilled workers of roughly three to one,[24] the migration of farm workers to the cities should approximately triple the productivity of those workers. If employment in industry and services rises by 10 million jobs a year over the coming two decades, migrants from the countryside will be the ones

[22]These trends are discussed in more depth in Perkins and Rawski, 2006.

[23]Because of the encroachment of urban and industrial development, China's arable land has been declining and has fallen from 130 million hectares in the late 1990s (Fu Jing, 2006, 1).

[24]Perkins and Rawski (2006).

filling those jobs.[25] The result will be the migration of 200 million farmers out of agriculture into the cities over the next two decades. We will explore the broader implications of this massive migration further below.

Migration from the countryside to the cities, rising education levels of the workforce in general, and a continued high rate of investment should keep China's GDP growing for at least the next two decades, but, in the absence of a high level of TFP growth, China's GDP growth will be in the 3 to 5% range. As the data in Table 1 indicate, TFP growth during the past 27 years of the reform period averaged 3.8% a year. This high TFP growth, however, was generated by a series of reforms that corrected some of the major distortions that hurt productivity growth during the command economy period between 1955 and 1978. In the 1979–1981 period, for example, China abolished the rural commune system of collective farming and went back to household agriculture. The result was a large jump in fam output between 1978 and 1984, but it was a one-shot jump. Agricultural value-added growth rates reverted part of the way back to the long-term trend rates of the pre-1978 period after 1984.[26]

The other major change in the first years of the reform period was the opening up of the economy to foreign trade. The rapid expansion of exports made possible the rapid expansion of inputs of key materials and equipment that certainly contributed in a major way to productivity growth and continues to do so to this day. But the gap between imported

---

[25]To be more precise, migrants into the urban workforce will take over many existing as well as new unskilled jobs, freeing up the better educated urbanites to fill the increases in higher skilled jobs.

[26]Between 1978 and 1984 the primary sector value-added rose at an annual rate of 7.3% per year. From the end of 1984 through 2004 that rate was 3.8% per year. Between 1957 and 1978, the gross value of agricultural output grew at only 2.3% per year (Rural Society and Economy Investigation Team of the National Bureau of Statistics, 2000, 33) as contrasted to a gross value output rate of increase from 1984 to 2004 of 5.7% per year. The gross value growth rate figures particularly for the most recent years are higher than the value-added data largely because agriculture was making increasing use of purchased inputs in the more recent years. Greater efficiency in the use of inputs that may also have been occurring would have brought the value-added growth rates closer to those for gross value of output. A major reason why agricultural growth in the post-1984 period was higher than in the pre-1978 period was that farmers were freer to plant higher valued crops rather than having to concentrate mainly on grain crops.

and domestically produced technology is not as great today as it was in those early years.

Beginning in 1984, China also experienced an explosion in industrial productivity when it freed up most industrial inputs to be sold on the market rather than allocated by administrative means in accordance with the central plans. The main beneficiaries were the township and village enterprises (TVEs) that were owned or controlled by localities. Unlike large state-owned enterprises, the TVEs responded to market forces because that was the main way to make money. The TVEs also faced hard budget constraints because the local governments lacked the resources to bail them out if they experienced losses — again unlike the large state firms that could go back to the banks for loans that they might or might not pay back. Prior to the 1984 reforms, however, TVEs had to apply to the central planners for administrative allocation of key inputs, an application process where they received a low priority. With the reforms, they could purchase what they needed, albeit at higher prices than the previous state-set prices. The TVE boom that ensued lasted into the mid-1990s and was the main force sustaining the high rate of industrial growth in that period. But by the late 1990s, the TVE boom had also lost much of its momentum.

Finally, it was in the late 1990s that FDI in China took off. In 1990 and in the years immediately preceding, FDI averaged between \$3 and \$4 billion per year, but by 1995 that figure had jumped to \$37.5 billion, and in 2004 it passed \$60 billion for the first time. The money itself was not so important, since China had large alternative sources of foreign exchange (mainly export earnings that reached \$149 billion in 1995, \$224 billion in the year 2000, and \$762 billion in 2005). What did matter for productivity growth were the technology, the management expertise, the quality control, and the access to foreign markets that accompanied the FDI. It is likely that FDI accounts for a large share of the 3.1% annual TFP growth in the first six years of the 21st century (see Table 1). But it is also likely that the sharp increase in FDI since the early 1990s will not continue long into the future. FDI into China appears to be leveling off at the current high levels, and annual realized FDI has only increased on average by 3.7% per year since 1997. Thus, continuously rising FDI is not likely to be a major source of TFP growth, although continued high levels of FDI will no doubt contribute to future TFP growth.

What then will support high TFP growth in the future if many of the past sources appear to have run out of steam? One source is likely to be the continued privatization of much of the modern sector of the Chinese economy. China has never had a formal privatization program, and, in fact, the word privatization is not used by the government to describe what is going on in industry and services. Furthermore, it is not easy to precisely estimate the size of the private sector in China, because ownership classifications keep changing. Between 1999 and 2002, for example, the state-owned enterprise share of industrial output in firms with sales above 5 million yuan fell from 30.56 to 15.59%. But most of this drop occurred because state-owned enterprises in large numbers were listing on the Shanghai and Shenzhen stock exchanges and were reclassified as shareholding enterprises. The share of state-owned industrial enterprises and state-controlled shareholding enterprises also declined, but only from 48.92 to 40.78%.[27] Outside of agriculture, the one area that is largely and unambiguously privatized is urban housing. Housing that was typically owned by the state industrial enterprises was sold usually at bargain prices to the occupants and most new housing is being bought by individual families.

Most of the shareholding, former state-owned enterprises, however, still operate much like they did in the recent past when they were formally state owned. The government and the Communist Party still have the major say in selection of management, and the government in fact still has majority control of the shares in most of these enterprises. There are a few "independent" directors on the boards, but there is little evidence that these independent directors have much influence. If shareholding is to really involve more than just a vehicle for raising capital and is to truly transform state-owned enterprises into modern market- and profit-oriented corporations, the government and the party will have to become minority shareholders at the most and will have to allow boards of directors elected by the majority shareholders to select top management. The Chinese Communist Party has surrendered direct power over the economy in other sensitive areas, notably in agriculture, so there is no reason to doubt that they will not do so in this area as well, but they had made little progress in this regard by 2006.

[27]Yusuf, *et al.*, (2006, p. 80).

The TVEs are proceeding much more rapidly toward true privatization. In the late 1980s and early 1990s, most were classified as collectives since that was a politically more acceptable term and it reflected the fact that the local community, mainly through local governments, had a major role in the operation of these local enterprises. Local governments still have a major role in these enterprises, but management is increasingly in the hands of a private owner. In the current climate that is friendlier to outright private ownership, TVEs apparently no longer feel a need for the kind of political protection provided by being collectively owned.[28]

Goods and services in China have been distributed mostly through market mechanisms since the middle to late 1990s. The dual price system set up in the mid-1980s, where goods were partly distributed through markets and partly through government administrative channels, died a natural death.[29] Firms with goods to sell preferred to offer them on the market, where prices were higher, and they used various methods to avoid use of the administrative channels. Firms purchasing goods knew that, if they wanted their key inputs on time, they were more likely to get them through the market than from the planners. The government, which introduced the dual price system mainly to appease powerful state enterprises that did not want to pay higher prices, had little incentive to stop the steady erosion of the quantity of goods allocated through administrative channels.

Markets for factors of production — labor, land, and capital — are less well developed than in the case of goods and services. There is a fairly well developed urban land market, although it is plagued with political influence and other distortions. There is no regular market for rural land, however, and there are inefficiencies created by farmers who leave their land for the city but use various methods to hold onto their rights to the land. In such cases, the land is often underutilized, and incentives to invest in the land are weak. In other parts of the country, the local authorities periodically redistribute

---

[28]From the beginning there was always considerable regional variation in the ownership classification of TVEs. In Guangdong Province, outright private ownership was acceptable early on, whereas in major TVE centers such as Wuxi in Jiangsu Province, outright private ownership in the 1980s was generally not acceptable. William A. Byrd and Qingsong Lin (1990). *China's Rural Industry: Structure, Development, and Reform*. New York: Oxford University Press.

[29]For a discussion of the origins of the dual price system see Hua, *et al.*, (1993, pp. 119–131).

the land under their jurisdiction to reflect changes in the demographic makeup of their localities. These interventions do sometimes serve equity considerations, and so moving toward greater efficiency by letting the market handle rural land transactions may not be politically acceptable. Corrupt land deals in the rural areas, whether they make more efficient use of the land or not, are a major source of political tension and violence. Typically, these land deals involve local officials pushing farmers off their land to make way for a factory or other commercial use.[30]

The main inefficiency in the urban labor market is the differential treatment of officially registered urban residents versus new migrants from the rural areas who are still registered as rural residents. We will discuss this issue further below. Government-directed administrative allocation of labor, the primary method of skilled labor allocation prior to the reform period, has largely disappeared.

In terms of the impact on economic growth, however, the largest negative influence at present arises from the underdeveloped and politically distorted nature of China's capital markets. Like most developing countries, China's capital markets are underdeveloped. The main financial institutions are the commercial banks, and these banks since early on in the reform period have lent mainly to the less efficient state enterprises.[31] Because the state enterprises were used to having their investment needs met through the government budget, they often treated bank loans as virtual grants and made no effort to pay them back. The result, as is now well known, was a massive buildup of nonperforming loans in the banking system.[32]

---

[30]One estimate based on statistics from the Ministry of Land and Resources reported in the Chinese press is that one in two construction projects between October 2004 and May 2005 were built on land acquired illegally. (Fu Jing, 2006).

[31]Prior to the reform period the banks lent mainly to state enterprises as well (and to rural communes) because state enterprises plus some collectives were all there were. But prior to the 1980s, loans were only for working capital while investment capital was supplied directly from the government budget. With the reforms, the system of having most industrial investment handled through the budget was abandoned and replaced with loans for investment from the commercial banks to the enterprises.

[32]For an in-depth discussion of the origins of the nonperforming assets of the banking system, see Lardy (1998).

China has been struggling with how to clean up the balance sheets of the commercial banks and is doing so with some success. Non-performing assets officially have fallen from 35% in 1999[33] to around 8% in 2005. The true figures are widely believed to be higher than these official estimates, but there is no doubt that the share of nonperforming loans has declined, although even officially it is still at a high level. Equally serious from an efficiency point of view, the banks continue to direct a large portion of their loans to the state-owned or state-controlled sector because loans to the state sector are seen as politically safe even if they often are not commercially safe. The more dynamic private sector (other than enterprises with large amounts of foreign direct investment) has difficulty getting access to capital. This situation is beginning to change, but slowly.

The Shanghai and Shenzhen stock exchanges are similar to the banks in that they mainly serve the capital needs of the state sector. Firms allowed to list on these exchanges are overwhelmingly state-owned enterprises or state-controlled shareholding enterprises. Other financial institutions, notably the insurance companies, are still in the early stages of development and are not yet major players on the Chinese capital markets. Thus, China's financial system has a long way to go to be the kind of efficient system that can sustain economic growth. From a forecasting point of view, that situation can be seen as either an advantage for the future or a disadvantage. It is a disadvantage if China fails to fundamentally reform and develop its financial institutions, particularly the commercial banks, up to international standards. In that case, the inability of dynamic non-state firms to access capital could be seriously hampered and China could even end up in a situation similar to that in Japan during its fourteen years of economic stagnation (1991–2004). Japan's stagnation was to a significant degree the result of a banking system loaded down with nonperforming assets that was reluctant to lend to anyone other than the government and already established firms such as Toyota.

[33]This figure was given by the then-governor of the central bank, Dai Xianglong. The transfer of a substantial portion of these bad loans to separate asset management companies reduced the nonperforming assets still in the banks to 25% of total assets. The criteria used in arriving at these percentages, however, are seen by many as understating the total (Lardy, 2001).

The weak state of China's financial system, however, also can be seen as an advantage for future productivity growth. If China continues to take forceful steps to strengthen its financial system and put it in the service of the whole economy, not just the favored state sector, China could achieve large efficiency gains. Our own estimate is that reforms in the financial system will continue at a steady pace and will be aided by China's commitments under the WTO to open its financial sector to full foreign participation and competition. China has done well to date with a very weak financial system. It should do better as it gradually weeds political considerations out of its financial decision making.

In a full market economy, it is not just the allocation of goods and services or allocation of factors of production that is handled through decentralized decisions of the enterprises themselves. The basic direction of industrial development, other than in the defense industry, is largely left to market forces. Issues such as bankruptcy and mergers or acquisitions are also handled by the parties directly involved — the creditors and debtors in the case of bankruptcy, and the firms acquiring or being acquired in the case of mergers and acquisitions. These transactions are subject to rules laid down by the legislature, but enforcement of those rules is left to independent judges. In much of East and Southeast Asia, in contrast, it is the executive branch of the government that takes the lead in these areas.

The most influential model for state-led growth in Asia was that developed by the Ministry of International Trade and Industry (M1TI) in Japan and altered to fit the somewhat different conditions of South Korea, particularly during the reign of President Park Chung Hee in the 1960s and 1970s. The executive branch of the government did not try to comprehensively plan industrial development. Instead, it attempted to determine which industries would be critical to the next stage of development and then actively promoted those industries through directed bank loans (the government either owned the banks outright or had enormous influence over bank lending decisions). The executive branch also provided access to foreign exchange and critical imports (in the early stages of development when foreign exchange was scarce and was tightly controlled). Implementation was actually carried out by private firms for the most part, but these were private firms willing to do the bidding of the government.

In this kind of industrial policy, if an enterprise failed because it faithfully carried out the wishes of the government planners, the government was obligated to help the firm get out of difficulty (by forgiving past loans or by lending more funds to tide the firm over, for example). If the firm failed because of its own shortcomings, the government still might intervene to save the firm but might replace the existing management. If the government felt that a different industrial structure was appropriate, it could pressure firms to merge with others or get out of particular lines of business in order to reduce "excessive" competition. This pressure did not always have the desired effect (MITI's failed attempt to force consolidation in the Japanese automobile industry is one of the best known examples), but, more often than not, the private firms tried to implement what the government desired. In South Korea after the financial crisis of 1997–1998, the government used its control over the banking system (itself largely bankrupt) to force some firms into liquidation (Daewoo) and to pressure others to give up some components in order to concentrate on what the government felt the particular firm did best.

China, more or less by default, has inherited this kind of an industrial policy, but has tried to implement such a policy under conditions very different from those that prevailed in Japan and South Korea. When China abandoned comprehensive central planning, it did not move toward a system of *laissez-faire* markets patterned on those of, say, Hong Kong. Instead, China retained an active interest in promoting particular industries, notably automobiles, and thus the MITI-Korean approach has had great appeal. China also had to deal with thousands of enterprises that began to experience financial losses once prices for their products had to be adjusted to reflect competitive market forces as opposed to the prior system of government-set monopoly prices. In addition, enterprises under comprehensive planning were typically single factories that were little more than subordinate offices of giant industrial ministries. When these enterprises were made into truly independent firms, China ended up with one of the least concentrated industrial organizations anywhere in the world. Consolidation of this fragmented industrial organization structure was clearly desirable, but how was this consolidation to be accomplished?

Thus, China's government by the 1990s faced all kinds of decisions about the future path of industry, and the question was what to do about it. The full market approach would have been to leave these issues to be dealt with by the individual enterprises in response to market forces. But China was not in a position to do that because institutions critical to allowing markets to make these decisions efficiently did not exist. Specifically, China's judicial system was extremely weak and completely incapable of handling complex issues such as bankruptcies and mergers. China's courts were not terribly effective at resolving even simpler commercial disputes. Judges were not well trained, and they certainly were not independent of the executive branch of the government. After decades during which the judicial system was neglected or abandoned (Mao at one point abolished the legal profession), judges had limited authority and their decisions could be overruled — or simply ignored — and not just by high government officials.

Consequently, the Chinese government had to have an activist industrial policy, but it lacked an essential ingredient possessed by those implementing industrial policy in Japan and South Korea. In Japan and South Korea, industrial policy was carried out by technocrats, and decisions were made mainly on technical grounds and not for political or for rent-seeking purposes (corruption). Corruption and politics certainly existed in these two countries but they played a minimum role in industrial policy, at least in the early stages of their development (the 1950s and 1960s in Japan and the 1960s and 1970s in South Korea).[34] In China, it is hard to imagine a major industrial policy decision that would not be influenced by politics and/or rent-seeking. China's ranking in the Transparency International Index discussed above makes it clear that corruption is pervasive in Chinese decision making. Technocrats do play some role in Chinese industrial policy decisions, but almost never do they have the primary or final say on major issues. Furthermore, China's very size makes an activist industrial policy emanating from Beijing difficult. South Korea's Park Chung Hee could meet with the leaders of all of the major industries and firms once a month and could listen to their concerns and

[34] In South Korea, particularly by the 1990s, industrial policy became increasingly politicized and corrupt, and that was one of several reasons why South Korea began to try to replace its active industrial policy with a more market-oriented system, but this proved difficult to do in practice.

try to solve the problems they were having with the government. It is difficult to imagine anything comparable being attempted by President Hu Jintao or Premier Wen Jiabao. There were 219,000 industrial enterprises above a certain minimum size (in 2004), and they were scattered across the country.[35]

Again returning to the issue of forecasting China's future productivity growth, China's current situation with regard to industrial policy can be seen in both a positive and a negative light. On the negative side, China clearly has no choice for the immediate future other than to pursue an activist industrial policy with a good deal of government intervention, however inefficient that intervention might be. The institutions needed to avoid this outcome, notably the legal and regulatory system, are simply too weak to take many tasks over from the executive branch of the government. On the positive side, if China does set out to build the necessary legal and regulatory institutions and moves steadily away from an activist MITI-style industrial policy, the results are likely to be a big boost in productivity.

Will China take this path? There is no question that China is gradually trying to strengthen its legal institutions, and more and more people are going to the courts in an attempt to resolve disputes. On the other hand, the Chinese government is still full, in its upper ranks, of former planners who see an active role for themselves and for the government. While there is little doubt that China has the potential to make major improvements in the supporting institutions of a full market economy, it is much less clear whether the Chinese leadership sees activist intervention in industrial policy in a negative light. If it persists with the system as it exists today, growth over the long run could suffer.

III. Sources of Political Tension

Failure to continue to vigorously push reform of the supporting institutions of a full market economy, therefore, could slow economic growth significantly, but no plausible pace of economic reform is likely to bring growth to a halt or even to bring growth to a level of less than 5% a year.

---

[35]The arguments in these paragraphs are developed at greater length in Perkins, 2004.

Social tensions and the political changes that could result, in contrast, could have a larger impact and could even bring growth to a halt. We do not think that this no-growth scenario is likely, but the social tensions in China today are real enough and could lead to fundamental political changes that could interrupt growth, at least for a time.

The tensions that are getting the most coverage in the Western press are largely connected with misappropriation of land by corrupt local officials. These land deals gone bad appear to be a major source of the rising number of officially reported incidents that have involved some form of higher level police and government intervention. Basically, given the weakness of the courts, local people, particularly in the rural areas, sometimes make known their complaints with authority by resorting to demonstrations and violence. The long-term solution to this problem is to define rural property rights clearly, strengthen the courts so that they can be a fair and efficient way of resolving property rights disputes, and strengthen local cadre elections so that more of the corrupt local officials are weeded out. Accomplishing these changes will be a formidable task, but at least it is reasonably clear what needs to be done.

Other sources of potential and actual social tension in China do not have such straightforward "solutions." At the most general level, rapid economic development, wherever it occurs, eases some sources of social and political tension and exacerbates others. High rates of growth, for example, are usually accompanied by rapidly rising wages and household incomes, and that usually contributes to political stability. This has been the case in China. Large portions of the urban population in China, in particular the younger cohorts who are best positioned to take advantage of the many new economic opportunities, are busy getting rich and do not have the time or the inclination to participate in political protests. On the other hand, rapid economic growth also means rapid structural change in both the economy and the society, and structural change inevitably leaves many people behind and requires others to fundamentally change their way of life. This, in turn, can lead to serious discontent among those most affected.

In urban China, for example, tens of millions of employees of the loss-making state-owned enterprises have been let go or forced to take early retirement. In theory, their pensions were guaranteed and a safety net of welfare payments and retraining existed for those no longer employed. In practice, the funds to maintain these support systems were often missing or only a fraction of what was called for in the regulations. Local governments and the state enterprises that were expected to pay for these benefits often did not have the money required. Most of the people let go in this way were in the older age cohorts, and older age cohorts are less likely to be in the vanguard pushing for fundamental political change. It is worth noting, however, that China's leaders in the past stated openly that one of the greatest single obstacles to completing state enterprise reform was the fear of the political consequences of letting so many workers go.

Potentially more disruptive to the political system are three other structural changes that are occurring. Two of these are changes that normally accompany rapid economic growth but have special features peculiar to China that make the process potentially more disruptive. A third is a feature peculiar to China and its one-child policy. These three structural changes by no means exhaust all of the possibilities for social and political tension, but they are among the most important.

One structural change that always accompanies economic growth, rapid or otherwise, is a population shift out of agriculture and the rural areas into industrial and service sector jobs in the cities. As already indicated in our analysis of China's growth prospects, China over the next two decades is likely to experience a massive movement of labor of this kind, the largest rural to urban migration in world history. If China follows the pattern of Japan and South Korea at comparable stages in their economic growth, the share of China's population in agriculture could fall from 50 to 10% of the total over the next two decades. In 2004, there were 757 million people in rural China and 353 million of those are farm workers. A conservative estimate of the movement of farm workers would be a movement out of agriculture mainly to the cities of at least 200 million workers by 2025. If their families go with them, the migration out of the rural areas could reach 400 to 500 million.

But what kind of welcome can these worker migrants and their families expect from the urban population and urban governments? For most of the period of Communist Party rule, China has had a household registration system, the *hukou* system, that assigns people to a residence in either an urban or a rural area. The *hukou* system itself dates back to imperial times, but its use to vigorously restrict rural to urban migration is a modern phenomenon. Under the system as it operated until recently, if a family had a rural *hukou*, it had few rights when moving to the city. Only urban residents were entitled to place their children in the public schools in the cities. Health insurance (when it existed at all) applied only to the regular workers in the enterprises who also had urban registration. Migrants faced the usually impossible task of paying the high costs of urban medical care out of pocket. Furthermore, the massive housing construction that China has undertaken in the urban areas since 1978 has been built, for the most part, for existing urban residents. Migrants were expected to live in factory dormitories or on the construction sites where they worked — anywhere other than in the new housing being constructed by the state and by private developers. China, in effect, has had a two-class system, with a relatively privileged urban population and an underprivileged rural and migrant population. The result has been that many migrants leave their families back in the countryside. Those that do bring their families have to find ways to support themselves and to create their own schools for their children without government support and, not infrequently, with local government harassment.

Dumping another several hundred million people into this system over the coming two decades would appear to be a formula for high tension on an unprecedented scale. The central government in Beijing at least appears to be aware of the problem. Steps have been taken to further weaken the household registration system, replacing it with rules that make it somewhat easier to transfer official residence to an urban location. This, however, has been mainly for people with regular long-term urban employment, a status that does not apply to large numbers of migrants. There has also been a national government decision to allow migrant children to attend urban public schools in part because, according to the national government, the one-child family policy has led to unused capacity in these urban schools. (There has been less effort to deal with the health situation, but that reflects the general disarray in Chinese health care financing and is not peculiar to the migrants.) Perhaps most importantly, there is not as of yet a major effort to provide these urban migrants with minimally adequate housing for their families.

The current shortcomings in the way China is handling rural-to-urban migration could be a source of social and political disaster, with hundreds of millions of young, discontented people struggling to survive in the cities and resorting to crime and demonstrations against perceived abuses. Or this situation could be an opportunity for the Chinese leadership. The recent decision concerning education for migrant children is a good illustration of the latter. If local urban governments really cooperate in this endeavor, families will move to the cities, in part, in order to get a better education for their children. Families trying to push their children up the income and social status ladder are less likely to be involved in antisocial activities. Better education for migrant children will no doubt mean that the number of migrants will increase relative to what otherwise would have been the case, but China will benefit in the long term from having children who have better educational opportunities than they could have received in most rural areas.[36]

Housing for the migrants could also be a major opportunity, not just a high cost burden. As will be discussed later in this chapter, China needs to shift demand from its current heavy reliance on the growth of exports to greater reliance on the domestic market. What better place to start than a large-scale housing program that will use domestically produced resources (cement and steel) and lots of labor in general and migrant labor in particular. Furthermore, done well, such a housing program could provide a foundation on which to build a stable urban society that includes most of the population of China. The Peoples Action Party in Singapore gained a large measure of its support from first undertaking a large-scale urban public housing program that housed virtually the entire low-income end of the population, and then proceeded to sell off that housing to those who lived in it at favorable prices and financing terms. Granted that Singapore had to accommodate fewer than 2 million people in this way and China

[36]China's leadership is also trying to put more resources into rural schools, but rural schools in most developing countries suffer from a handicap that is very difficult to overcome. It is extremely difficult to get well-trained teachers to go to the rural areas to teach. Even those from the rural areas that go on to get sufficient education to be comparable to urban teachers usually do so in order to get out of the rural areas, not to return to them to teach.

will have to accommodate 500 million or perhaps as many as 25 million a year, the principle is much the same.

Given the way the Chinese governmental system is structured, including the way the various levels of that system are financed, local governments would have to play a major role in this effort, and that is part of the problem. The national government appears to recognize the issues at stake, but it is far less clear that the same can be said of local urban governments. Many of the latter appear to look on migrants as a necessary nuisance and to spend as little money on them as possible.

Another source of potential social tension in China arises directly from the one-child per family policy. Because of traditional Chinese values and because of the weakness of the current pension systems, Chinese families, like families elsewhere in many developing countries, have a distinct preference for male children. In the Chinese system, female children marry into their husband's family and in the eyes of many are "lost" to the family into which they were born. With modern methods for determining the sex of children and with the ready availability in China of abortion, many families are opting to abort female fetuses and allow male fetuses to go to term. The practice is illegal in China, but it is extremely difficult to enforce the law The result in terms of child sex ratios is shown in Table 3. Over a 20-year period, the ratio has gone from fewer males than females to nearly 123 males for every 100 females. If this situation continues for another two decades, in absolute numbers, one is talking about 25 million excess males in the potentially volatile 15–24 age group.

This kind of change for so large a population has no precedent and that makes it virtually impossible to predict the consequences. It is

Table 3. Sex ratios (number of males per 100 females by age group in 2004).

Aged 20–24	Ratio 96.85
Aged 15–19	Ratio 107.42
Aged 10–14	Ratio 112.43
Aged 5–9	Ratio 119.10
Aged 0–4	Ratio 122.69

Source: National Bureau of Statistics, 2005, 97.

difficult, however, to see this situation as anything other than a major source of potential instability and other forms of antisocial behavior.

The biggest source of potential pressure for political change is from a more conventional source for which there is a great deal of international experience. China today is a nation where a large proportion of the population is still poor and not very well educated relative to the populations of middle and high-income nations. Based on a large sample survey in 2004, only 19.2% of China's population, over the age of six or a total of 235 million people had either a secondary school or tertiary-level education. In terms of income, the top 40% of the urban population or 217 million people had an income per capita of renminbi 8,300 yuan or more or roughly 22,000 yuan per family ($1,000 and $2,700 at the official exchange rate or $4–5,000 and $10,800–13,500 at the PPP exchange rate). In the rural areas, the per capita income of the top 15% of the population in 2004, or another 190 million people, averaged over renminbi 5,000 yuan.[37] There is no widely accepted definition of "middle class," but we use the term here to refer to people who are reasonably well educated, are likely to have supervisory or white-collar jobs above the clerical level, or are well-off farmers who can afford to send their children all the way through secondary school. These are people who have significant amounts of discretionary income and have some knowledge of what is happening in the rest of China and even in the rest of the world from television, reading, and even the Internet (there are more than 100 million people with regular access to the Internet in China). It is likely that a substantial majority of the top 40% of the income earners in the urban areas and some of the top 15% in the rural areas could be considered "middle class" in this sense.

Put differently, these are the people most likely over time to want to have more participation in the major political decisions that affect their lives than they have at present, given the way the Chinese Communist Party and hence the government is organized. They are the kind of people who, if upset enough with the current system, may not go to the streets themselves but will support the activities of students and others who do,

[37]These data are all from or derived from National Bureau of Statistics, 2005, and are mainly based on. rural and urban household surveys taken annually.

as happened in South Korea in 1987 or in China in 1989. Their numbers in China today, however, are still relatively small, perhaps 200 to 300 million adults, about 20% of the total population. Over the next 20 years, these numbers and their share of the total population will rise rapidly. In income terms, 7% per capita growth a year will produce incomes four times the present level. In 2004, there were 4.5 million new entrants into tertiary-level institutions and 8 million new entrants into senior secondary schools. Even though the number of people in the relevant age groups is beginning to decline because of the one-child policy, these enrollment figures will continue to rise rapidly over the coming two decades.

Any precise estimate involves some weakly supported assumptions, but it is likely that at least another 250 million will graduate from senior high school, with over 140 million of those going on to university.[38] Because the percentage of those educated who will die over these coming years is very small, the net increase in the population educated to these levels will be almost the same as this increase in enrollments.[39] Thus, in 2025, the Chinese educated and relatively "high-income class" or "middle class" will total over 500 million people or nearly 40% of the total adult population at that time. A high percentage of those will be under the age of 60. By 2025, most of these people will reside in urban areas. Will these

---

[38]This assumes that enrollments and graduates of secondary schools will average over 12 million per year (the current enrollment level in 2004 was 8 million) and that more than 7 million a year will go on to university (the current enrollment level in 2004 was 4.5 million). Because the size of the relevant age cohorts is declining due to the one-child policy the percentage of the relevant age cohorts going on to upper secondary and tertiary education will be higher than the absolute rise in numbers of enrollments and graduates.

[39]Only 1.7% of the total population in 1964 (census data) or 12 million people had either a secondary level or some tertiary level of education and most of that education occurred after 1949. Presumably, most of the people dying over the next 20 years will be those born before 1949 (who will be aged 76 or older) and those born in the 1950s, who will range in age from 65 to 75 in 2025. The number of graduates of tertiary schools in the 1950s was 480,000 and the number of graduates of senior secondary schools was 1.2 million (National Bureau of Statistics, *Zhongguo tongji nianjian*, 1989, 799–800). To that should be added several tens of thousands of tertiary-level students from before 1950 and an unknown but small number of secondary school graduates who would still be alive in 2005. The total number of university graduates in China in the period 1913–1947 was 210,000 and 174,000 were estimated to be still alive in 1960 (Orleans, 1961, p. 126).

people continue to remain passive politically? Will they remain passive even if China goes through several years of poor economic performance or some other social or political strain? We will have to wait until 2025 to find out the answer to these questions, but from the perspective of 2006, continued passive acceptance of the political status quo does not seem very likely. Will the transition to a new political order be peaceful or violent? Again, even in Asia, there is no common pattern that one can point to. The transition in Taiwan was led by then President Chiang Ching-kuo, the transition in South Korea came after large student rioting supported by the middle class, and the transition in Japan came only after defeat in World War II.

Finally, there are international events that could fundamentally alter what, overall, are the favorable prospects for continued Chinese economic growth. This chapter is not the place to discuss at length the various foreign policy challenges faced by China. Suffice it to say that a major war in the Straits of Taiwan would fundamentally alter all of the forecasts of future economic growth described above.

IV. The Impact of Future Economic Growth

This chapter is primarily about trying to understand the path of (Chinese economic growth over the next two decades. One cannot leave the subject, however, without some comments on the implications of this high growth rate for the international economy, the environment, and the world balance of military power.

As discussed briefly above, China's exports in 2005 reached $762 billion and were 6% of total world trade. China's foreign exchange reserves by the end of 2006 were projected to pass $1 trillion.[40] The growth rate of exports since the year 2000 has averaged 23% per year, and the figure in the most recent years has been higher. If these rates were to continue for the next two decades, China's exports would rise 62-fold and trade as a share of Chinese GDP would rise to 3 or 4 times China's GDP in 2025. Even in 2005, Chinese exports were 34% of Chinese GDP, an extraordinarily high figure for a large country. Large countries in terms of population size tend

[40]David Barboza (2006). "China's Surge Raises Fears of Runaway Economy," *New York Times,* July 19.

to have much lower trade ratios than small countries.[41] Japan in the year 2000, by way of comparison, had an export-to-GDP ratio of roughly 11%. Chinese total exports in 2025 would be several times the current level of total world exports! There is no question, therefore, that Chinas' export growth rate in percentage terms will come down and will come down sharply sometime within the next few years, or within the next decade at the latest. Even a slower real-growth rate of say 10% a year, given the absolute size of the expansion of China's exports at that rate, will put an adjustment strain on countries around the globe, both recipients of those Chinese exports and competitors with China for the same markets. Whether the World Trade Organization could manage those strains is an open question.

China, therefore, clearly must generate most future increases in aggregate demand from domestic sources. China's trade ratio as a share of GDP, already extraordinarily high for such a large country, is likely to level off in the near future. A level or slightly declining trade ratio implies that China's future exports will grow at the same real rate as Chinese GDP or 6 to 8% a year. Even that rate will require major adjustments on the part of other trading nations.

One likely change that would both help slow the export growth rate and also slow the rapid increase in China's foreign exchange reserves would be a major revaluation of the Chinese currency. In addition to the need to slow exports for reasons already given, it makes little sense for China to keep on building up foreign exchange reserves. The rate of return on these reserves is very low, given that it is mostly invested in US and other foreign government bonds. These bonds do give China some leverage over US policy in a range of areas, a noneconomic motive for holding them, but the magnitude of that leverage is not as large as it is sometimes portrayed.[42]

---

[41]The relationship between country size measured in terms of population and the ratio of trade to GDP was first noted by Simon Kuznets.

[42]The Chinese government, for example, has already decided to diversify its foreign exchange holdings and it could in the future decide to get out of US Treasury bonds altogether. But these bonds would still be sold to someone, albeit at a somewhat higher rate of interest. How high the interest rate rise would have to be would be a function not just of the market for US government bonds but of the worldwide market for instruments of this kind and of bonds in general. The rise would thus be much smaller than would be the case if the US Treasury bond market operated in isolation from other capital markets.

Another obvious impact of China's growth on the world economy is on the demand for energy and for petroleum — and natural gas in particular. China's rising demand for oil is widely seen as contributing to high oil prices in 2006, although events in the Middle East often had a bigger impact. The basic nature of China's growing demand is not complicated. China has vast quantities of coal, but coal is creating so many environmental problems that there is a strong desire on the part of the Chinese government to switch out of coal, to a limited degree, and substitute petroleum and natural gas. When the rapid increase in the number of automobiles and other four-wheeled motorized vehicles is added to this situation, China's demand for oil is increasing at a rate faster than that of energy in general; and demand for energy in general is growing at roughly half the rate of GDP if one believes the official statistics. The rate of energy demand growth according to these same official statistics appears to have picked up markedly since the year 2000.[43] The share of petroleum in total energy demand fell from 22.5% in 1978 to 17.5% in 1995, but since then rose to 24.6% in 2000 before falling back to 22.7% in 2004.[44]

On the supply side, China's supply of petroleum from domestic sources has grown very slowly — at 1.7% a year to 175 million tons (roughly 3.5 million barrels per day) — causing imports to rise rapidly to roughly equal domestic production. Since production in some of China's older fields is declining and new fields are coming online only slowly, most future demand is likely to be met by imports. Forecasts of what this might involve depend critically on the assumptions made to derive those forecasts — notably, the assumption about the likely improvement in energy and petroleum use efficiency. Will China match the experience of

[43] Chinese energy consumption and production figures are a bit treacherous, in part because reporting from small coal mines is often inaccurate. Thus, for example, the government repeatedly orders the closing of many of these mines but local authorities and mine owners regularly keep the mines open. Eventually, they stop reporting production in those mines. Total energy demand grew according to official figures between 1978 and 2004 at an average annual rate of 4.9% as compared to GDP growth at a 9.1% rate. But from the end of 2000 through 2004, energy consumption grew at 10.9%.

[44] These percentages should be used with caution. Some of the fluctuation in the percentage oil contributes to energy demand may only reflect the inaccuracies in the estimates of coal consumption. (National Bureau of Statistics, 2005, p. 255).

Japan with highly efficient use of energy or will it match the wasteful practices of the United States? At present, China is one of the world's least efficient users of energy when measured as units of energy per unit of GDP. China in 2004 used roughly 0.7 kg of energy per US dollar of GDP as contrasted to Japan, which used only 0.14 kg per US dollar of GDP, and the United States, which used 0.24 kg.[45] Much of China's inefficiency reflects the years under central planning, when little if any effort was made to improve energy efficiency and supplies of energy, given China's low level of GDP, were plentiful. Supplies relative to China's GDP are no longer plentiful and the incentives of a market economy, the severity of the pollution problem, and the low income of much of the Chinese population are all causing the country to put much more effort into raising energy efficiency levels. Whether that will bring Chinese energy use to efficiency levels achieved by countries such as Japan remains to be seen, but the efficiency level is bound to rise markedly. If as a result of these efficiency measures, petroleum-use growth fell a little below GDP growth over the next two decades, China by 2025 would probably be importing oil at a rate of roughly 17 million barrels per day.[46] The US Energy Department estimates, in contrast, that China in 2025 will be importing 10.9 million barrels per day, a relatively conservative estimate.[47] At the extreme upper end is environmental analyst Lester Brown's estimate for Chinese domestic oil consumption of 99 million barrels per day in 2031 if present Chinese policies continue unchanged.[48]

If China does require oil imports of 11 to 17 million barrels a day, the country will probably have the foreign exchange to pay for it. At $70 per

---

[45]These calculations were made by the author. China reports its consumption of energy in terms of a "standard coal equivalent," whereas Japan and others report data in terms of standard crude oil equivalent. The Chinese data were taken from the National Bureau of Statistics, 2005, and GDP was converted into US dollars at 8.1 yuan = $1.00. The Japanese and US energy consumption data came from Japan External Trade Organization (2002, p. 75).

[46]This assumes that oil demand grows at 6% per year to reach 22 million barrels per clay in 2025, with 5 million barrels per day supplied from domestic sources.

[47]This estimate assumes total Chinese demand of 14.2 million barrels per day and domestic production of 3.3 million barrels per day.

[48]Lester Brown's point is that such a level of imports would be impossible given the size of the world oil market among other reasons (AFP, 2006).

barrel, the higher figure would cost China $434 billion per year in 2025, when China's total exports (in today's prices) would be around $3 trillion. But would prices in real terms stay at $70 with Chinese imports of this magnitude? It would all depend on a combination of world efforts to cut back on the demand for petroleum-products together with the supply response of petroleum-producing nations. That is a subject for another essay.

High energy consumption along with industrial development in general, of course, also has major implications for the environment. Recent visitors to Chinese cities regularly comment on the poor air quality. Many rivers are filled with chemical wastes from nearby factories. There are now many environmental laws on the books, and China's environmental protection authorities have become increasingly vigorous over time in the difficult task of trying to enforce these laws. But is the environmental situation in China serious enough to alter our forecast of long-term growth?

Clearly, China has been forced to face up to the environmental consequences of rapid economic growth at a much lower per capita income than was the case in the United States, Europe, or Japan. But is the problem significantly worse in China than in these earlier advanced countries and is the cost of dealing with the problem large enough to affect economic growth? There are various ways of measuring the level of pollutants in Chinese air and water. Here in Figure 1, we only present the data for the total number of particulates in the air in China and compare it with similar measures for Tokyo and Seoul from earlier periods. The figure is from a recent study by economics professor Thomas Rawski.[49] Other tables in that study compare some of China's most polluted cities with Pittsburgh. The main point of this figure is to show that China's level of air pollution, bad as it is, is not significantly different from the situation in Tokyo in 1968, Pittsburgh in 1920, or Seoul in the early 1980s. Furthermore, as the figure makes clear, the level of pollution in China's major cities, while still very high, is coming down despite continued rapid economic development. Efforts to reduce pollution are having an effect.

How expensive is this ongoing effort to control pollution? By the mid-1990s, the Dutch Sinologist Eduard Vermeer estimates that China was

---

[49]Thomas Rawski (2006, figure 2).

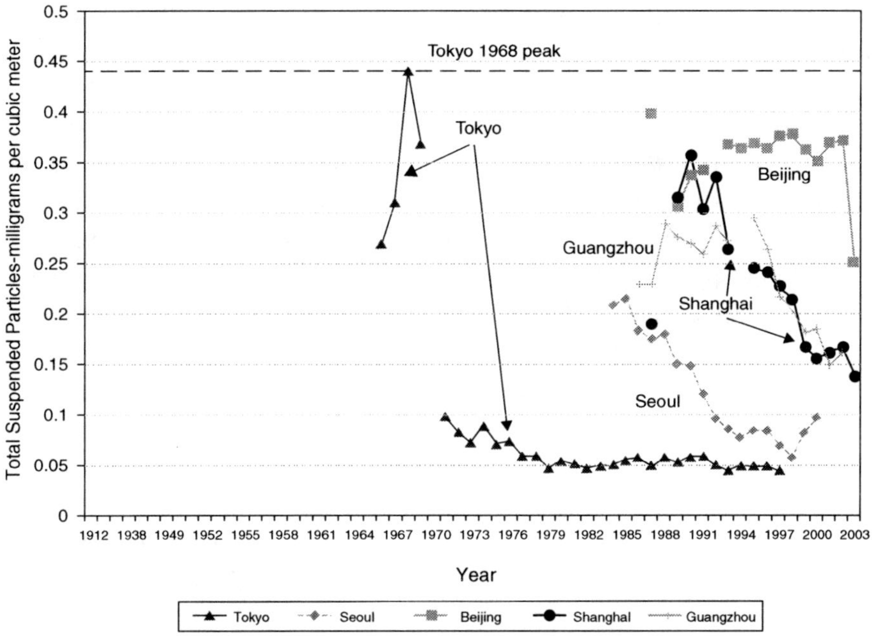

Figure 1. Air pollution in China and its neighbors.

Source: Thomas G. Rawski, "Urban Air Quality in China: Historical and Comparative Perspectives" (Working Paper, International Center for the Study of East Asian Development, Kitakyushu, Japan, 2006).

spending 1.4% of GDP on the prevention and treatment of pollution.[50] That is a large figure in absolute terms but it clearly is not going to be a major influence slowing overall Chinese GDP growth. At a 4:1 incremental capital–output ratio, roughly China's current level, this expenditure on pollution treatment and control would reduce growth by 0.35% per year. If a reduction in pollution levels increased overall health and efficiency in the cities, the impact on growth would be that much less.

While China appears quite capable of eventually reducing air and water pollution emanating from its factories at an acceptable cost, reducing particulates and SO_2 will not slow China's impact on CO_2 emissions resulting from the consumption of hydrocarbons. China's rapidly

[50]Vermeer, 1998, 956.

increasing contribution to global warming, therefore, will continue. It will be some time before China's impact on global climate change is comparable to that of the United States, but China's impact is significant today and will grow along with the projected rise in China's use of coal and petroleum. If global warming is to be slowed and eventually reversed, clearly China is going to have to play a major role in reducing its consumption of hydrocarbons per unit of GDP. Put differently, given that China under any realistic assumptions will continue to experience steadily rising emissions of CO_2 even if it makes significant strides toward greater efficiency in energy use, the rest of the world, and especially the United States, will have to make far greater efforts than at present if global warming is to be contained. How China, the United States, and the rest of the world should go about achieving these reductions is a subject for another essay.

Finally, a few words are in order about the impact of continued Chinese growth on the size of the Chinese military budget. For many years after the start of the reform period, China held down its military expenditures. In real terms, there was scarcely any increase in expenditure at all. As a result, Chinese military expenditures as a share of GDP actually declined significantly. Beginning in 1997, however, Chinese military expenditures began to grow at a pace similar to the rapid growth of GDP Estimates of the change in military expenditures in real terms are presented in Table 4 on the following page. Real expenditures by 2003 nearly doubled the level of 1997, and the rate of growth has continued since. The question of why China began expanding defense expenditures in 1997 is not known, but there are several plausible explanations. The level of Chinese military technology prior to 1997 was stuck in an earlier era and it probably made little sense for China to invest more in the production of obsolete fighter aircraft, tanks, or infantry weapons. There is also the possibility that China was influenced by the first US attack on Iraq in 1991 following Iraq's invasion of Kuwait. In that brief war, American high-tech weapons obliterated a Soviet-weapons–equipped Iraqi military in a matter of a few weeks. Given that China's military was also equipped with Soviet-type weapons, many of them less advanced than those of Iraq, it is reasonable to assume that China's military planners saw a need to fundamentally rethink and upgrade their military

Table 4. Chinese Official and Estimated Defense Expenditures.

Year	Official defense budget (billion yuan, current prices)	Official defense budget (as a share of GDP)	Estimated defense budget (official budget × 2; billion yuan, current prices)	"Real" national defense expenditures (billion yuan, 2003 prices)
1978	16.78	0.046	33.56	Na
1980	19.38	0.043	38.76	Na
1985	19.15	0.021	38.30	113.7
1990	29.03	0.016	58.06	97.2
1991	33.03	0.015	66.06	102.8
1992	37.79	0.014	75.58	104.6
1993	42.58	0.012	85.16	95.6
1994	55.07	0.012	110.14	96.0
1995	63.67	0.011	127.34	95.5
1996	72.01	0.011	144.02	100.3
1997	81.26	0.011	162.52	109.1
1998	93.47	0.012	186.94	120.0
1999	107.64	0.013	215.28	133.1
2000	120.75	0.013	241.50	140.0
2001	144.20	0.015	288.40	157.9
2002	170.78	0.016	341.56	180.0
2003	190.79	0.016	381.58	190.8

Source and methodology: Perkins, 2005, 380. The figure for real expenditures was obtained by first doubling the size of the officially reported military budget because of the widespread view that the official budget understates total expenditures by at least that much (Shambaugh, 2002). These figures are divided into wages of military personnel and military equipment and the former is deflated by a state sector wage index and the latter by a price index for industrial products (the ex-factory price index).
Note: Na = data not available for price deflation.

technology and equipment.[51] Finally, once military modernization was underway in the 1990s and was increasing at roughly the same rate as GDP, politics, notably the need of the civilians in charge of the

[51] I am indebted for this insight to a participant in the discussion following this lecture at the American Enterprise Institute.

government to keep the military content, ensured that military expenditures would continue to grow regardless of external threat projections or the lack thereof.[52]

Whatever the motives for the change in growth of military expenditures in the 1990s, therefore, there is every reason to think that China will continue to expand its military expenditures in the years to come. Barring a security crisis affecting China or a fundamental change in the strategic challenge facing China, a plausible assumption is that continued rapid GDP growth will enable China to expand military expenditures at a rate similar to the growth rate of GDP. China's almost certain long-term goal is to move from being able to defend the Chinese homeland to being able to reach military parity with the United States. That goal depends as much on the progress of Chinese military technology as it does on the country's willingness to spend money on defense, but over time, the size of the Chinese defense budget could match that of the United States. Parity with the United States in dollars spent, however, will not be reached within the two-decade time frame with which this discussion is concerned.[53] China long before that, however, will almost certainly have the second largest defense budget in the world, and it is not far away from that target today. At present, depending on just what exchange rate one uses, China is already in a group of nations (France, Germany, Japan, and Russia) that are next after the United States in total military expenditures, with the United States' expenditures being far ahead of all four combined.

V. Implications for United States Policy

This Chapter is not primarily about United States foreign policy, but there are some clear implications for the United States if the Chinese economy

[52] Shambaugh (2005, pp. 82–85).

[53] Any precise discussion of when China might achieve parity involves assumptions about the US military budget that are outside the frame of reference of this essay. Parity in terms of actual military capacity requires a judgment about the level of US and Chinese military technology at some future date, a judgment that is well beyond the capacity of the author of this essay.

continues its rapid growth. China's rapid growth of exports and imports is already receiving the attention of American politicians, policymakers, and the general public. Even if this export growth slows markedly down to the rate of growth of GDP as suggested above, China will be on the regular agenda of American trade negotiators for decades to come. This will be the case even though China today has a trade and foreign investment regime that is much more open than were those of South Korea, Taiwan, or Japan at a comparable stage of development. Given the absence in China of a legal system capable of rigorously enforcing intellectual property rights, for example, there will be ongoing demands from American producers of intellectual property followed by efforts by the Chinese to meet those demands at least partway. These negotiations may involve tension between the two parties, but ultimately protection of property rights is in the interest of both; it is just that it is more in the interest of the United States at this stage of its development than it is of China at its stage of development.

China's current account surplus situation, however, may or may not be an ongoing problem. If China does what it probably should do for its own sake and revalues its currency in a major way, that current account surplus would shrink and possibly disappear. No Chinese revaluation, however, will solve the US current account deficit, and thus the bilateral trade deficit between China and the United States is likely to continue.[54] The US deficit is a product of Americans' spending more for goods and services that the rest of the world produces than they are earning on sales of goods and services to that world. No plausible amount of Chinese trade liberalization or revaluation will solve that problem. The solution lies mainly in America.

The impact of China on the world energy market and the market for other minerals is not really an item for negotiation. It is simply a fact to

[54] Over time, it is possible that the bilateral China–US current account deficit will shift in part to being a deficit with countries other than China, just as what was once a US–Japan, Korea, Taiwan deficit turned into a US–China deficit when those other East Asian countries shifted much of their labor-intensive manufacturing and assembly facilities into China. These other countries still produced much of the value-added in the goods going to the US market but the final production and assembly were in China, so these were defined as "Chinese goods."

which the rest of the world will have to adjust. Energy security does have some implications for China's military security, notably the protection of the sea lanes that carry petroleum destined for China. For the most part, however, these are the same sea lanes that bring oil to Japan and South Korea, so the interests of the major parties in Northeast Asia should be aligned most of the time.[55] Outside of these kinds of security issues, rising mineral prices should generate all of the supply response that is feasible without any assistance from government policy of any of the major producers and consumers of energy.

The environmental situation does require government action, particularly action by the US government. China's air and water pollution problems are a Chinese problem and will be dealt with by China, no doubt with the help of environmentally supportive technology developed in part by companies in the United States and elsewhere. China's growing CO_2 emissions, however, require action of governments around the world to rein in the worldwide growth of CO_2. There is no acceptable way to slow the growth of China's CO_2 emissions below a level comparable to that of the more energy-efficient users around the world. It in fact will take a major effort by China to reach that slower level of growth. The country with the widest economic and technological discretion to do something about worldwide CO_2 growth is clearly the United States, either as part of an international agreement or unilaterally. Whether the US government has the political will to take advantage of this situation, however, remains to be seen.

The growth of China's military expenditures is also a fact that cannot be radically altered by the policies of the United States or by other outside powers short of war. The one exception to this statement is in the area of military use technology, where the United States and other nations already impose restrictions. Clearly, the rise of Chinese military power is gradually going to change the balance of military power in Asia. What is far less clear is whether this changing balance of power will alter significantly any of the current relationships between China and its neighbors. For the

[55]The most obvious exception to this statement would be if there were a war in the Taiwan Straits and the United States or some other power opted to try to embargo oil going to China, but scenarios of this sort are well beyond the scope of this chapter.

most part, the answer is probably that changes in these relationships will be modest. Border disputes do exist between China and India, between China and Japan over islands lying between the two countries, and between China and other claimants to islands in the South China Sea, but it is hard to see how a rational Chinese government would try to resolve these disputes by force alone. China probably could seize many of the disputed areas that it does not now control, but the main effect would be to create a ring of hostile nations around its borders no doubt backed by US power.

The one big exception to the above relatively benign view of Chinese power is Taiwan and the balance of power between China and Taiwan's implicit protector, the United States. If the Chinese military budget increases fourfold over the coming two decades and its military technology improves rapidly along with these expenditures, there will be a shift in the balance of power in the Straits of Taiwan. The potential costs to US support for Taiwan will go up, with implications for US policy that are difficult to predict and are way beyond the scope of this essay. We simply note here that the shift is real and the implications are profound for all of the parties involved.

Finally, there is the basic question of whether or not continued rapid growth in China is itself in America's interests. The unequivocal answer of this writer is yes. The alternatives are all much worse. A rapidly growing China integrated into the world economic system and the world political system is a China with a strong vested interest in stability. It does not follow that China will buy stability at all costs in order to continue rapid economic growth, but it will do so in most circumstances. Rapid economic growth is also the best hope, probably the only real hope, for the kind of domestic political changes in China that will build a foundation for long-term stability in China both domestically and internationally. Will these changes occur in a reasonable time frame? The obvious answer is we do not know — they may occur or they may not, but what is the alternative if one wants to achieve political reform? This statement about domestic political change fostering stability may seem like a contradiction to the earlier discussion of how the rapid rise of a large middle class could create political instability in China. Instability in the short run, caused by the population demanding full participation in the political process, may in fact be a cost that has to be paid to reach the kind of participation and pluralism in the political system that will fortify stability over the long run.

Could this growth all go wrong and lead to domestic crises that bring nationalistic politicians to the fore, politicians willing to use the military to back up claims to "lost" Chinese territory? The obvious answer is that this could happen, but that it is far more likely to happen if China is careening from one economic crisis to another. If growth slows or even stops altogether, job growth will disappear, incomes of those with jobs will stagnate or fall, and discontent will spread rapidly. The leaders of the government presiding over this end to growth will no doubt lose their jobs, and they will be replaced. China could have a rebellious population and a leadership playing the nationalist card, all in a country with a large nuclear arsenal and the missiles to deliver them. The risks of an increasingly rich and powerful China are to be preferred.

References

AFP (2006). "Lester Brown: China growth unsustainable on all counts, must change," May 26.

Barboza, D (2006). "China's Surge Raises Fears of Runaway Economy." *New York Times,* July 19.

Byrd, W and Q Lin (1990). *China's Rural Industry: Structure, Development, and Reform.* New York: Oxford University Press.

Chen, S and M Ravallion (2004). "How have the world's poorest fared since the 1980s?" Development Research Group. World Bank.

Fu, J (2006). "Curbs placed on land use rights, farmers to be better compensated." *The China Daily*, July 28, p.l.

Hua, S, Z Xuejun and L Xiaopeng (1993). *China: From Revolution to Reform.* London: MacMillan.

Japan Automobile Manufacturers Association. http://www.jama.org.2006.

Japan External Trade Organization (2002). *Nippon 2002: Business Facts and Figures.* Tokyo: JETRO.

Klein, LR, H Gao and L Tao (2005). "Estimation of China's inflation rate" (Draft Paper).

Kojima, R (2002). "On the reliability of China's economic statistics with special reference to GDP" *The Journal of Econometric Study of Northeast Asia* 4, (1) pp. 15–30.

Kristof, N (2006). "In China it's vs. netizens." *New York Times,* June 20.

Lardy, N (1990). *China's Unfinished Economic Revolution.* Washington: Brookings.

Lardy, N (2001). "China's worsening debts." *The Financial Times*, June 22.

Maddison, A (1995). *Monitoring the World Economy 1820–1992.* Paris: OECD Development Centre.

National Bureau of Statistics (1989). *Zhongguo tongji nianjian, 1989.* Beijing: China Statistics Press.

National Bureau of Statistics (2005). *China Statistical Yearbook, 2005.* Beijing: China Statistics Press.

Orleans, L (1961). *Professional Manpower and Education in Communist China.* Washington: National Science Foundation.

Perkins, DH (2005). "China's economic growth: Implications for the defense budget," *Strategic Asia 2005–06. Military Modernization in an Era of Uncertainty.* In Ashley J. Tellis and Michael Wills (eds.), Seattle: National Bureau of Asian Research, 2005.

Perkins, DH (2004). Corporate governance, industrial policy, and the rule of law, *Global Change and East Asian Policy Initiatives.* In Shahid Yusuf, M. Anjum Altaf, and Kaoru Nabeshima (eds.),Washington: World Bank and Oxford University Press, pp. 293–336.

Perkins, DH and TG Rawski. "Forecasting China's Economic Growth over the Next Two Decades." 2006 Draft, forthcoming in a volume edited by Loren Brandt and Thomas Rawski.

Plueger, G (2006). *Totalitarianism,* http://www.histoiy-ontheweb.co.uk. (2006).

Rawski, T (2001). "What's happening to China's GDP statistics?" *China Economic Review* December, pp. 347–54.

Rawski, T (2006). "Urban air quality in China: Historical and comparative perspectives." Unpublished Draft, June 25.

Rural Society and Economy Investigation Team of the National Bureau of Statistics (2000). *Xin Zhongguo wushinian nongye tongji culiao* [Fifty years of agricultural statistical materials of New China]. Beijing: China Statistics Press.

Shambaugh, D (2002). "Calculating China's military expenditure." Report prepared for the Council on Foreign Relations, Task Force on Chinese Military Power, June 25.

Shambaugh, D (2005). "China's military modernization: Making steady and surprising progress." *Strategic Asia 2005–2006: Military Modernization in an Era of Uncertainty.* In Ashley J. Tellis and Michael Wills (eds.), Seattle: National Bureau of Asian Research, 2005.

State Statistical Bureau (1982). *Statistical Yearbook of China, 1981.* Hong Kong: Economic Information and Agency, 1982.

Transparency International (2005). *Transparency International Corruption Perceptions Index.* http://www.transparency.org.

Vermeer, E (1998). "Industrial pollution in China and remedial policies." *The China Quarterly,* (156), Special Issue: China's Environment, December, pp. 952–985.

World Bank (2006). *Doing Business in China in 2006: Creating Jobs. Washington:* World Bank.

World Bank (2003). *Sustainable Development in a Dynamic World/World Development Report 2003.* New York: Oxford University Press.

Yusuf, S, K Nabeshima and DH Perkins (2006). *Under New Ownership: Privatizing China's State-Owned Enterprises.* Stanford: Stanford University Press.

THE FUTURE

CHAPTER 9

FORECASTING CHINA'S ECONOMIC GROWTH TO 2025*

Why attempt to forecast China's economic growth? Most importantly, the impact of China on the rest of the world and on the standard of living of its own people depends mainly on whether the nation continues to double the size of its gross domestic product (GDP) every 7 to 10 years or whether that growth slows markedly or even halts. China already influences the world economy through its booming exports, its demand for natural resources, its influence on global warming, and much else. A GDP four times the current level will multiply China's worldwide impact.

But there is another reason why forecasting Chinese growth is desirable in a volume dedicated to understanding China's present and past economic performance. The ability to forecast is one important test of whether the analysis has gotten the story right. There are many ways to forecast the future, some of which, like simple projections of recent trends, tell us little about the present and not much about the future.

But analytical forecasts based on a model that attempts to sort out the main influences that are likely to shape that future can deepen our understanding of the mechanisms driving Chinese growth. Even if the forecasts are a bit off the mark or downright wrong, a good model allows analysts to review a forecast's strengths and limitations and to identify specific shortcomings that contributed to the gap between predictions and ultimate outcomes. Put differently, the effort to forecast necessitates explicit judgments about which economic forces matter and which do not. If the forecast turns out to be wrong, future analysts and readers are in a position to understand why the forecast was wrong and what changes could have improved it.

*The authors gratefully acknowledge research assistance from Yifan Zhang, Tingting Huang, Ying Fang, and Zixia Sheng. Judith Banister, Loren Brandt, Nicholas Lardy, and Carsten Holz stand out among many colleagues who have provided valuable information and advice. The usual caveat applies.

The forecasting model used in this chapter is extremely simple. We start with the supply-side growth accounting equation. We use data from the past half century to determine how much of GDP growth can be attributed to larger inputs of capital, human capital, and labor and how much is due to rise in total factor productivity (TFP) or output per unit of these inputs. This approach has an important advantage in that it is possible to make informed quantitative judgments about the likely growth of labor, capital, and education over the next two decades.

The primary reason for starting with the growth accounting equation, however, is that it provides a basis for separating out the contribution of TFP and capital to China's economic growth. If rapid growth arises primarily from high rates of capital formation, then the forecasting agenda boils down to determining whether high rates of investment will continue. This in turn depends on whether personal savings of the Chinese population will remain high, whether Chinese corporations continue to be an independent source of high savings, and whether the Chinese government will run large fiscal surpluses or large fiscal deficits.

If growth is driven instead by TFP, the considerations critical to any long-term forecast are very different. Rising rates of savings and investment may contribute little to growth. What matters is whether investments deliver high rates of return. But what contributes to a high rate of return? Can a country achieve a high rate of return with a weak financial system? Was China's growth during the 1980s and 1990s the result of reforms that created a one-time rise in the level of TFP? Or, have these reforms created conditions that will promote sustained TFP growth over the coming decades?

The sources of TFP growth are inherently difficult to quantify. Determining the impact of financial reform or greater outward orientation is more complex than measuring an increase in the size of the labor force or in the number of college graduates. Still, we have far more knowledge than existed several decades ago about what kinds of reforms promote accelerated growth. In East Asia, in particular, we have the experience of South Korean and Taiwanese economic reforms in the 1960s through the 1980s and of Vietnamese reforms in the 1990s. We also have the econometric estimates of the "new growth economics" that give us some guidance as to what works and what does not in the relationship between policy, institutional reform, and growth.

There is a fundamental difference between forecasting growth over a 20-year period, which is the focus of this essay, and short-run predictions targeting the next year or two. Because short-term outcomes depend on a host of economic variables and can be strongly influenced by external shocks, short-run forecasting requires a model that captures how the many different sources of change in the economy impact overall performance. The model thus will depend on a large number of equations. Given that we have few estimates of such equations in the Chinese context, short-term forecasts call for a wide variety of assumptions about the parameters of such equations. Such assumptions invariably involve high error margins. Utilizing short-term models to project longer-term growth is particularly dangerous because rapid shifts in economic structure — such as changes in income distribution or in the relative size of the state and private sectors — seem likely to shift the underlying structure embedded in short-term forecasting models.[1]

Long-term growth, by contrast, is largely independent of sudden shocks or short-term changes in consumption behavior. It is mainly driven by the growth rate of productivity, which in turn is heavily influenced by research and development expenditures, the availability of capital to turn the discoveries of R&D into final demand products, and the growth of the labor force.

Long-term growth in developing countries is both a bit simpler and a bit more complicated. It is simpler because efforts to develop and commercialize new technologies typically contribute little to economic growth in poor nations. China may be an exception as the scale of domestic R&D spending increases (see Chapter 9 in this volume) and as multinational firms transfer a growing array of research activity to the People's Republic. Productivity growth in developing countries, however, depends mainly on how fast these countries can adapt the technology and management practices of higher-income economies to their particular situations.

Because developing countries are not, for the most part, in the business of pushing out the frontiers of knowledge, they can avoid the dead ends that technological leaders inevitably encounter. Developing

---

[1] While these more elaborate models are an unreliable basis for forecasting long-term GDP growth, they can be very useful in sorting out the impact of various levels of growth on sector demand and much else.

nations may also benefit from opportunities to avoid expensive and time-consuming investments, for example, by building cell-phone networks rather than connecting telephone wires to customers' homes or shops. These advantages give developing countries the potential to grow much faster than high-income nations, at least for a time.

A half century of international development experience demonstrates that low-income nations can capture this unique opportunity for accelerated growth only if they orient their economic systems to take full advantage of being followers. Since we know something about the structures that generate productivity growth, we can compare what China has accomplished in this regard with what has worked elsewhere. Comparisons of this sort do not lead to precise quantitative estimates of the contribution of reform to growth, but they do provide a benchmark for comparing Chinese economic institutions and policies with circumstances in countries that have succeeded in building extended periods of high-speed growth into their economies.

I. Structure of This Chapter

We begin by measuring the supply-side sources of growth between 1952 and 2005 with as much rigor as is possible given the limitations of Chinese data. Making the measurements is a straightforward if time-consuming task. Interpreting the results is quite another matter. Most analysts select a time period, compile the data, determine whether the contribution to growth of capital is greater than that of TFP or vice versa, and leave it at that. In our view, this approach is inadequate because it fails to examine the dynamic interaction between productivity and accumulation. In China and other nations that experience major economic or institutional reforms, the growth of capital is itself in part the result of acceleration in TFP growth. We see China's recent development as first and foremost a story about productivity growth supported by the growth of factor inputs, notably, capital. From this perspective, China's ability to sustain high rates of GDP growth in the future will depend critically on the capacity to generate continuing growth in TFP.

TFP growth, however, is far from the whole story of either China's past or its future. The next section of this chapter, therefore, looks at the likely future growth of factor inputs. Will the savings rate remain high and will high savings continue to be translated into high rates of investment and capital stock growth? We can be reasonably precise about labor force growth, but considerably less precise about what share of that labor force will end up in high-productivity industrial and service-sector employment as contrasted to low-productivity agriculture or failing state enterprises.

The analysis of Chinese productivity dynamics will begin with a brief review of what our growth accounting equation and our knowledge of Chinese reforms since 1978 can tell us about what drove productivity growth over the past quarter century. Many of the reforms that led to high productivity growth in the past, however, are not likely to continue to provide a comparable stimulus to growth in the future.

The effort to understand where future reforms might impact productivity growth is unavoidably speculative. It begins with a brief look at cross-country econometric growth equations to see what guidance they give us about China's likely growth path over the next two decades. We then focus on key economic institutions, policies, and social issues that are likely to affect future growth.

Finally, we will turn from our supply-side approach to look briefly at demand-side issues. Foremost among these is the question of whether and for how long China can continue to expand the share of domestic output exported to its trading partners. If demand-side limits oblige China to rein in export growth, which seems inevitable, will the domestic market suffice to push the economy ahead without losing momentum?

This chapter cannot encompass the multiple forces that could shape China's GDP growth over the coming two decades. We concentrate on economic factors and make only passing reference to political events that could fundamentally alter the country's growth prospects. Will rising incomes and education lead to pressure for fundamental political change, for example, and might the ensuing political changes result in protracted instability? Will war in the Taiwan Straits upset China's growing economic integration with the rest of the world?

Nor can we explore the implications of the GDP growth rates that we project for agriculture and other economic sectors, for China's environment, or for energy demand. Answering those kinds of questions is a very different kind of exercise involving other kinds of models and analysis.

II. Measuring Supply-Side Sources of Growth

To measure the sources of growth from the supply side during 1952–2005, we begin with a conventional production function,

$$Y = f(K, H, t), \tag{9.1}$$

where "Y" is GDP, "K" is the stock of fixed capital, "H" is the education-enhanced labor force, which is measured in a way that includes the increase in quality of labor due to the rise in human capital, and "t" represents shifts over time in the production function or changes in the productivity of the factor inputs. To get this equation into a measurable form, we differentiate with respect to t and rearrange terms to arrive at the following standard growth accounting equation,

$$g_{\mathrm{y}} = s_{\mathrm{k}}^{*} g_{\mathrm{k}} + s_{\mathrm{l}}^{*} g_{\mathrm{h}} + a, \tag{9.2}$$

where "g_{y}" is the growth rate of GDP, "g_{k}" is the growth rate of the capital stock, "g_{h}" is the growth rate of the education-enhanced labor force, and "a" is the increase in TFP. The parameters "s_k" and "s_l" are, in the calculation we shall make, the shares of capital and labor in total national income. To construct the equation in this way, one must assume constant returns to scale. We could avoid this assumption by estimating "s_k" and "s_l" directly, but we do not believe that currently available Chinese aggregate data can support reliable econometric estimates of these parameters.[2]

The main challenge in estimating the sources of growth for China during 1952–2005 is to obtain reliable time series for the key variables. Any large, low-income nation faces unavoidable obstacles to the accumulation of comprehensive and accurate statistical information. In China, the use of Soviet-inspired accounting methods, the subsequent shift to conventional national accounts, and episodes of widespread data manipulation add to the difficulties surrounding national economic statistics. As a result, the data that we use to measure output, capital, labor, and schooling are beset by issues of reliability as well as a variety of conceptual or theoretical problems. We defer detailed discussion of

---

[2]We ignore the numerous controversies surrounding this widely utilized method of analysis. Our calculations follow Robert Solow's (1957) original exposition of this approach measuring the sources of growth.

these issues to an appendix.[3] Here, we summarize the choices we have made in assembling key statistics and briefly explain how our data series differ from standard official statistics and from estimates by other researchers.

Official measurements of the level and growth of China's total output have attracted a steady stream of criticism from Chinese and international analysts who argue that distortions inherent in the methods of compiling official data may lead to an overstatement of output growth.[4] There is evidence, for example, that output data for township and village enterprises may mix current and constant prices, imparting an upward bias to growth measures for inflationary years during the early and mid-1990s.

The disruption of regular economic reporting during the Great Leap Forward (1958–1960) and the early years of the Cultural Revolution calls for the application of large error margins for data in those years. More recently, some analysts have argued that political pressures may have elevated China's official growth rates in the aftermath of the Asian financial crisis of 1997–1998.[5]

Although most studies emphasize possible overstatement of Chinese growth, there is good reason to suspect substantial downward bias in official growth measures. Despite multiple adjustments, the complete elimination of long-standing under measurement of China's service sector may require further revision. The coincidence of rapid output growth, rising product quality, and falling prices visible in many manufacturing sectors (e.g., autos, home appliances, and electronics) raises the possibility that quality adjustments could produce sharp increases in measured output growth.[6] Work by Klein and others indicates that international pricing

[3]The appendix, which describes the sources and methods used to obtain data for our calculations and analysis, is posted at http://post.economics.harvard.edu/faculty/perkins/papers.html.

[4]Perkins (1980) and Ren (1997, Chapter 2) review early controversies. Recent contributions include Maddison (1998), Meng and Wang (2000), Young (2003), and Holz (2003, 2006).

[5]Rawski (2001); Lardy (2002) provides an opposing view.

[6]Following adjustments tor quality change to price indexes, "the real growth rates for both semiconductor output and intermediate inputs were revised up substantially" in the United States national accounts (Grimm, 1998).

conventions such as those currently used by China underestimate quality improvements and hence overstate price increases used to deflate data in current prices.[7]

Despite these strictures, some of which we regard as well founded, we regard standard official data, including revisions announced by China's National Bureau of Statistics (NBS) during 2005–2006, as the best available benchmark for appraising the long-term evolution of China's economy.[8] We therefore take the most recent NBS measures of nominal and real output and growth as the starting point for studying the sources of growth in China's economy. We do, however, make one important adjustment to official growth measures in order to remove distortions arising from the peculiar structure of relative prices during China's socialist plan period. Following Soviet example, China's government assigned high values to industrial goods and set low prices for agricultural and resource products soon after the 1949 creation of the People's Republic. This price arrangement generated monopoly profits for industry, which provided the main source of government revenue, typically exceeding 20% of GDP.

These arrangements, while intended to create a mechanism for financing government investments under successive five-year plans, had an accidental effect on GDP growth. With industry growing more rapidly than agriculture, the use of official prices that artificially

[7]Lawrence Klein and his coauthors, for example, use a technique developed for a related purpose during the Second World War to show that the official Chinese price indexes tend to overstate the increase in price (Klein *et al.*, 2005). Reiitsu Kojima (2002) anticipated some of the revisions undertaken by the NBS, with analysis showing that underreporting of the service sector remained even after attempts were made to better account for output in this sector.

[8]As we were preparing this chapter, China's NBS revised its GDP estimates from 2004 back to 1993, mainly by increasing the size and share of the services sector. This service-sector adjustment accounted for 93% (or RMB 2.1 trillion) of the total upward adjustment in GDP of RMB 2.34 trillion in 2004 (Xu, 2005, p. 1). These adjustments respond to well-known gaps in official data (see Keidel, 1992). The revisions considerably alter the share of the various producing sectors in GDP, but do not substantially affect the shares of consumption, investment, and net exports on the expenditure side of China's national accounts.

exaggerated the relative price of fast-growing manufactures distorts both the overall growth rate of GDP and the GDP share of investment spending (much of which goes to purchase equipment and other overpriced manufactures).

Meaningful analysis of the sources of growth requires that we remove the effect of these price distortions. As Branstetter and Lardy explain in their contribution to this volume (Chapter 16), the dismantling of trade restrictions during the 1990s initiated a broad convergence of Chinese commodity prices to international norms. This steep reduction in domestic distortions allows us to use prices of the year 2000 to recalculate both the GDP and the capital series.

Recalculating Chinese GDP item by item in 2000 prices is well beyond our capacity and would be a major task even for China's NBS. Starting with official series for nominal value added in the primary, secondary, and tertiary sectors, we use the implicit price indexes derived from nominal and real growth rates in each sector to derive series of sector output valued in 2000 prices and combine the resulting sector data to form a new series of aggregate output valued in 2000 prices.

The resulting GDP series provides the output data used in our decomposition of growth into input and productivity components. This procedure does not eliminate all price distortion in the GDP growth estimates: official regulation, for example, continues to hold domestic energy prices below world market levels. However, this revision does eliminate the implausibly high relative prices for manufactures that we see as the most important source of distortion in China's official GDP statistics.

Our approach to the measurement of inputs focuses on the available supply of capital and labor. We seek to measure the stock of fixed assets and the non-student population between the ages of 16 and 65. These input measures make no adjustment for changes in utilization rates, unemployment levels, or the standard retirement age. Our series of annual TFP observations simply record trends in output value per combined unit of capital and labor. The results incorporate the combined impact of changes in output per unit of employed resources and variations in the utilization of both capital and labor.

Chinese capital stock data are built up by adding new investment valued at current prices to the undeflated sum of past investments, with or without deductions for depreciation, major repairs, and scrap. The resulting figures combine amounts valued in prices of many years and are therefore unsuitable for productivity analysis. Beginning with Chen *et al.* (1988), analysts routinely apply the perpetual inventory method to build capital stock estimates from standard data on annual investment outlays.

We adopt the same approach, but apply a new deflator for fixed investment that uses the shares of construction and equipment in investment spending to combine separate indexes of construction costs and equipment prices. The new deflator parallels the NBS index of investment costs for 1992–2005; however, it improves on the crude improvisations that various researchers have used to estimate trends in investment costs prior to 1992.

The perpetual inventory method also requires information about depreciation rates and about the initial stock of fixed assets. Available data indicate that until very recently, depreciation rates used by Chinese accountants reflected the physical rather than the economic service lives of buildings and equipment (Gao, 1985, pp. 70–71; Yearbook, 1994, p. 29). We derive capital stock measures using two depreciation rates: 9.6%, a figure derived by Zhang *et al.* (2004, p. 39) from an earlier study of service lives and an alternate rate of 7% to facilitate sensitivity analysis.

We actually have a figure for the national total of fixed assets in 1952, the initial year of our study. Since this figure is known to be incomplete (Ishikawa, 1965, pp. 109–110), we assume that the initial value of the fixed capital stock in 1952 is either the same as 1952 GDP (a 1:1 capital output ratio) or is double the size of 1952 GDP (a 2:1 capital output ratio). Which initial capital stock assumption is used has little influence on the growth rate of the capital stock in the post-1978 reform period, but a major influence on the capital stock growth rate in the 1950s and, to a lesser degree, the 1960s.

We measure annual labor input as the non-student working-age population, meaning persons aged 16–65. We decompose the annual labor totals into five categories based on educational attainment: no diploma (L_1), primary school (L_2), junior high school (*chuzhong* (L_3)), high school

(L_4), and college (L_5).[9] Standard Chinese sources provide these data only in connection with the population censuses of 1982, 1990, and 2000. Interpolation between the census results is not feasible because of major inconsistencies in the education component of successive census compilations.

Results from the 1990 census show substantially higher education levels than what we derive by combining the 1982 census outcome with subsequent graduation figures. The 2000 census also reveals a wider expansion of educational attainment than what is implied by the 1990 census findings and subsequent graduation rates. These inconsistencies arise from two factors: China's expanding array of non-traditional training programs and a thriving trade in forged credentials. In addition, official labor totals appear to incorporate definitional changes that introduce an enormous jump in the employed population between 1989 and 1990.[10]

Faced with these difficulties involving both numbers of workers and the growth of educational attainment, we have chosen to construct new time-series measures of the working-age population and the dispersion of education. We begin with the 1982 census totals and use information on births, age-specific mortality rates and annual numbers of graduates to obtain totals for earlier and subsequent years. The appendix explains the details of this procedure.

In addition to deriving time-series estimates of Chinas non-student working-age population, we use information about education-linked wage differentials in 2000 shown in Table 1 to construct a new measure of "education-enhanced" labor. We assume that wage differentials reflect differences in productivity. The analysis of wage data, for example, shows that junior high school graduates earned 34.6% more on average than primary graduates with similar demographic characteristics in 2000.

---

[9]We group graduates of specialized (*zhongdeng zhuanye xuexiao*) and vocational (*zhiye zhongxue*) secondary schools together with recipients of regular high school (*gaozhong*) diplomas.

[10]The reported level of year-end employment (*congye renyuan*) rises by 54.6 million during 1985–1989 and by 40.38 million during 1990–1995, but jumps by 85.8 million during the single year of 1989–1990 (Labor Yearbook, 2001, p. 9).

We attribute this difference to education-linked productivity variation and record each junior high graduate as equivalent to 1.346 primary graduates in tabulating the education-enhanced work force H.[11] In formal terms,

$$L = L_1 + L_2 + L_3 + L_4 + L_5 \tag{9.3}$$

$$H = w_1L_1 + w_2L_2 + w_3L_3 + w_4L_4 + w_5L_5. \tag{9.4}$$

In Eq. (4), the w coefficients are the "Mincer coefficients" or education-linked wage differentials shown in Table 1, with w_2, the coefficient for primary graduates, set equal to unity.

Table 1 summarizes the outcome of our labor analysis. Our measure of working-age non-students aged 16–65, denoted by L, has grown substantially, but at declining rates. The new labor force series L eliminates the implausible bulge in the official totals for 1989–1990. Our measure of the working-age non-student population L grows at an annual rate of 2.52%

Table 1. Nonstudent working-age population, 1952–2005 headcount, educational attainment, education-enhanced total.

		Percentage of workers in each education category					
Year	Headcount L (Age 16–65)	No diploma	Primary	Junior high	Senior high	Tertiary	Ratio H/L
1952	313,346,294	73.9	19.6	4.8	1.4	0.4	0.90
1965	372,783,230	56.8	30.2	9.2	3.0	0.8	0.98
1978	506,667,822	39.6	33.4	20.6	5.7	0.7	1.07
1990	722,042,872	27.6	33.5	25.8	12.1	1.0	1.18
2000	808,414,668	18.5	34.4	30.6	14.7	1.8	1.26
2005	849,636,604	15.1	32.8	33.6	15.7	2.7	1.31
Mincer weights from 2000 wage data		0.818	1	1.346	2.010	3.277	

Source: Appendix. Working-age population includes ages 16–65.

[11]The wage differentials in Table 1 are based on analysis of rural wages by deBrauw and Rozelle (2004) and of urban wages by Junsen Zhang *et al.* (2005). Alan deBrauw, Xiaoqing Song, and Yaohui Zhao generously provided unpublished data and answers to many questions.

during 1978–1995 and rises by 2.09% in 1989–1990 in comparison with officially measured employment, which rises at an average rate of 3.15% during 1978–1995 and by an implausible 17.03% during 1989–1990.

The ratio H/L measures the average educational attainment of the working-age population included in the headcount total L. The initial 1952 figure of 0.90 indicates that the average educational level of Chinese workers was below the primary school level. The ratio H/L attained a value of close to 1.0 (actually 0.98) in 1965, indicating that the average worker at that time still had only a primary school level of education. By 2005, H/L had increased to 1.31, nearly equivalent to the junior high school level (for which the same ratio would equal 1.346). By recognizing only the diplomas issued by traditional educational institutions, our calculation understates the growth of human capital since the reform period began because we ignore the impact of non-traditional training programs, some of which no doubt increased the subsequent productivity of the trainees.[12]

Although we expect that education is negatively related to mortality, our calculations apply age-specific mortality rates without regard to educational attainment level, adding a further downward bias to our estimates of human capital growth. We conclude that our estimates understate the growth of human capital. We believe that the extent of this bias remains modest.[13]

III. The Historical Growth Accounting Results

The results of our efforts to estimate the sources of Chinese GDP growth during 1952–2005 appear in Table 2 and Figure 1. The results from our

---

[12]Many did not increase trainee productivity. Hsi-sheng Ch'i, for example, finds that efforts to expand training programs outside the regular school system "greatly increased the number of cadres with impressive academic degrees or certificates without meaningful improvement of their educational levels" (1991, p. 107).

[13]An alternate measure of education-enhanced human capital incorporating the education stock reported in the 1990 and 2000 population censuses exceeds the measure shown in Table 1 by 4.7% in 1990, 11.1% in 2001, and 7.4% in 2005. Insertion of the new index in our TFP calculations reduces the estimated rate of annual TFP growth during 1982–2005 by 0.1–0.2 percentage points, raises the share of GDP growth attributable to labor and human capital from 12.5 to 14.4%, and reduces the share attributable to productivity growth from 45–46% to 43–44%. We are grateful to Albert Park for recommending this sensitivity analysis.

Table 2. Average annual growth of GDP, fixed capital, labor, and TFP, with contributions to TFP growth, 1952–2005.

		Average growth of inputs				Percentage shares of GDP growth attributable to		
			Labor input			Education-enhanced labor		
		Fixed capital	Raw labor	Education enhanced	Average TFP growth			
Period	GDP	*K*	*L*	*H*		*K*	*H*	TFP
1952–2005	7.0	7.7	1.9	2.6	2.1	47.7	21.4	30.9
1952–1978	4.4	5.8	1.9	2.5	0.5	56.3	32.7	11.0
1952–1957	6.5	1.9	1.2	1.7	4.7	12.7	14.9	72.4
1957–1978	3.9	6.7	2.0	2.7	–0.5	73.7	39.7	–13.4
1957–1965	2.4	5.2	1.5	2.1	–1.0	93.1	49.5	–42.6
1965–1978	4.9	7.7	2.4	3.1	–0.2	67.7	36.7	–4.4
1978–2005	9.5	9.6	1.9	2.7	3.8	43.7	16.2	40.1
1978–1985	9.7	9.2	3.4	4.5	3.2	40.6	26.6	32.8
1985–1990	7.7	6.9	2.5	2.9	3.1	38.8	21.5	39.7
1990–1995	11.7	9.1	1.4	1.9	6.7	33.3	9.5	57.3
1995–2000	8.6	10.5	0.9	1.6	3.2	52.7	10.5	36.8
2000–2005	9.5	12.6	1.0	1.8	3.1	57.1	10.6	32.3

Source: Appendix.

Notes: Values are in percent; calculations assume that 1952 capital stock is two times that year's GDP; assumed depreciation rate is 9.6%.

reconstructed input and output series broadly resemble the findings of previous studies built on simpler methods.[14] Careful analysis of the new results, however, clarifies the dynamics of China's post-reform growth spurt.

Beginning with the period that covers the first Chinese five-year plan (1953–1957), GDP grew rapidly, in large part due to an increase in TFP, which accounts for nearly three-quarters of measured GDP growth. Our estimate of GDP growth in this period (6.5%) is well below the official Chinese figure (9.2%), but close to the T.C. Liu–K.C. Yeh reconstruction

[14] See Kraay (1996) and Wang and Yao (2001), among others.

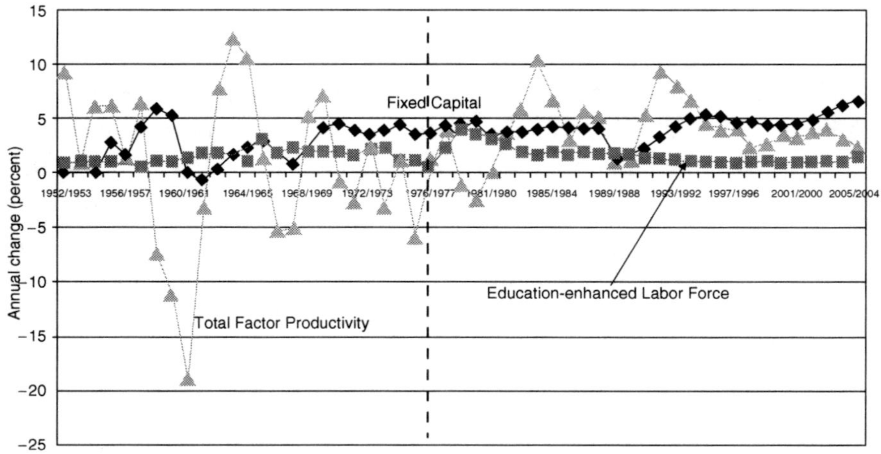

Figure 1. Sources of annual GDP growth, 1952–2005 annual change in fixed capital, education-enhanced labor and TFP.

of official estimates made years ago, using prices from 1933, when China approximated a fully-open market system.[15] This agreement between our estimate of GDP growth and the Liu–Yeh result based on 1933 prices enhances our confidence that the 2000 prices underlying our data more closely approximate the relative scarcities of industrial and agricultural products during the 1950s than do the official prices of the time.

Since the assumption about the initial 1952 level of capital stock heavily influences the capital stock growth rate in this early period, the appendix provides alternative calculations, using different assumptions about the initial capital stock. A high initial capital stock estimate for 1952 lowers the contribution of capital and raises the impact of TFP in accounting

[15] Liu and Yeh, it should be noted, made estimates of GDP growth for this period, using the underlying official data but adjusting for the distortions in the 1952 prices and that is the figure that we use here. They also had an estimate, and it was the one that they preferred, which made adjustments in the underlying data series that brought down the rate of growth of GDP in the 1953–1957 period in 1933 prices to 4.6%. These small differences are now mainly of historical interest, although they led to heated debate at the time. Liu and Yeh (1965, p. 120) and elsewhere. Liu and Yeh do not actually calculate the reconstructed Chinese GDP growth rate in 1933 prices, but a rough estimate can be obtained from the difference between their adjusted estimate and the reconstructed estimate in 1952 prices.

for GDP growth, and vice versa. Only a detailed analysis of China's capital stock in the early 1950s, building on the work of Shigeru Ishikawa (1960, 1965), can determine which of these estimates best reflects the reality in China at that time. The calculations presented here report only the results based on assuming that the initial capital stock was twice GDP in 1952, with a depreciation rate of 9.6% per year.[16]

China achieved impressive growth of TFP during the first five-year plan period despite undertaking the collectivization of agriculture (1955–1956) and the state takeover of virtually all industry. Offsetting the disruptive impact of these political movements was in part the high rate of capital formation that had risen from very low levels prior to 1949 when total investment probably did little more than cover depreciation if that. Productivity growth mainly reflected continued recovery from the long-term impact of the war with Japan (1937–1945) and the final phase of China's civil war (1945–1949) between the Kuomintang and the victorious Communists.

Recovery from war typically unleashes a quick productivity surge due to the reactivation of capital and labor idled by military strife and the associated chaos. Under these circumstances, simple measures such as restoring electricity and reopening transport routes can deliver major jumps in output. In China, the new government's swift restoration of monetary stability following a decade-long hyperinflation provided a further push toward higher productivity by stimulating the resumption of cultivation and trade in cotton and other commercial farm products (Perkins, 1966).

From 1958 to the eve of the reform period that officially began in December 1978, China's growth slowed markedly. The average GDP growth rate in year 2000 prices fell to 2.41% from 1957 through 1965 and then rose to 4.87% from 1965 through 1978, producing an average growth rate over the entire period of 3.92% (as contrasted to an official growth rate mainly in 1957 prices of 5.4% for the whole period).[17]

---

[16] The lower initial capital stock figure (equal to GDP in 1952) produces implausibly low TFP growth in the first five-year plan period when recovery from wartime disruption should have, and in the estimates in the table, did enable substantial improvements in productivity. A lower depreciation rate (we also used 7% in our complete calculations in the appendix) has much less influence on the estimates.

[17] National Bureau of Statistics (1999, p. 4).

It would have been remarkable if China had actually maintained a growth rate of over 5% a year between 1957 and 1978. This period began with the Great Leap Forward (1958–1960) that left much of industry in shambles and caused a steep decline in agricultural output that led directly or indirectly to excess deaths amounting to tens of millions in the resulting famine of 1959–1961. Compounding these punishing reversals, the Soviet Union withdrew its technical assistance in 1960. Together with China's prohibition of foreign direct investment, political hostility from the far left toward foreign technology in general, and the US-led trade embargo, China effectively was left on its own with only the most limited access to the superior technologies available in the outside world. Despite some modifications in the early 1970s, China's costly economic isolation hardly changed until after the death of Mao Zedong in 1976.

Finally, there was the Great Proletarian Cultural Revolution that reached a peak of disruption in 1967–1968, but which continued to paralyze economic decision making throughout its formal existence from 1966 to 1976. As the data in Table 2 indicate, the disruption to the economy caused by the Cultural Revolution, while considerable, was substantially less than what occurred during the Great Leap Forward.

Given this long and formidable list of setbacks, the real question about the 1958–1978 period is how GDP grew at all. The answer is that the growth was primarily made possible by high and rising rates of capital accumulation, which replaced productivity enhancement as the dominant contributor to GDP growth (see Table 2 and Figure 1). The share of gross investment in GDP (measured in current prices) rose from 17.5% in 1957 to 29.5% in 1978. Data in Table 2 show that capital formation dominated the growth picture during the two decades following 1957, accounting for 93% of GDP growth during 1957–1965 and 68% of GDP expansion during 1965–1978. TFP, not surprisingly, declined, making a sharp negative contribution to overall growth during the years that encompassed the Great Leap Forward.

The growth that did occur in this period did not provide much help to China's population, which grew at an annual rate of 1.9% during 1957–1978 in spite of the famine in 1959–1961. If we subtract capital formation from output growth, we find that real per capita consumption during

1957–1978 rose slightly more than 2% per year in 2000 prices.[18] Most of that increase occurred in the urban areas or was eaten up by government consumption. As a result, our calculations confirm work by Lardy (1984), Bramall (1989), and others indicating that China's rural majority experienced little or no improvement in living standards during the two decades prior to the start of economic reforms.

The dramatic change after 1978 is the story that is most relevant to our interest in the future performance of China's economy. Instead of the trendless swings in annual TFP changes typical of 1952–1978, the data underlying Figure 1 show annual TFP turning upward in 1976–1978, dipping briefly in 1978/1980, and then rising in each year beginning with 1981/1982. Following negligible growth averaging 0.5 per year during the 1952–1978 plan era, including an actual decline during 1957–1978 (Table 2), TFP grows at an annual rate of 3.8% during 1978–2005 and accounts for 40% of overall growth during this interval of nearly three decades. The size and persistence of this productivity surge is unprecedented in Chinese history. Although TFP growth did average 4.7% during 1952–1957, this spurt covered only five years and, as noted earlier, is partly attributable to recovery from the ravages of war and hyperinflation.

The rise in the contribution of capital did not occur independently of the rise in productivity. The rate of capital accumulation in China did not rise after 1978 as a result of efforts by government and the private sector to shift a higher share of resources away from consumption and toward investment. The rate of capital accumulation in current prices as a share of GDP actually declined slightly in the early 1980s and again in the late 1980s before rising again later on (Figure 2). The higher growth rate of the capital stock (and hence of the contribution of capital to growth) resulted from the same savings and investment effort being applied to a higher growth rate of GDP. Thus, it was the jump in productivity growth leading to a higher GDP growth rate that made possible the greater contribution of capital. Put differently, the story of the 1979–2005 period in

[18]This is a rough estimate obtained by subtracting gross fixed capital formation in 2000 prices in 1957 and 1978 from GDP in 2000 prices for those same years. The resulting figure for "consumption" thus includes government consumption and changes in net exports as well as household consumption.

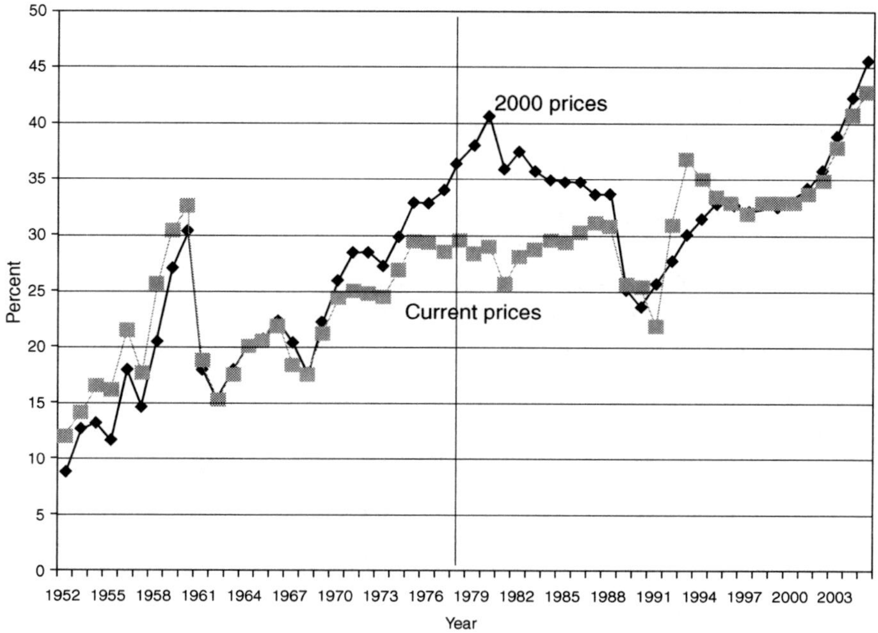

Figure 2. China: Fixed capital formation proportions, 1952–2005.

China is a story of reforms generating high TFP growth that in turn led to a higher level of capital formation growth than would otherwise have been the case.

This pattern recalls the experience of Japan during its 20-year growth spurt from the early 1950s. Calculations by Denison and Chung (covering 1953–1971) and by Shinohara (covering 1960–1970), for example, show that TFP accounted for just over half of Japan's 9 plus percent rate of GDP growth in this period.[19] The GDP share of gross fixed capital formation averaged 20.1% in the early 1950s, then rose to 24.5% in the latter half of the 1950s, and finally to over 30% of GDP during the 1960s,[20] where it remained throughout the 1970s even though the Japanese GDP growth rate slowed markedly. Thus in Japan, as in China, it was TFP growth that

[19] Both results reproduced in Ito (1992, pp. 48–49).

[20] These figures are from Ohkawa and Rosovsky (1973), but Ito (1992) shows an even more dramatic rise in the capital formation rate.

drove accelerated growth of GDP, leading to a rise in the rate of capital formation. In Japan in the 1970s and into the 1980s, it was a deceleration in TFP, not a decline in the rate of gross fixed capital formation that accounted for most of the initial slowdown in growth in that period.

The Chinese and Japanese data on the contribution of TFP to GDP growth are similar to the data for South Korea and Taiwan. Reform in all four cases led to a jump in productivity that in turn led to a rise in the growth rate of the capital stock. This close connection between reforms that led to high TFP followed by high growth and hence higher rates of growth of capital has been missed in some earlier studies because of the way the data were presented. There were two major economic reform periods in both South Korea and Taiwan, the turn outward to promote manufactured exports in the early 1960s and the major effort at economic liberalization (reduction in the role of government in limitations on imports and much else) beginning in the mid-to-late 1980s. In both reform periods in both countries, the growth accounting data indicate that there was a burst in TFP followed by a rising rate of growth of the capital stock (Perkins and Sabin, 2001).

The picture for China as shown in the yearly growth accounting data in Figure 1 is most like the story for South Korea and Taiwan. The pace of institutional reform in China in qualitative terms breaks down into four major periods. The first period, 1979–1984, was the period of the opening up of foreign trade, the return to household agriculture, and the freeing up of rural and many consumer markets. The second period of reform followed closely on the first in 1985 through 1988 and involved the freeing up of industrial inputs for sale on the open market that led in turn to the boom in township and village enterprises that sustained high growth until the hiatus in June 1989 and conservative backlash to reform in the latter part of that year and in 1990. The third phase of reform came after Deng Xiaoping's trip to China's south in 1992 and his call for more not less reform. The fourth phase of fundamental institutional and policy changes came in the mid-to-late 1990s with the rapid rise in foreign direct investment, China's decision to do whatever was necessary to join the World Trade Organization (WTO), and the government's disguised but clear decision to reduce sharply its role in the ownership and control of the industrial sector.

The primary question addressed in this essay, however, is not about the past, but about whether China's high growth will continue into the future. Will China continue to enjoy major spurts in TFP followed by accelerated growth in the capital stock or will a new pattern of capital and TFP growth emerge, perhaps one that is still robust but perhaps less volatile than in the past? Previous interludes of reform and accelerated TFP growth were a product of the return of household farming, the shift from plan to market, the removal of most restrictions on domestic and international trade, and other fundamental changes that accompany the transition from a central planning to a market economy. That transition, while not complete, has moved China far toward the market economy end of the economic systems spectrum. Future reforms of this sort will not have the same impact as the freeing up of industrial inputs for sale on the market or the large increase in foreign direct investment. Future agricultural reforms in particular are not likely to have much of an impact on GDP growth, because that sector now accounts for less than 15% of GDP. The shift of labor out of agriculture and into industry and services will continue to be important, but only so long as the secondary and tertiary sectors create new jobs.

Thus, future productivity and GDP growth in China over the coming two decades depends primarily on what happens to growth in output and productivity in industry and services. One suspects that these new sources of reform and productivity growth in industry and services are likely to come in a continuing stream of important but smaller and less volatile steps that raise efficiency and upgrade technology year after year. What some of those changes might be in the subject of the discussion that follows. We begin, however, with a discussion of some of the future sources of growth that are a bit easier to predict than the pace of innovation and productivity growth.

IV. China's Growth Prospects

Will the savings and investment rate remain high?

Even if productivity is the main driving force behind high GDP growth, sustained growth at the levels attained during the past quarter century will require the continued expansion of China's stock of fixed capital at something approximating the 9% annual growth that has prevailed since the reform period began. This is because it is difficult to conceive of sustained productivity growth in the absence of the large investments needed to introduce new technologies. In a market system, it is equally improbable to expect investment to remain at high levels if productivity is not growing rapidly. Productivity growth is a central component in the large number of profitable investment opportunities needed to keep investors willing to invest.

In China, the continuing role of official actors in investment choice complicates the relation between growth of investment and productivity. Because of China's consistent record of poor investment decisions, a subject to which we shall return, a decline in the expenditure share devoted to fixed investment could improve the quality of project selection and execution and contribute to a higher rate of TFP growth.

Even though China has become a magnet for overseas investment, annual increments to the capital stock come mostly from domestic sources of investment, which in turn are largely financed by domestic savings.[21] Assuming robust investment opportunities, it is therefore the level of domestic savings over the coming two decades that will largely determine the pace of investment in China and the growth rate of the capital stock.

Savings in China come from three sources: household saving that accounts for a little over half of total savings, enterprise saving that accounts for roughly one-third of the total, and government saving that has averaged around 15% of the total since the 1990s (Yu, 2005). Among these three components, only the household segment is amenable to systematic analysis and forecasting.

Chinese households have recorded high savings levels throughout the reform era. In recent years, both rural and urban households save roughly one-quarter of disposable income, with household savings amounting to about one-sixth of GDP (Kuijs, 2006). There are several reasons for high household savings during the past two decades, not all of which will

[21]Working with data from a cross section of nations, Feldstein (1983) observed a strong correlation between domestic saving and domestic investment. Jiang (2006) finds that foreign direct investment represents only a small fraction of China's overall capital formation, demonstrating that recent Chinese experience conforms to the same pattern.

continue with the same force into the future. One current motivation is to accumulate funds that can be used to purchase expensive durable goods including, for a small but growing part of the population, automobiles. The recent privatization of urban housing has provided an even greater reason for urban households to save. These motivations for saving will continue, but their impact could decline over the coming decades if financial institutions continue to expand the availability of home mortgages, auto loans, and other forms of consumer credit. Since slow growth of aggregate demand has prompted Beijing to strenuous efforts to raise consumer spending during the past decade, policy restrictions are unlikely to slow the expansion of consumer loans and mortgages.

The main motivation for high household savings in China, however, is to save for retirement and to meet the rapidly rising costs of health care and education. None of these factors acted as important determinants of household saving during the plan era. Urban workers expected to receive generous pensions provided by their work units. Rural households were unable to accumulate substantial savings; their retirement incomes depended on whatever reserves their collective farms could accumulate and whatever income their children could share with them. Access to education and medical care was largely determined by non-monetary considerations.

Chinas reforms changed all this. Mass layoffs and privatization introduced new uncertainty into urban pension arrangements, while the demise of collectives eliminated the collective reserves on which elderly villagers had depended. Ability to pay became increasingly prominent in the allocation of education and especially health care. Following these changes, multiple studies have shown that Chinese household behavior now fits the life cycle model of savings behavior that economists routinely apply to market economies.[22] This approach postulates an inverse relationship between dependency and savings: children and retirees consume more than they earn, while adults in the prime working ages accumulate savings to benefit their children and finance their own retirement.

China's government lacks the financial resources to establish a public retirement or social security system that will provide ample pension

[22] Kraay (2000), Modigliani and Cao (2004), and Yu (2005).

income to more than a small segment of the population.[23] This circumstance is unlikely to change dramatically during the next two decades. This means that most households must depend primarily on their own resources for retirement income. The same story applies to health care: most Chinese must expect to pay the bulk of their medical expenses. Given these realities, what then does the life cycle savings model tell us about the likely level of household savings over the next decade or two?

Table 3 provides data and projections for China's population and divides the demographic total into two categories: working-age persons

Table 3. Population and dependency ratio, 1990–2045.

		Percentage share			
		Working age 16–65		Dependents	
Year	Population (millions)	Including	Excluding	Including	Excluding
1990	1,130	65.4	64.1	34.6	35.9
2000	1,263	66.7	64.5	33.3	35.5
2005	1,308	68.8	65.3	31.2	34.7
2015	1,390	70.6	66.4	29.4	33.6
2025	1,457	67.9	63.4	32.1	36.6
2035	1,489	64.1		35.9	
2045	1,497	61.4		38.6	

Source: Data for 1990 from official census results for that year. Numbers of high school and college students are from Appendix. Other data are from China population projections posted at http://genderstats.worldbank.org/hnpstats/dp.asp, accessed November 12, 2006.

Notes: Dependents are defined as persons aged under 16 and over 65. We assume that high school and college students are of working age.

[23]The Chinese government is actively discussing and experimenting with a national pension system, and one will no doubt be in place sometime in the next decade or two, the time frame with which we are concerned. That said, however, the resources needed to finance this system will remain meager over this period and pensions, other than for a relatively narrow elite, are likely to remain a small part of what most families will depend on in their retirement years.

(between 16 and 65 years of age) and dependents. One immediate observation from these data is that the dependency ratio, meaning the share of persons above or below working age, is very low.

China's low dependency ratio follows from recent demographic history. The one-child-family policy instituted in the early 1970s led to a marked decline in the number and proportion of young people, and the earlier baby boom that began in the 1950s is only now beginning to approach retirement age (see Chapter 5).

Although the age structure of China's population ensures rapid future increases in the proportion of retirees (Howe and Jackson, 2004), the projections in Table 3 show the dependency ratio declining to 2015, whether or not working-age high school and college students are counted as dependents. Although the dependency ratio begins a steep ascent of about 3 percentage points per decade from 2015, it is only after 2025 that this ratio climbs above the low figures observed during 1990–2005. The predictions of the life cycle model, which associates low dependency with robust household savings, therefore indicate that household saving in China is likely to remain high throughout the two decades to 2025.

It is difficult to say much about the future savings of business and government, the other major sources of domestic saving in China. Prior to the reform period, the primary source of saving was enterprise profit that was generated by monopoly pricing of consumer manufactures. The state collected these profits in the form of turnover and profit taxes and used the revenues to fund virtually all investment other than that done by the rural communes. Under the reform, the expansion of entry and price flexibility eliminated this system. Enterprise profits fell sharply (see Figure 1 in Chapter 4) and then recovered to some extent. Industrial profits remain highly concentrated. In 2003, just five sectors (out of a total of 39) accounted for half of all industrial profits; in 2005, the same five sectors — oil and gas, ferrous metallurgy, electric power, electronics, and transport equipment, earned 42% of total industrial profits.[24] Although we may speculate that concentration of profits is conducive to high savings, any detailed forecast of business savings requires predictions about profit trends in these and the

---

[24]Yearbook (2004, pp. 520–521); Yearbook (2006, pp. 506–507). These data exclude enterprises outside the state sector with annual sales under RMB5 million.

other 34 industrial sectors, as well as construction, commerce, finance, transport, communications, and other branches of economic activity, a task far beyond our competence. In thinking about the future, all we can say is that we see no reason to expect enterprise profits and savings to fall substantially as a share of GDP. If investment opportunities remain robust, enterprises will make substantial profits and will plow a large portion of those profits back into investment.

Forecasting the level of government savings mainly involves reaching a judgment about the likely path of government revenue and, more importantly, how that revenue will be used. The recent shift in government policy toward greater efforts to ameliorate the distributional consequences of rapid growth could boost subsidies for the poor and other welfare expenditures at the expense of government savings. We think it more likely that increased effort to reduce poverty is likely to concentrate on raising investment in education and rural infrastructure rather than subsidizing consumption. Our best guess is that government will continue as a substantial contributor to domestic saving.

In summary, therefore, there is every reason to believe that China's rate of saving and investment will remain high for the next two decades. Inadequate saving is unlikely to constrain China's economic growth between now and 2025.

Future growth of the labor force and human capital

Since infants born in 2005 will enter the work force in 2021, forecasting China's working-age population to 2025 is not difficult. To accomplish this, we assume that the annual number of births remains constant during 2005–2009 and apply age-specific mortality rates for 2005 to the ensuing two decades. Results appear in Table 4. They show that China's workforce, which we define to include non-students aged 16–65, will continue to grow slowly until about 2015, and then begin to decline, resulting in a terminal 2025 figure that matches the projected total for 2010.

Our focus, however, is not on total numbers, but rather on the portion of the labor force that is employed outside agriculture and particularly on the changing educational attainments of Chinese workers. We consider these issues in turn.

Table 4. Projection of working-age non-student population ages 16–65: size and composition, 2005–2025.

	Labor force and graduates (millions)									
		Annual graduates		Educational composition of non-student workforce (percent)						
Year	Working-age non-students L	Senior high	Tertiary	No diploma	Primary	Junior high	Senior high	Tertiary	Ratio H/L
2005	849.6	8.3	3.1	15.1	32.8	33.6	15.7	2.7	1.31
2010	558.3	9.9	5.0	11.6	29.3	36.6	17.8	4.7	1.39
2015	913.4	12.8	5.0	9.5	25.3	37.8	20.2	7.2	1.48
2020	903.6	11.5	6.9	7.4	21.9	38.2	21.7	10.8	1.58
2025	885.6	12.8	6.6	5.7	19.4	37.0	23.2	14.7	1.69

Source: Appendix.

Notes: H/L is the ratio of education-enhanced workforce (H) to the actual workforce headcount (L). Values of 1 (respectively 1.35, 2.01 and 3.28) indicate that the average worker has earned a diploma at the primary (respectively junior high, senior high, tertiary) level.

The growth accounting results summarized in Table 2 indicate that a rising workforce has contributed 1 percentage point and often more, to overall growth ever since the 1950s. Should we be concerned that the stagnation and, after 2015, decline in numbers might detract from future growth? We think not, and for two reasons.

To begin, China's long history of labor market segmentation, which dates to the 1950s, institutionalized a large productivity gap between urban and rural workers (see Chapters 6, 17, and 19). Survey data for 2000, for example, show that wages of urban primary school graduates were more than double the earnings of rural workers with similar educational qualifications.[25] Assuming that this wage gap reflects differences in the marginal labor productivity of rural and urban workers, we may anticipate that the transfer of workers from rural to urban occupations, which accounted for a substantial share of output growth during 1978–2005

[25] Based on urban and rural survey results underlying Zhang *et al.* (2005) and deBrauw and Rozelle (2004). As explained in the chapter on labor (see Chapter 6), adjusting for differences in urban and rural prices would reduce this wage differential; adjusting for differential non-wage benefits, however, would push in the opposite direction.

(see Chapter 17), will continue to spur future growth. The presence of urban scale economies (see Table 19.9) means that shifting workers from rural to urban occupations can increase the productivity of existing urban workers as well as that of the migrants themselves.

Economists analyze rural–urban migration from the perspective of the Harris–Todaro model, which assumes that migration is an increasing function of the gap between urban and rural incomes and of the migrants' probability of obtaining urban employment. The migration of villagers to China's cities and towns, which Chinese sources describe as a "tide of workers" (*mingongchao*), is already the largest in human history.

Government initiatives to remove barriers limiting migration — for example, by abolishing the administrative distinction between "urban" and "rural" residents, allowing trade unions to assist migrants' efforts to claim unpaid wages, and providing medical benefits for migrant workers — promise to improve pay and working conditions, which should increase the flow of migrants (Zheng *et al.*, 2005; Chen, 2006; Zhu, 2006).

China's recent declining rate of job creation obliges us to hesitate before concluding that the continued transfer of large numbers of workers from rural to urban occupations seems likely to offset the drag on the economy arising from the near-term slow labor force growth and eventual decline in the overall labor force. Employment growth in China's secondary and tertiary sectors dropped sharply during the past decade. One study found that annual creation of formal employment during 1995–2004 was no more than half as much as during 1990–1995 (Rawski, 2006).

Slow employment growth is partly due to restrictions on the inflow of rural migrants, however. The main difficulty is an array of policies, including official support for capital-intensive projects and sectors, low interest rates for favored borrowers, and policy discrimination against private business, which have the effect of tilting investment spending in directions that limit employment growth (Chapter 6, section "Causes of Unemployment and Slow Job Creation"). These policies, each with its own rationale, are "formulated without consideration of their effects on aggregate employment" (see Chapter 6) and have the unintended consequence of restricting the growth of employment.

Given the importance that China's present administration has placed on efforts to accelerate the growth of employment, we anticipate that, despite the legacy of migration restrictions and of policies and institutional arrangements that constrain job creation, continued migration out of China's countryside will deliver sufficient productivity increases to offset the negative impact of slow growth and eventual shrinkage of the labor force on overall economic expansion. In terms of our growth accounting equation, this productivity boost shows up in TFP because lack of sufficient data makes it difficult to separate the labor force in our equation into its rural and urban components.

How does the addition of human capital change this picture? Over the next two decades, growing numbers of high school and college graduates will reshape China's labor force. Our projections assume that the expansion of Chinese high school and college enrollments during 2005–2025 will parallel Japanese enrollment patterns during the two decades from 1955, when Japan's share of agriculture in its national labor force approximated China's 2005 share. The details are left to the appendix, but we assume that the proportion of high school (*gaozhong*) graduates among successive cohorts of 18-year-olds will rise from the 2005 figure of 42% to 82% by 2005 and that the proportion of successive cohorts earning tertiary diplomas will rise from 16.0 to 44.5% between 2005 and 2025.

Our labor force projections, summarized in Table 4, show that junior high school graduates will continue to constitute the largest segment of Chinese workers, accounting for a steady proportion slightly above one-third of the total. But the distribution of educational attainment among the remainder of the workforce will shift dramatically between 2005 and 2025, with the share of high school and college graduates doubling from 18.4 to 37.9%, while the proportion with primary school diplomas or less drops from nearly half to only one-fourth.

As more students earn higher-level diplomas, their subsequent contribution to GDP will rise. Our projections show the annual numbers of high school and university graduates rising from 11.4 million in 2005 to 17.8 million in 2015 and 19.4 million in 2025, with new university graduates exceeding 6 million in both 2020 and 2025 (Table 4).

Table 5, which summarizes the results of our projections, shows that, under plausible assumptions about demographic and educational change, the education-enhanced workforce will continue to contribute positively to overall growth between 2005 and 2025 even as the number of workers reaches a

Table 5. Productivity consequences of input projections and 6 or 9% growth, 2005–2025.

		Average growth of inputs (percent)				Annual growth of GDP (percent)			
			Labor input				Attributable to		
Period	Annual GDP growth (percent)	Fixed capital (*K*)	Raw labor (*L*)	Education enhanced labor (*H*)	Average TFP growth (percent)	Fixed capital (*K*)	Education enhanced labor (*H*)	TFP growth	TFP share of GDP growth (percent)
Version 1									
2005–2015	9.0	9.8	0.7	2.0	3.6	4.2	1.1	3.6	40.4
2015–2025	9.0	8.2	–0.3	1.0	4.9	3.5	0.6	4.9	54.4
2005–2025	9.0	9.0	0.2	1.5	4.3	3.9	0.8	4.3	47.4
1978–2025	9.3	9.4	1.2	2.2	4.0	4.0	1.2	4.0	43.1
1952–2025	7.5	8.1	1.4	2.3	2.7	3.5	1.3	2.7	36.3
Version 2									
2005–2015	9.0	9.0	0.7	2.0	4.0	3.9	1.1	4.0	44.5
2015–2025	9.0	6.6	–0.3	1.0	5.6	2.8	0.6	5.6	62.4
2005–2025	9.0	7.8	0.2	1.5	4.8	3.3	0.8	4.8	53.4
1978–2025	9.3	8.8	1.2	2.2	4.2	3.8	1.2	4.2	45.6
1952–2025	7.5	7.7	1.4	2.3	2.9	3.3	1.3	2.9	38.3

(Continued)

Table 5. (*Continued*)

		Average growth of inputs (percent)				Annual growth of GDP (percent)			
			Labor input			Attributable to			
Period	Annual GDP growth (percent)	Fixed capital (*K*)	Raw labor (*L*)	Education enhanced labor (*H*)	Average TFP growth (percent)	Fixed capital (*K*)	Education enhanced labor (*H*)	TFP growth	TFP share of GDP growth (percent)
Version 3									
2005–2015	6.0	8.1	0.7	2.0	1.4	3.5	1.1	1.4	23.1
2015–2025	6.0	5.6	–0.3	1.0	3.0	2.4	0.6	3.0	50.7
2005–2025	6.0	6.8	0.2	1.5	2.2	2.9	0.8	2.2	37.0
1978–2025	8.0	8.4	1.2	2.2	3.1	3.6	1.2	3.1	39.1
1952–2025	6.7	7.5	1.4	2.3	2.2	3.2	1.3	2.2	32.4
Version 4									
2005–2015	6.0	7.3	0.7	2.0	1.7	3.1	1.1	1.7	28.7
2015–2025	6.0	4.0	–0.3	1.0	3.7	1.7	0.6	3.7	61.7
2005–2025	6.0	5.7	0.2	1.5	2.7	2.4	0.8	2.7	45.4
1978–2025	8.0	7.9	1.2	2.2	3.3	3.4	1.2	3.3	41.8
1952–2025	6.7	7.1	1.4	2.3	2.3	3.1	1.3	2.3	34.5

Memo item: average TFP growth 1978–2005: 3.8% (Table 20.2)

Source: Appendix.

Notes: Versions 1 and 2 assume 9% GDP growth; versions 3 and 4 assume 6% growth. The ratio of fixed capital formation to GDP declines linearly from the 2005 figure of 42.3% to a terminal 2005 level of 35% (versions 1 and 3) or 25% (versions 2 and 4).

peak and begins to decline. This is because the anticipated productivity benefits from the continuing spread of education outweigh the slow growth and subsequent decline in the actual number of working age adults.

Future growth of TFP

As the earlier discussion indicates, it is possible to base forecasts of trends in factor inputs at least in part on solid information about demographics, school enrollment, savings potential, and investment behavior. No comparably solid foundation exists for estimates of the likely future path of TFP. Since TFP growth accounted for two-fifths of China's overall GDP increase between 1978 and 2005, this poses a major difficulty for our effort to derive a reasonable forecast for economic performance over the coming decades. In order to create the firmest possible foundation for our predictions, we adopt the following step-by-step approach:

- Use our projections of capital and labor input to examine the productivity implications of assumed 6 and 9% annual GDP growth during 2005–2025.
- Review the findings of cross-national studies of economic growth for possible relevance to China's economic future.
- Examine the likely future productivity impact — both positive and negative — of specific dimensions of China's economy: further market-oriented reform, research and development, the financial and legal systems, and health and environmental degradation.
- Supplement our discussion of these supply-side issues with a brief excursion into the implications of China's expenditure accounts for future growth prospects.

We then conclude by reviewing China's prospects for sustained productivity growth.

Productivity implications of expected growth of capital, labor, and education

We begin with a series of calculations that investigate the productivity implications of combining specific assumptions about the growth of GDP and fixed capital with the labor force projections summarized in Table 4. Table 5 presents both assumptions and results.

To make the calculations underlying Table 5, we assumed annual GDP growth of 9% (versions 1 and 2) or 6% (versions 3 and 4) throughout 2005–2025. These are not predictions, but simply the starting point for our analysis. We project fixed capital using the perpetual inventory method with annual depreciation of 9.6%. Our capital stock projections assume that the GDP share of fixed investment declines linearly from the 2005 figure of 42.3% to a terminal 2025 level of 35% (versions 1 and 3) or 25% (versions 2 and 4).

Together with our projected labor force outcome (Table 4), these assumptions produce four growth scenarios, corresponding to various combinations of assumed growth rates (9 or 6%) and capital formation paths (fixed investment shrinking to 35 or 25% of GDP).

The first thing to note about these projections is that, despite the anticipated expansion of education, the contribution of labor and human capital to projected growth during 2005–2025 is only 0.8% annually, well below the 1.5% figure derived for 1978–2005 in Table 2. Excluding rural–urban migration that shows up in TFP in our calculations, without the increase in high school and university enrollments, the contribution of labor and human capital growth over the coming two decades would be close to zero.

A second observation is that under widely varying assumptions about the growth of GDP and investment, the average annual contribution of fixed capital to overall GDP growth during 2005–2025 varies only between 2.4 and 3.9%. Put differently, if China has to rely entirely on inputs of labor (including education) and fixed capital for growth over the next two decades, the nation's GDP growth rate cannot exceed 4.7% per year — a figure that is only half the 9.5% rate attained during 1978–2005 (Table 2).

The central issue in forecasting China's future rate of growth, therefore, involves projecting the likely rate of growth of TFP. That will be the focus of the discussion that follows. One conclusion emerges from these projections alone. To sustain a growth rate of 9% per year for another two decades, China would have to push the annual growth of TFP growth above 4% — higher than the 3.8% growth attained during 1978–2005 and far above the 3.1–3.2% rate recorded during 1995–2005. We think such an increase in TFP growth is unlikely. Nor do we think that China can substitute a rapidly rising (as contrasted to our assumption of a falling) rate of capital formation to fill this gap. Our initial conclusion, therefore, is that China's GDP is not likely to grow by 9% a year for the coming two decades. Simply maintaining the TFP growth rates of the recent past will be an enormous challenge, and, as is evident from the four different projections in Table 5, those rates will produce a GDP growth rate in the range of 6 to well under 9% a year.

When the projections for the two decades (2006–2015 and 2016–2025) are separated out, it is clear that China will have much more difficulty achieving a rate of growth above 6% in the second of these two decades. All of these projections, the reader should recall, assume that China's economy enjoys a peaceful environment both externally and internally. Assuming a peaceful environment, our belief is that Chinese GDP will grow at a rate of from 6 to 8% per year for the next decade and sometime, in the second decade the economy will slow to a rate of GDP growth that could be as low as 5%, to a rate as high as 7% per year. In the second decade, the rate of growth will depend not only on the level of TFP achieved, but also on the rate of growth in the first decade. A slower rate of growth in the first decade will make possible a somewhat higher growth rate in the second.[26]

Would this level of economic performance for China be unprecedented or is there experience elsewhere that would lend credence to these forecasts? An approach that provides some guidance as to how long China can sustain high growth is one that looks at other nations with similar economies that earlier experienced a sustained (several decades or more) rate of GDP growth comparable to that achieved by China over the past 27 years. There are many economies that have achieved high growth rates for a decade or less starting at low levels of per capita income and a few that have grown at 7–9% per year for longer, but only

[26]This statement is based on the view that a slower rate of growth will leave more early stage economic reforms and structural changes for the second decade (slower rural–urban migration in the first decade followed by faster migration than would otherwise be the case in the second decade, for example) hence making possible somewhat faster growth.

three can be said to have economies similar to that of China.[27] Those three are Japan, the Republic of Korea, and Taiwan. In all three of the economies, growth proceeded for either two decades (Japan) or three decades (Korea and Taiwan) at rates that averaged more than 8% per year. But all three eventually slowed down never to grow at rates that high again. In Japan, this accelerated growth began in the 1950s when full recovery from World War II was achieved and continued until 1971 when the growth rate dropped precipitously never to recover to "miracle" levels. In South Korea and Taiwan, the slowdown was not quite so sudden or sharp, but was pronounced nonetheless and began in 1990 for Taiwan and 1992 for Korea.

As the data in Table 6 indicate, this slowdown came at a similar level of per capita income, remarkably similar when GDP per capita is

Table 6. Increase of per capita GDP before and after growth deceleration in three East Asian economies.

	Per capita GDP			Average annual growth of GDP per capita			
		When slowdown begins calculated using		Before slowdown		After slowdown	
Economy	Slowdown begins	PPP (dollars)	Exchange rate GDP (dollars)	Period	Growth rate	Period	Growth rate
Japan	1971	13,800	16,500	1960–1970	10.5	1971–1979	5.2
Taiwan	1990	13,370	10,880	1980–1989	8.1	1990–1999	6.3
Korea	1992	13,370	8,810	1982–1991	9.1	1992–2005	5.3

Sources: World Bank (1981, p. 137); Heston *et al*., (1982); Directorate General of Budget, Accounting and Statistics (2005, p. 153); Bank of Korea (2006, pp. 162–163).

Notes: US dollars at 2005 prices and percent per year; PPP per capita GDP figures in current prices were converted to 2005 prices using the GDP deflator for the United States, the main source of international prices used in making the PPP calculations.

[27] A number of oil-rich countries and even a small country with diamonds (Botswana) have managed to grow rapidly for sustained periods. There are also the city states of Hong Kong and Singapore. But none of these countries is both large in terms of population, possesses at the start a large and poor agricultural sector, and has built its economic growth on manufacturing.

calculated in purchasing-power parity (PPP) terms and converted into prices of a comparable year (2005 prices in the case of this table). When these three economies' per capita GDP passed US$13,000 in PPP terms, the GDP growth rate in the years that followed dropped and did not recover to the levels of the previous decades for even one year. According to the World Bank (World Bank, 2007, p. 288), Chinese PPP GDP per capita in 2005 was $6,600 and the Penn World Tables figure for 2004 updated to 2005 would be about $6,300. Because China does not participate in the United Nations project that calculates PPP GDP figures, these Chinese estimates are subject to more than the usual margin for error. Nevertheless, given that China's GDP per capita in US dollars using the official exchange rate was US$1,717, given that the Chinese currency is widely accepted to be significantly undervalued, and given that developing countries at this level of income typically have a PPP GDP per capita that is two or three times their per capita GDP calculated using the official exchange rate, these Penn and World Bank estimates are plausible.

If one accepts the Chinese estimates of PPP per capita GDP and our GDP growth rate forecasts of 6–8% or something over 5.4–7.4% per capita per year,[28] then China would reach the slowdown point within ten years (at 7%) or 14 years (at just over 5% per year). Thus, these international comparisons reinforce our view that China should be able to achieve 6–8% GDP growth for another decade (if reforms proceed at a determined pace) but it will be unprecedented for the growth rate to proceed at that pace for another full decade.

Being unprecedented does not mean it cannot happen, but we have no basis for believing that China will outdo the performance of Japan, South Korea, or Taiwan. This international comparison, therefore, reinforces what we have said based on our growth accounting estimates. Given a continued effort comparable to that achieved by Japan, South Korea, and Taiwan, China's economy has the potential to grow at a high rate, as high as 8%, for another decade and perhaps a bit longer. But when China's GDP reaches PPP $13,000 (in 2005 prices) a decade or a bit more from now, it

[28]These per capita figures assume a population growth rate that continues at the current rate of 0.6% per year.

is likely that the GDP growth rate will begin to decline on a sustained basis. Whether it will come down sharply, as in the case of Japan, or more gradually as in the case of South Korea, remains an open question.

None of these projections will be realized, however, unless China is able to maintain a high rate of growth of TFP. What kind of evidence can we bring to bear on the question of whether Chinese TFP over the coming two decades will continue at its recent pace or whether it will begin to slow down or even disappear altogether? Our approach to this question is first to look at what we can learn from the various econometric efforts that use an array of variables to study the determinants of economic growth in large numbers of nations. We will concentrate on those variables that might have something to do with TFP. Second, we will then turn to a brief review of well-known sources of inefficiency in specific Chinese sectors and institutions, inefficiency whose elimination could help sustain TFP growth. Some of these latter issues are also discussed at greater length in other chapters in this volume.

Econometric estimates of the sources of growth

A number of researchers have used data from many economies to conduct statistical studies that attempt to pinpoint factors that can be associated with higher or lower rates of long-term growth. The resulting econometric growth equations are not ideal for our purposes, because they typically relate various explanatory variables to the growth rate of GDP rather than to the growth rate of TFP. Furthermore, these equations do not include a variable for capital formation, because the level of capital formation is endogenous and hence the estimates of its relationship to growth will be biased when estimated econometrically. Thus, the explanatory variables used could work as much through capital as through TFP to raise the growth rate of GDP. Variables such as the working population and the total population, for example, are an indirect way of measuring the dependency ratio and hence the likely level of savings and investment.

Despite these difficulties, econometric studies of growth do provide plausible links to productivity growth. Comparing these links with Chinese circumstances reinforces the perception of China as an economy with strong growth prospects.

Jeffrey Sachs and Andrew Warner find a strong positive association between economic openness and growth (Sachs and Warner, 1995). Openness is clearly tied more closely to productivity than to capital formation. In Chapter 16 on China's international economic relations, Branstetter and Lardy show that the dramatic opening of China's economy predates Beijing's 2001 entry into the WTO. Looking ahead, both domestic policy (e.g., the "Go Global" (*zou chuqu*) program that promotes overseas investments by Chinese firms) and China's WTO obligations, which call for further liberalization of trade in services as well as commodities, point to future increases in China's participation in many forms of cross-national exchange.

China earns high marks for openness in terms of the specific criteria employed by Sachs and Warner. In their analysis, "open" economies have tariff rates below 40% (China's weighted average tariff rate was 12% in 2001), subject no more than 40% of imports to quotas and licensing (China applied such measures to only 21.6% of imports in 2001),[29] maintain moderate export taxes (China has few taxes on exports), and keep the black market premium for foreign exchange below 20% (with China's *renminbi* widely seen as undervalued, there is no black market premium).

Sachs and Warner also find links between geography and growth. Specifically, their work associates slow growth with states that are landlocked, have short coastlines, and/or are located in the tropics. China avoids each of these potential obstacles. The reasons underlying the superior economic performance of nations located outside the tropics and endowed with long coastlines are not entirely clear. Chinese experience suggests that the negative impact of isolation has more to do with the attitudes of people and their governments than with physical limitations. Many chapters in this volume, particularly the studies of trade, industry, and science, demonstrate that China's dramatic shift from isolation (imposed by politics rather than geography) to growing openness contributed to the economic boom of the last three decades.

Development economists find a negative association between large resource exports and growth, apparently because of management difficulties associated with dominant natural resource exports whose revenues

---

[29] These tariff data are from Bhattasali *et al.* (2005, pp. 214–215).

experience wide price fluctuations. From this perspective, China's growth prospects benefit from its growing dependence on imports rather than exports of crude oil, iron ore, and a variety of other resource products: one study finds that "by 2020, China's domestic resources will fully supply only 9 of 45 mineral varieties" (You and Qi, 2004, p. 13).

Robert Barro finds that high levels of government consumption (as a share of GDP) tend to retard economic growth (Barro, 1997). Collection of taxes to fund public consumption, including excessive levels of subsidies and welfare outlays, could divert funds from investment. As Wong and Bird note in Chapter 12 on the fiscal system, China's formal tax system "remains weak," with budgetary revenue and extrabudgetary funds each amounting to roughly 20% of GDP. Despite recent increases in defense budgets, China's public spending avoids excessive consumption outlays, perhaps because, as Wong and Bird emphasize, responsibility for most social expenditures rests with poorly funded local administrations. Data for 2005 show that the combined budgetary expenditures of central and local governments amounted to 18.5% of GDP, of which roughly one-third may be classified as investment related.[30]

Most cross-national studies include a variable for education. Because growth promotes school enrollment, so that the causation between education and growth runs in both directions, analysts typically make use of education levels at the start of the period being considered. China's 2000 census found that the average adult had received 8.28 years of education or 2.28 years of secondary schooling (Census Research, 2005, p. 1649). The China Health and Nutrition Survey reports a 75% secondary school enrollment rate in 2000 among youths aged 12–18, much higher than the 53% sample average among 98 countries in Barro's cross-national study (see Table 7.7; Barro, 1991, p. 438). At the beginning of the 21st century, China had a high level of schooling given its per capita income. With educational attainments expected to rise further, these growth equations lead us to anticipate that high and growing levels of educational attainment should add momentum to future Chinese growth.

[30]Yearbook (2006, pp. 57, 286). Investment-related spending includes outlays on capital construction, innovation, science and technology promotion, prospecting, and operating funds for education, science, and health.

Alesina and others find that cross-national data reveal a positive link between political stability and economic growth (Alesina and Perotti, 1994; Alesina *et al.*, 1996). Chinese experience confirms this observation. Political turmoil slowed China's economy at many points during the century prior to the establishment of the People's Republic of China in 1949 and again during the chaos of the Great Leap Forward and the Cultural Revolution (1958–1976).

During the reform era, China's economy has clearly benefited from a combination of relative political stability (notwithstanding the uncertainty surrounding the Tiananmen incident of June 1989) and policy focus on economic growth. While this chapter avoids engaging with political issues, we see the continued presence of a stable, growth-oriented political environment as an essential support for the continuation of sustained productivity growth.

Table 7 summarizes our reading of China's current position with respect to variables commonly employed in cross-national regression studies intended to pinpoint the determinants of economic growth. In general, these observations show that China is well situated to continue the strong economic performance of the recent past.

Table 7. China's prognosis for variables included in cross-national growth studies.

Variable (expected correlation with growth)	Chinese prognosis
Openness to trade (+) and foreign investment (+)	Exceptional
Geography (+)	Favorable — long coastline
Tropical location (–)	Favorable — outside tropics
Rich resource endowment (–)	Good (China lacks resources)
Government consumption as share of GDP (–)	Good (Ratio is moderate)
Education/human capital (+)	Good to excellent
Political stability (+)	Good (late 1970s–present)
Quality of Institutions	
Law/Property rights (+)	Fair
Corruption (–)	Poor/Fair
Administrative Competence (+)	Good, perhaps excellent
Growth-oriented policy environment (+)	Excellent
Democratic institutions (+)	Poor

Cross-national growth studies typically also include dummy variables for different regions of the world; the estimated coefficient for East Asia is invariably positive, meaning that, after controlling for the other explanatory variables, East Asian performance turns out to be unexpectedly strong. Exceptional growth in East Asia during the 1960s and 1970s provided important motivation for China's reform effort: "no sooner had the Chinese opened their eyes to the outside world after the Cultural Revolution than they exclaimed how far China had lagged behind" (Hua *et al.*, 1993, p. 27).[31] Now, such studies identify China itself as exceptional in the same fashion: Bekaert, Harvey, and Lundblad find that "standard growth regressions substantially under-predict … Chinese growth.… China is a huge outlier with the bulk of its past growth unaccounted for by the standard variables" (2006, pp. 22, 34).

Table 7 points to institutions as the single area in which Chinese circumstances fail to provide the conditions that cross-national studies associate with rapid economic growth. To examine the adequacy of Chinese institutions and policies to support sustained growth of productivity over the coming decades, one must get beyond these econometric estimates and focus on the specific situations facing China along a number of dimensions. To do that, we draw in part on a few general trends in the development of market-related institutions in China and in part on studies by others of such growth-related issues as the cost of dealing with environmental problems.

Can Chinese institutions support continued rapid growth?

The role of the state

Although the experiences of Singapore and a few enterprises in Korea (POSCO), the United States (Tennessee Valley Authority), and elsewhere demonstrate that state ownership and management can coexist with economic success, recent Chinese experience supports the view that a higher degree of state involvement in ownership and direct management of economic activity is likely to reduce the future increase of TFP.

[31] Hua *et al.* (1993, p. 27); see also Shirk (1993, p. 35) and Lin *et al.* (2003, p. 140).

Chapter 17 in this volume and many other studies associate state intervention and especially public ownership with low growth of output, employment, and productivity, slow progress toward the transfer of labor out of farming and other aspects of structural change, low investment returns, and large seasonal fluctuations in economic activity.

At the outset of China's reforms in 1978, the state controlled virtually all aspects of the economy. Markets governed only the allocation of a few consumer goods and rural sidelines, and even then, prices were set by the state. Private activity was essentially limited to the household plots of farmer families, which occupied about 5% of China's cultivated acreage.

Since that time, a long sequence of reforms has pushed market forces to the fore in determining the prices of virtually all goods and most services. Among factors of production, wages and urban land prices have moved into the market orbit, while official preferences still exert strong control over the price of capital and especially the price of foreign exchange (see Chapter 14 in this volume).

Ownership of resources has experienced substantial, though less dramatic, change. Early reform initiatives included the dismantling of collective farms and the restoration of family farming, which effectively privatized farm equipment and livestock, while ownership of land (including mineral deposits) remained in the hands of the state.

Ownership in the secondary and tertiary sectors is more complex, but the trend toward private control is clear (Garnaut *et al.*, 2005). Virtually all retail commerce and much wholesale commerce are in private hands. Even nominally state-owned department stores mainly rent space to individual traders. Although the state has maintained its control over the finance and utility sectors, as well as railway, airline, and telecommunications networks, privatization has begun to infiltrate these activities, although its extent remains modest.

Industry provides a well-documented illustration of the shift away from state control. Table 8 tracks the output shares of different ownership forms between 1980 and 2005. Despite shifts in category definitions and in the scope of industrial output, the trend toward private ownership is clearly evident. The output share of state-owned enterprises plunges from 81% in 1980 to 15% in 2005.

Table 8. Changing ownership structure for Chinese industrial output, 1980–2005.[a]

Year	State ownership[b]	Shareholding and limited liability corporations	Collective	Foreign invested[c]	Domestic private
1980	80.78	n.a.	18.51	0.01	0.00
1985	73.12	n.a.	25.48	0.43	0.01
1990	54.60	n.a.	35.62	1.88	5.39
1995	38.50	4.06	37.10	15.85	3.40
2000	34.92	12.52	17.07	26.07	4.46
2005	15.06	25.73	4.42	30.20	22.36
Output share					
Profit share	5.1	33.4	3.8	29.1	18.5
ROA	3.3	6.4	6.3	6.4	6.7

n.a., category for which no data is provided; ROA, annual pretax profits as percent of total assets.
[a] Percentage shares of gross output at current prices.
[b] Data for 2000 and 2005 include corporations with 100% state ownership.
[c] Includes firms with partial or full ownership by overseas Chinese and non-Chinese interests.
Sources: For 1980 and 1985, Industrial Census (1985, 3, pp. 88–89); for 1990, Industrial Yearbook (1991, p. 3); for 1995, Industrial Census (1995, General volume, p. 6); for 2000 and 2005, Yearbook (2001, p. 401; 2006, p. 505).
Notes: Omission of minor categories causes annual shares to sum to less than 100%. 1980 and 1985 data limited to "independent accounting units."
1995 data exclude private, individual, and village-level firms with sales below RMB1 million.
2000 and 2005 data exclude nonstate firms with sales below RMB5 million.

Even if we assume effective state control of all corporations, the combined share of state-owned and corporate firms in 2005, at 41%, is only half the size of the 1980 starting point. While state influence permeates the operations of many corporations, the assumption of across-the-board state control is excessive: China's 2004 economic census found that the sources of capital for shareholding entities included a state share of 52%, but for limited liability corporations, the state's capital share (36.2%) was considerably less than the share of private Chinese stakeholders (47.2%) (State Council Economic Census Group, 2005, Table 8).

Even when state ownership is substantial, industrial companies show a growing tendency to pursue commercial interests, as when petroleum refiners, squeezed between rising costs for imported crude oil and controlled domestic prices of gasoline, reduced their production and domestic sales of gasoline, thus creating regional gasoline shortages in order to draw attention to the negative impact of price controls on their finances.[32]

Equally impressive is the growing scale of privately controlled industrial activity. The 2005 data in Table 8 show 52% of industrial output coming from domestic private firms and from firms with partial or full foreign (including overseas Chinese) ownership. With the 2004 Economic Census listing the combined share of private and foreign capital as 97.8% for domestic private firms, 85.9% for firms with investment from Hong Kong, Macao, or Taiwan, and 88.1% for firms with other foreign ownership, these enterprises surely fall into the category of private ownership despite pockets of official influence (State Council Economic Census Croup, 2005, Table 8).

Recent developments demonstrate a continuing shift away from state ownership. The 2004 Economic Census reported that the number of state enterprises in the entire economy dropped by 177,700, while the number of collectives fell by 402,000 between 2001 and 2004, indicating declines of over 45% in each of the two most prominent forms of public ownership. At the same time, the entry of 658,000 private enterprises employing eight or more persons pushed the balance of ownership further away from the public sector (State Council Economic Census Group, 2005).

We anticipate further declines both in the number of state firms, especially at the provincial and local levels, and in the state sector's output share. In addition, the proliferation of public offerings and the conversion of non-tradable corporate shares held by state-sector entities into tradable shares will further dilute public ownership of corporate firms.

As the share of public ownership shrinks, the issue of state intervention in the operation of the economy, rather than direct state ownership, comes to the fore. The chapters in this volume identify many areas of China's economy in which official intervention is no more intrusive than in many leading market economies. The planning, financing, and implementation of capital formation, which absorbs over 40% of aggregate

[32]"As the pump prices were not rising as fast as global crude markets, so firms responded by cutting down on domestic supplies while boosting exports" (Zhan, 2006b).

expenditure, represents the biggest exception to this observation. The institutions surrounding investment behavior pose a considerable threat to China's forward momentum. At the same time, weaknesses in these institutions create opportunities for improvements that can stimulate future productivity growth.

The disproportionate role of the state sector in investment spending is widely understood. Despite their declining output share and consistently low profitability (Table 8), state-owned units absorbed one-third of investment funds in 2005 (Yearbook, 2006, p. 187). As Allen, Qian, and Qian point out in Chapter 14, bank loans, share offerings, and bond issues flow mainly to state-controlled entities. The unfortunate consequences of extensive official involvement in investment decisions are well documented. Even after 25 years of reform, Table 9 shows that investment spending displays Soviet-style seasonality, with low activity during the

Table 9. Completed investment in fixed assets: monthly share of annual total.

	1975	1990	2000	2002	2003	2004	2005
January/February	6.4	3.4	3.9	4.3	4.5	5.6	5.6
March	5.1	4.9	5.3	5.6	6.0	6.4	6.4
April	6.0	5.2	5.7	6.5	6.5	6.8	6.6
May	7.2	6.2	6.7	7.5	7.8	7.5	7.6
June	9.1	8.6	9.5	9.8	10.5	10.9	11.0
July	7.4	7.5	7.6	8.2	8.6	9.0	8.9
August	7.3	7.2	7.5	8.3	8.5	8.6	8.7
September	8.9	8.7	9.4	9.9	9.7	10.0	10.1
October	8.0	8.7	9.1	9.4	9.3	9.4	9.4
November	9.8	9.5	10.3	9.9	9.7	9.8	9.9
December	24.8	30.1	25.0	20.7	18.8	15.9	15.8
Q1&Q2	33.8	28.3	31.1	33.7	35.3	37.3	37.2
Q4	42.6	48.3	44.4	39.9	37.8	35.1	35.1

Sources: *Fixed Asset Yearbook* (1997, p. 77); *China Monthly Economic Indicators* (2001, 1, p. 36; 2003, 2, p. 32; 2003, 12, p. 32; various issues for 2004–2005); *China Monthly Statistics* (various issues, 2005–2006); http://www.stats.gov.cn/was40/detail (accessed March 25, 2004).

Note: Values are in percent.

first quarter, minipeaks in June and September, and a fourth-quarter rush. Chinese sources provide a flood of anecdotes chronicling poor investment decisions. Zhang Hanya, secretary general of the China Investment Association, reports a failure rate of 42% for medium- and large-scale projects during the eighth five-year plan period (1991–1995) (Gao *et al.*, 2004). Failed investment efforts often arise because "local governments and officials ... invest in 'image projects' ... to enhance their performance record" (GDP, 2004).

Recent studies deploy firm-level industrial data to explore the macroeconomic consequences of China's largely unreformed investment system. Using data from more than 100,000 enterprises, Hsieh and Klenow (2006) find that equalizing the marginal product of labor and capital across enterprises within specific four-digit industries could raise output by approximately 100%.

Dollar and Wei (2006) employ a smaller data set, but focus precisely on the link between ownership and returns to capital. Preliminary results show that "the average return to capital is more than 50% higher for private firms [and also for foreign-invested enterprises] than for wholly state-owned firms ... [These results] suggest that state-ownership is systematically associated with lower returns to capital."

It is evident that reductions in state ownership and official intervention in the economy, particularly in the realm of investment decisions, have the potential to propel substanlial productivity gains over the coming decades. The benefits of an improved investment mechanism extend far beyond reducing the number of failed projects and the scale of bad debt. Policies that channel investment funds to state-sector projects and artificially reduce interest rates to improve the profitability of state-sector borrowers are largely responsible for the slow pace of job creation visible since 1995 (Rawski, 2006).[33]

Despite these difficulties, important steps have moved China's economy toward greater commercialization of investment, by which we mean

[33]A government economist finds that, on average, investment outlays per new job amount to RMB220,000 in large enterprises, RMB120,000 in medium-sized firms, but only RMB80,000 at small companies (SMEs), so that "promoting SMEs will be more cost effective in job creation" (Zhao, 2002).

a structure in which decisions governing investment outlays rest primarily in the hands of decision makers whose choices reflect the costs and likely returns to alternative allocations of funds. Substantial privatization has placed increasing shares of assets and profits under the control of profit-seeking entrepreneurs and managers. Removing restrictions on the sale of formerly non-tradable corporate shares, while still incomplete, represents another important advance. Ongoing expansion of the market for corporate ownership rights is also highly significant. Business mergers and acquisitions, which increasingly cut across sector, provincial, and national boundaries, can activate assets formerly trapped in low-yielding circumstances.

The emerging agenda for China's State Asset Supervision and Administration Commission (SASAC), established in 2003, represents another significant development. SASAC's objective is to represent the state's interest as the owner and investor in over 150 centrally controlled state enterprises, including China's large "petroleum, petrochemical, electricity, automobile, and telecom enterprises, as well as those that evolved from the old military industry ministries, Chinese government conglomerates based in Hong Kong, the big state-trading and import–export companies, specialized construction companies and research institutes, and quite a few high-tech enterprises including Great Wall Computer and Alcatel Shanghai Bell" (Naughton, 2003, p. 3). Provincial and local commissions will perform similar functions at lower levels of government. This initiative may eliminate longstanding difficulties arising from the absence of any effective agent to implement ownership of state enterprises by "all the people." SASAC, which "formulates its agenda in terms that a Wall Street investment banker would understand," aspires to collect dividends from profitable state enterprises, channel these funds into a capital management budget, and gradually shift the management of state ownership interests into the hands of public companies operated by investment specialists (Naughton, 2005, p. 7; 2006).

Recent initiatives at both the central and local levels illustrate the potential productivity benefits of implementing these ambitious plans. In addition to managing the government's interest in centrally controlled state firms, the national SASAC has systematized procedures for management buyouts at provincial and local state enterprises, enhanced the marketability of shares in state firms, expanded listings of state-controlled enterprises, announced plans to accelerate bankruptcies, and supported M&A activity involving centrally controlled firms in the energy and electronics sectors, among others (Li, 2005; Naughton, 2005, 2006; Wang Ying, 2005, 2006a, b). At the local level, Shenyang's municipal SASAC "plans to sell a 49% stake in China's top machine tool manufacturer, Shenyang Machine Tool Group "… to diversify the company's ownership and improve its competitiveness" (Wu, 2006).

Reforming the financial sector

Along with the actions of SASAC and other official agencies, the progress of reform efforts in China's financial and legal systems is likely to exert a powerful influence on the outcome of efforts to improve the quality of day-to-day economic decision making.

We see three levels at which fundamental change in China's financial sector can improve the prospects for sustained productivity growth: cleaning up bank balance sheets, promoting entry and reform to increase the range and quality of financial services offered to Chinese firms and households, and removing politics from the allocation of financial resources.

Chapter 14 by Allen, Qian, and Qian chronicles the recent decline in the share of non-performing loans in the banking system. Whatever the exact level of bad loans, preventing the future accumulation of non-performing debt is a key reform objective. Japan's recent experience illustrates the danger associated with high levels of bad loans. Japan's floundering banks sought to protect their weak balance sheets by propping up heavily indebted clients with additional loans while denying credit to potentially dynamic start-up companies. The result was a decade and a half of near stagnation for Japan's economy. With state firms, including many weaklings, absorbing huge amounts of capital and private companies pushed to the margins of the formal financial system (see Chapter 14 in this volume), China's economy could drift into comparable difficulties. To avoid such dangers, China needs to commercialize its financial markets by dismantling long-standing arrangements that favor state firms with preferential access to bank loans and preferential opportunities to tap domestic and international stock and bond markets. The productivity and employment benefits associated with these reforms (and the cost of inaction) will increase as the economy becomes more complex.

Improving the scope and quality of financial services by expanding entry and upgrading existing institutions can provide important support for raising productivity growth during the coming decades. Two key measures have opened the door to long-term development of China's weak financial sector. China's entry into the WTO included a promise to offer national treatment to foreign banks, investment firms, and insurance companies, China's subsequent decision to sell equity stakes in key financial institutions to international firms ensures the implementation of this promise by installing global leaders of international finance within the core of China's financial sector. By selling equity stakes in China's largest banks and insurance companies, China's leaders have implicitly acknowledged both the central importance of commercializing the financial sector and the inadequacy of their own prior reform efforts.

The injection of global financial heavyweights and offshore reporting requirements into key banks and insurance firms should increase pressures to control the fraud and embezzlement that have plagued China's financial sector. Even more important than curbing criminality is the effort to install business rather than politics as the foundation for allocating funds. This will entail rolling back longstanding arrangements under which offices of the Communist Party selected the officers of financial institutions, government quota systems controlled access to stock market listings, "high-risk financial projects ... ended up getting bank loans, usually under orders from government departments," and local bank offices, "with little choice, frequently ignored routine risk calculations and limits on the size of loans ... at the behest of party and government officials" (Sender, 2004; Gao, 2005).

Past efforts to improve China's financial system "have done enough *not* to slow down the growth of the economy" (see Chapter 14, section "Summary and Concluding Remarks"). Looking forward, this minimal standard is unlikely to suffice. China's financial system falls far short of arrangements that can offer positive support to (rather than merely permitting) sustained growth of output and TFP.

Recent changes have pushed China's financial system in the right direction. The weak starting point provides ample opportunities for productivity-enhancing improvements in performance. To underwrite continued growth and productivity increase, China needs to raise its financial sector to the level currently operating in Korea and Taiwan. This is not a high standard. Achievement of this outcome — or better yet, one that matches the considerably more effective financial mechanisms currently operating in Hong Kong and Singapore — depends most of all on China's success in wringing politics out of lending and investment decisions.

Strengthening the legal system

Chapter 11 on law recounts many flaws in China's legal, judicial, and enforcement regimes. The question of how China's economy developed so fast in the face of these weaknesses remains open. Perhaps economists overstate the importance of having governments enforce property rights and uphold contract provisions. Perhaps flaws in China's legal system are less costly than they appear from outside. Perhaps, as both the law and finance papers suggest, Chinese participants have developed alternative mechanisms that partially replace what theorists regard as essential institutional arrangements. The extensive participation of China-based firms in cross-national networks of manufacturing, finance, research, and design demonstrates that, whatever its shortcomings, China's legal system has not decisively blocked national development to date, nor has it prevented Chinese firms from joining in increasingly complex webs of transactions. At the same time, we cannot doubt that weaknesses of the legal system, beginning with such elementary matters as employers (including government-run firms) refusing to pay wages or electricity purchase agreements being "scrapped because local governments felt that the original contracts were too expensive," impose very large costs on China's economy (Xie, 2005; Defaulting, 2006).

Two areas, intellectual property rights (IPR) and disposition of business property, stand out as particularly important for China's long-term growth prospects. Although the active involvement of official agencies makes the extent of Chinese technological piracy quite unusual,[34] developing nations, including the United States, have typically ignored IPR enforcement at early stages of their growth. The reason is obvious: for nations with little in the way of intellectual property, the benefits of piracy outweigh the cost to domestic innovators.

The rapid expansion of domestic R&D spending described in Chapter 9 on science and technology, together with China's growing success in attracting R&D operations from foreign companies, means that the value of domestic intellectual property, and therefore the potential cost of weak IPR protection, has entered a steep upward trajectory. As more and more Chinese firms join the "battle against pirates and counterfeiters" and Chinese innovators focus on "strengthening … defenses … [against] other enterprises … copying … technology … without paying any royalties," the future course of public policy seems clear (Liu Weiling, 2005a, b).

Rapid intensification of official efforts to curb IPR violations appears to have begun. Official regulations have outlawed the installation of pirated software in government offices and, most recently, in newly manufactured computers (Poon, 2006). IPR enforcement is emerging as a new dimension of competition among localities. Beijing's municipal government has ordered enterprises to use authentic computer software and plans to establish a hotline to receive IPR complaints, while Guangdong plans to "redouble efforts to improve the system for technological innovations while improving measures to protect intellectual property rights" (Guan, 2006; Zhan, 2006a). Initial results impress often critical foreign media, which note that "China Moves From Piracy to Patents" and that "China Makes Genuine Progress Against Sellers of Fakes" (Ortolani, 2005; Dickie and Minder, 2006).

The disposition of assets for firms undergoing bankruptcy or restructuring is equally important, especially because these categories encompass large numbers of firms and large amounts of assets. The emergence of national and regional SASAC agendas for the management of

---

[34] During the late 1980s, for example, one of the authors encountered a pirated version of an American company's virus-detection software distributed by China's Ministry of Public Security.

state-owned assets represents an important advance, as does the expansion of mergers and acquisitions based on commercial criteria rather than official decisions. Despite these gains, the commercialization of firms now trapped in bureaucratically controlled enterprise groups (*jituan*) holds the prospect of considerable gains in productivity.[35]

It is too early to tell whether China's new bankruptcy law, which took effect in June 2007, will establish a system in which legal precepts rather than official preferences govern the timing of bankruptcy declarations and the disposition of assets held by bankrupt firms. In North America and the European Union, these decisions are made by the firms involved subject to rules set down by the legislature and enforced by an independent and competent judicial system or by independent regulatory bodies. In China, as in much of East and Southeast Asia, these decisions are often made by the executive branch of the government. The courts lack the independence, competence, and authority to determine and enforce the resolution of issues surrounding bankruptcies, mergers, or acquisitions.

The central point here is that the absence of competent and effective judicial or regulatory processes pushes such decisions into the hands of government or party administrators in spite of the high costs associated with official intervention in business decisions. As Perkins (2004) argues, efforts to establish an independent judiciary as the chief arbiter of issues surrounding the disposition of business property will hasten the improvement of corporate governance and the protection of minority shareholder interests, both of which can contribute to future productivity growth.

V. Do Social Issues Pose Major Obstacles to China's Development?

In addition to possible political instability, numerous observers suggest that social issues could pose major obstructions to China's future growth

---

[35] A 2005 visit to a Chinese firm listed on the Hong Kong stock exchange revealed a passive operation completely dependent on instructions from group headquarters. This firm had no discretion over the selection of component suppliers or the disposition of its output. Despite rapidly eroding demand for its main product, the company was not permitted to develop a substitute, because the group headquarters had assigned that task to another enterprise (Interview, July 2005).

(e.g., Wolf *et al.*, 2003; Pei, 2006). We focus successively on public health and environment.

Public health

The SARS scare of 2002–2003 and the longer-term issues surrounding AIDS/HIV have drawn international attention to the limitations of China's public health system. Despite many shortcomings, China's response to both SARS and AIDS/HIV suggests that health authorities have sufficient administrative and financial resources to prevent threats to public health from inflicting severe damage on China's economic prospects.

In the case of SARS, crude but effective official and community action rapidly defused a potentially dangerous situation by curtailing interaction between suspected disease carriers and the general public. Following the collapse of initial efforts to deny the spread of this disease, the official response shifted to "massive, swift, and concentrated action from the center. Strong quarantine measures were introduced, and SARS 'bounties' were paid to help in contact and case finding. The Health Minister was sacked and epidemic monitoring systems tightened up" (Ma *et al.*, 2006, p. 289). Economic damage, though substantial, was confined to the first half of 2003, after which rapid growth resumed (Rawski, 2005).

The official Chinese response to HIV/AIDS followed the same sequence of denial followed by strong action to limit the spread of disease. Recent policy measures include steeply rising appropriations for combating HIV/AIDS; efforts to expand the availability and reduce the cost of medications; investigation and regulation of blood collection networks; imposition of compulsory premarital health checks in Yunnan, the province most seriously affected; and limited offers of free testing and treatment (Ma, 2005; Wu and Sullivan, 2005; Ma *et al.*, 2006; Yunnan, 2006; Zhang, 2006).

Specialists agree that this disease could spread to as many as "10 million infected over the next decade *in the absence of effective measures*" (Ma *et al.*, 2006, p. 289; italics in original). They also report that in 2002 "the Chinese government succeeded in reducing the cost of annual antiretroviral treatment … to US$4,000–5,000 … with significant price reductions … since 2003" (Ma *et al.*, 2006, p. 293).

We can crudely reckon the direct cost of treating HIV/AIDS under worst-case assumptions: 10 million HIV/AIDS victims with the government bearing the full annual treatment costs of US$5,000 per person. At RMB7.5 per dollar, the annual cost becomes RMB375 billion. Although spending of this magnitude would impose substantial pressure on official budgets, Chinas government, which increased its revenues by RMB525 billion during 2004–2005 alone, is fully capable of mobilizing funds on this scale without major economic disruption.

We conclude that public health issues, barring some worldwide health catastrophe on the model of the 1918 pandemic or worse, are unlikely to impose major obstacles to the growth of China's economy during the coming decades.

Environment

Environmental issues are widely seen as possible barriers to future growth. The questions that matter for our forecast of the future are whether cleaning up the undoubtedly widespread environmental degradation will cost so much that it will cut significantly into investment in new production or whether that degradation will reduce the health of the labor force enough to materially influence the labor force's contribution to growth. We focus on issues surrounding air quality and water supply.

Focusing on urban air quality, Roumasset, Burnett, and Wang find declining levels of particulates and sulfur dioxide and conclude that "the statistical picture of pollution trends contrasts starkly with bleak qualitative reports" (see Chapter 8). Rawski and Sheng (2007) provide evidence that concentrations of dust and soot outside major cities reached a peak around 2000 and subsequently began to decline, suggesting a general trend toward improved air quality.

International comparison of trends in urban concentrations of particulates and sulfur dioxide can provide historical perspective on Chinese air quality. Figure 3 compares trends in concentrations of sulfur dioxide in major Chinese cities with circumstances in the United States, Japan, and Korea. The average for Chinese major cities consistently falls below the readings for Tokyo in 1968, for Seoul in 1990, and in recent years, for New York in 1972. The Chinese average for 1984 matches the 1984

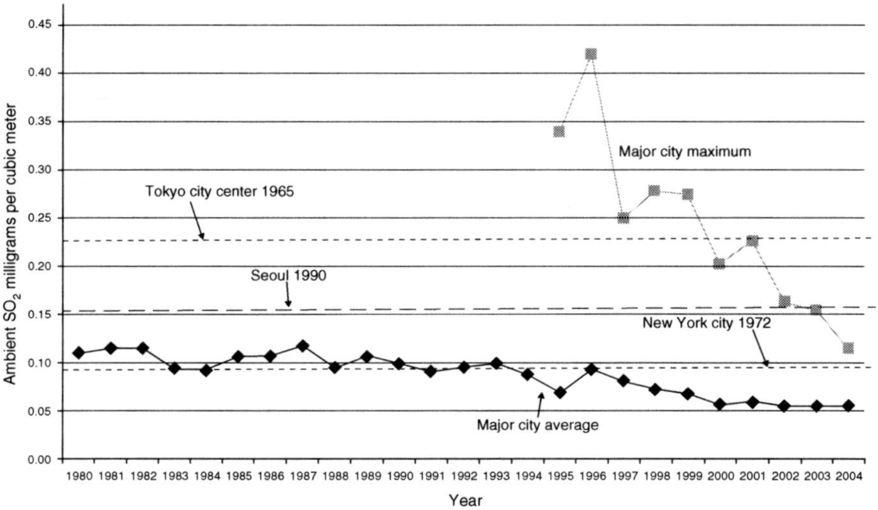

Figure 3. China: SO_2 levels in major urban areas, 1980–2004, with international comparisons.

reading for Pittsburgh, which was named "America's most livable city" in the following year. Even the worst of major Chinese cities now reports lower concentrations of SO_2 than Tokyo in 1965 or Seoul in 1990. These observations demonstrate that air quality in major Chinese cities, although well below current standards in today's rich nations, can hardly pose unprecedented hazards to human health or economic growth.

Cross-national data for total suspended particulates (TSP) reinforce the observation that the magnitude of Chinese urban air pollution is not unusual. Figure 4 plots primary-sector labor force shares for China, Japan, and Korea against urban TSP concentration for Tokyo, Kitakyushu, and Seoul and compares these observations with the arithmetic average of readings for approximately 30 major Chinese cities. The share of the primary sector (mainly agriculture) in the national labor force is a standard development indicator that declines with rising levels of per capita income.

Each series shows a declining trend in atmospheric concentration of particulates. In Japan, the decline begins when the primary-sector labor force share stands in the range of 20–30%. In Korea, the decline starts with primary labor share in the 25% range. In China, by contrast, ambient concentrations of TSP begin their downward march much earlier in the

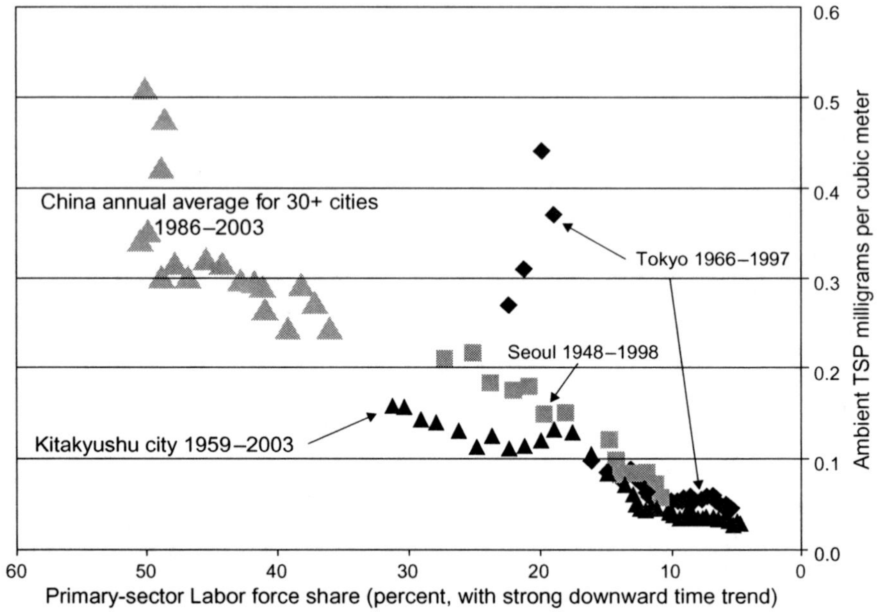

Figure 4. Primary labor force share versus urban TSP concentration.

development process, when the share of primary-sector workers in the national labor force is approximately 50%.[36] These data indicate that the spread of new technologies and especially of awareness about the damaging effects of pollution have prompted China to move toward abatement of urban air pollution at an earlier stage of the development process than occurred in Japan or Korea.

While air quality appears to be improving, China's greatest difficulties with water lie in the future. Elizabeth Economy notes that "[f]or many regions in China, diminishing water supplies pose today's greatest social, economic, and political challenges … the Ministry of Water Resources predicts a 'serious water crisis' in 2030, when … China's per capita water resources are estimated to decline to the World Bank's scarcity level" of 2,000 cubic meters per capita per year from the 2005

[36]The Chinese data on primary-sector labor force share in Figure 4 come from Chapter 17. Use of official Chinese labor data, which appear to overstate the share of primary sector workers, would accentuate the observations in the text.

level of roughly 2,150 (Economy, 2004, pp. 67–68; Yearbook, 2006, p. 412). With water tables falling, 400 of 660 cities reporting water shortages, and over 100, including the capital, reporting "very severe" supply problems, it is evident that current arrangements are not sustainable (Water, 2005).

China's water resources are unevenly distributed, with available supplies concentrated in the south, while northern regions cope with extreme supply limitations. One study indicates that 1993 levels of per capita water resources are at 225–356 cubic meters per person for North China's major river basins (Wolf *et al.*, 2003, p. 78). Although these figures may be too low, data for 2005 show 10 province-level units with per capita water resources less than 1,000 cubic meters. These water-short regions, which include the two most populous provinces, Henan and Shandong, as well as Beijing, Tianjin, and Shanghai, account for 34.8% of China's population (Yearbook, 2006, pp. 101, 412). With urbanization and industrialization generating higher levels of waterborne effluents, the water-short areas confront growing difficulty with the quality as well as the quantity of water.

Statistics on water usage show a steep tilt toward agriculture. In 2004, the farm sector absorbed 65% of total water consumption.[37]

Price increases, structural change, and regulatory controls can help save water. Nationwide data show the average price of water rising from RMB1.63 to RMB3.61 per cubic meter between 1993 and 2001 for agricultural use and from RMB8.2–8.7 to RMB22.8–24 for household and industrial use between 1994 and 2001 (Liu Wei, 2005, p. 217). In Beijing, "the current price is 3.7 yuan … more than 30 times the price in 1991" (Xin, 2006). With the Minister of Water Resources insisting that water prices "must be used as a major way" to promote efficient usage, further increases seem inevitable.

Water usage declined from 537 to 465 tons per RMB10,000 of GDP between 2002 and 2003, but these figures are "about four times the global average" (Zhao, 2004; Liang, 2005). This decline may persist as development shifts output and employment toward services and away from

[37]Li (2006). Wolf (2003, p. 78) cites data showing that agriculture absorbed 77–78% of overall water consumption in 1993.

farming and water-intensive manufacturing industries. Policymakers have also imposed "Norms of Water Intake" to "mandate rational and efficient use of water" in seven water-intensive industries (Zhao, 2004).

Each of these measures promises important benefits. However, the dominant share of agriculture in water consumption and the difficulty of collecting water fees from farm operators[38] mean that an effective response to growing water shortages will almost certainly include substantial reductions in farmland and agricultural employment, particularly in North China. Compulsory shrinkage of farm activity has also begun: Chicheng county, Hebei, which "provides almost half the water for Miyun Reservoir" in nearby Beijing, shifted cultivated acreage from rice to corn and "dropped sheep grazing ... to ... only a quarter" of the 2001 figure "in a bid to provide abundant water resources for Beijing" (Yang, 2006).

In environmental matters, as in the health sector, cost is not a major issue. News that anticipated costs for the initial phase of "China's massive south–north water diversion scheme" would rise "by around 80% ... to a total 225 billion yuan," with "the entire project ... expected to cost 500 billion yuan ... before 2050" appeared as a routine announcement that reflected no sign of alarm (Diversion, 2006). A figure of 500 billion yuan spread out over one decade would amount to roughly 0.4% of average annual gross capital formation each year and spread over two decades would be less than 0.2% of gross capital formation each year.[39]

Table 10 shows that annual investment in remediation and prevention of pollution, which does not include expenditures on water

---

[38]Liu Wei cites a 2002 report from the Ministry of Water Resources, noting that "in the past three years," presumably referring to 1999–2001, "50 of 100 water authorities collected at least 75% of fees imposed on agricultural water users, 30 attained a collection rate of 50–75%, and 20 collected less than half of the user fees. Among urban units, the collected rate exceeds 90%" (2005, p. 220).

[39]Chinese gross capital formation in 2005 was 7,956 billion yuan. If it grew at 7% a year for two decades, it would reach over 30,000 billion yuan in 2025. Gross capital formation throughout the period would average around 16,000 billion yuan per year. Five hundred billion yuan spread over ten years would be 50 billion per year and over twenty years 25 billion yuan per year.

Table 10. Investment in prevention and remediation of environmental pollution, 1991–2005.

	1991	1995	2000	2005
Environmental investment	17.0	30.7	101.5	238.8
As percent of GDP	0.84	0.68	1.13	1.30
As percent of annual investment	3.09	1.88	3.08	2.69

Sources: Data for 1991 and 1994 from Vermeer (1998, p. 956). Data for 2000 and 2005 from Yearbook (2004, p. 454; 2006, pp. 189, 444).

Notes: Values are in billion current yuan and percent; annual GDP and investment are in current prices.

diversion projects, has jumped from under 1% of GDP in the early and mid-1990s to 1.1–1.3% in 2004–2005, figures that approach comparable totals for the United States, Japan, and Germany around 1990, when annual spending on environmental protection and pollution control ranged from 1.3 to 1.8% of GI5P (O'Connor, 1994, pp. 177–178). For China, these outlays amount to no more than 3% of annual investment spending. Although these are sizable figures, high levels of current and projected future saving and investment mean that China's economy can easily support a much larger burden of expenditure on environmental remediation without endangering its prospects for rapid growth of output and productivity.

What of the possible impact of global warming on China's development prospects? When and if global warming leads to a major rise in the sea level, China, along with many other nations, will face large expenditures to move people out of flooded areas, notably in the lower reaches of the Yangzi River, or to build dikes to protect low-lying coastal cities. Of greater relevance to the next two decades, the challenge for China, and for other nations, is to restrict CO_2 emissions so that the worst effects of global warming do not occur. Success in this regard will eliminate the need for remedial investments to control coastal flooding. Efforts to limit CO_2 emissions mainly involve improving the efficiency of energy use, an area in which China lags far behind international best practice. Japan's successful efforts to raise energy efficiency did not damage its economic prospects. We see no reason to expect similar conservation efforts to undermine Chinese economic growth.

We conclude that issues surrounding public health and environment, while confronting China's policymakers with a broad array of complex and difficult problems, seem unlikely to pose fundamental obstacles leading to downward revision of China's prospects for economic growth between now and 2025.

The demand side of the sources of growth

Most of the discussion in this chapter has approached the question of future growth from the supply side of the issue. But there are also elements on the demand side that will determine whether or not China will be able to sustain rapid growth over the next one to two decades. The contributions of the main expenditure categories to annual growth in China since 1979 are presented in Figures 5 and 6. There are two trends worthy of note in these figures. The first is that household consumption as a share of GDP declined steadily over time and came to just under 40% GDP in 2004 and 2005. The change in household consumption as a share of the change in GDP also fluctuated around a declining trend line and fell to a very small level below 30% of the increment to GDP in the years after 2001. The change in

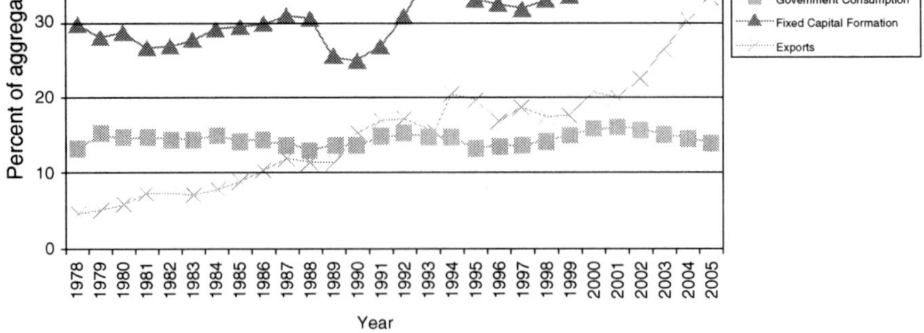

Figure 5. Principle components of GDP expenditure, 1978–2005.

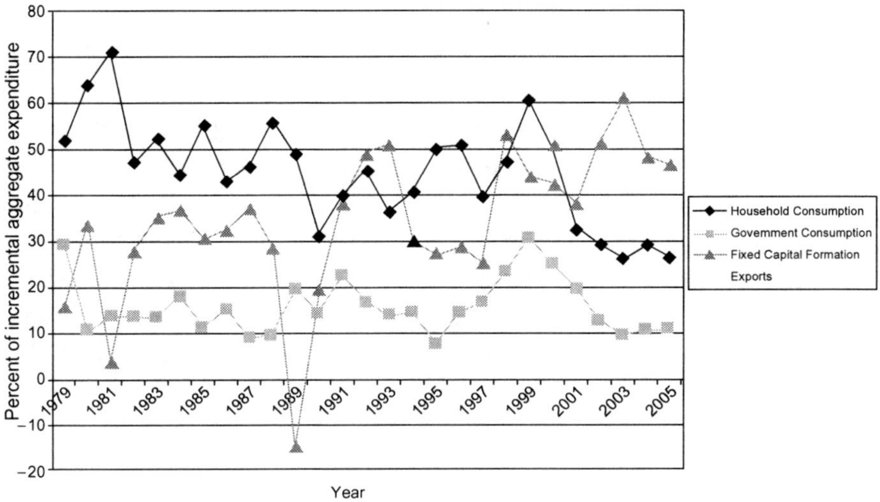

Figure 6. Principle components of incremental expenditure on GDP, 1978/1979–2004/2005.

government consumption as a share of the change in GDP fluctuated year to year as well, peaking in the late 1990s when, as discussed earlier in this chapter, the Chinese government pump primed in an effort to keep the financial crisis of those years from depressing the growth rate of GDP.

The most notable trend in these charts, however, is that the annual change in exports accounted for a rising share of incremental expenditure on GDP and in the years 2003–2005 accounted for over half of that change in GDP. Put differently, without the extraordinarily rapid growth of exports in recent years, China very likely would have experienced a shortage of aggregate demand, and, unless the government had taken steps to prime the pump as in 1997–1999, the growth rate of GDP would have fallen markedly because of inadequate aggregate demand.

This contribution of the annual rise in exports to GDP was achieved thanks to a growth rate of exports over the past decade that averaged 17.7% per year (2005/1995) and averaged 29.9% per year over the last five years (2005/2000). There is a large import component to these exports, so the net impact on aggregate demand is moderated, but the point remains — Chinese growth in recent years has been highly dependent on an unusually high export growth rate.

It is highly unlikely that an export rate of growth of this magnitude can be sustained for even one more decade let alone two decades. Exports in 2005 reached US$762 billion. At a growth rate of 15% per year, lower than the average of the past ten years, exports in 2015 would reach US$3 trillion and would by then be growing at US$450 billion per year. China's factories could probably produce this many toys, shoes, textiles, computers, cars, and television sets per year, but where would they find the markets for these goods? And if they could find the markets, would the importing countries tolerate for long the rapid adjustment that accommodating this massive import surge would require? This seems highly unlikely.

If China needs to sustain high export growth rates for exports to continue to be a main source of growth in GDP from the demand side, how high would that export growth rate have to be? If one assumes that GDP continues to grow at 9% a year over the next decade (or in current prices 12% per year with inflation at 3% annually), then a growth rate of exports (in current prices) at 12% a year would produce an annual increment to aggregate demand equal to around a quarter of Chinese GDP in the year 2014.[40] An export growth rate of 7% a year (in current prices), in contrast, would contribute only about one-tenth of the increment to GDP in the year 2014. For exports to be a major element in sustaining aggregate demand, therefore, they will have to grow at something like 9% per year in real terms or 12% annually in nominal terms. Total exports at that rate would reach nearly US$2 trillion by the year 2015, for an average annual increase of more than US$200 billion. Achieving even this lower figure will be a major challenge.

China, therefore, is probably going to have to find a way to stimulate domestic demand as the export share of increments to aggregate demand declines. How it achieves this shift inward in demand, however, could have a major impact on whether the country will be able to sustain a high GDP rate of growth over the next one to two decades. If demand has to be supported as it was in 1997–1999 by government running a fiscal deficit in order to fund expanded government consumption plus state investment

[40] These calculations used the recently revised GDP figure for 2004 of RMB15,988 billion yuan (National Bureau of Statistics, 2005b).

in road and airport construction across the country, sustained productivity growth at high rates seems unlikely. High productivity growth is more likely to come from a higher growth rate (and a higher share of GDP) of consumer spending that in turn stimulates a higher or at least high growth rate in private investment. This chapter is not the place to outline the policies required to stimulate this increase in consumer demand, but it is an achievable goal.

VI. Conclusion

Our objective in this chapter has been to forecast the broad outlines of Chinese economic growth to the year 2025. The central ingredients in our forecast are analyses of the likely path of factor inputs (labor, human capital, and physical capital) and, of most importance, TFP.

We began by reviewing the performance of China's economy between 1952 and 2005. During China's plan era (roughly, 1952–1978), GDP growth was sustained almost entirely by increases in capital and labor inputs with TFP actually at negative levels during the two decades 1957–1978. Beginning in the late 1970s, China's turn to economic reform brought dramatic change, with productivity emerging as a key driver of accelerated growth, both directly and, through its stimulus to the acceleration of capital formation, indirectly. TFP recorded average annual growth of 3.8% between 1978 and 2005, with the pace slackening somewhat during the final decade.

We then used straightforward and, we believe, uncontroversial assumptions to project the growth of fixed capital, labor, and education to 2025. These projections show that the growth of labor, capital, and education alone can propel China's GDP growth at a maximum rate of less than 5% during 2005–2025, well below the average rate of 9.5% recorded during 1978–2005.

We then focus on productivity, beginning with the TFP implications underlying assumed annual GDP growth of 6 or 9% between 2005 and 2025. Because the productivity expansion required to support 9% annual growth seems unrealistically high (it is higher than what was achieved during 1978–2005), we focus on the likelihood that China can attain sufficient TFP growth to drive the economy forward at an average annual rate in the neighborhood of 6–8% during the two decades ending in 2025. That range does seem feasible over the next decade to 2015, but the upper end of this range appears to be unrealistically high for the entirety of the second decade from 2016 to 2025.

There are two reasons for our conclusion that the likely range of growth rates in this second decade falls between 5 and 7% per year. First, the rate of TFP required to sustain a growth rate of 8% is higher than the TFP rate sustained by China during 1978–2005 and much higher than TFP growth during 1995–2005. Second, the three economies that in earlier times were most like China's economy today (Japan, South Korea, and Taiwan) each sustained a growth rate for several decades similar to that achieved by China from 1979 through 2005, but each saw the rate of GDP growth rate fall sharply when per capita GDP rose above $13,000 measured in 2005 prices, using the PPP method. China's current per capita GDP in PPP terms is roughly $6,600 and, at a per capita growth rate of 6–7% a year, will surpass $13,000 in 10 to 12 years.

These projections assume that China continues to enjoy a stable domestic and international political environment over these next two decades. But even if the political environment is stable, growth rates in the 6–8% range in 2006–2015 and in the 5–7% range in 2016–2025 are not a sure thing. These rates, even the lower end of the ranges, assume that China will continue to pursue economic reform and will maintain a high rate of savings and investment throughout these two decades. That China will sustain a high rate of investment or capital formation will not be seen as controversial by most economists who study the Chinese economy. Our belief that Chinese TFP will continue to grow at a high rate is likely to be more controversial.

In addition to dividing the sources of growth between factor inputs and TFP, one can also look at future growth prospects in terms of moving to the production possibility frontier and moving that frontier outward. Capital formation moves the frontier outward by expanding old industries and starting new ones. R&D expenditures also move the frontier outward and protection of IPRs is one way of ensuring that innovators have the incentive to develop new products and new ways of producing old products. Protecting IPRs in turn requires a legal system that is equitable, efficient, and can enforce its judgments — conditions that do not exist today. As we have shown above, however, China is clearly taking strides to raise R&D, protect IPRs, and strengthen the legal system, but there is a long way for China to travel before it has a system that compares in these areas with the more advanced industrial and postindustrial economies. Having a long way to go means that the expansion outward of the production frontier would slow in the absence of vigorous pursuit of reform in these areas, but it also means that the frontier will keep moving outward if China continues to strengthen its R&D together with steady improvement in the incentives for innovation and the capacity of the legal system to enforce those incentives.

Many of China's potential sources for continued productivity growth come not from moving the production frontier outward, but through moving toward the existing frontier from its current position that is well inside that frontier. Certain reforms discussed in this chapter and in other chapters in this book will play a central role in this regard. The two that we have emphasized in this chapter are the reform of ownership and finance.

China's productivity prospects will benefit from further reforms aimed at getting the state out of direct ownership and management of industrial and service sector enterprises. State ownership and management is clearly associated with lower rates of return than private ownership and management. China has made a great deal of progress in this regard, but, as in other areas, there is still a long way to go. Furthermore, even where private ownership and management exist, state administrative intervention remains necessary to manage efficiently such critical areas as bankruptcy and mergers and acquisitions. Reducing state administrative intervention, however, requires finding a substitute for administrative regulation in these and other areas, and that brings us back to the need to create and strengthen an independent, fair, and technically competent legal or regulatory system.

Moving toward the frontier depends critically on improving China's financial system. The waste connected with a system of investment allocation that is heavily influenced by politics and rent seeking is enormous. Again China has made progress in this area, but decisions particularly by the state owned banking system are still heavily influenced by politicians.

Other areas discussed briefly in this chapter that involve approaching the frontier include reallocation of labor from low-productivity activities in the rural areas to much more productive work in industry and urban services. We have also looked briefly at the challenge China faces in shifting a larger portion of aggregate demand from dependence on exports to a greater dependence on domestic demand.

Finally, in this chapter, we have looked at shocks to the economic system that could derail economic growth. A period of political instability is in this regard probably the greatest danger to China's continued growth, but the conditions that could bring this about are outside the scope of this book. We do, however, consider other potential shocks to the system, such as a major health crisis prompted by a pandemic, such as what might occur with SARS or H5N1 Avian Flu or if HIV/AIDS becomes more prevalent in the population. Some have suggested that China's current environmental situation could be a shock to the system that derails growth, but to do so the cost of cleaning up the environment would have to cut deeply into total capital formation and in China, as we have shown, this is unlikely to be the case. Even the severe water problems of North China and the cost of transferring large amounts of water from the Yangzi River north are well within China's financial capacity.

Our overall belief, therefore, is that China's economy will continue along a path of rapid growth over the next two decades. Our forecast envisions annual growth averaging 6–8% in real terms. While considerably below the 9.5% real growth recorded during 1978–2005, two decades of expansion at rates between 6 and 8% will deliver large increases in the absolute and relative scale of China's economy and in the standard of living available to China's nearly 1.5 billion citizens.

References

Alesina, A, S Ozler, N Roubini, and P Swagel (June 1996). "Political instability and economic growth." *Journal of Economic Growth,* 1(2), pp. 189–211.

Alesina, A and R Perotti (1994). "The Political Economy of Growth: A Review of the Recent Literature." *The World Bank Economic Review,* 8(3), pp. 351–371.

Bank of Korea (2006). *Economic Statistics Yearbook 2006.* Seoul: Bank of Korea.

Barro, RJ (May 1991). "Economic Growth in a Cross Section of Countries." *Quarterly Journal of Economics*, CVI(2), pp. 407–443.

Barro, RJ (1997). *Determinants of Economic Growth: A Cross-Country Empirical Study.* Cambridge, MA: MIT Press.

Bekaert, G, CR Harvey, and C Lundblad (2006). "Financial openness and the Chinese growth experience." Paper presented to the NBER China Working Group Meeting, Cambridge, MA, October 13, 2006.

Bhattasali, D, S Li, and W Martin (2005). *China and the WTO: Accession, Policy Reform, and Poverty Reduction Strategies.* Oxford: Oxford University Press and World Bank.

Bramall, C (1989). *Living Standards in Sichuan, 1931–1978.* London: Contemporary China Institute, School of Oriental and African Studies, University of London.

Census (1990). *Zhongguo 1990 nian renkou pucha ziliao* [Materials from China's *1990 Population Census*]. Beijing: Zhonguo tongji chubanshe.

Census Research (2005). "State Council Population Census Management Office and National Bureau of Statistics, Division of Population and Social Science and Technology Statistics, eds." *2000-nian renkou pucha guojiaji zhongdian keti yanjiu baogao* [Research Report on National-Level Key Topics From the 2000 Population Census]. Beijing: Zhongguo tongji chubanshe.

Chao, L (2005). "Water-Saving More Urgent Than Ever." *China Daily,* May 6, 2005, p. 2.

Chen, H (2006). "Medical Insurance Regulation Benefits Migrant Workers." *China Daily,* May 16, 2006, p. 3.

Chen, K, GH Jefferson, TG Rawski, H Wang, and Y Zheng (1988). "New estimates of fixed investment and capital stock for Chinese slate industry." *China Quarterly,* 114, pp. 243–266.

Ch'i, H-S (1991). *Politics of Disillusionment: The Chinese Communist Party under Deng Xiaoping, 1978–89.* Armonk, New York and London: M. E. Sharpe.

China Monthly Economic Indicators. Beijing.

China Monthly Statistics. Beijing.

deBrauw, A and S Rozelle (March 12, 2004). "Reconciling the returns to education in rural China." Unpublished paper.

Defaulting (2006). "No more wage defaulting." *China Daily,* 4.

Dickie, Mure and Raphael Minder (2006). "China makes genuine progress against sellers of fakes." January 17, 2006, *Financial Times*, p. 6.

Directorate General of Budget, Accounting and Statistics (2005). *Statistical Yearbook of the Republic of China 2004.* Taipei: Directorate General of Budget, Accounting and Statistics.

Diversion (2006). "Water Diversion Project Bill Sees 80% Rise," from www.chinaview.cn. [Accessed December 30, 2006].

Dollar, D and S-J Wei (2006). "Das (Wasted) Kapital: Firm Ownership and Investment Efficiency in China," in NBER China Workshop, Cambridge, MA.

Economy, E (2004). *The River Runs Black: The Environmental Challenge to China's Future.* Ithaca: Cornell University Press.

Feldstein, M (1983), "Domestic Saving and International Capital Movements in the Long Run and the Short Run." *European Economic Review*, 21, pp. 129–151.

Fixed Asset Yearbook (1997). *Zhongguo guding zichan touzi tongji nianjian 1950–1995* [China Yearbook of Fixed Asset Investment 1950–1995], Beijing: Zhongguo tongji chubanshe.

Gao M, S Xisheng, and Z Xing (July 27, 2004). "Zhang Hanya: touzi tizhigaige hexin jiushi fangquan," *Jingji cankaobao* [Economic reference news], from jjckb.xinhuanet.com/www/Article/200472794126-1.shtml [Accessed October 8, 2004].

Gao, P (1985). *Gongye qiye guding zichan guanli* [Fixed Asset Management for Industrial Enterprises]. Taiyuan: Shanxi renmin chubanshe.

Gao, S (2005). "Shifting the government's role." *China Daily,* February 11, 2005, p. 6.

Garnaut, R, L Song, S Tenev, and Y Yao (2005). *China's Ownership Transformation: Process, Outcomes, Prospects.* Washington, DC: International Finance Corporation.

GDP (2004). "GDP not the only goal." *China Daily,* February 17, 2004, p. 6.

Grimm, BT (February 1998). "Price Indexes for Selected Semiconductors, 1974–96." *Survey of Current Business*, from http://bea.gov/bea/an/0298od/maintext.htm [Accessed February 18, 2007].

Heston, A, R Summers, and B Aten (October 1982). *Pernn World Table Version 6.1.* Philadelphia, PA: Center for International Comparisons at the University of Pennsylvania (CICUP).

Holz, C (2003). "'Fast, clear and accurate:' How reliable are Chinese output and economic growth statistics?" *China Quarterly,* 173, pp. 122–163.

Holz, C (March 2006). "China's reform period economic growth: How reliable are Angus Maddison's estimates?" *Review of Income and Wealth*, 52(1), pp. 85–119.

Howe, N and R Jackson (2004). *The Graying of China,* Washington, DC: Center for Strategic and International Studies.

Hsieh, C-T and PJ Klenow (2006). "Misallocation and manufacturing TFP in China and India," in NBER China Workshop, Cambridge, MA.

Hua, S, X Zhang, and H-P Luo (1993). *China: From Revolution to Reform.* Houndmills, Basingstoke, Hampshire, England: Macmillan.

Industry Census (1985). *Zhonghua renmin gongheguo 1985 nian gongye pucha ziliao* [Materials on China's third industrial census in 1985], Vol. 3. Beijing: Zhongguo Tongji chubanshe.

Industry Census (1995). *Zhonghua renmin gongheguo 1995 nian disanci quanguo gongye pucha ziliao hui bian* [Compendium of materials from China's 3rd national industrial census in 1995], general volume. Beijing: Zhongguo tongji chubanshe.

Industry Yearbook (2001). *Zhongguo gongye jingji tongji nianjian 2001* [China Industrial Economy Statistics Yearbook 2001]. Beijing: Zhongguo tongji chubanshe.

Ishikawa, S (1960). *Chûgoku ni okeru shihon chikuseki kikô* [China's mechanism of capital accumulation]. Tokyo: Iwanami Shoten.

Ishikawa, S (1965). *National Income and Capital Formation in Mainland China: An Examination of Official Statistics*. Tokyo: Institute of Asian Economic Affairs.

Ito, T (1992). *The Japanese Economy.* Cambridge, MA: MIT Press.

Jiang, W (2006). "M&As emerge as key drawcard for foreign investment." *China Daily,* September 9–10, 2006, p. 5.

Keidel, A (1992). *How Badly Do China's National Accounts Underestimate China's GNP?* Washington, DC: Rock Creek Research Inc E-8042.

Klein, LR, H Gao and L Tao (2005). "Estimation of China's inflation rate." Draft Paper 2005.

Kojima, R (2002). "On the reliability of China's economic statistics with special reference to GDP." *The Journal of Econometric Study of Northeast Asia,* 4(1), pp. 15–30.

Kraay, A (1996). *A Resilient Residual: Accounting for China's Growth Performance in Light of the Asian Miracle.* Washington, DC: World Bank Policy Research Department.

Kraay, A (2000). "Household Savings in China," *World Bank Economic Review,* 14.3, pp. 545–570.

Kuijs, L (2006). "How Will China's Saving-Investment Balance Evolve?" *World Bank China Office Research Working Paper* 5. Washington, DC: World Bank.

Lardy, NR (2002). "Evaluating Economic Indicators in Post-WTO China." *Issues & Studies,* 38.4–39.1, pp. 249–268.

Lardy, NR (1984). "Consumption and living standards in China, 1978–83," *China Quarterly,* 100, pp. 849–865.

Li, W (2005). "Electronics giants may soon merge." *China Daily,* July 26, 2005, p. 9.

Li, Z (2006). "China issues new regulation on water management, sets fees for usage," from www.worldwatch.org/node/3892. [Accessed January 9, 2007].

Lin, JY, F Cai, and Z Li (2003). *The China Miracle: Development Strategy and Economic Reform,* Revised edn. Hong Kong: Chinese University Press.

Liu, T-C and KC Yeh (1965). *The Economy of the Chinese Mainland: National Income and Economic Development, 1933–1959.* Princeton, NJ: Princeton University Press.

Liu, W (2005). *Zhongguo shui zhidu de jingjixue fenxi* [Economic analysis of China's water system]. Shanghai: Shanghai renmin chubanshe.

Liu, W (2005a). "Bad Medicine." *China Business Weekly,* November 7–13, 2005, p. 9.

Liu, W (2005b). "Prince of Patents." *China Business Weekly,* October 31–November 6, 2005, p. 9.

Ma, L (2005). "Shaanxi Offers Free AIDS Treatment." *China Daily,* July, 15, 2005, p. 3.

Ma, SJ, S Hillier, K-L Zhang, J-J Shen, F Lu, M Liu and C-G Jin (2006). People's Republic of China. In *The HIV Pandemic: Local and Global Implications,* E. J. Beck, N. Mays, A. W. Whiteside, J. M. Zunega, and L.-M. Holland, eds., pp. 282–299. New York and Oxford: Oxford University Press.

Maddison, A (1998). *Chinese Economic Performance in the Long Run.* Paris: Development Centre of the Organisation for Economic Co-operation and Development.

Meng, L and X Wang (2000). "Dui Zhongguo jingji zengzhang tongji shuju kexindu de guji [An evaluation of the reliability of China's statistics on economic growth]," *Jingji yanjiu* [Economic research], 10, pp. 3–13.

Modigliani, F and SL Cao (March 2004). "The Chinese saving puzzle and the life-cycle hypothesis." *Journal of Economic Literature,* XLII, pp. 145–170.

National Bureau of Statistics (1999). *Comprehensive Statistical Data and Materials on 50 Years of New China.* Beijing: China Statistics Press.

National Bureau of Statistics (2005b). "Key Achievements If the First National Economic Census with New Changes of China's GDP Aggregates and Its Structure." Press Release, Beijing, December 20, 2005.

Naughton, B (2003). "The state asset commission: A powerful new government body." *China Leadership Monitor*, 8, 2003, from http://www.hoover.org/publications/clm/issues/2904721.html. [Accessed December 5, 2006].

Naughton, B (2005). "SASAC Rising." *China Leadership Monitor,* 14, 2005, from http://www.hoover.org/publications/clm/issues/2903741.html [Accessed December 6, 2006].

Naughton, B (2006). "Claiming profit for the State: SASAC and the capital management budget." *China Leadership Monitor,* 18, 2006, from http://www.hoover.org/publications/clm/issues/3294311.html [Accessed December 6, 2006].

O'Connor, D and Organisation for Economic Co-operation and Development Centre (1994). *Managing the Environment with Rapid Industrialisation: lessons from the East Asian Experience, Development Centre Studies.* Paris: OECD.

Ohkawa, K and H Rosovsky (1973). *Japanese Economic Growth: Trend Acceleration in the Twentieth Century.* Stanford: Stanford University Press.

Ortolain, A (2005). "China moves from piracy to patents." *Wall Street Journal,* April 7, 2005, p. B4.

Pei, M (2006). *China's Trapped Transition: The Limits of Developmental Autocracy.* Cambridge, MA: Harvard University Press.

Perkins, DH (1966). *Market Control and Planning in Communist China.* Cambridge, MA: Harvard University Press.

Perkins, DH (1980). Issues in the Estimation of China's National Product. In *Quantitative Measures of China's Economic Output,* Alexander Eckstein (ed.), pp. 246–273. Ann Arbor, MI: University of Michigan Press.

Perkins, DH (2004). "Corporate Governance, Industrial Policy, and the Rule of Law." In *Global Change and East Asia Policy Initiatives*, Shahid Yusuf, M. Anjum Altaf, and Kaoru Nabeshima, (eds.), pp. 293–336. Oxford: Oxford University Press and World Bank.

Perkins, DH and L Sabin (2001). Productivity and Structural Change. In *Industrialization and the State: The Changing Role of the Taiwan Government in the Economy, 1945–1998,* Li-min Hsueh, Chen-kuo Hsu, and Dwight H. Perkins (eds.), pp. 151–174. Cambridge, MA: Harvard Institute for International Development.

Poon, T (2006). "China requires legal operating software in PCs." *Wall Street Journal,* p. B3.

Rawski, TG (2001). "What's happening to China's GDP statistics?" *China Economic Review,* 12.4, pp. 347–354.

Rawski, TG (2005). SARS and China's Economy. In *SARS in China: Prelude to Pandemic?* Arthur Kleinman and James L. Watson (eds.), pp. 105–121. Stanford: Stanford University Press.

Rawski, TG (2006). Recent Developments in China's Labor Economy. In *Restructuring China*, Tomoyuki Kojima and Katsuji Nakagane (eds.), pp. 16–47. Tokyo: Toyo Bunko.

Rawski, TG (2006). "Urban air quality in China: Historical and comparative perspectives." Unpublished draft.

Rawski, TG and S Zixia (2007). "Overall trends in China's air quality." Unpublished manuscript.

Ren, R (1997). *China's Economic Performance in an International Perspective*. Paris: OECD.

Sachs, JD and A Warner (1995). "Economic reform and the process of global integration." *Brookings Papers on Economic Activity,* 1, pp. 1–118.

Sender, H (2004). "Chinese banks slowly learn to walk on own." *Wall Street Journal,* July 9, 2004, p. C1, C4.

Shirk, SL (1993). *The Political Logic of Economic Reform in China, California Series on Social Choice and Political Economy; 24.* Berkeley: University of California Press.

Solow, RM (1957). "Technical Change and the Aggregate Production Function." *Review of Economics and Statistics,* 39(3), pp. 312–320.

State Council Economic Census Group (2005). *Diyici quanguo jingji pucha zhuyao shuju gongbao diyihao* [Report #1 of the Main Data from the First National Economic Census]. Issued by the Office of the State Council Leading Small Group for the First National Economic Census and the National Bureau of Statistics, from http://news.xinhuanet.com/fortune/2005-12/06/content_3883969.htm [Accessed December 6, 2005].

Vermeer, EB (December 1998). "Industrial Pollution in China and Remedial Policies." *The China Quarterly*, 156, pp. 952–985. Special issue: China's Environment.

Wang, Y and Y Yao (2001). "Sources of China's economic growth, 1952–99: Incorporating human capital." *World Bank Policy Research Working Paper* 2650. Washington, DC: World Bank.

Wang, Y (2005). "Coal giant bids for Chemical Co." *China Daily,* July 1, 2005, p. 11.

Wang, Y (2006a). "Power companies build portfolios." *China Daily,* September 28, 2006, p. 11.

Wang, Y (2006b). "Sinopec 'buys out subsidiaries'." *China Daily,* February 9, 2006, p. 5.

Water (2005). "New concept wanted to solve water shortage." *China Daily,* May 11, 2005, p. 4.

Wolf, C, Jr., KC Yeh, B Zycher, N Eberstadt, and S-H Lee (2003). *Fault Lines in China's Economic Terrain.* Santa Monica, CA: RAND.

World Bank (1981). *World Development Report 1981: National and International Adjustment*. Washington, DC: World Bank.

World Bank (2007). *World Development Report 2007: Development and the Next Generation*. Washington, DC:

Wu, Y (2006). "Engineering firm seeks investors." *China Daily*, November 28, 2006, p. 10.

Wu, Z and S Sullivan (2005). China, in *Fighting a Rising Tide: The Response to AIDS in East Asia.* T. Yamamoto and S. Itoh (eds.), pp. 76–95. Tokyo: Japan Center for International Exchange.

Xiaofeng, G (2006). "Beijing issues IPR policies for companies." *China Daily,* April 14, 2006, p. 3.

Xie, Y (2005). "Foreign firms quit power sector." *China Daily,* January 20, 2005, p. 11.

Xin, D (2006). "Water conservation helps stop money going down the drain." *China Daily*, September 12, 2006, p. 1.

Xu, D (2005). "Revised GDP for 2004 up by 16.8%." *China Daily,* December 21, 2005, p. 1.

Yang, C (2006). "Storing more water." *China Business Weekly,* September 4–10, 2006, p. 8.

Yearbook, Annual. *Zhongguo tongji nianjian* [China Statistical Year book]. Beijing: China Statistics Press.

You, W and Q Jianguo (2004). "China's Long Term Development Trend and Environmental Economy," *Caimao jingji* [Finance and trade economics]. 10, pp. 11–17.

Young, A (2003). "Gold into base metals: Productivity growth in the People's Republic of China during the reform period." *Journal of Political Economy,* 111, pp. 1220–1261.

Yu, Y (2005). "China's rise, twin surplus, and the change of China's development strategy." Preliminary draft. Institute of World Economics and Politics, Chinese Academy of Social Sciences.

Yunnan (December 2, 2006). "China's worst AIDS-hit province orders compulsory pre-marital HIV tests." *People's Daily Online*, from english.people.com.cn/200612/02(print20061202_327576.html [Accessed December 8, 2006].

Zhan, L (2006a). "Guangdong Vows to Encourage Self-Innovation." *China Daily,* February 28, 2006, p. 3.

Zhan, L (2006b). "No reason to panic over lack of oil in Guangdong." *China Daily,* April 29–30, 2006, p. 2.

Zhang, F (2006). "HIV/AIDS cases grow 30% in China." *China Daily 22 November*, from http://www.chinadaily.com.cn/china/2006-11/22/content_739378.htm [Accessed December 8, 2006].

Zhang, J, W Guiying, and Z Jipeng (2004). "Estimates of tangible capital stock for China's provinces, 1952–2000," *Jingji yanjiu* [Economics Research], 10, pp. 35–44.

Zhang, J, Y Zhao, A Park, and X Song (2005). "Economic returns to schooling in urban China, 1988 to 2001." *Journal of Comparative Economics,* 33, pp. 688–709.

Zhao, H (2004). "Nation forms quota rules to conserve water supply." *China Daily,* October 16–17, 29004, p. 2.

Zhao, X (2002). "Unemployment Aid Needed." *China Daily,* October 31, 2002, p. 4.

Zheng, C, Y Wu, and N Guo (2005). "Rural dwellers to be granted urban rights." *China Daily,* November 2, 2005, p. 3.

Zhu, Z (2006). "Unions help migrant workers win back wages." *China Daily,* January 6, 2006, p. 2.

↜ CHAPTER 10 ↝

CHINA'S INVESTMENT AND GDP GROWTH BOOM: WHEN AND HOW WILL IT END?

I. China's Investment and GDP Growth Boom: When and How Will It End?

East and Southeast Asia, with nearly a third of the world's population, has over the past half-century become the most rapidly growing region in the world. With the exception of the Philippines and Myanmar, all of the economies in the region have experienced at least one decade — and often several decades — of per capita GDP growth rates of 5% a year and more. No other major part of the developing world has experienced anything comparable — whether it is South Asia (despite the recent high growth of India) or Sub-Saharan Africa, or most of Latin America. China's high growth of the past three plus decades is extraordinary in the broader developing country context but is not unique in the East Asian context. Other economies, notably the Republic of Korea (1963–1997) and Taiwan (1961–1997), have grown somewhat longer at rates of 5% per capita or more a year. Korea and Taiwan did not grow as rapidly as China during their high growth period, but Japan grew just as rapidly in the 1950s and 1960s although only for two not three plus decades (Table 1 and Figure 1). China's experience is unique, however, in one respect in that it grew at a very fast 9% rate for a long period starting from a lower per capita income than the other fast developers (Figure 2).

China is also unique in one other respect — it continues to grow at a very high rate and there is no sign to date that this growth rate will slow. But that uniqueness will not last indefinitely. China's GDP per capita growth rate will slow down — the only questions to be answered are: when and how? If growth should continue at current rates for another three decades, China's GDP in 2040 would reach US$80 trillion — five and a

Table 1. Growth rates of GDP per capita in East and Southeast Asia.

	1955–1960	1961–1970	1971–1980	1981–1990	1991–2000	2001–2010
China	4.2	1	4.3	7.7	9.3	9.8
Hong Kong	na	7.7	6.9	5.4	2.3	3.4
Taiwan	3.4	7	7.9	6.4	5.7	2.3
Japan	7.3	9.8	3.3	4	0.9	0.8
Republic of Korea	1.6	5.7	5.4	7.5	5.1	3.7
Mongolia	na	na	3.4	4.2	–0.8	5.1
Indonesia	na	1.8	5.4	4.4	2.7	4
Vietnam	na	na	na	na	5.9	6
Philippines	3	1.8	3.1	–0.9	0.8	2.8
Thailand	2.6	5.1	4.3	5.9	3.5	3.4
Malaysia	1.3*	3.4	5.3	3.1	4.4	2.6
Cambodia	na	na	na	na	na	6.5
Singapore	na	4.4	7.2	4.9	4.6	2.5
Laos	na	na	na	na	3.5	5.4
Brunei	na	na	13.5	–1.2	2.3	7.1

Source: World Bank, WDI Online, 2011 except for Taiwan that comes from various issues of Directorate General of Budget, Accounting, and Statistics, *Statistical Yearbook of the Republic of China*, and the data for 1955–1960 come from various sources.

Note: na. Reliable data were not available to the author for these years.

half times the current size of the US economy. An increase in GDP equivalent to the size of the entire US economy would occur within eight years in the second decade and every four years in the third decade. If China's foreign trade grew at even half its current rate, in 30 years, Chinese exports would reach US$28 trillion. It is hard to imagine the magnitude of the adjustments that the rest of the world would have to make to accommodate any such transformation of China's economy. The price of energy would soar, established export markets of the rest of the world would disappear almost overnight and much of the world's trade would involve importing from China and exporting to China. This is not going to happen, at least not within a short period of three or four decades.

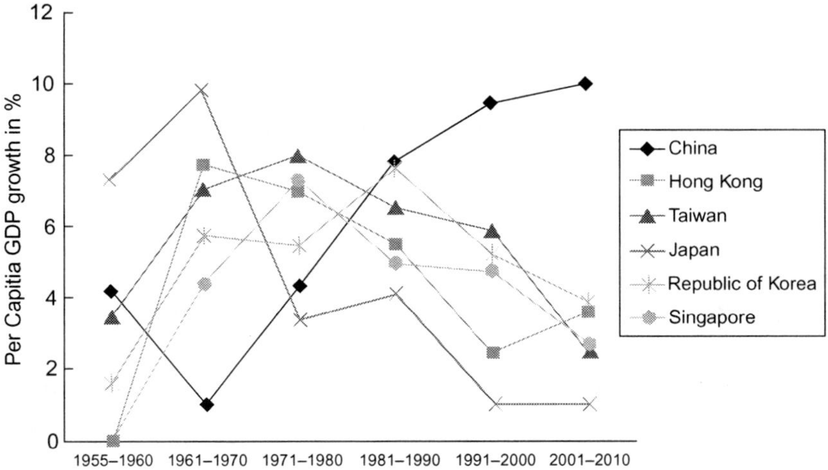

Figure 1. Growth rates of high-income East Asian economies.

Source: This figure was derived from the data in Table 1.

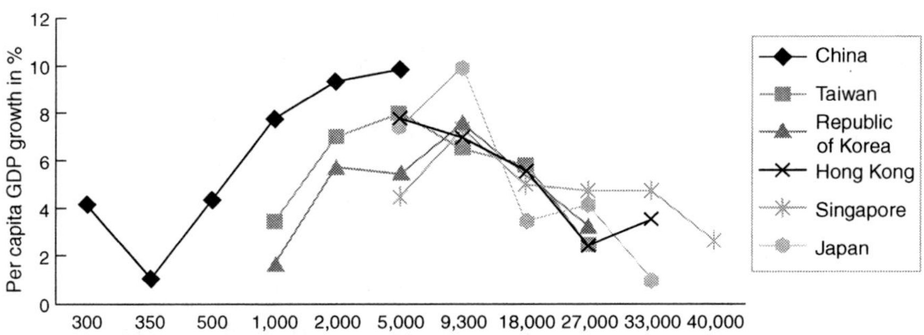

Figure 2. Growth of East Asian GDP at different levels of per capita GDP.

Sources and explanation of Figure 2: The GDP growth rates are the average growth rates per decade and are from the same sources as the data in Table 1. The PPP per capita income data in 2005 prices were taken from Alan Heston, Robert Summers and Bettina Aten, Penn World Tables 7.0, Center for International Comparisons of Production, Income, and Prices at the University of Pennsylvania, May 2011. Matching the average growth rates per decade to a particular level of per capita GDP is not precise. The per capita GDP at the midpoint of each decade was used for each country. To keep the x-axis from becoming unreadable, the data for each country in each decade were placed above the per capita income on the x-axis that was closest to the actual figure. An alternative would have been to take the annual growth rates and the annual per capita GDP figures for each year and each country, or the three or five year moving average of the growth rates and the per capita incomes but that effort was beyond the scope of this paper and its author.

The remainder of this essay is devoted to trying to understand what is likely to cause China's growth to slow down and what causal factors will bring that about. We will also speculate on when that is likely to occur, but no really precise estimate of the timing of the slowdown is possible. We can, however, eliminate the implausible time frames and suggest a narrower range of possibilities.

This analysis begins by looking at when the other high-income countries of the world experienced a marked decline in their per capita growth rates. We then turn to an analysis from the supply side of the past sources of growth in China and what these sources imply for the future. This discussion is followed by an analysis of China's changing economic structure on the demand side and the implications that this has for future growth prospects.

II. GDP Growth Rates and Per Capita Income

The first piece of relevant evidence in considering when China's growth is likely to slow down is international data on the relationship between levels of per capita income and the rate of growth of GDP. The data for East Asia are presented in Figure 2. As the chart indicates, China began its high-growth period at a level of per capita GDP (PPP GDP in 2005 prices) that was half the level of the Republic of Korea and Taiwan and roughly one-tenth the level of Japan, Hong Kong and Singapore. As this chart also makes clear, China's per capita income has not yet reached the levels where decline began in the other five economies. Table 2 presents estimates of the level of per capita GDP at the time that growth slowed in each of these other five economies. The first phase of slowdown was at between \$13,000 and \$16,000 per capita in PPP terms. There was then a second slowdown that began at anywhere from \$17,000 to \$29,000.

As it turns out, the period of the first slowdowns is not unique to the economies of East and Southeast Asia. As the data in Figure 3 indicate, all countries that achieved a per capita income of over \$20,000 have experienced a slowdown in their per capita GDP growth rate when they reached a level of between \$10,000 and \$16,000 per capita (PPP in 2000 prices). There are plausible arguments that can be made, however, about why this

Table 2. Date and per capita GDP of sustained slowdowns in East Asian GDP growth rates.

	Year of first decline	Per capita GDP	Year of second decline	Per capita GDP
China	?	?	?	?
South Korea	1992	12,862	1997	17,567
Taiwan	1990	13,658	1998	21,308
Hong Kong	1982	15,012	1995	27,098
Singapore	1982	15,889		
Japan	1970	14,797	1992	29,418

Note: These data are taken from WDI online and the Penn World Tables. Dating a sustained slowdown involves judgment but the basic criterion used here is a drop in the average annual growth rate for more than a decade by greater than 1.5% per year.

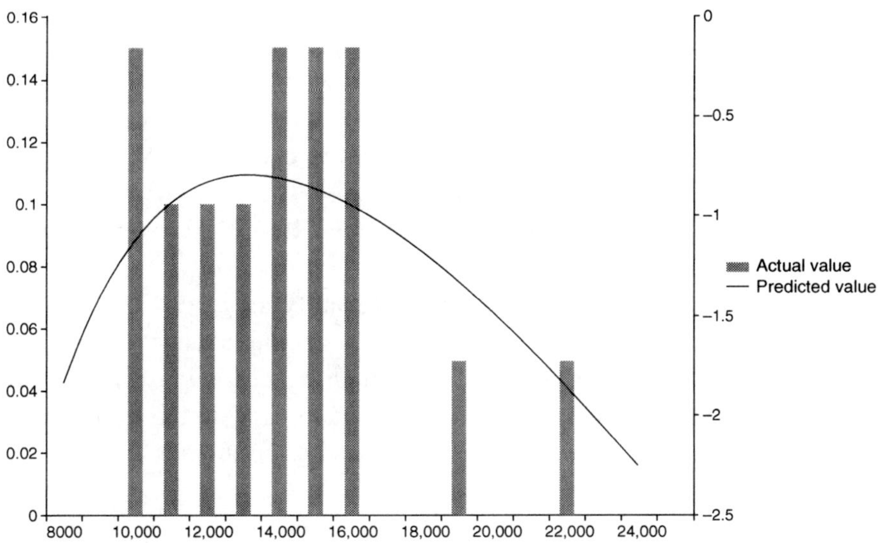

Figure 3. Per capita income at which GDP growth decelerated.

Source: Barry Eichengreen, Dwight H. Perkins, and Kwanho Shin (2012). *From Miracle to Maturity: The Growth of the Korean Economy.* (Cambridge: Harvard Asia Center Series), Chapter 2.

Note: This is a sample of 20 sustained decelerations with some countries represented by two different episodes of deceleration in this figure.

relationship seems to prevail across a wide range of countries at different points of time in the second half of the 20th and 21st centuries.

There is nothing in these charts that proves that there was a causal relationship between these levels of income and the slowdown in the GDP growth rate and no such evidence exists. There are plausible arguments that can be made about why this relationship exists, however. In the same study that produced Figure 3, we regressed the slowdown point on logistic curves (the variable and the variable squared) of per capita income, the dependency ratio of the working population to the non-working population and the share of employment in manufacturing. This regression indicated that there was a significant relationship between the GDP growth slowdown point and a rising per capita income, a rising dependency ratio, and a fall in the share of manufacturing and by implication a rise in the share of services in GDP.[1] In the East Asian case, the high-growth period in each of the countries of the region coincided with a low dependency ratio that typically was related to and probably caused the high savings rates in the East Asian countries. And the high savings rates, given the imperfections in the international capital markets, had much to do with the high East Asian investment rates. Manufacturing also typically grows more rapidly than services, although the recent experience of India suggests that this may not always be the case. Thus, when a country's employment in manufacturing begins to decline, the GDP growth rate also has a tendency to decline.

At a more general level, but one not readily subject to quantitative analysis, the early stages of growth in developing countries generally involve following well-trod paths. The main innovation in these early stages is to adapt proven successful development paths to the local conditions in one's own country. There are plausible arguments that can be made, however, about why this relationship seems to prevail across a wide range of countries at different points of time in the second half of the 20th and 21st centuries. With the notable exception of the UK in the early 19th century, all economies at the most general level during the early phases of their growth tend to follow the path laid down by other countries that

[1]Barry Eichengreen, Dwight H. Perkins and Kwanho Shin (2012). *From Miracle to Maturity: The Growth of the Korean Economy.* Cambridge, MA: Harvard University Press.

preceded them in entering into modern economic growth. In the case of the Republic of Korea and Taiwan, the model that had the greatest influence was the earlier development path of Japan. For Malaysia, Indonesia and Thailand, the main influence was both Japan and the modified versions of the Japanese model followed by Korea and Taiwan. China began by following the growth model of the Soviet Union, tried without success in the 1958 to 1976 period to find a unique path of its own, and then switched after 1978 to a model that looked increasingly like that of Korea, Taiwan and Japan but with important differences. Vietnam since 1986 or 1989 had been heavily influenced by the example of China. Hong Kong and, to a large degree, Singapore followed a very different development path influenced by their British colonial experience and the fact that they were both major ports long before entering into sustained rapid economic growth.

Modifications of the earlier Japanese growth model worked well in the 1960s through the early 1980s in Korea and Taiwan, but worked less well in Malaysia and Thailand and did not work at all when attempted in Indonesia in the 1990s. By the time China switched to a similar growth path, it was no longer possible to restrict imports with high tariff and quantitative barriers and other measures that violated World Trade Organization rules. Hostility to foreign direct investment (FDI) also made little sense in a world where supply chains made most large companies truly international. As time passed and the economies became more complex in all of the East and Southeast Asian economies, they all had to make adjustments from their original growth model and following what others had done no longer worked, research and development (R&D), for example, plays almost no role in the early stages of rapid growth, but over time that is no longer true. Countries can no longer depend on low wages to stay competitive as they move into industries where low wages provide few advantages. Innovation in technology and production methods becomes more important and economies begin to make the inevitable mistakes that go with true innovation. Why this happens at $13,000 or $14,000 per capita or a bit more or less would require research that is far beyond the scope of this essay. The point is that it does occur and when countries must innovate both with respect to particular industries and technologies and with respect to their overall growth model, they inevitably begin to make mistakes. Mistakes (R&D that produces new products that turn out not to be viable, corporate strategies that try but fail to move into new kinds of markets, etc.) lead to slower growth for a given level of investment.

We will pursue this question of why growth becomes more difficult as per capita incomes rise and the economy becomes more complex in the sections of this essay that follow. Here, we mainly note that China's GDP per capita in purchasing power parity terms is already around $8,000 per capita and that at a growth rate of 9% per year it would reach $16,000 in eight years which is at the upper range of when most other countries have experienced their first decline in their GDP per capita growth rate.[2]

III. Supply-Side Challenges

A full exposition of all of the supply-side challenges that face China today and in the coming decade would be incomplete even with a book-length manuscript. Here, we will present only two kinds of analysis that have a bearing on the growth-related issues facing China. First is to use a Solow sources of growth analysis for China to better understand the fundamental difference between China's high-growth decades and its earlier much slower growth period. That will then be used to better understand, at this very general level, China's likely sources of future growth. Second, we will briefly discuss the case for why economic and institutional reforms going forward are more complex and likely to be more difficult than those

[2]We still do not have a completely reliable measure of per capita GDP for China in purchasing power parity (PPP) terms. The most systematic effort to estimate PPP for China was carried out by the Asian Development Bank and the World Bank (Asian Development Bank, 2007, *Purchasing Power Parities and Real Expenditures* (Manila: Asian Development Bank)) but used only urban data in China to derive its purchasing power parity prices and this is widely believed to bias downward the resulting per capita GDP PPP estimates. However, even deriving per capita GDP using the official exchange rate China's per capita GDP in 2011 was $5,100 and if one accepts the widely held view that the official Chinese exchange rate is undervalued by perhaps 25%, then the per capita figure becomes $6,700. In developing countries, the PPP per capita GDP is almost always higher, often considerably higher than the official exchange rate calculation mainly because the price of non-tradables (notably services) is much lower relative to tradables in developing countries. Thus, a PPP figure of $8,000 is probably a conservative estimate of 2011 PPP per capita GDP in China.

Table 3. The sources of growth in China, 1952–2005.

	GDP	Fixed capital	Raw labor	Education enhanced	TFP growth
1952–1957	6.5	1.9	1.2	1.7	4.7
1958–1965	2.4	5.2	1.5	2.1	–1
1966–1978	4.9	7.7	2.4	3.1	–0.2
1979–2005	9.5	9.6	1.9	2.7	3.8

Source: This is a shortened version of Dwight H. Perkins and Thomas G. Rawski (2008). Forecasting Chins's Economic Growth to 2005, In *China's Great Economic Transformation*. Loren Brandt and Thomas G. Rawski (eds.). Cambridge: Cambridge University Press, p. 839.

of the first decades of rapid growth that mainly involved dismantling the centrally planned command system and replacing it with a market based economic system.

The data on the sources of growth in China over the past six decades are presented in Table 3. The growth rate prior to the Deng Xiaoping reforms that began in 1978 was slow[3] and entirely explained by the increase in capital and the labor force. In fact, total factor productivity (TFP) throughout the period was negative. Per capita household consumption grew at an even slower rate than GDP because most of the increase in GDP went to investment goods to make more investment goods (machinery to make more machinery much of it of low quality). The share of household consumption in GDP fell, as a result, to 48.8% in 1978 from 62.4% in 1956–1957.

The sharp rise in the rate of growth after 1978 is almost entirely explained by the rise in TFP. The rate of investment as a share of GDP actually fell by several percentage points in the early 1980s before

[3]The GDP growth rates in Table 4 are lower than the official growth rates for this period although the growth rates in the table are based entirely on official data. The problem with the official figures is that in the 1950s through the 1970s they are based on state-determined prices that following the practice of the Soviet Union were heavily biased toward the faster-growing industrial sector thus artificially raising the rate of GDP growth. The estimates in the table revalued the official data for the primary, secondary and tertiary sectors using the year 2000 market prices that give a much lower weight to the secondary sector.

beginning to rise again. The increase in the growth rate of the capital stock was driven mostly by the higher rate of GDP growth that produced a higher rate of growth of capital despite the decline in the percentage share of gross capital formation.

There is no difficulty in explaining what brought about this rise in TFP. China opened up to imports of high-technology and higher-quality goods in general even before the formal reform period that began in late 1978. Higher imports had to be paid for and hence the rapid expansion of labor-intensive manufacturing exports in order to supply the needed foreign exchange. From 1979 through the early 1980s, the Commune system, really the collective system based on 20 to 30 family production teams, was disbanded in favor of household-based agriculture and farm output boomed partly due to increased fertilizer use but in large part because of the superior incentives of a household-based system. In October 1984, the government began to try to reform the industrial sector then dominated by large state-owned enterprises. Inputs were freed up to be sold on the market at market-set prices although lower state-set prices continued in force for the politically powerful large state-owned enterprises. The performance of the state enterprises did not improve much, but the availability of industrial inputs on the market led to an unexpected boom in what came to be called township and village enterprises (TVEs). There were enormous gaps between what the state enterprises produced and what consumers and other enterprises wanted and the TVEs rushed in to fill those gaps. The tragedy of June 4, 1989 brought a brief end to the forward thrust of reform but then Deng Xiaoping made his famous trip to the south in 1992 and declared that even the more radical economic reforms were a good thing and the boom began anew. The 1990s saw first a large increase in enterprises established by FDI. China, after decades of prohibiting FDI, formally welcomed it in the 1980s but it was not until the 1990s that the relevant laws governing FDI were in place. The boom in FDI from that point on accounted for much of the very rapid increase in exports and China's industrial economy became firmly imbedded in global supply chains. Then in the latter half of the 1990s, Zhu Rongji led the effort to join the World Trade Organization, not so much to promote exports that were rising rapidly without membership, but to force the state enterprises to face vigorous foreign competition if they were to survive. Several tens of millions of redundant state enterprise workers were retired or dismissed. Finally, the last years of the 1990s and the first decade of the 21st century witnessed a massive state-led investment in infrastructure which will be discussed further in the next section on demand-side issues.

The point of this very brief recitation of the major reforms is twofold. These reforms clearly explain much of the 9% growth in GDP and high rate of TFP growth during these three plus decades. Second, these reforms may have been difficult in a political sense although Deng Xiaoping's power overrode the special interest objections of state-owned enterprises and conservative cadres, but there was nothing terribly complicated in a technical sense. Much of what was involved was the dismantling of systems that did not work. Getting rid of the Commune system mainly involved Deng quietly stepping in at key moments to stop cadres from blocking what was happening spontaneously in the villages. Once back to household farming, the households did not need to be trained in how to farm on their own and the incentives once they were able to sell on the market were clear and appropriate. Rural areas, particularly those in the most developed part of the country, had also already acquired substantial experience with small-scale enterprises under the Rural Small-scale Industry Program and these skills, plus some innate entrepreneurial skills, were well placed to respond to the market incentives that opened up in 1984. Export of manufactures to western markets did not begin in 1978. China had been exporting labor-intensive manufactures to western markets since the break with the Soviet Union in 1960 but politics kept a tight rein on expanding either exports or imports. When the tight rein was removed, those producing and marketing manufactured products for exports knew what to do, or, more accurately, they knew where to get the necessary expertise to expand rapidly. They turned to the formidable marketing machine of Hong Kong. Writing the laws needed to provide foreign direct investors with adequate security and incentives was not difficult — there were lots of models to follow around the world. The one difficult problem was figuring out how to reform the state-owned enterprises, but China in the late 1990s had the strong leadership needed to make a good beginning.

The most difficult intellectual challenge to the various supply-side reforms was that China in the 1980s had no directly relevant model to follow. China got information on what to do from a wide variety of sources — the

World Bank and other development economists, people knowledgeable about the development experiences of its neighbors, economists experienced with the pre-1989 efforts at economic reform in Eastern Europe, Hong Kong entrepreneurs, and many others. There was a general notion among many of the more radical reformers who had the ear of top government officials in the 1980s that the nation should make much greater use of markets. But the approach was to try a particular reform in parts of the country and, if it had a positive impact, promoting it in the rest of the country and abandoning the effort if it did not work. Eventually by the 1990s, China recognized that what it was doing was moving toward a full market-driven economy, or a 'socialist market economy' as it is now described. But there was never a fully consistent theoretical framework that was applied by the reformers from the beginning as was later tried in Eastern Europe and the Soviet Union with at best mixed success. In the end, China had a coherent and consistent development model that had many features in common with its neighbors, but it did not start out trying to implement such a model. It developed a viable model by an iterative process.

The situation that China faces at the beginning of the second decade of the 21st century is very different from the challenges of the past three decades. To begin with, to maintain a 9% rate of growth of GDP or a slightly lower rate in per capita terms, China must sustain a high rate of TFP growth. Some hypothetical projections of the required level of TFP growth are presented in Table 4. These projections were originally done in 2005, but a part of their message is if anything even more valid as of 2011.

Table 4. Hypothetical projections of the future sources of GDP growth.

	GDP	Fixed capital	Raw labor	Education enhanced	TFP growth
1979–2005	9.5	9.6	1.9	2.7	3.8
2006–2015	9	9.8	0.7	2	3.6
2016–2025	9	8.2	–0.3	1	4.9
2006–2015	6	8.1	0.7	2	1.4
2016–2025	6	5.6	–0.3	1	3

Source: This is a shortened version of a table in Dwight H. Perkins and Thomas G. Rawski (2008). Forecasting China's Economic Growth to 2025. In *China's Great Economic Transformation*, Loren Brandt and Thomas G. Rawski (eds), pp. 852–853.

The principal message is that to maintain a 9% rate of GDP growth, TFP would have to grow initially at the same rate as it did on average throughout the reform period. After 2015, however, TFP would have to accelerate to an unprecedented 4.9% annual rate. The reason for this is that the labor force will actually begin to decline slightly during this later period. Furthermore, while the education of that labor force will continue to rise, it will do so more slowly than in the past because China has already achieved near universal education through the first nine years and well over half of the relevant age cohort completes 12 years of education (high school or upper middle school graduation). Attendance at university is a much lower share of the age cohort, but there are now over 21 million students enrolled at the tertiary level and the number is rising steadily. It takes much longer, however, to train teachers for quality higher education and there is also a problem of finding jobs for university graduates if their numbers rise too quickly. The flow of rural to urban migrant workers will continue for some time in large part because many families leave their children in the village with their grandparents even when both parents are working in urban areas. Surveys suggest that over 80% of the registered rural population between the ages of 18 and 40 is now mainly working in the cities. As their children come of working age they too will move to the cities to find work and this will make a modest contribution to productivity growth.

The hypothetical projections in Table 4 made in 2005 indicated that the GDP growth rate was likely to slow down, if only modestly, in the near future. Growth in fact retained its torrid pace despite the global recession that began in 2008 in the United States and spread worldwide but not to China.

What kept growth high was a steady increase in the rate of investment as a share of GDP, a jump over three years of nearly 6% or an annual average rise of 2% (Table 5). This growth in investment took place in the context of underemployed labor and excess industrial capacity. Because of these underemployed resources, this rise in the rate of investment contributed directly to a higher growth rate of GDP.[4] In growth accounting terms,

[4]If there is full employment of resources, then an increase in the investment rate will be at the expense of consumption and the growth rate in GDP in that year would not be any higher than it otherwise would have been. If there are underemployed resources and no major resource bottlenecks, however, an increase in the investment rate will increase the GDP growth rate in that year.

Table 5. China's rising investment rate, 1995–2010.

	Investment as a share of GDP (annual average rate in %)
1995–1999	37.6
2000–2002	36.5
2003–2005	41.8
2006–2007	41.8
2008	43.9
2009	47.5
2010	48.6

Source: National Statistical Office, *Zhongguo tongji zhaiyao, 2010,* p. 36.

TFP for the period 2006–2010 represented over one-quarter of the 11.5% GDP growth rate and for the global recession years of 2008–2010 TFP was 1.4% of a GDP growth rate of 9.8%.[5] In short, the GDP growth rate of recent years has been driven mainly by the massive increase in capital made possible by a high and rapidly rising rate of investment. This is not a strategy for maintaining a high GDP growth rate that is likely to be sustainable over the next decade.[6] We shall return to the implications of this massive rise in investment and fixed capital in the discussion of aggregate demand that follows this discussion of supply side issues.

Beyond 2011, the question remains as to whether China can sustain a high growth in TFP for another decade or more. There are no longer major

[5]These figures use the same methodology followed in 'Dwight H. Perkins and Thomas G. Rawski (2008). Forecasting China's Economic Growth to 2025. *China's Great Economic Transformation*. In Loren Brandt and Thomas G. Rawski (eds). Cambridge: Cambridge University Press'. The specific assumptions were a 9.6% depreciation rate for the fixed capital stock and a capital share in national income of .45. The educated labor growth rate used is the same as in Table 5 of this essay.

[6]Maintenance of this rate of growth of fixed capital would require a steadily rising rate of capital formation as a share of GDP. Alternatively, if the share of fixed capital investment in GDP did not rise further but leveled off, the growth rate of the capital stock would revert to the growth rate of GDP and high GDP growth could only be maintained if that additional capital was very productive (i.e., capital productivity or TFP would have to accelerate well above the levels of recent years).

boosts in productivity that can come from simply dismantling the most inefficient components of a Soviet-type economic system. Central planning and the command economy no longer exist. The institutional changes that will promote high productivity growth in the future are not so easily or quickly implemented. We have already mentioned the increasing role of R&D investments. Increasing the money going to R&D is part of the task but one must have the skilled personnel and well-functioning research institutes to use the money effectively. China is making great progress on this front but world class research results cannot be achieved quickly. China also needs a legal system that is skillfully administered, efficient, and fair. Creating such a system, given the almost total absence of a judiciary and lawyers three decades ago in 1978 when the reform process began, will take another generation or more.

In addition, if investment is to be used efficiently, the role of politics in investment decisions will have to be reduced much further than is currently the case. The current increased reliance on state infrastructure investment in that respect is a move in the wrong direction. Furthermore, this massive infrastructure investment will have to be maintained in the future. The recurrent costs involved in maintaining roads, railroads, government buildings and housing are often neglected by governments and households around the world, but they show up as costs in one way or another. In the absence of recurrent cost expenditures, the capital and housing stock deteriorates and the productivity of that capital falls. With appropriate recurrent cost expenditures, the productivity of capital does not fall but it does not rise either. Most of these recurrent cost expenditures show up in the national accounts as an increase in either government or household consumption.[7] In summary, the challenges to maintaining a very high rate of TFP growth over the next decade are formidable.

IV. Demand-Side Challenges

China's high investment rate is a direct result of its low and falling rate of household consumption as a share of GDP If China had not raised the

---

[7]I am indebted to Malcolm McPherson for pointing out the relevance of recurrent costs to this discussion of productivity.

share of investment in GDP, the absorption of labor in the modern sector would have been slower and much industrial capacity, notably in the investment goods sector, would have been underutilized. China has had a potential insufficient aggregate demand problem since the late 1990s and it has dealt with it by expanding investment. It also for a time expanded its export surplus but that surplus fell back quickly to more normal levels. This changing demand structure is presented in Figure 4. In Figure 5, we compare China's decline in household consumption as a share of GDP with the trends in other parts of the world. In Figure 6, the rates of investment as a share of GDP among the high performing East Asia economies are compared.

China's low household consumption share as a percentage of GDP is only partly due to the high household savings ratio that reflects the weakness of the social safety net during the first three decades of economic reform. The decline in the share of household consumption, as contrasted with the level of the share instead largely reflects the fact that rural and urban incomes, while they have grown rapidly in real terms, have lagged behind the growth rate of GDP both during the period of the command

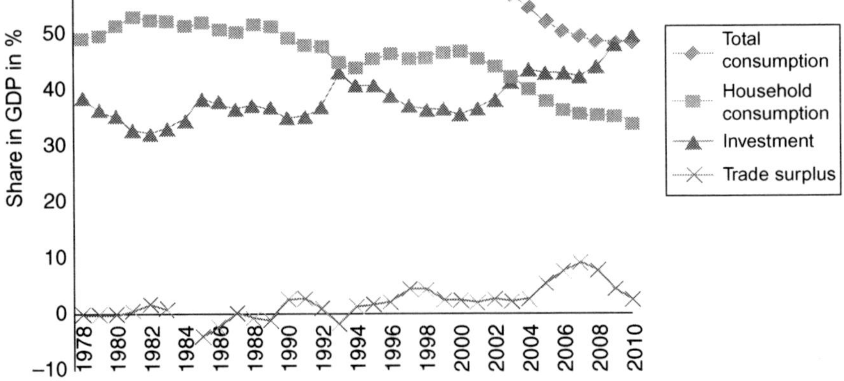

Figure 4. China GDP expenditure breakdown, 1978–2010.

Source: National Statistical Office: *Zhongguo tongji zhaiyao 2011*, p. 36.

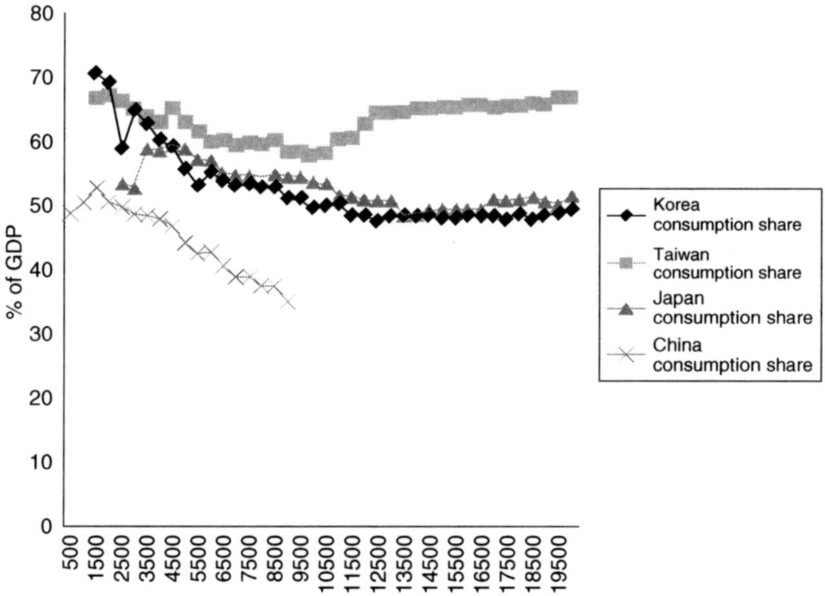

Figure 5. East Asian consumption shares (% of GDP).

Source: The data for the Republic of Korea, Taiwan and Japan are from Alan Heston, Robert Summers and Bettina Aten, Penn World Tables Version 6.3, Center for International Comparisons of Production, Income and Prices at the University of Pennsylvania, August 2009. The Chinese consumption share data were derived from data in National Statistical Office, *Zhongguo tongji zhaiyao 2011*, p. 36 and the purchasing power parity GDP data are based on the Penn World Tables 6.3. The Chinese official consumption shares were used in preference to the Penn World Table shares even though they were based on Chinese market prices rather than purchasing power parity consumption good prices because the Penn World Tables make a number of assumptions to derive the Chinese data about which this author is skeptical.

Note: The data on the x-axis are per capita GDP in purchasing power parity terms.

economy, when wages and rural incomes were stagnant, and during the post-1978 reform period, when wages and rural incomes grew rapidly but at rates that were still below the rate of growth of GDP. During the command economy period, stagnant incomes and a falling consumption share represented government policy and the Soviet-style economic model. In the post-1978 reform period, it was mainly market forces that determined the rate of growth of wages, particularly after 2000.

The low household consumption share when combined with government consumption expenditures leaves a gap that must be filled to maintain

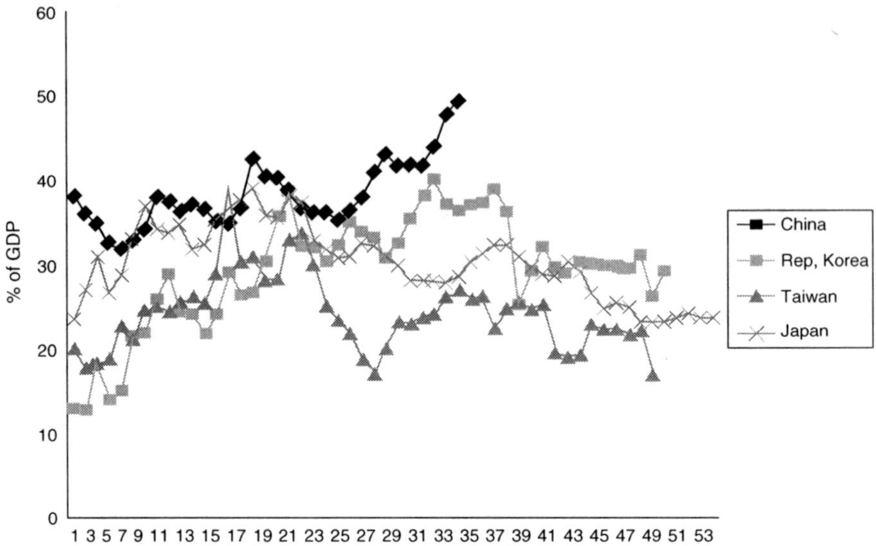

Figure 6. East Asian post-1950 investment shares (% of GDP).

Source: National Statistical Office, *Zhongguo tongji zhaiyao* 2011, p. 36 and Alan Heston, Robert Summers and Bettina Aten, Penn World Tables 6.3. The Penn World Tables shares are based on purchasing power parity prices while the Chinese data are based on current market prices so they are not strictly comparable.

full use of a nation's resources. In most countries that gap is between 20 and 30% of GDP with the economies of East Asia at the high end and the United States at the lower end. The gap can be filled in part by a trade surplus but few countries run a trade surplus larger than a few percent of GDP. The remainder of the gap must be filled by several different types of investment. Conventional textbooks tend to focus on investment that produces products for consumers or for export markets or produces investment goods that will in turn be used to produce consumer or export products. These investments are driven by market demand that produces a rate of return sufficient to cover the cost of borrowing (or is equal to or higher than rates of return on available alternative investments). Most investment in housing in market economies is also driven by market demand. In a full market economy, much infrastructure investment is demand driven in the sense that investors can recoup their investment in a highway with the use of tolls, airports can charge the airlines that in turn can pass the cost on to their passengers, etc. In the more typical case, however, much infrastructure is built by government and paid for with taxes or financed by bonds that are paid back using taxes. Military expenditures are a case where the government rather than consumers provides all of the demand although the actual investment may be carried out by private firms under government contracts.

China is a market economy in most respects and much of its investment is carried out for profit by private and public firms in response to market forces. However, because household and government consumption is such a low share of GDP, investment to produce consumer products, related investment products, and exports amounted roughly to only about 17% of GDP.[8] That left roughly 27% of GDP that had to be covered by something else. Military production may have accounted for a few percent of that difference but most of the gap in the years 2005–2010 was filled by either housing or infrastructure investment. Most of the infrastructure investment was carried out by the state while much of the housing investment was carried out by private contractors or by state companies motivated by the same market forces as the private sector. In the future, however, much of the housing will have to be for low-income migrants and urban residents who cannot afford commercially built housing and thus the state will either have to build this housing or contract with private firms to build it. Together, the state going forward could be responsible for providing investment of 15 to 20% of GDP. In addition, government consumption expenditure will rise as the recurrent costs of maintaining the large increases in infrastructure and public housing are added.

A high share for infrastructure and housing investment and the resulting recurrent cost expenditures is not unique to China. Both Japan after World War II and the Republic of Korea after the end of the Korean War were faced with economies where virtually all infrastructure and urban

[8]This figure was obtained from the 9.31% rate of growth in consumption plus net exports in the 2005–2010 period and multiplying by the incremental capital output ratio in that same period of 3.95/1. The 3.95/1 incremental capital output ratio is based on the average rate of investment in the 2005–2010 period of 44.2% of GDP and a GDP growth rate of 11.2%. To simplify the calculations, I have assumed that the incremental capital output ratio is the same for both investment in consumption goods plus net exports and for housing and infrastructure investment.

housing had been destroyed. Thus, an enormous building program was clearly needed to replace what had been destroyed as well as new infrastructure required by a rising and increasingly prosperous population. In Japan, this process of building infrastructure and housing from scratch presumably accounts in large part for the high rate of investment during the first 19 years after the country regained its independence with the end of the US occupation in 1952 (see Figure 6). In the case of Korea, the investment boom started modestly in the early 1960s and carried through at rates well over 30% of GDP to the financial crisis of 1997–1998 before falling back to 30% or less from 1998 on, a high investment rate period of 36 years. The high investments of the last seven or eight years of the boom in the 1990s, however, are widely perceived to be the product of out of control large conglomerates expanding unwisely into all kinds of new endeavors. The investment boom that involved to a significant degree the recovery from wartime destruction plus the need to catch up to housing and infrastructure needs appropriate for an economy of Korea's income level probably ended after about 30 years, or at the beginning of the 1990s. In Taiwan's case, investment never reached the high shares of Korea or Japan, leveling off at around 30% of GDP and then falling after 20 or 21 years to levels a bit above 20% of GDP. Taiwan never experienced the level of destruction of either Japan or Korea and the infrastructure needs of a population concentrated along a 200-mile narrow strip of land (much of Taiwan is covered by high mountains with limited population) were less than in Korea and Japan to start with. It is also worth noting that Taiwan's GDP, after the decline in the rate of investment in the mid-1980s, continued to grow through the 1990s at a pace similar to that of Korea in that period even though Korea had a much higher rate of investment.

China had long recovered from wartime destruction by 1978, but China had also experienced a quarter century during which housing and infrastructure investment were largely neglected. The Soviet command model put all of its emphasis on industry and particularly heavy industries that could produce investment goods and military hardware and China adopted this aspect of the model as well as many others. The Soviet model also stressed producer goods over consumer goods and the latter included housing. The result was that China began the three reform decades with a very small stock of urban housing and a weak and badly overburdened transport system.

The effort to expand transport capacity did not begin in earnest until the 1990s (Table 6) but housing construction began on a large scale almost from the beginning of the reform period (Table 7). There is little question

Table 6. Expansion of China's railroad and highway systems, 1955–2010.

	Railroad length 1,000 km	Railroad freight billion to n/km	Road length 1,000 km	High speed road length 1,000 km	Road freight billion ton/km
1955	25.6	98.2	167.3	0	3.4
1978	51.7	534.5	890.2	0	27.4
1988	56.2	987.8	999.6	0.1	322.1
1998	66.4	1256.1	1278.5	8.7	548.3
2010	79.7	2764.4	3730.2	74.1	4339.1

Sources: National Statistical Office, 2009, *Xin Zhongguo 60 nian*, pp. 650 and 654; National Statistical Office, 2011, *Zhongguo tongji zhaiyao 2011*, pp. 150 and 153.

Table 7. Urban housing development, 1978–2010.

	Urban population (millions)	Urban housing per capita (living space) (sq. meters)		Implied urban housing stock (constructed space) (million sq. meters)		Housing stock completed (preceding decade total) (million sq. meters)
1978	172.45	3.6		621		
1990	301.95	6.7	13.7	2023	4137	9075
2000	459.06		20.3		9319	11089
2010	665.57		31.6		21032	14528

Sources: National Statistical Office, 2011, *Zhongguo tongji zhaiyao 2011*, pp. 40, 53, and 103; National Statistical Office, 1991, *Zhongguo tongji nianjian 1991*, p. 269; and National Statistical Office, 2009, *Xin Zhongguo 60 nian*, p. 608.

Note: The two different measures of per capita housing space appear to refer to actual living space (the smaller number) in contrast to total constructed residential space (the larger number). The housing stock completed each decade probably includes some rural housing stock. The total for the three decades adds up to considerably more than the implied total urban housing stock derived from the per capita figures, but there was considerable demolition of older urban residential buildings so that is not surprising. The implied housing stock figures were obtained by multiplying the urban population by the number of square meters per capita. The urban population only includes registered urban residents but migrants with rural registration had little access to regular urban housing and lived crowded into single rented rooms, in tents, construction sites, and other similar areas.

that most of the urban housing constructed through 2010 was needed despite publicity surrounding the fact that some newly constructed residences were unoccupied for long periods after being completed. Some of this empty housing reflects the fact that prosperous Chinese individuals have few reliable investment choices and a residence that is empty for several years may still be a better investment than putting the money in a bank account that pays a negative real interest rate. Most such investors assume that real estate prices will continue to rise at the rapid rates of the recent past, even though many feel that Chinese commercial housing prices are already out of reach for most of the urban population.[9]

The issue relevant to this essay is whether there continues to be a need to construct new housing at the rate of the first decade of the 21st century, 1.45 billion square meters a year? If the issue were whether the registered urban population required an investment of this magnitude (over RMB3 trillion per year), there is some doubt that this level would be justified for a country with China's per capita income. The official urban population increased by 20 million persons a year (some of which involved redrawing urban boundaries) and it would take "only" 632 million square meters of new housing to accommodate each additional 20 million persons at the average amount of housing per capita in 2010, or less than half the rate of new completed housing space over the past decade. To that one would have to add an unknown amount to replace older housing being demolished. However, if one adds in the need to house more than 100 million migrant families that are currently working in the cities but often leaving their children back in the village, and then adds all of the new migrants coming in as they become old enough to be eligible for urban employment, then over the next decade there is a need for housing for perhaps 300 million additional people. At a more modest 20 m^2 per person, the migrant population could easily require another 6 billion square meters. Spread out over 10 to 15 years that would be 400 to 600 million additional

[9]Analyses in 2011 of the urban housing market and of the empty apartment issue (and in some cases temporarily empty new towns) include, Roselea Yao, May 26, 2011 'No Room for Squares: China's Housing Supply and Demand', *China Insight Economics,* GaveKalDragonomics; and Tom Miller, September 1, 2011, 'Don't Fear the Suburbs: Understanding China's "Ghost Towns,"' *China Insight Economics,* GaveKalDragonomics.

square meters of needed housing per year. The government by 2010 began to shift in a major way toward promoting low-cost housing while at the same time attempting to rein in the pace of construction of higher-priced commercial housing. If this shift in resource allocation succeeds, the overall level of housing construction will fall perhaps by 10% or more from the average level of the first decade of the 21st century. The one relatively safe forecast, going forward, is that there is not likely to be a market for a 2009–2010 level that begins at 1.8 billion m^2 of new commercial housing each year and rises steadily thereafter.[10]

The prospects for the continued expansion of transport infrastructure also face the question of how much more is really needed. In the 1970s, almost all of China's roads had two lanes, many were unpaved, and long-distance highways were often jammed, even though the number of vehicles on the road was a tiny fraction of what it is today. But China now has four times the length of highways of all kinds, most of them now paved, and it has a multi-lane high-speed highway system that rivals that of the United States. There are no doubt many areas where there are still bottlenecks and the demand for new highways is in part a product of how fast private automobile ownership is allowed to rise, but there does not appear to be a need for a continued highway expansion program on the scale of the past decade. The plan for a nationwide high-speed rail system is a long way from completion, but there is already a question of whether there is adequate demand for what, for a majority of the Chinese people, is an expensive way to travel. That plus quality and safety questions suggest that investment in this area is also likely to slow down over the coming decade. Government has also put a large investment into new and improved airports and no doubt a few areas, notably Beijing, could justify building a large new commercial airport given the congestion of the runways at Capitol Airport. But all, or virtually all, of the provincial capitals have new airports and the government is planning major investments in another 45 new airports. Many of the smaller airports already in existence handle only a few dozen flights a day. Investments in airports that receive limited use are investments with a low rate of return and hence only modest contributors to future growth.

---

[10]To maintain a constant share of a rising GDP, the area constructed each year would also have to rise.

Thus, this massive public investment program in the coming decade is likely to experience sharply diminishing returns[11] and some of it will probably be cut back. The question then becomes whether consumers can pick up the slack and keep growth going at top speed. Certainly, the government has wanted consumers to play this role, but the government has only a limited influence on the forces that will determine whether and when consumer spending will rise. What the government can control are expenditures on health and education and subsidies to the poor and government expenditures in these areas have increased significantly in recent years, but as a percent of GDP the level of these expenditures has been small. Government can and is currently trying to expand the coverage of health insurance, of a national pension system, and other social welfare measures and this should have some impact over time by lowering the rate of savings of the average household. It takes time, however, to build efficient national health and pensions systems and thus the impact on savings will only be felt over a long period.

[11]A counterargument that Chinese investment in general and in most sectors is highly productive and has in fact experienced increasing productivity is based on the fact that the rate of profits in all major sectors of the economy, state and non-state, have risen markedly. One of the most sophisticated efforts of this sort is by Feng Lu, Guoqing Song, Jie Tang, Hongyan Zhao and Liu Liu, 'Profitability of Chinese Firms, 1998–2006' (forthcoming). The rise in profits has clearly been the case at least for the years for which the analysis has been done. Profits of firms, however, are not a very good measure of the contribution of investment in infrastructure to economic growth. Investment of state firms building the infrastructure, for example, depends on what the state is willing to pay these firms to carry out this construction and that payment may have little relationship to the contribution of the investment to economic growth or to any kind of market force. Similarly, while some housing investment is constructed to meet private market demand, some of that demand is speculative and could represent a bubble. There is also the fact that the privatization of the housing market involved very large state subsidies to existing residents of properties and those subsidies have provided much of the demand for new housing (and hence commercial profits) when owners of subsidized properties trade up (or down) to new housing. In addition, much of the profitability in housing and in office buildings comes from speculation in land or the use of political connections to get access to land. The profitability of manufacturing that produces goods for the domestic consumer market or for export, in contrast, is a measure that is likely to reflect the social contribution of those investments to economic growth, but the discussion in this paper is only raising questions about infrastructure and housing investment.

What the government cannot control in any major way is the level and growth of rural household incomes and of wages because these are primarily driven by market forces. Household incomes from these sources, like household consumption, are an unusually small share of National Income in China. The reason, as pointed out earlier in this essay, is that the growth of wages and rural incomes has lagged behind the rapid growth of GDP. Chinese wage data indexes are based on the annual changes in the average wage of all workers in a given sector which gives one some idea of how wages have lagged GDP. The wage indexes for state enterprises and urban collective enterprises, and the index of per capita consumption in the rural areas is presented in Figure 7. Wages in the urban collective sector are the closest we can come to a wage index for unskilled workers. Unskilled worker wages in turn are likely to be determined by the incomes of rural to urban migrants who will move to take urban jobs when incomes for unskilled labor in urban areas are significantly higher than what could be earned staying in the rural areas. The flow of migrants thus holds down urban wage growth to no more than the growth of rural incomes. In Figure 7, we have used rural real consumption because of doubts about the

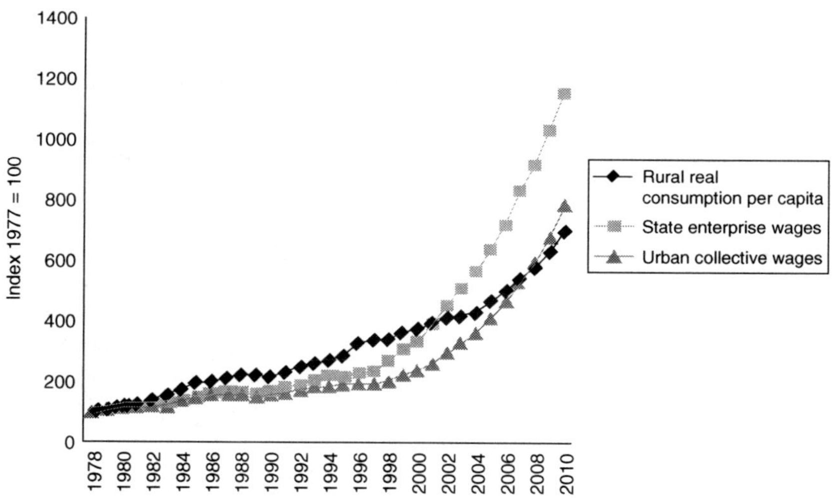

Figure 7. Urban wages and rural incomes, 1978–2010.

Source: This figure was derived from data in National Statistical Office, 2011, *Zhongguo tongji zhai yao 2011*, pp. 48, 103; and National Statistical Office, 2009, *Xin Zhongguo 60 nian*, pp. 610 and 616.

reliability of the rural real net income per capita index. As Figure 7 indicates, urban collective wages actually grew more slowly than average rural consumption per capita through the 1990s, but then accelerated markedly thereafter. From 2002 through 2010, urban collective real wages averaged an increase of 13.0% per year and in 2010 the rise was 16.5%. That and much anecdotal evidence all point to an end of the rural labor surplus.[12] Backing up this view is evidence that most of the young working age people in rural areas have moved to the cities. One survey suggests that over 80% of all registered rural residents between the ages of 18 and 40 are out of farming and mostly working in the cities.[13] Since few older rural residents are in a position to migrate to work in the cities, net migration from the rural areas will largely come from rural teenagers as they finish their formal education and move to the cities. Alternatively, if adequate housing and education for migrants is provided, these school-age children will instead move to the cities where their parents are working and enter the urban workforce from there.

A tight labor market will not restore the share of household consumption in GDP to more normal levels quickly, however. If GDP grows at 9% and household income and consumption grow at 12% in real terms, household consumption would rise to 47% of GDP in a decade and total consumption, assuming a modest increase in government welfare, health and education expenses could add another 16% for a total consumption of 63%. Government recurrent cost expenditures might add several per cent more. Assuming net exports fell to zero, gross capital formation

---

[12]For analysis of the likely end of the labor surplus in China see Cai Fang and Wang Meiyan (2011). 'Chinese Wages and the Turning Point in the Chinese Economy', *East Asia Forum* (www.eastasiaforum.org) and also Cai Fang, Du Yang, and Wang Meiyan (2009). 'Migration and Labor Mobility in China', Human Development Reports Research Paper, United Nations Development Programme.

[13]The survey as reported to me by Scott Rozelle is in Jikun Huang *et al.* (2010) 'China's Labor Transition and the Future of China's Rural Wages and Employment', Working Paper, China Center for Agricultural Policy, Chinese Academy of Sciences, Beijing, China. Personal observations of the author in 2009 in designated poor rural counties in eastern Qinghai Province indicate that most of the under-40 population was working in cities in western China with women coming back to have their babies, nurse them for a period, and then returning to work in the cities leaving the babies with their grandparents.

would be 37% of GDP, still a very high figure but well below the 2010 rate of 48.6%. Growth rates of GDP at 6% and household income and consumption at 9% would produce similar results. Whether this will in fact happen remains to be seen. As the data in Figure 2 indicate, among the other East Asian economies that experienced a decline in the share of household consumption in GDP during their period of high GDP growth, only Taiwan experienced a significant rise in the share of household consumption in GDP after the period of high growth ended. In the other economies, the share stopped falling but did not rise. However, given the much greater magnitude of China's falling household consumption share, it is plausible that the end of the labor surplus and the slowing of GDP growth would lead the consumption share to rise and not just level off. If that happens, the government will no longer need to mount such an enormous public investment and housing program.

Finally, the current growth strategy, with its reliance on large-scale state infrastructure investments, contributes to the inflationary pressures that the country has faced in recent years. Large infrastructure expenditures well ahead of demand for the services of that infrastructure raises expenditures on the demand side without providing adequate offsetting payments by users of that infrastructure and thus must be paid for with tax revenues or with loans that expand the money supply. China, for historical reasons, is averse to high rates of inflation and that will also contribute to pressure to limit the growth of investment demand as was the case in 2011.

V. Summing Up: When Will Growth Slow?

There is thus good reason to believe that China's growth rate will slow significantly in the not too distant future. A slower growth rate, it should be noted, does not necessarily mean a drop to an annual rate of 2 or 3% per capita. A more likely rate, barring a political crisis of some sort or a long-term global recession, would be 5 or 6% per capita initially falling further later.

The first piece of evidence that supports this view is that few countries have managed to sustain a high or rising growth rate when they reached $10,000 to $16,000 per capita PPP GDP. The exceptions, Norway, the

United Kingdom, and Israel, have little relevance to China's prospects. The forces that brought a slowdown elsewhere, including a rising dependency ratio and a gradual shift toward services as the main growth engine, are just as valid for China as other nations. This piece of evidence, however, does not suggest that a slowdown is imminent. Depending on just where one places China's current level of purchasing power parity income, China by this measure could grow at current rates for another eight years or so.

The second piece of evidence is that to grow rapidly well into the future, China will have to maintain a very high rate of growth in TFP. The beginning of a decline in the labor force is one reason why TFP will have to grow. High TFP growth, however, cannot be achieved by dismantling the inefficient structures of a Soviet-type economy — that has already been done. Maintaining high productivity growth will require greater reliance on R&D-based innovations and improved institutions including a better legal system. The current strategy for maintaining high growth, the large-scale housing and state investment program, has already produced a decline in the TFP rate of growth, not an increase.

Finally, the reliance on a high and rising rate of investment in infrastructure and housing to sustain high GDP growth is reaching its limits. There is still a considerable potential demand for more housing (mainly for migrant families), but not of the magnitude to justify a continued rise from the very high rates of housing construction and completion in 2009–2011. Infrastructure investments are also likely to slow down or at the least level off. At its current level of per capita income, China does not need to double the size of it's high-speed road system over the coming decade and the construction of four east–west nationwide high-speed passenger rail lines and four north–south lines, while no doubt needed at some point in the future, will probably be slowed down since existing levels of demand for such services probably will not justify a crash building program. A slowdown in these areas should also significantly reduce the demand for cement and steel, presumably leading to unused capacity in these sectors. There will be areas where there will be increased demand for government expenditures, notably in dealing with the severe water shortage in the north and the cost of cleaning up the polluted air of most urban centers, but the demand is not likely to completely substitute for the crash infrastructure building programs of the past decade. None of the expenditures of this type will contribute to high TFP growth. The current development strategy, therefore, while it has done wonders in sustaining a high rate of GDP growth in an adverse global context, is not a strategy that is likely to sustain high growth for another decade.

Over time, there is reason to believe that household consumption as a share of GDP will rise and China will experience a reversion to a more normal GDP structure and growth that is driven to a substantial degree by consumer demand rather than government demand. This rise, however, will take time.

It is impossible to put a precise time frame on when this inevitable deceleration in growth will occur, because it depends in part on how long the government will continue to try to prop up the growth rate with its current state-led investment model. There are certainly powerful forces pushing the government to continue with such a model — forces ranging from the fear of instability if the rate of job growth declines to pressures from major state heavy industries if the demand for their products falls, leaving them with substantial excess capacity. If these latter forces were absent, it would make sense for China to slow its GDP growth rate sooner rather than later, perhaps within two or three years. Whatever the policies of the government, high rates of GDP growth are not likely to be sustainable for more than another six to eight years. Even maintaining a rate of per capita GDP growth of 6% a year for the next six to eight years will involve a continued concerted effort to improve market-supporting institutions and create a world-class research and development effort as well as special efforts to use all the existing capital stock as efficiently as possible.

INDEX

J

Q

R

T

CPSIA information can be obtained at www.ICGtesting.com
Printed in the USA
BVOW02*0855070415

394974BV00003B/3/P

9 789814 612371